The Dark History of the Reincarnated Villainess

1

Akiharu Touka

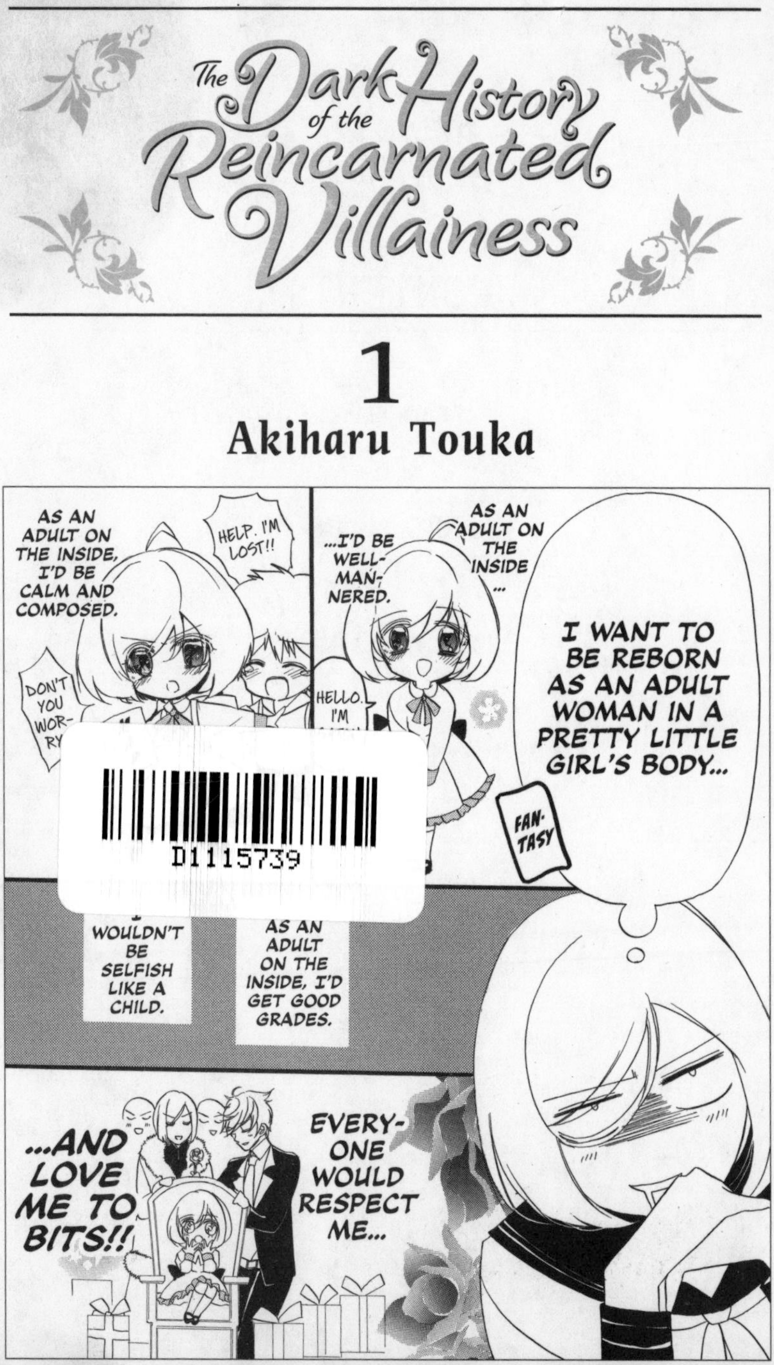

I WANT TO BE REBORN AS AN ADULT WOMAN IN A PRETTY LITTLE GIRL'S BODY...
FAN-TASY
AS AN ADULT ON THE INSIDE...
...I'D BE WELL-MANNERED.
HELLO. I'M
AS AN ADULT ON THE INSIDE, I'D BE CALM AND COMPOSED.
HELP. I'M LOST!!
DON'T YOU WOR-RY
AS AN ADULT ON THE INSIDE, I'D GET GOOD GRADES.
WOULDN'T BE SELFISH LIKE A CHILD.
EVERY-ONE WOULD RESPECT ME...
...AND LOVE ME TO BITS!!

The Dark History of the Reincarnated Villainess

VOL. 1

CONTENTS

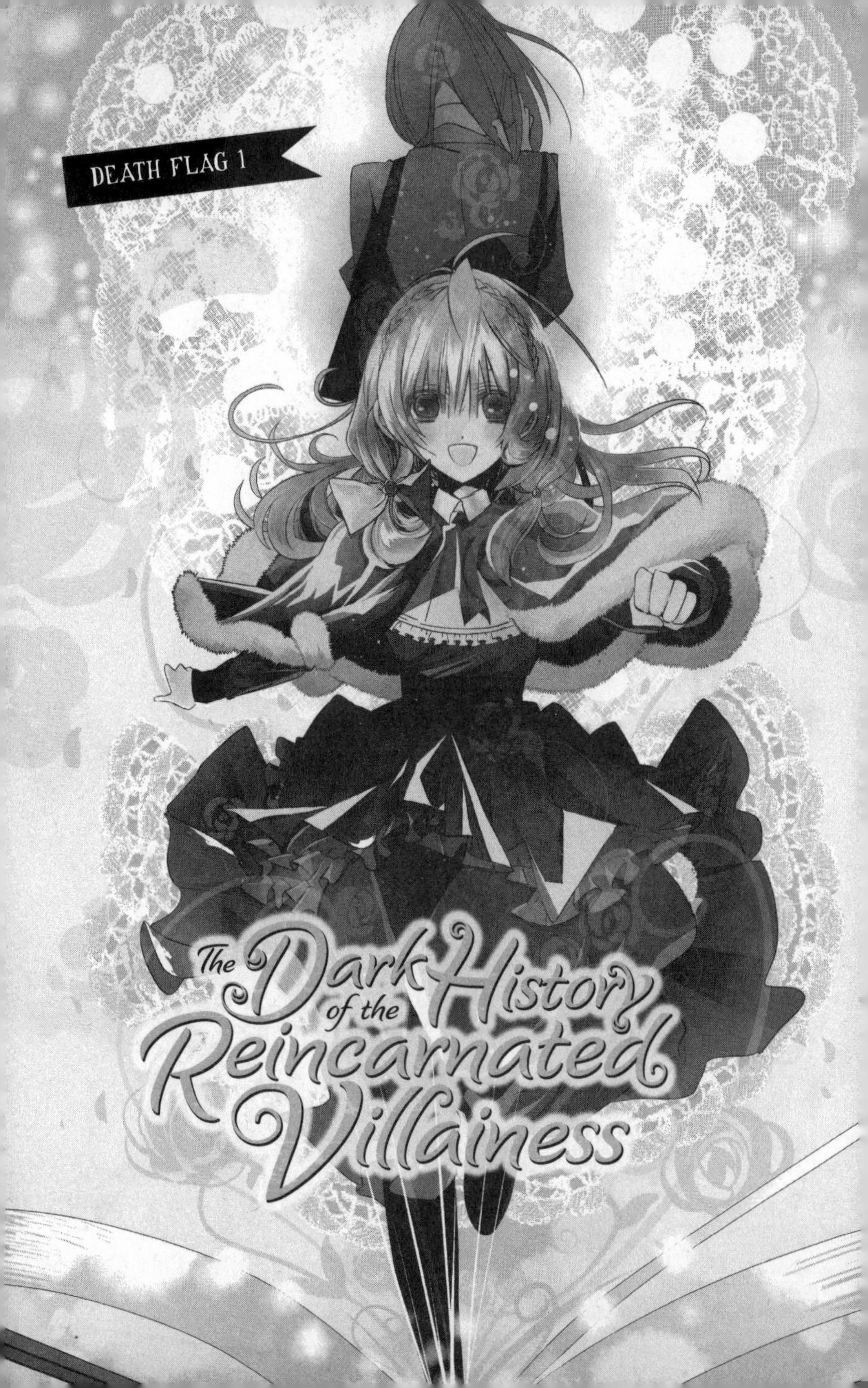
DEATH FLAG 1
The Dark History of the Reincarnated Villainess

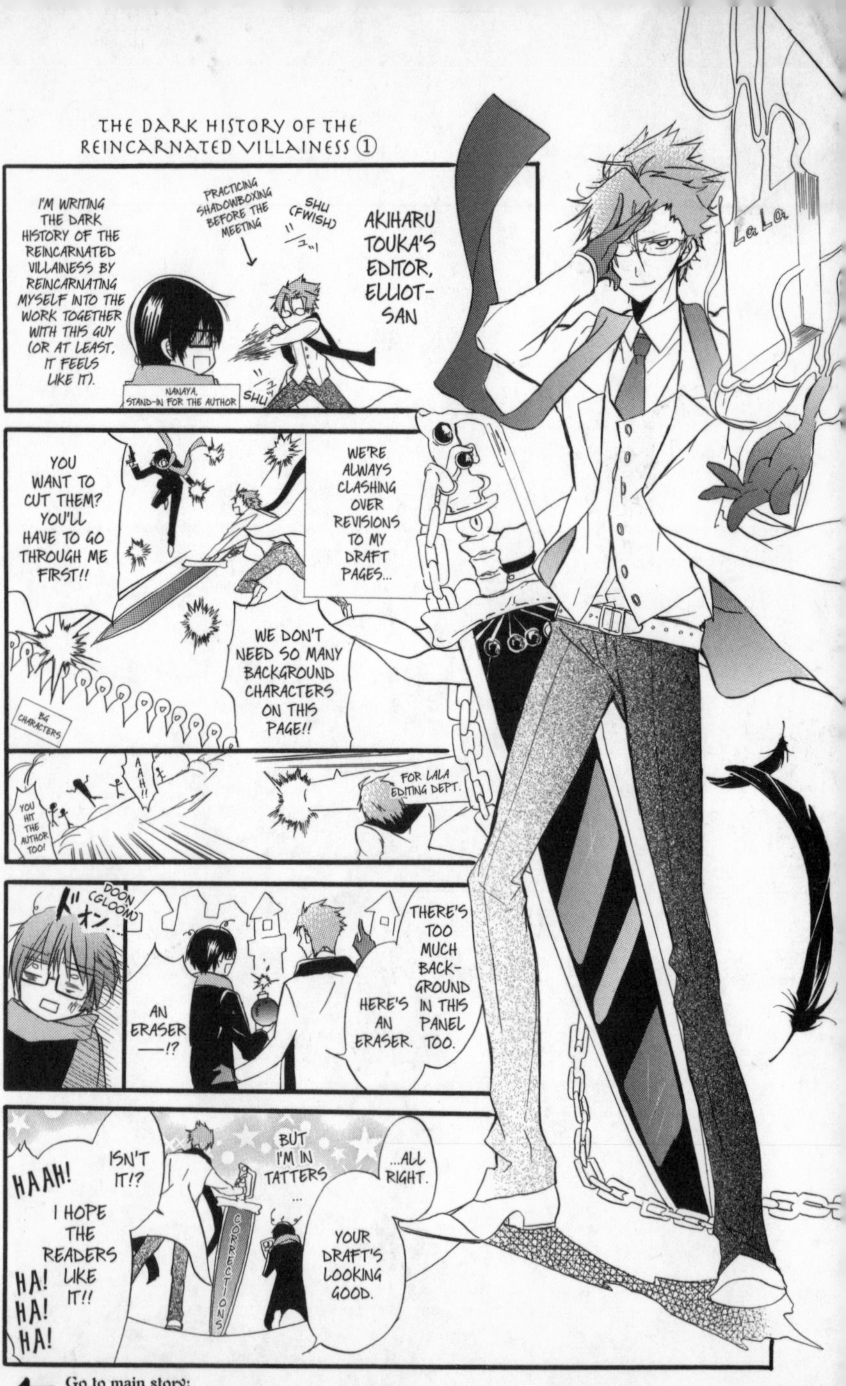
THE DARK HISTORY OF THE REINCARNATED VILLAINESS ①
LaLa
AKIHARU TOUKA'S EDITOR, ELLIOT-SAN
SHU (FWISH)
PRACTICING SHADOWBOXING BEFORE THE MEETING
I'M WRITING THE DARK HISTORY OF THE REINCARNATED VILLAINESS BY REINCARNATING MYSELF INTO THE WORK TOGETHER WITH THIS GUY (OR AT LEAST, IT FEELS LIKE IT).
NANAYA, STAND-IN FOR THE AUTHOR
SHU
WE'RE ALWAYS CLASHING OVER REVISIONS TO MY DRAFT PAGES...
YOU WANT TO CUT THEM? YOU'LL HAVE TO GO THROUGH ME FIRST!!
WE DON'T NEED SO MANY BACKGROUND CHARACTERS ON THIS PAGE!!
BG CHARACTERS
FOR LALA EDITING DEPT.
AAH!!
YOU HIT THE AUTHOR TOO!
THERE'S TOO MUCH BACK-GROUND IN THIS PANEL TOO.
HERE'S AN ERASER.
AN ERASER—!?
DOON (GLOOM)
...ALL RIGHT.
YOUR DRAFT'S LOOKING GOOD.
BUT I'M IN TATTERS...
ISN'T IT!?
HAAH! I HOPE THE READERS LIKE IT!!
HA! HA! HA!
CORRECTIONS

← Go to main story:
The Dark History of the Reincarnated Villainess!

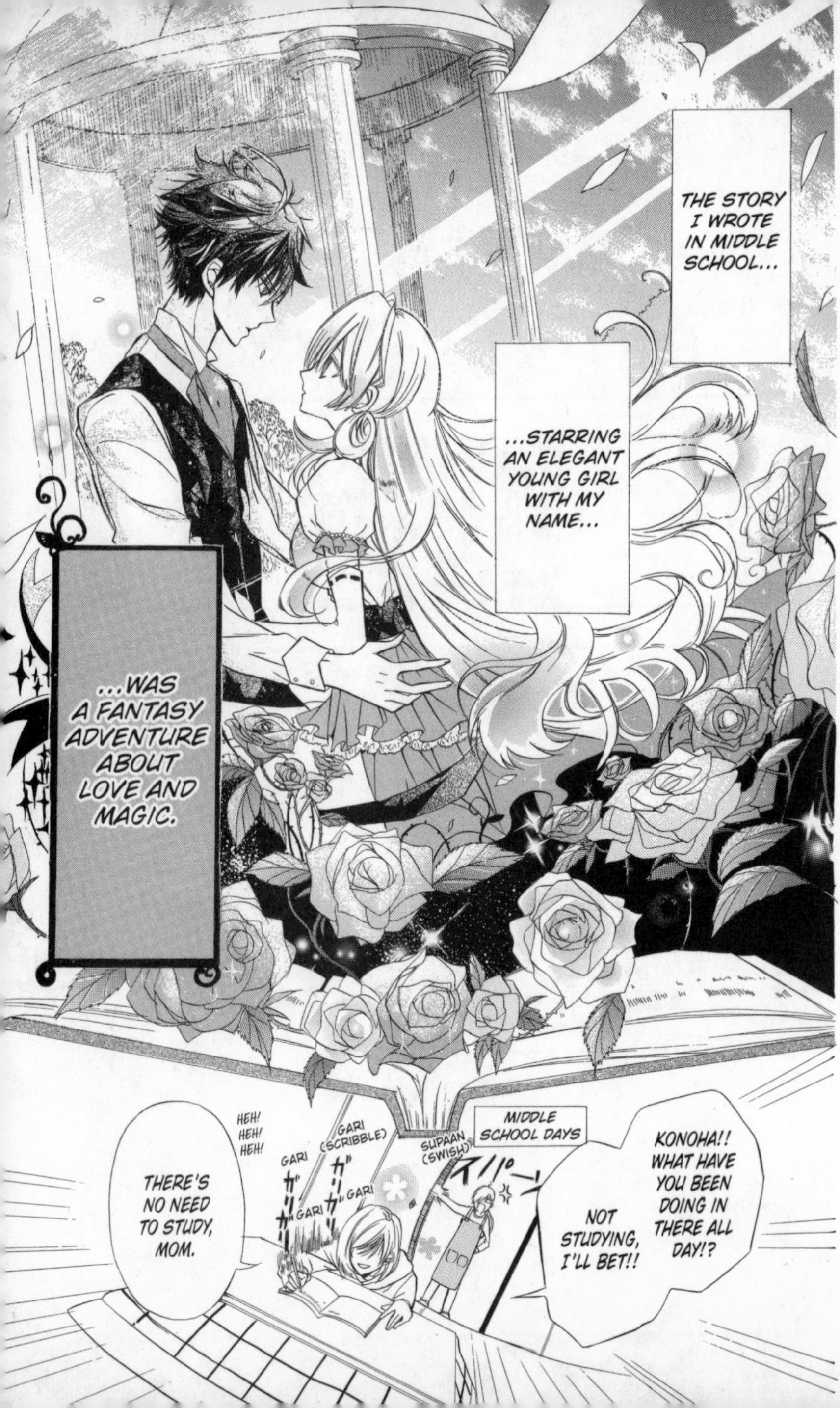
THE STORY I WROTE IN MIDDLE SCHOOL...
...STARRING AN ELEGANT YOUNG GIRL WITH MY NAME...
...WAS A FANTASY ADVENTURE ABOUT LOVE AND MAGIC.
MIDDLE SCHOOL DAYS
KONOHA!! WHAT HAVE YOU BEEN DOING IN THERE ALL DAY!?
NOT STUDYING, I'LL BET!!
SUPAAN (SWISH)
GARI (SCRIBBLE)
GARI
GARI
GARI
HEH! HEH! HEH!
THERE'S NO NEED TO STUDY, MOM.

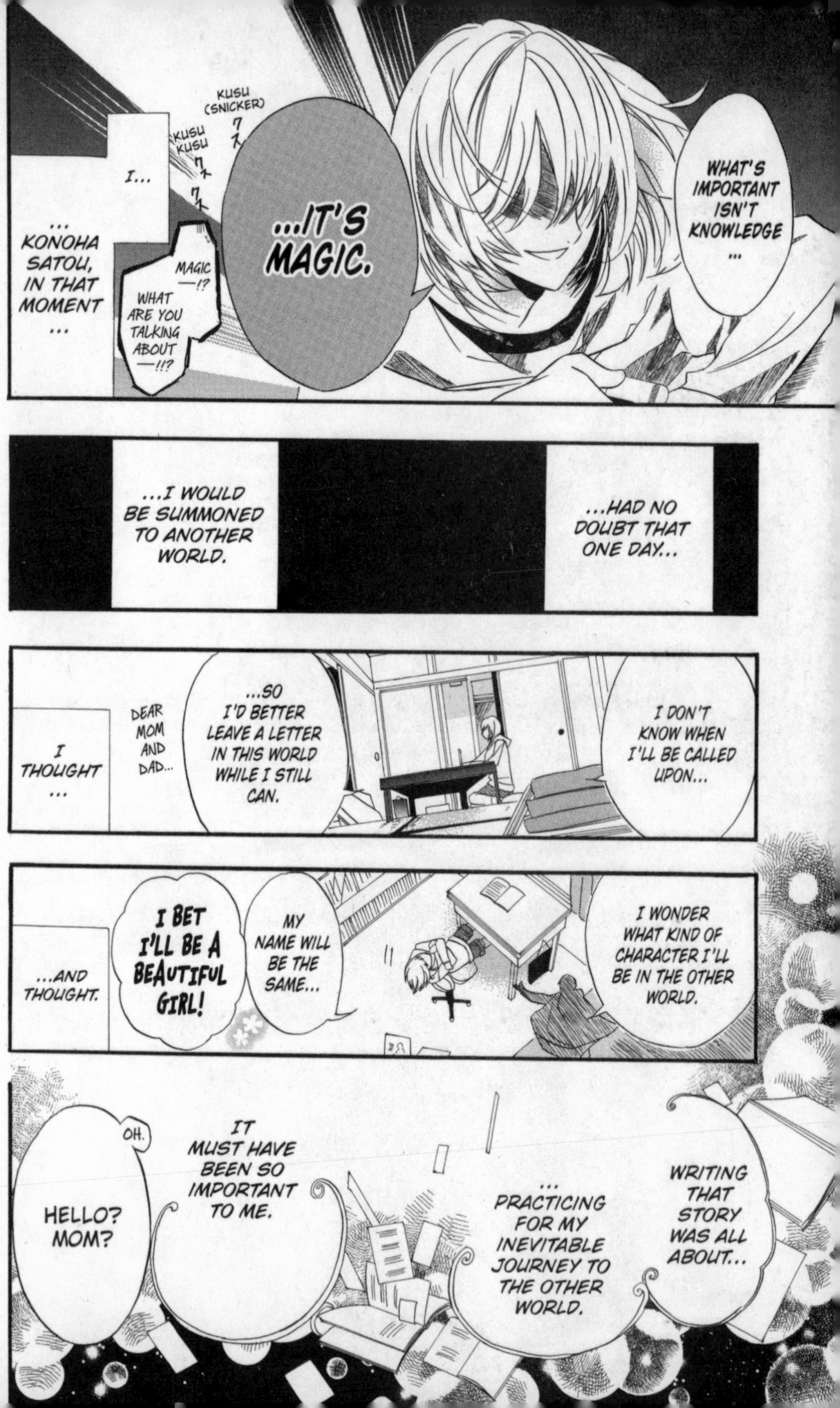
WHAT'S IMPORTANT ISN'T KNOWLEDGE...
...IT'S MAGIC.
KUSU (SNICKER)
KUSU KUSU
MAGIC—!? WHAT ARE YOU TALKING ABOUT—!!?
I...
...KONOHA SATOU, IN THAT MOMENT...
...HAD NO DOUBT THAT ONE DAY...
...I WOULD BE SUMMONED TO ANOTHER WORLD.
I DON'T KNOW WHEN I'LL BE CALLED UPON...
...SO I'D BETTER LEAVE A LETTER IN THIS WORLD WHILE I STILL CAN.
DEAR MOM AND DAD...
I THOUGHT...
I WONDER WHAT KIND OF CHARACTER I'LL BE IN THE OTHER WORLD.
MY NAME WILL BE THE SAME...
I BET I'LL BE A BEAUTIFUL GIRL!
...AND THOUGHT.
WRITING THAT STORY WAS ALL ABOUT...
...PRACTICING FOR MY INEVITABLE JOURNEY TO THE OTHER WORLD.
IT MUST HAVE BEEN SO IMPORTANT TO ME.
OH.
HELLO? MOM?

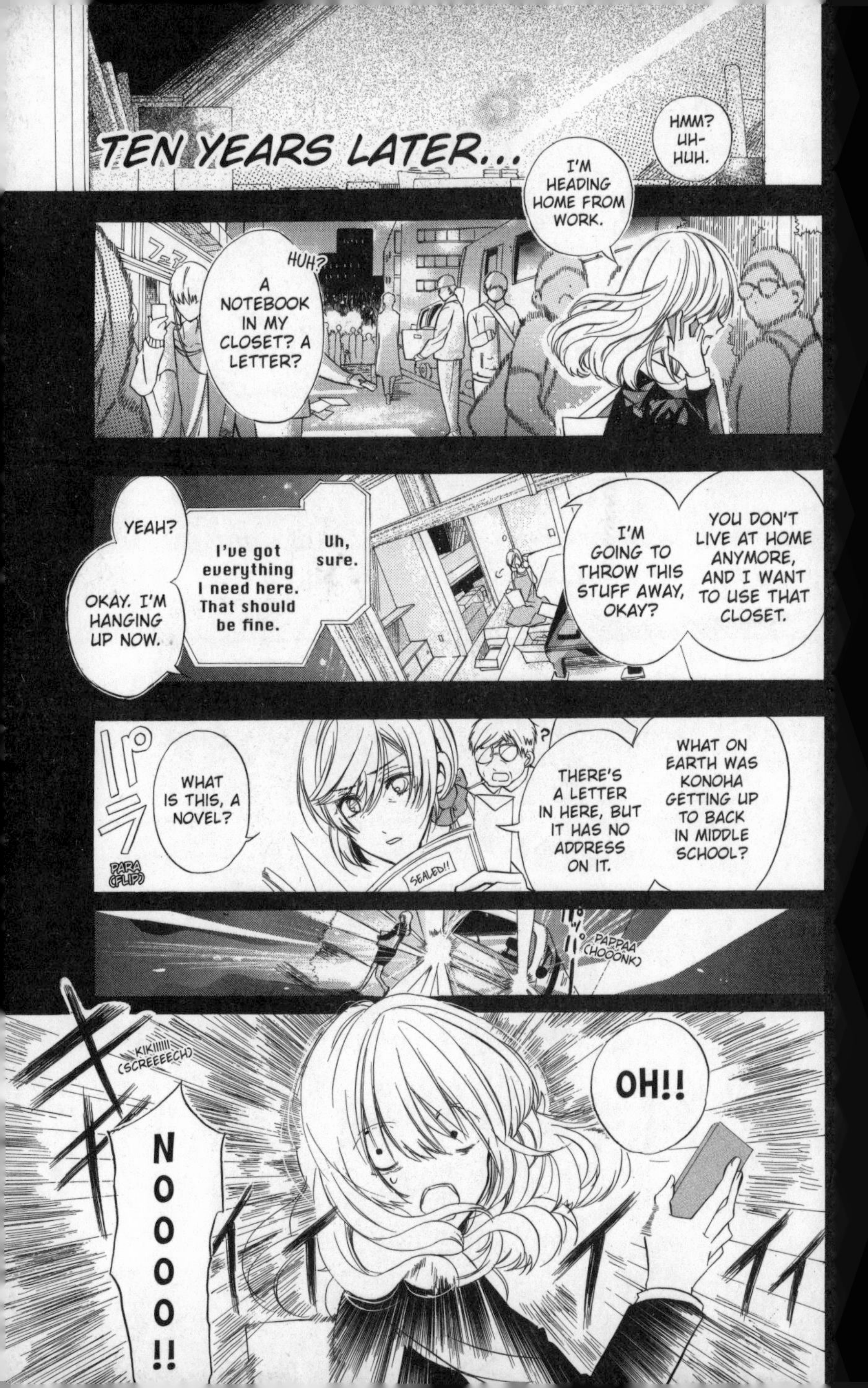
HMM? UH-HUH.
TEN YEARS LATER...
I'M HEADING HOME FROM WORK.
HUH?
A NOTEBOOK IN MY CLOSET? A LETTER?
YOU DON'T LIVE AT HOME ANYMORE, AND I WANT TO USE THAT CLOSET.
I'M GOING TO THROW THIS STUFF AWAY, OKAY?
Uh, sure.
I've got everything I need here. That should be fine.
YEAH?
OKAY. I'M HANGING UP NOW.
WHAT ON EARTH WAS KONOHA GETTING UP TO BACK IN MIDDLE SCHOOL?
THERE'S A LETTER IN HERE, BUT IT HAS NO ADDRESS ON IT.
SEALED!!
WHAT IS THIS, A NOVEL?
PARA (FLIP)
PAPPAA (HOOONK)
OH!!
KIKIIIIII (SCREEEECH)
NOOOOO!!

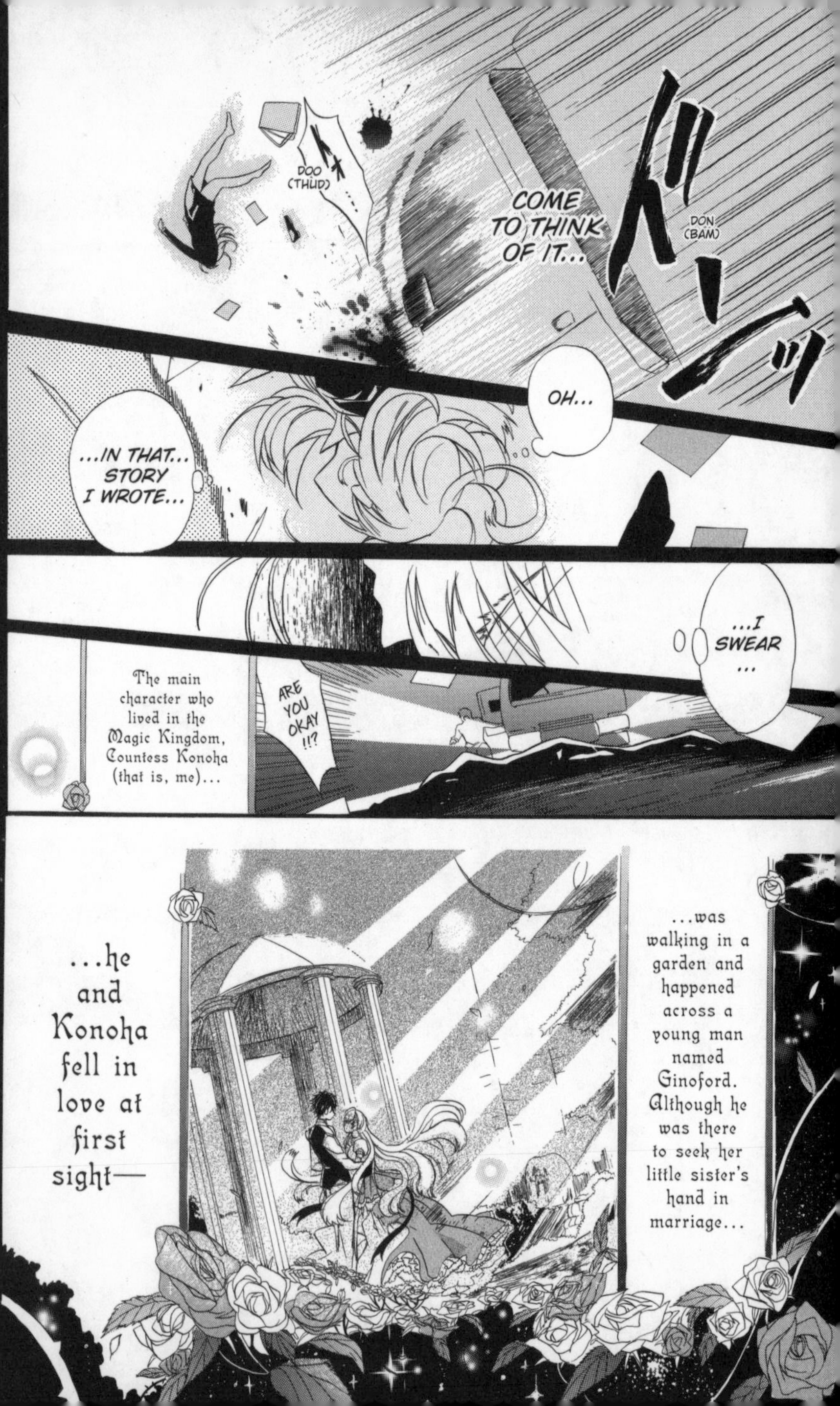
DON (BAM)
COME TO THINK OF IT...
DOO (THUD)
OH...
...IN THAT... STORY I WROTE...
...I SWEAR ...
ARE YOU OKAY !!?
The main character who lived in the Magic Kingdom, Countess Konoha (that is, me)...
...was walking in a garden and happened across a young man named Ginoford. Although he was there to seek her little sister's hand in marriage...
...he and Konoha fell in love at first sight—

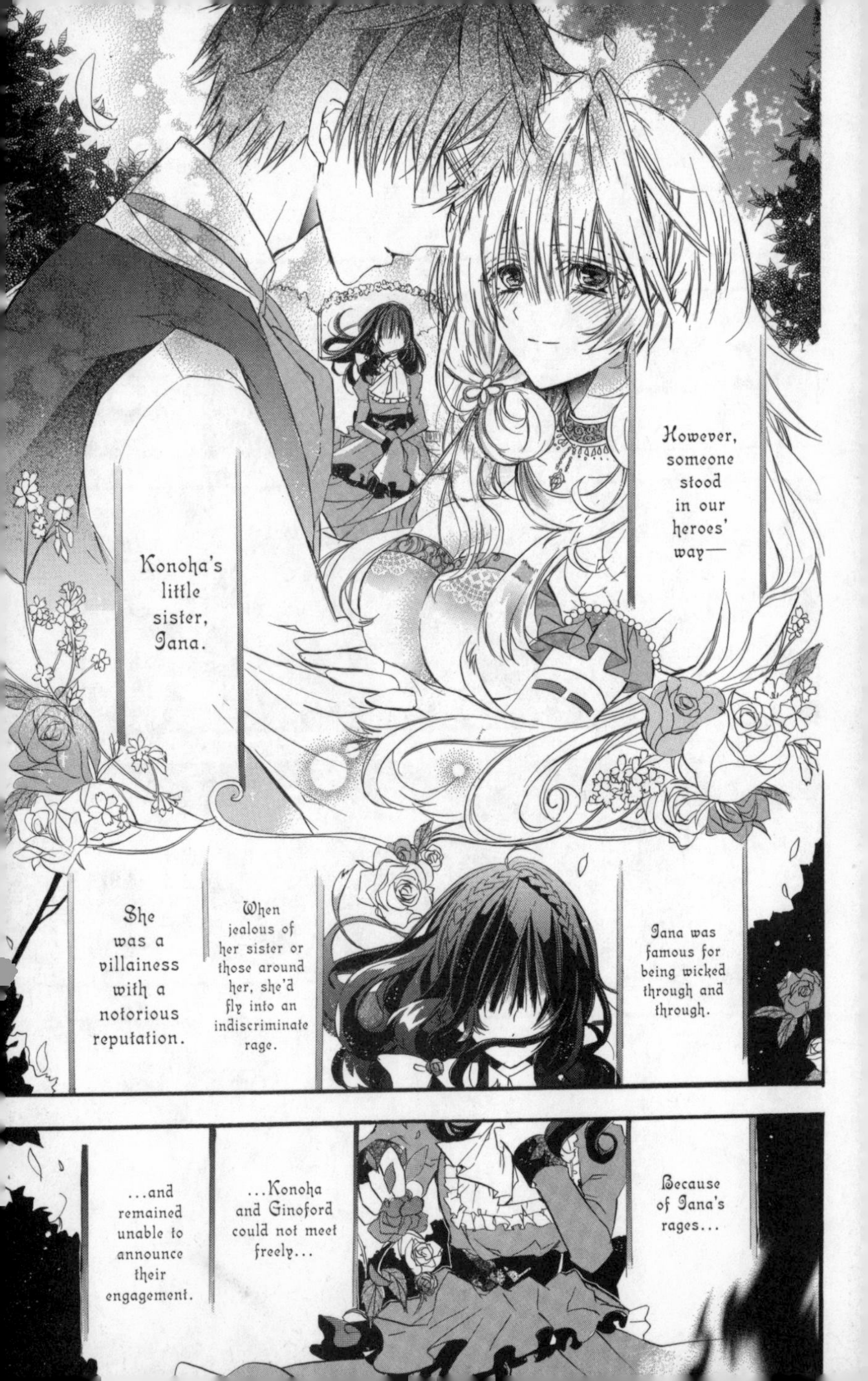
However, someone stood in our heroes' way—
Konoha's little sister, Iana.
Iana was famous for being wicked through and through.
When jealous of her sister or those around her, she'd fly into an indiscriminate rage.
She was a villainess with a notorious reputation.
Because of Iana's rages...
...Konoha and Ginoford could not meet freely...
...and remained unable to announce their engagement.

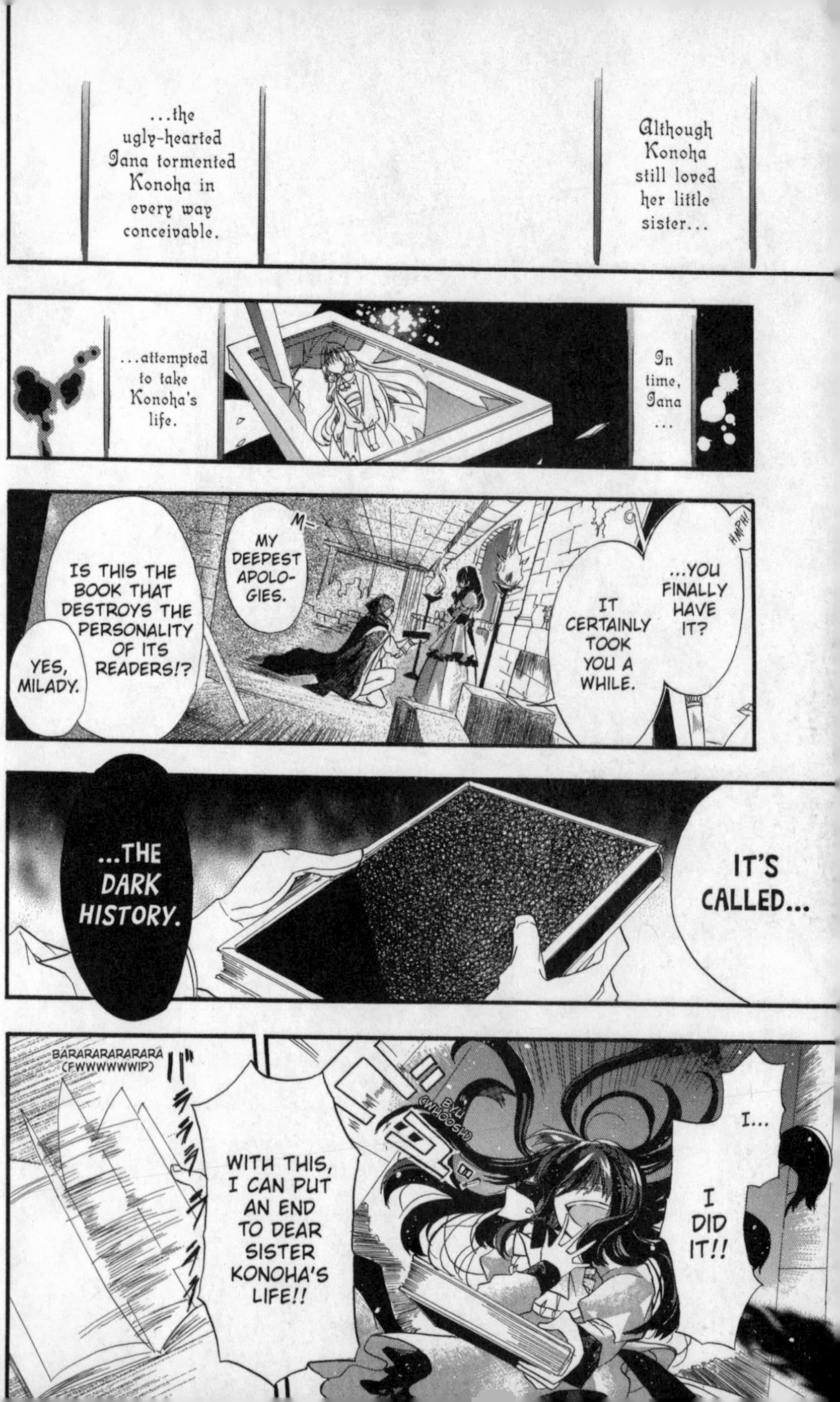
Although Konoha still loved her little sister...
...the ugly-hearted Iana tormented Konoha in every way conceivable.
In time, Iana...
...attempted to take Konoha's life.
HMPH!
...YOU FINALLY HAVE IT?
IT CERTAINLY TOOK YOU A WHILE.
M— MY DEEPEST APOLOGIES.
IS THIS THE BOOK THAT DESTROYS THE PERSONALITY OF ITS READERS!?
YES, MILADY.
IT'S CALLED...
...THE DARK HISTORY.
I...
I DID IT!!
BYU (WHOOSH)
WITH THIS, I CAN PUT AN END TO DEAR SISTER KONOHA'S LIFE!!
BARARARARARARA (FWWWWWWIP)

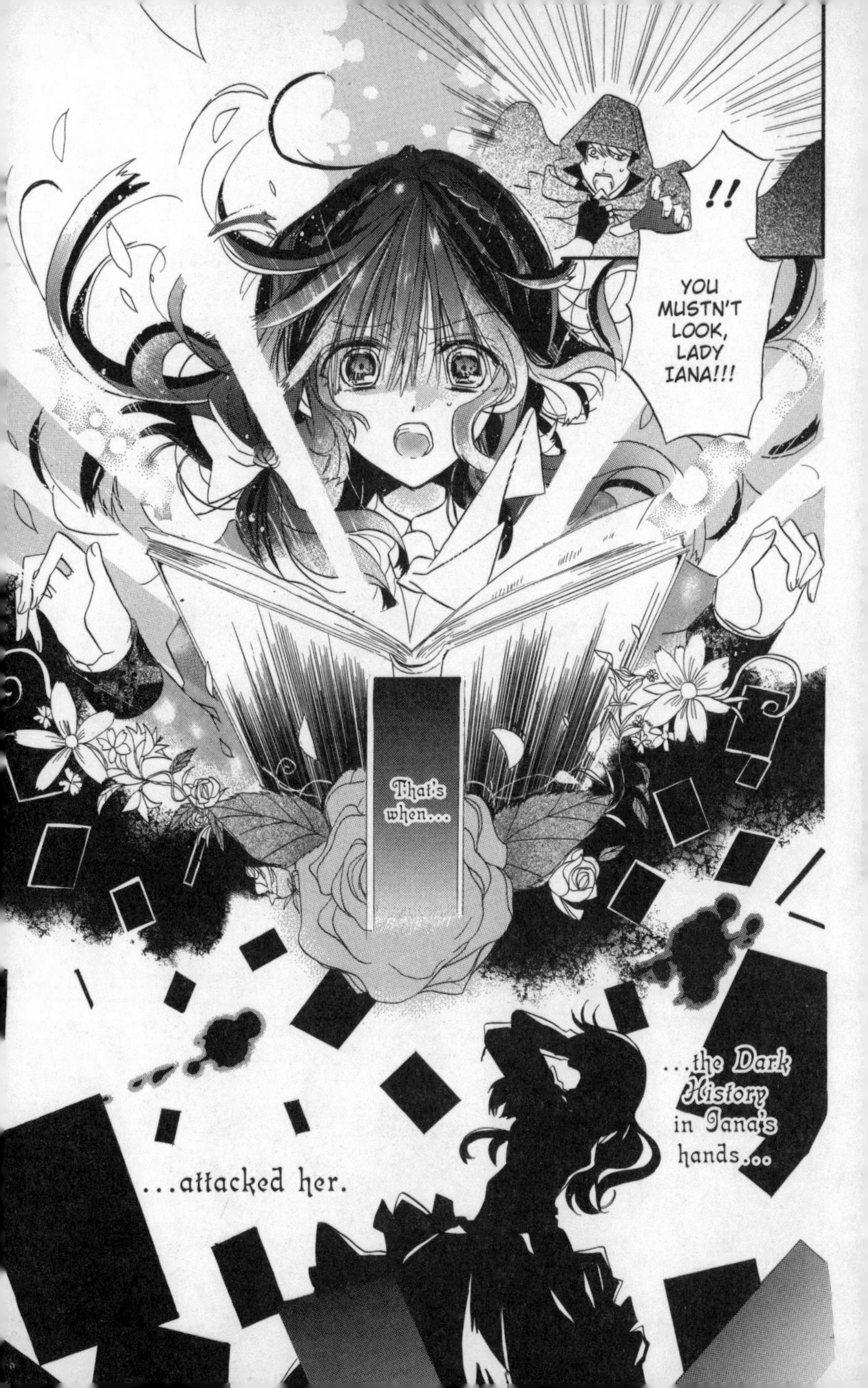
!!
YOU MUSTN'T LOOK, LADY IANA!!!
That's when...
...the Dark History in Iana's hands...
...attacked her.

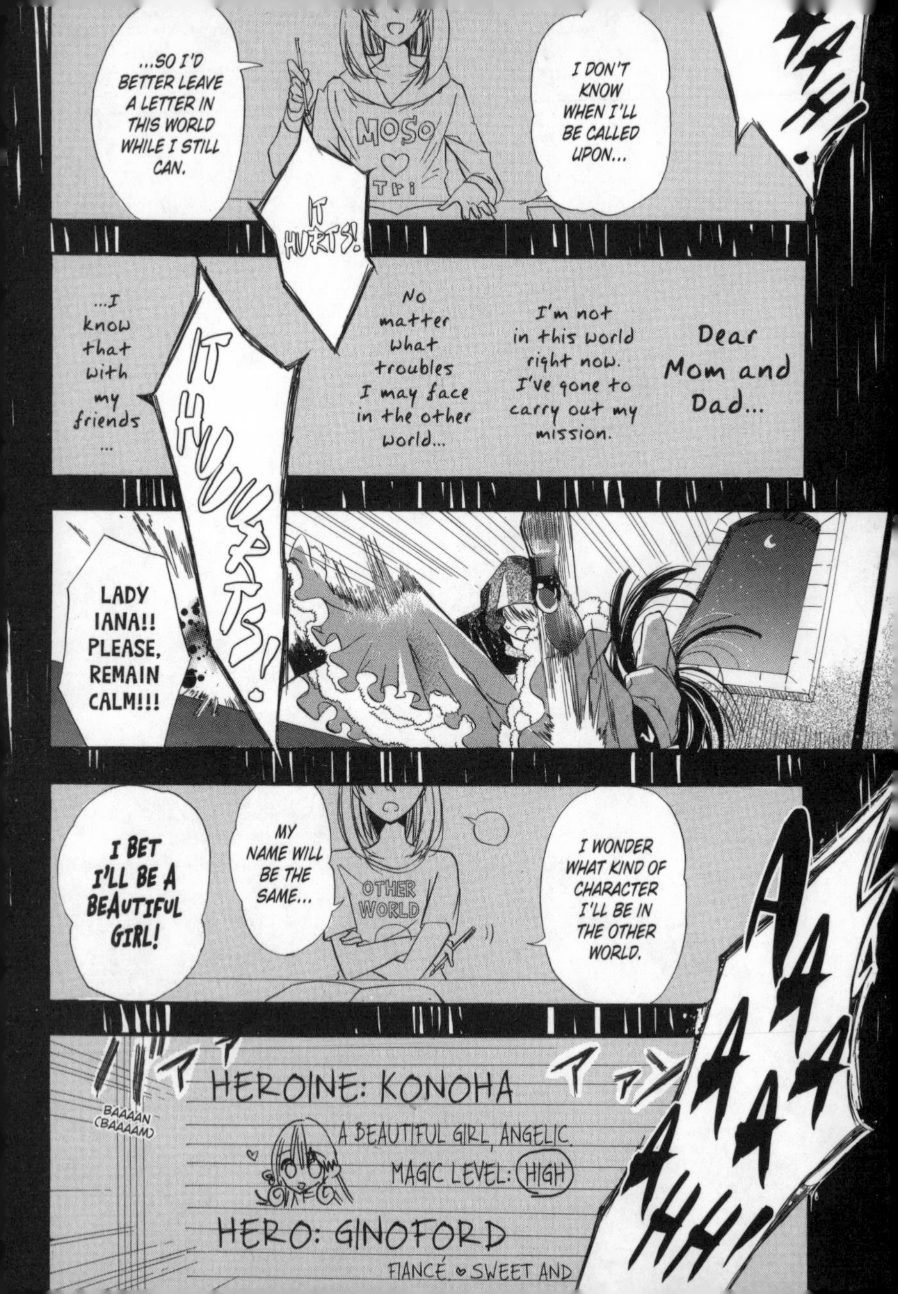
AAH!
I DON'T KNOW WHEN I'LL BE CALLED UPON...
MOSO ♥ Tri
...SO I'D BETTER LEAVE A LETTER IN THIS WORLD WHILE I STILL CAN.
IT HURTS!
Dear Mom and Dad...
I'm not in this world right now. I've gone to carry out my mission.
No matter what troubles I may face in the other world...
...I know that with my friends ...
IT HUUURTS!
LADY IANA!! PLEASE, REMAIN CALM!!!
AAAAAAAAAHH!
I WONDER WHAT KIND OF CHARACTER I'LL BE IN THE OTHER WORLD.
OTHER WORLD
MY NAME WILL BE THE SAME...
I BET I'LL BE A BEAUTIFUL GIRL!
HEROINE: KONOHA
A BEAUTIFUL GIRL, ANGELIC.
MAGIC LEVEL: HIGH
HERO: GINOFORD
FIANCÉ ♥ SWEET AND
BAAAAN (BAAAAM)

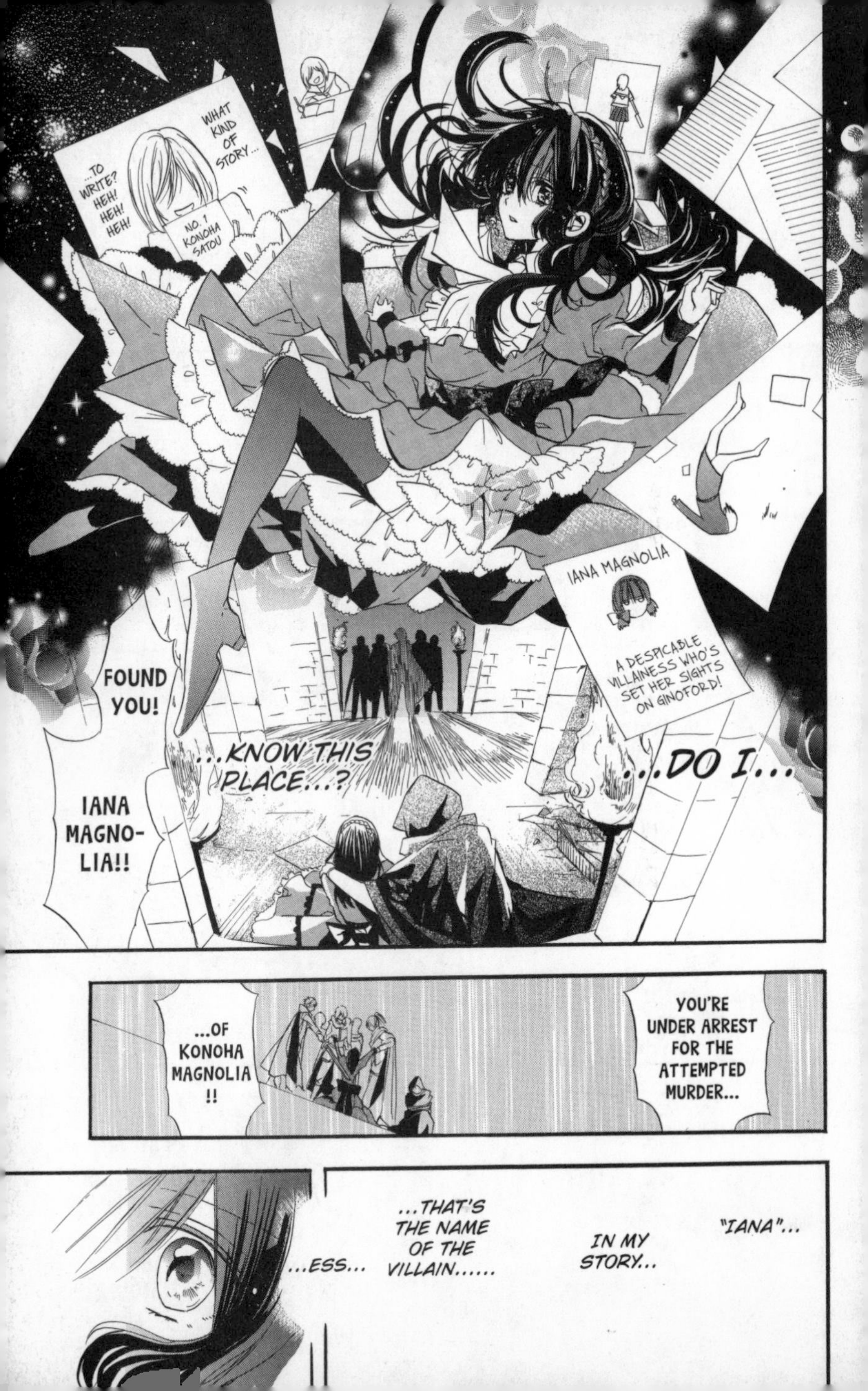

WHAT KIND OF STORY...
...TO WRITE? HEH! HEH! HEH!
NO. 1 KONOHA SATOU
IANA MAGNOLIA
A DESPICABLE VILLAINESS WHO'S SET HER SIGHTS ON GINOFORD!
...DO I...
...KNOW THIS PLACE...?
FOUND YOU!
IANA MAGNOLIA!!
YOU'RE UNDER ARREST FOR THE ATTEMPTED MURDER...
...OF KONOHA MAGNOLIA !!
"IANA"...
IN MY STORY...
...THAT'S THE NAME OF THE VILLAIN......
...ESS...

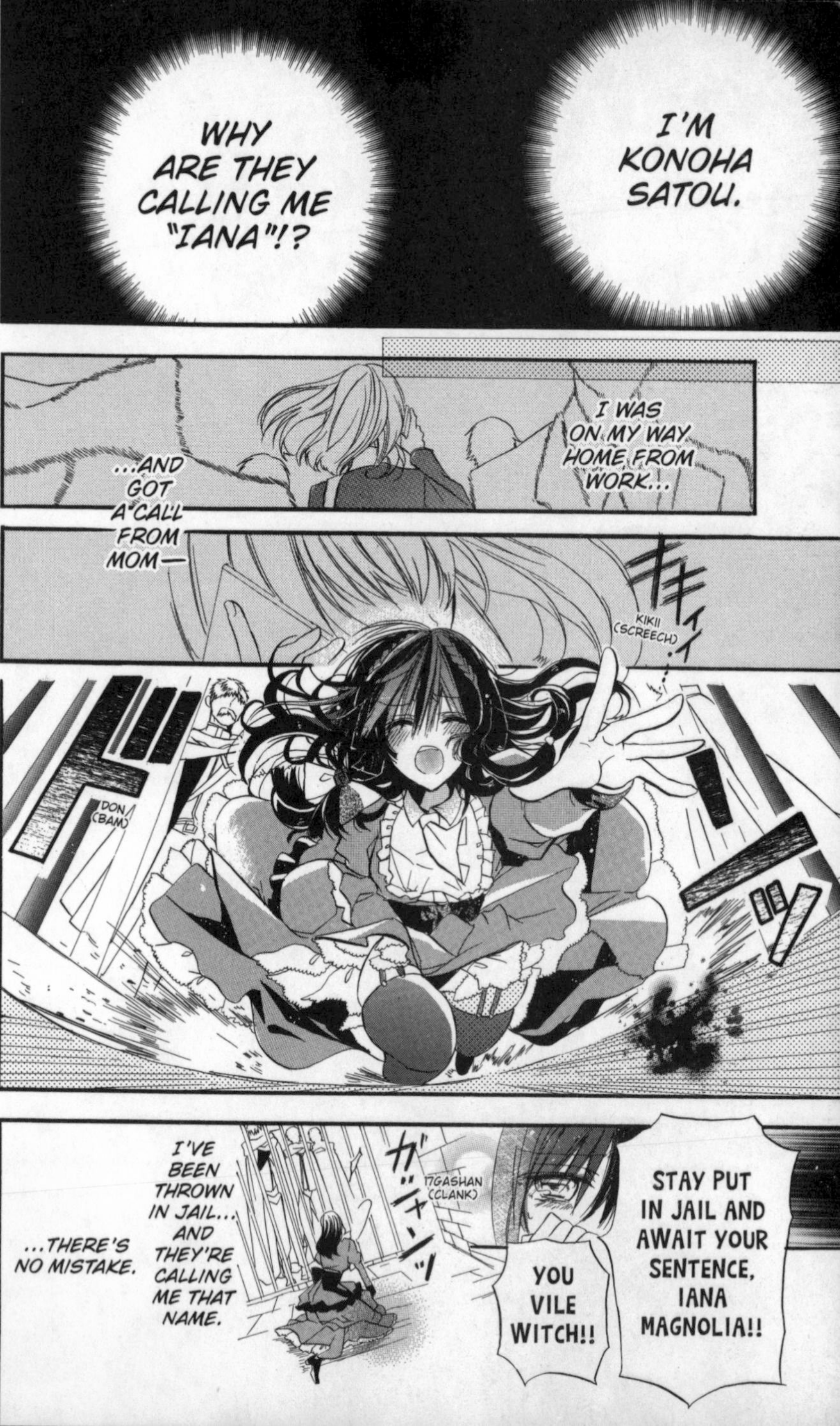
I'M KONOHA SATOU.
WHY ARE THEY CALLING ME "IANA"!?
I WAS ON MY WAY HOME FROM WORK...
...AND GOT A CALL FROM MOM—
KIKII (SCREECH)
DON (BAM)
STAY PUT IN JAIL AND AWAIT YOUR SENTENCE, IANA MAGNOLIA!!
YOU VILE WITCH!!
GASHAN (CLANK)
I'VE BEEN THROWN IN JAIL... AND THEY'RE CALLING ME THAT NAME.
...THERE'S NO MISTAKE.

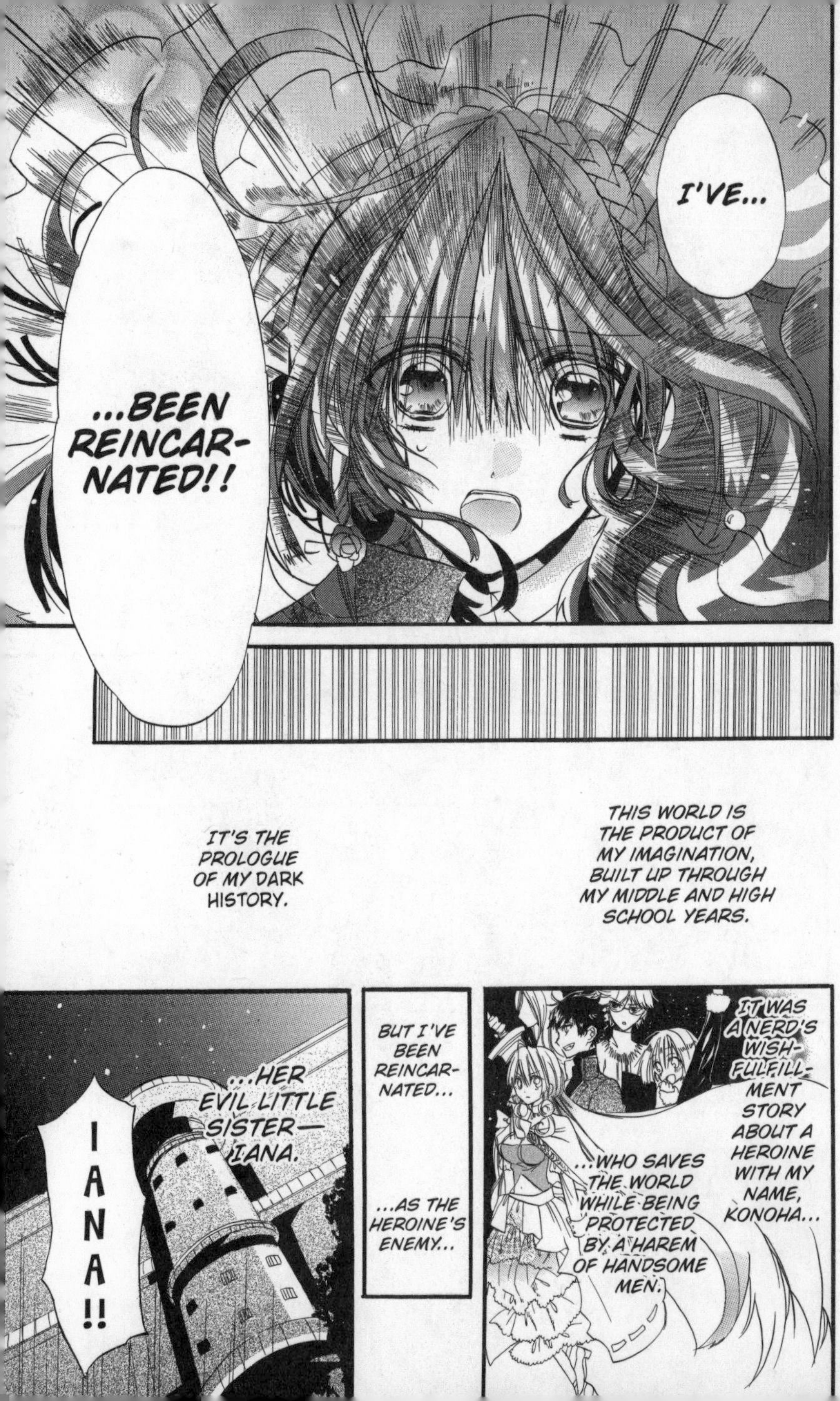
I'VE...
...BEEN REINCAR-NATED!!
THIS WORLD IS THE PRODUCT OF MY IMAGINATION, BUILT UP THROUGH MY MIDDLE AND HIGH SCHOOL YEARS.
IT'S THE PROLOGUE OF MY DARK HISTORY.
IT WAS A NERD'S WISH-FULFILL-MENT STORY ABOUT A HEROINE WITH MY NAME, KONOHA...
...WHO SAVES THE WORLD WHILE BEING PROTECTED BY A HAREM OF HANDSOME MEN.
BUT I'VE BEEN REINCAR-NATED...
...AS THE HEROINE'S ENEMY...
...HER EVIL LITTLE SISTER—IANA.
IANA!!

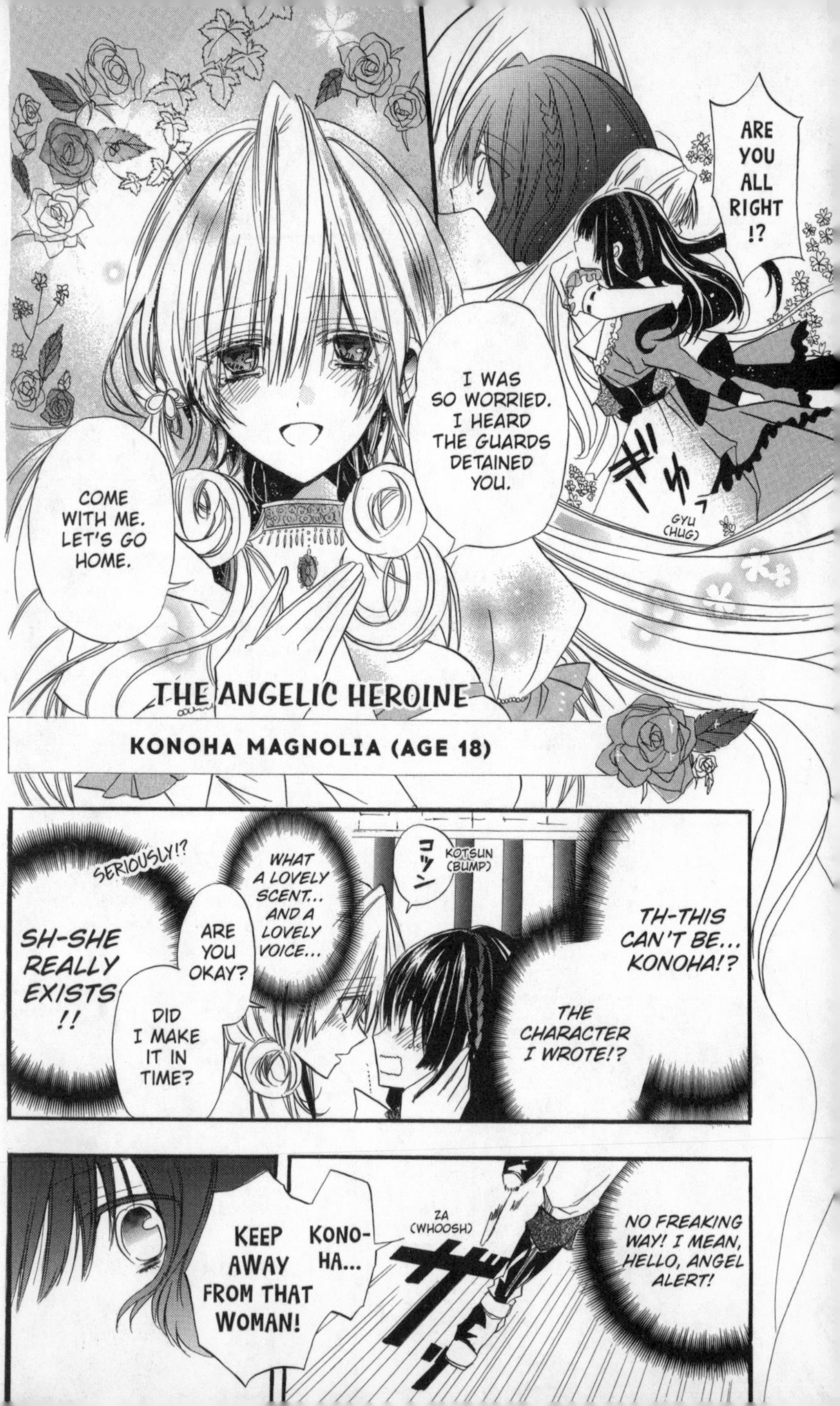
ARE YOU ALL RIGHT!?
GYU (HUG)
I WAS SO WORRIED. I HEARD THE GUARDS DETAINED YOU.
COME WITH ME. LET'S GO HOME.
THE ANGELIC HEROINE
KONOHA MAGNOLIA (AGE 18)
TH-THIS CAN'T BE... KONOHA!?
THE CHARACTER I WROTE!?
KOTSUN (BUMP)
WHAT A LOVELY SCENT... AND A LOVELY VOICE...
ARE YOU OKAY?
DID I MAKE IT IN TIME?
SERIOUSLY!?
SH-SHE REALLY EXISTS!!
NO FREAKING WAY! I MEAN, HELLO, ANGEL ALERT!
ZA (WHOOSH)
KONOHA...
KEEP AWAY FROM THAT WOMAN!

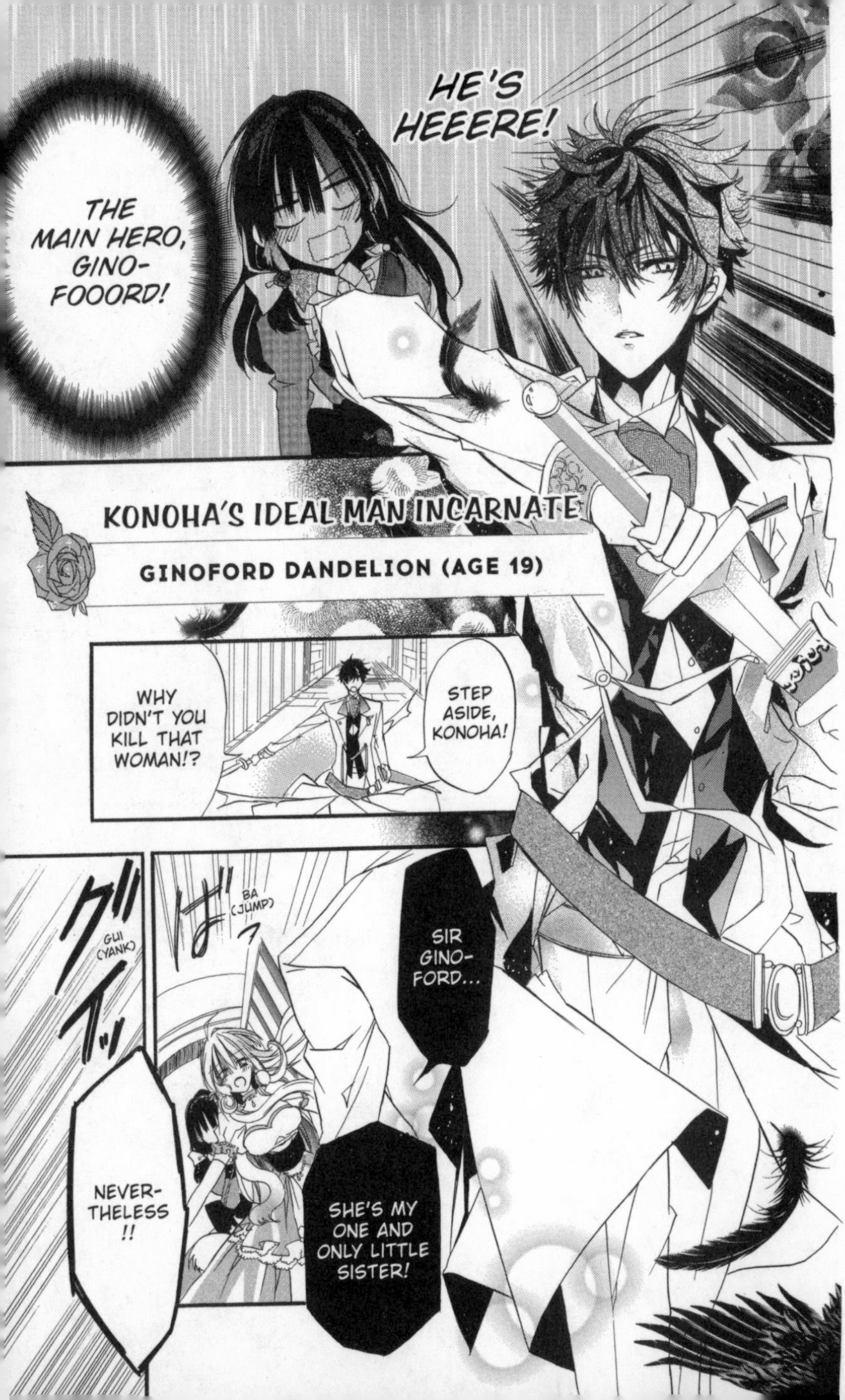

HE'S HEEEERE!
THE MAIN HERO, GINO-FOOORD!
KONOHA'S IDEAL MAN INCARNATE
GINOFORD DANDELION (AGE 19)
STEP ASIDE, KONOHA!
WHY DIDN'T YOU KILL THAT WOMAN!?
SIR GINO-FORD...
SHE'S MY ONE AND ONLY LITTLE SISTER!
BA (JUMP)
GUI (YANK)
NEVER-THELESS!!

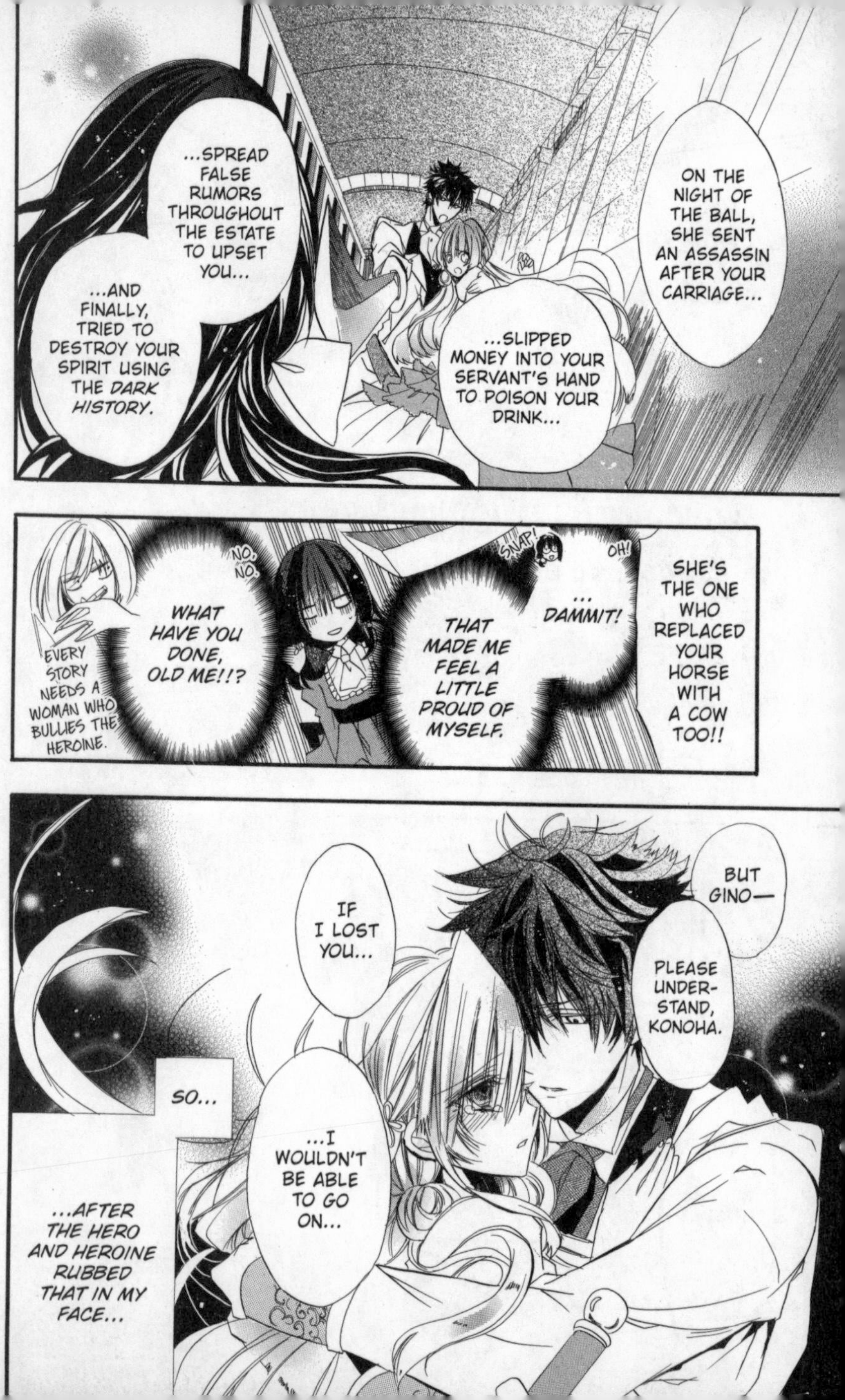
ON THE NIGHT OF THE BALL, SHE SENT AN ASSASSIN AFTER YOUR CARRIAGE...
...SLIPPED MONEY INTO YOUR SERVANT'S HAND TO POISON YOUR DRINK...
...SPREAD FALSE RUMORS THROUGHOUT THE ESTATE TO UPSET YOU...
...AND FINALLY, TRIED TO DESTROY YOUR SPIRIT USING THE *DARK HISTORY*.
SHE'S THE ONE WHO REPLACED YOUR HORSE WITH A COW TOO!!
OH!
SNAP!
...DAMMIT!
THAT MADE ME FEEL A LITTLE PROUD OF MYSELF.
NO. NO.
WHAT HAVE YOU DONE, OLD ME!!?
EVERY STORY NEEDS A WOMAN WHO BULLIES THE HEROINE.
BUT GINO—
PLEASE UNDER-STAND, KONOHA.
IF I LOST YOU...
...I WOULDN'T BE ABLE TO GO ON...
SO...
...AFTER THE HERO AND HEROINE RUBBED THAT IN MY FACE...

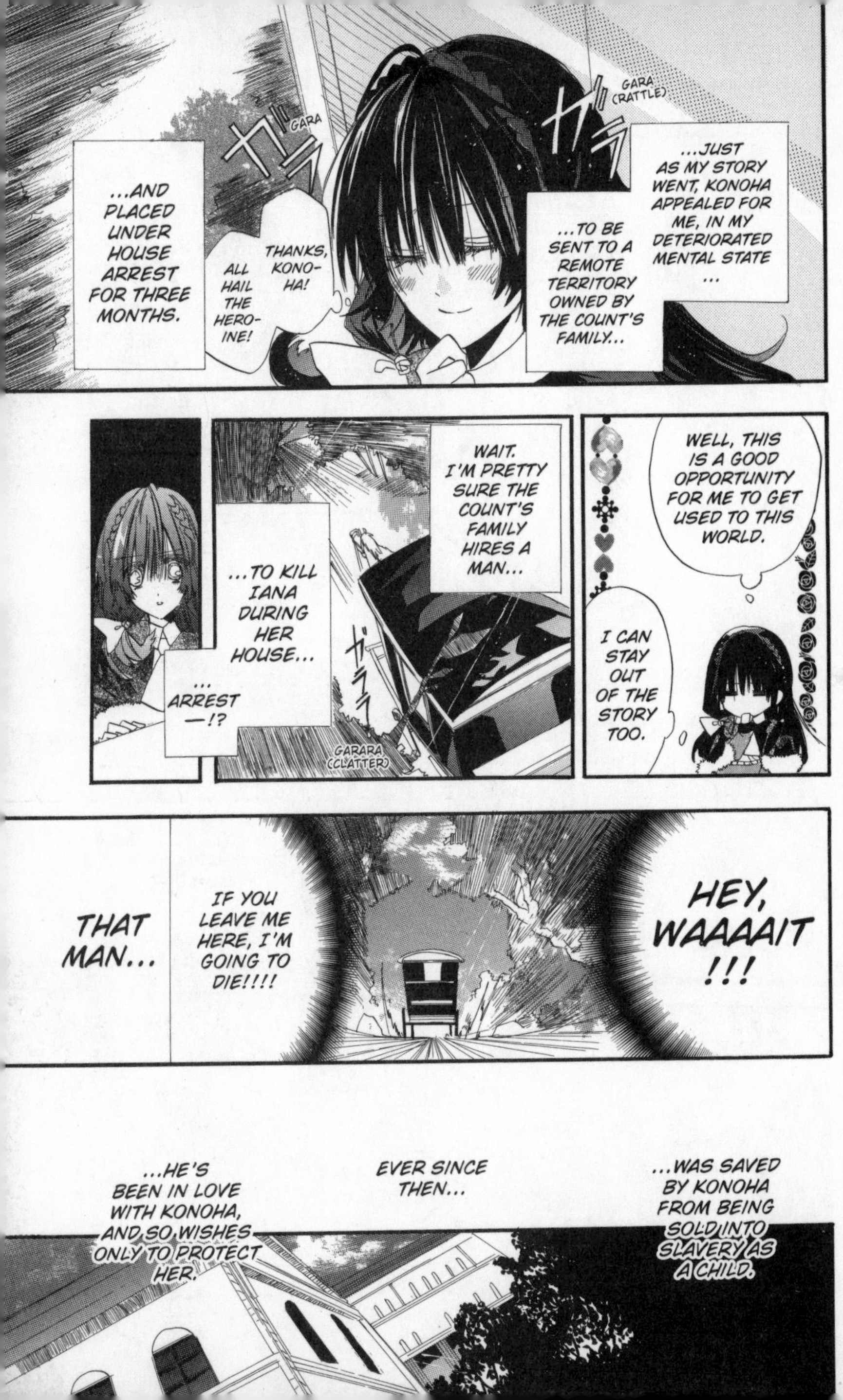
GARA (RATTLE)
...JUST AS MY STORY WENT, KONOHA APPEALED FOR ME, IN MY DETERIORATED MENTAL STATE ...
...TO BE SENT TO A REMOTE TERRITORY OWNED BY THE COUNT'S FAMILY...
THANKS, KONOHA!
ALL HAIL THE HEROINE!
GARA
...AND PLACED UNDER HOUSE ARREST FOR THREE MONTHS.
WELL, THIS IS A GOOD OPPORTUNITY FOR ME TO GET USED TO THIS WORLD.
I CAN STAY OUT OF THE STORY TOO.
WAIT. I'M PRETTY SURE THE COUNT'S FAMILY HIRES A MAN...
...TO KILL IANA DURING HER HOUSE...
GARARA (CLATTER)
... ARREST—!?
HEY, WAAAAIT!!!
IF YOU LEAVE ME HERE, I'M GOING TO DIE!!!!
THAT MAN...
...WAS SAVED BY KONOHA FROM BEING SOLD INTO SLAVERY AS A CHILD.
EVER SINCE THEN...
...HE'S BEEN IN LOVE WITH KONOHA, AND SO WISHES ONLY TO PROTECT HER.

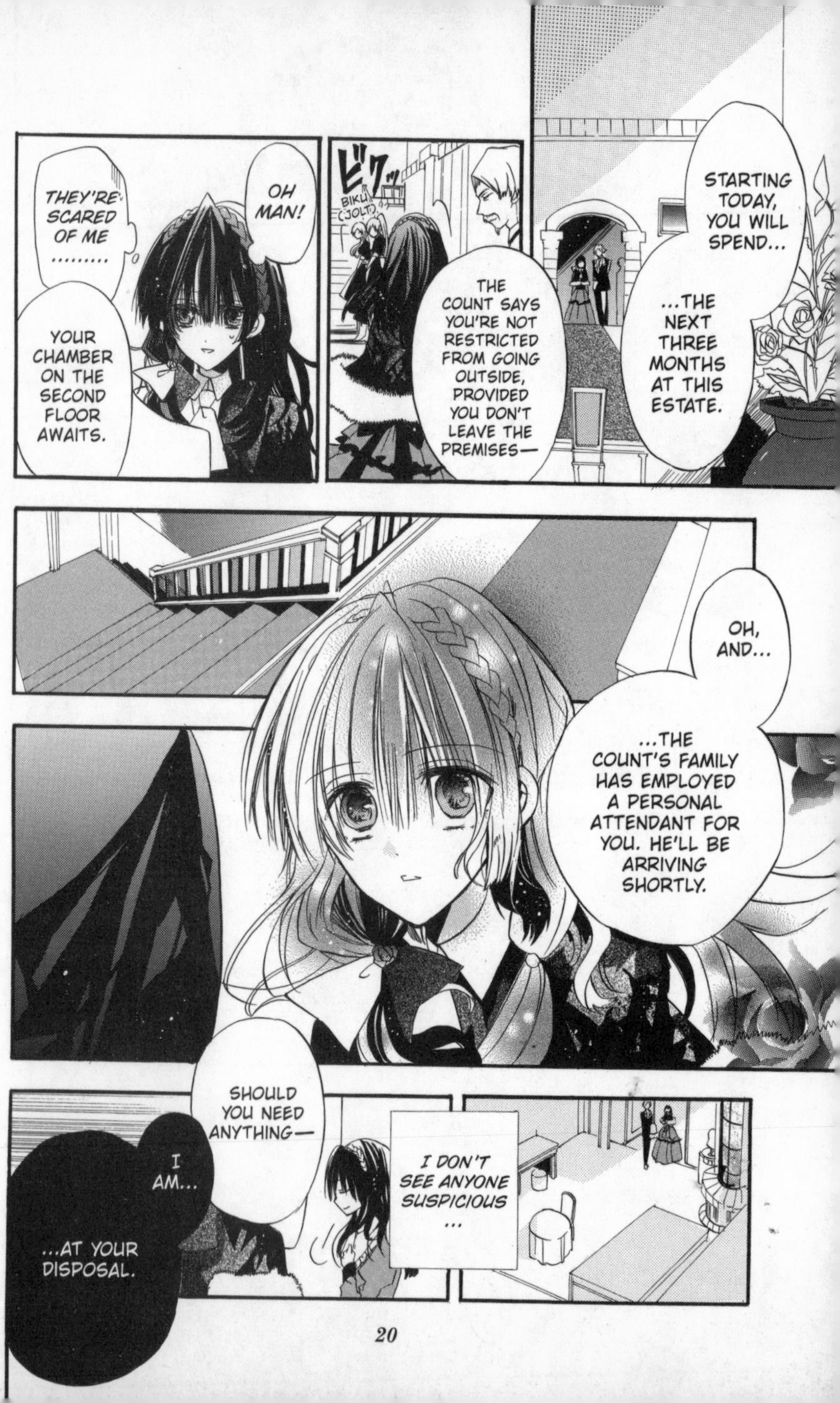

STARTING TODAY, YOU WILL SPEND...
...THE NEXT THREE MONTHS AT THIS ESTATE.
ビクッ
BIKU (JOLT)
THE COUNT SAYS YOU'RE NOT RESTRICTED FROM GOING OUTSIDE, PROVIDED YOU DON'T LEAVE THE PREMISES—
OH MAN!
THEY'RE SCARED OF ME ....
YOUR CHAMBER ON THE SECOND FLOOR AWAITS.
OH, AND...
...THE COUNT'S FAMILY HAS EMPLOYED A PERSONAL ATTENDANT FOR YOU. HE'LL BE ARRIVING SHORTLY.
SHOULD YOU NEED ANYTHING—
I DON'T SEE ANYONE SUSPICIOUS ...
I AM...
...AT YOUR DISPOSAL.

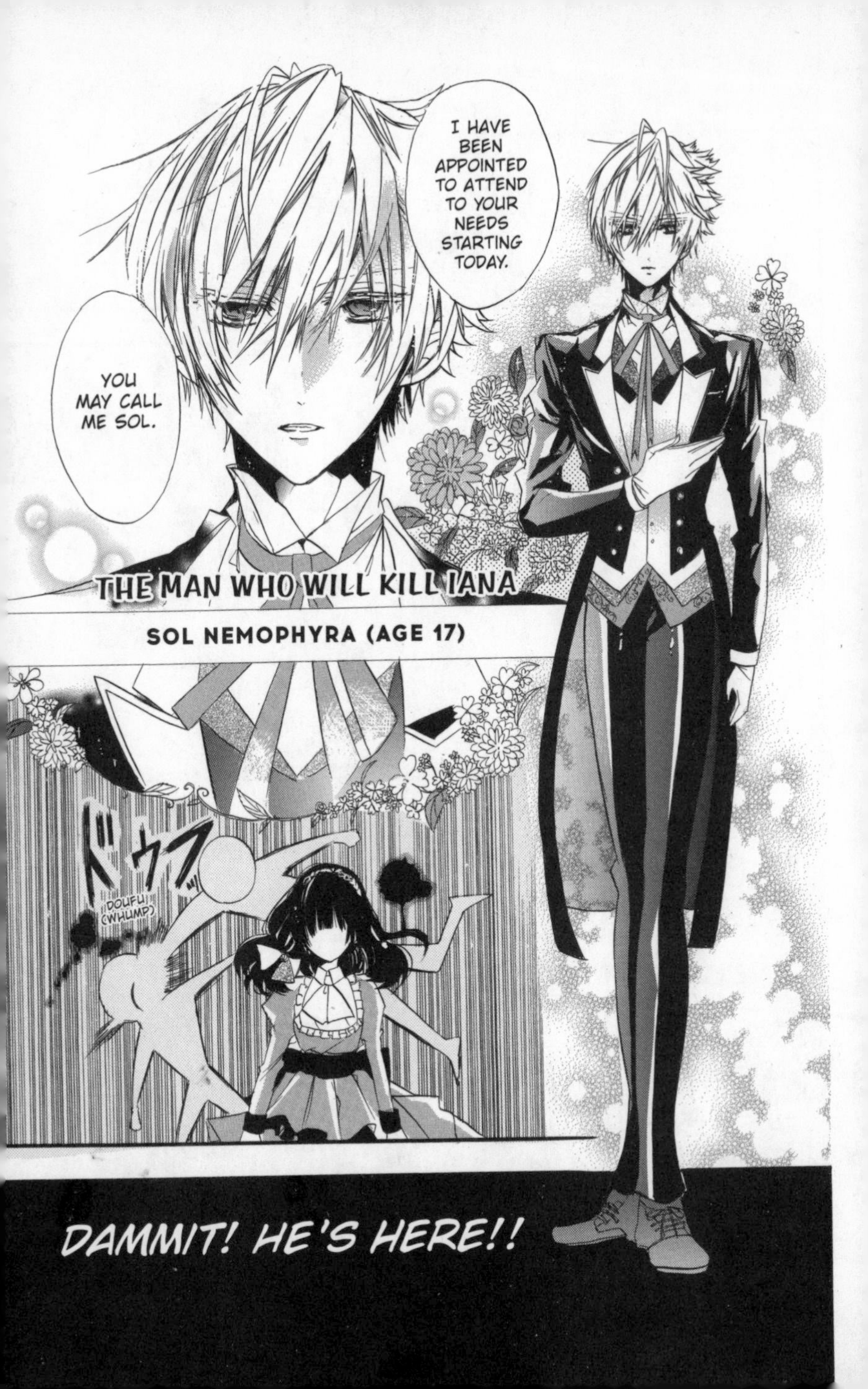
I HAVE BEEN APPOINTED TO ATTEND TO YOUR NEEDS STARTING TODAY.
YOU MAY CALL ME SOL.
THE MAN WHO WILL KILL IANA
SOL NEMOPHYRA (AGE 17)
ドゥフ
DOUFU (WHUMP)
DAMMIT! HE'S HERE!!

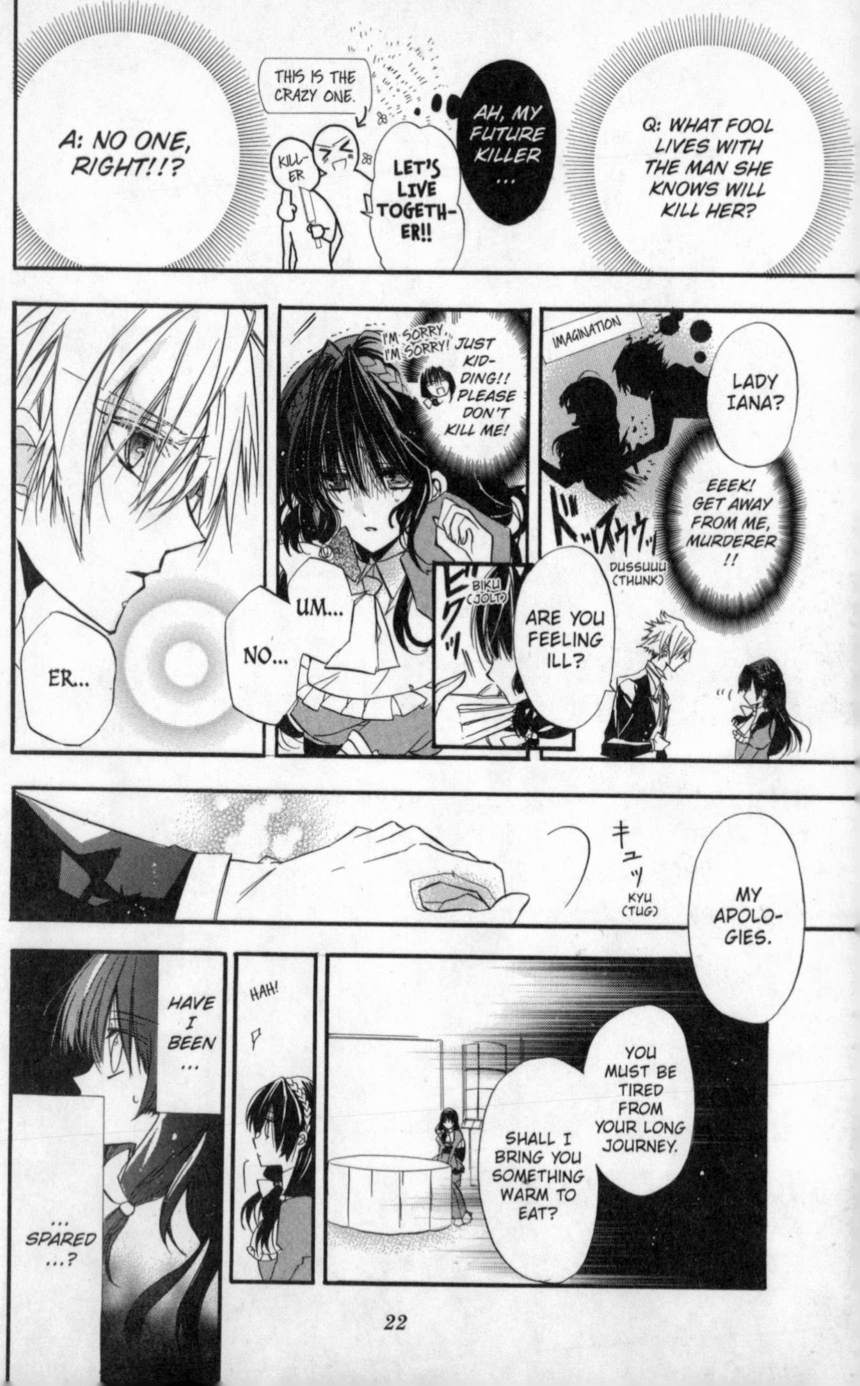
Q: WHAT FOOL LIVES WITH THE MAN SHE KNOWS WILL KILL HER?
AH, MY FUTURE KILLER ...
LET'S LIVE TOGETH-ER!!
THIS IS THE CRAZY ONE.
KILL-ER
A: NO ONE, RIGHT!!?
IMAGINATION
LADY IANA?
EEEK! GET AWAY FROM ME, MURDERER !!
ドッスウッ
DUSSUUU (THUNK)
ARE YOU FEELING ILL?
ビクッ
BIKU (JOLT)
JUST KID-DING!! PLEASE DON'T KILL ME!
I'M SORRY I'M SORRY!
UM...
NO...
ER...
MY APOLO-GIES.
キュッ
KYU (TUG)
YOU MUST BE TIRED FROM YOUR LONG JOURNEY.
SHALL I BRING YOU SOMETHING WARM TO EAT?
HAH!
HAVE I BEEN ...
... SPARED ...?

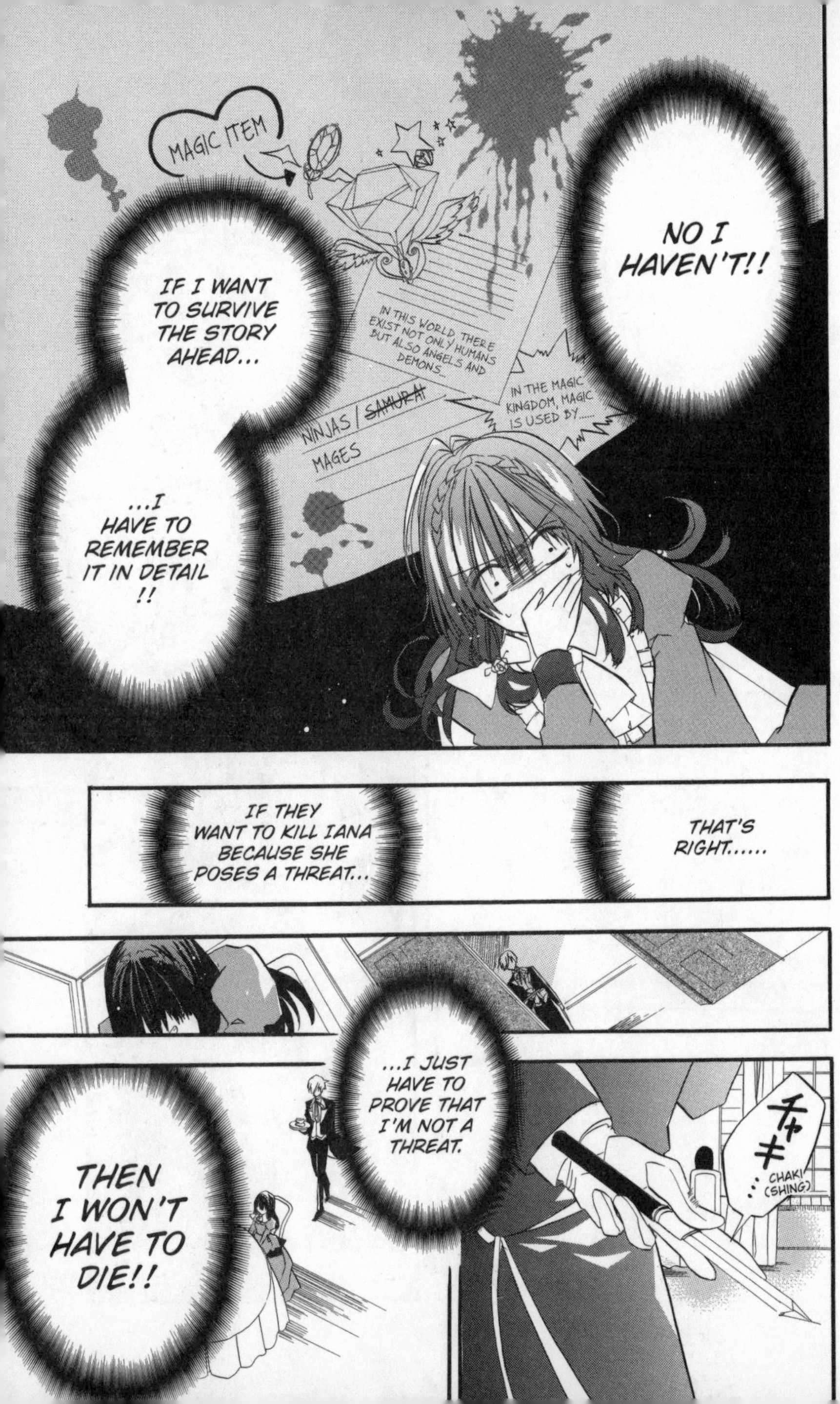
NO I HAVEN'T!!
MAGIC ITEM
IN THIS WORLD, THERE EXIST NOT ONLY HUMANS BUT ALSO ANGELS AND DEMONS...
IN THE MAGIC KINGDOM, MAGIC IS USED BY......
NINJAS / SAMURAI
MAGES
IF I WANT TO SURVIVE THE STORY AHEAD...
...I HAVE TO REMEMBER IT IN DETAIL!!
THAT'S RIGHT......
IF THEY WANT TO KILL IANA BECAUSE SHE POSES A THREAT...
チャキ
CHAKI (SHING)
...I JUST HAVE TO PROVE THAT I'M NOT A THREAT.
THEN I WON'T HAVE TO DIE!!

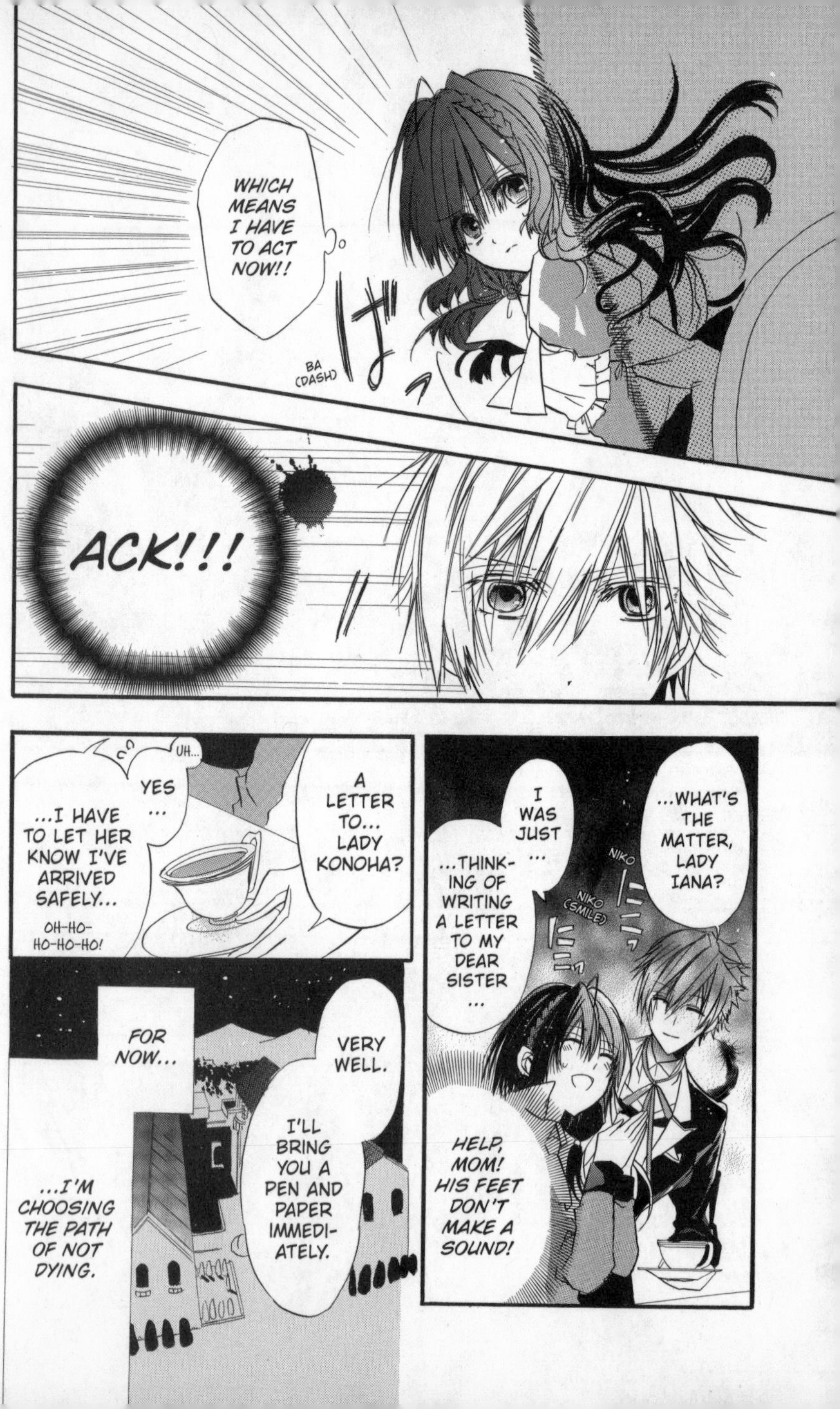
WHICH MEANS I HAVE TO ACT NOW!!
BA (DASH)
ACK!!!
...WHAT'S THE MATTER, LADY IANA?
NIKO
NIKO (SMILE)
I WAS JUST ...
...THINKING OF WRITING A LETTER TO MY DEAR SISTER ...
HELP, MOM! HIS FEET DON'T MAKE A SOUND!
A LETTER TO... LADY KONOHA?
UH...
YES ...
...I HAVE TO LET HER KNOW I'VE ARRIVED SAFELY...
OH-HO-HO-HO-HO!
VERY WELL.
I'LL BRING YOU A PEN AND PAPER IMMEDIATELY.
FOR NOW...
...I'M CHOOSING THE PATH OF NOT DYING.

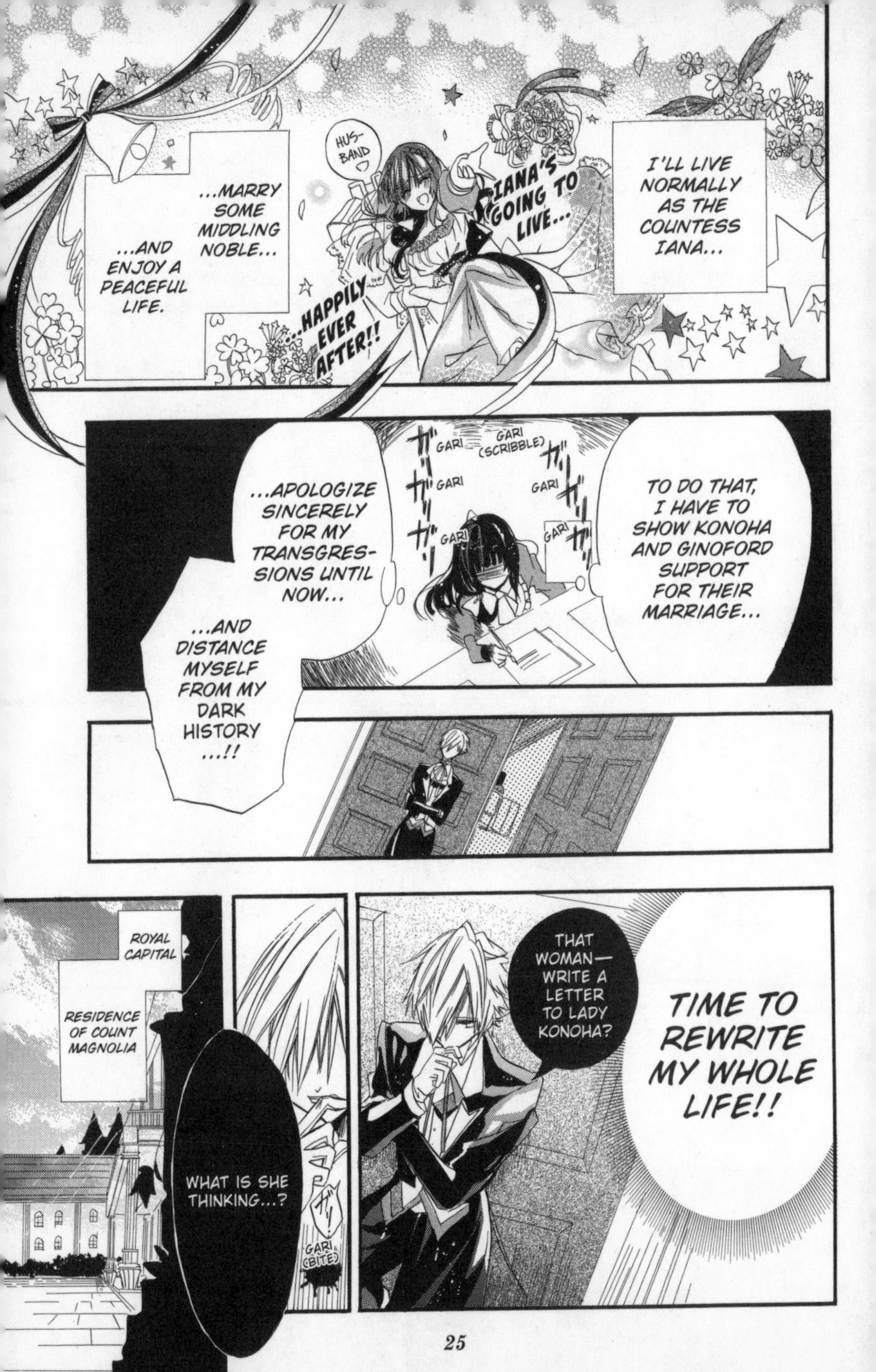
I'LL LIVE NORMALLY AS THE COUNTESS IANA...
IANA'S GOING TO LIVE...
HUS-BAND ♡
...MARRY SOME MIDDLING NOBLE...
...AND ENJOY A PEACEFUL LIFE.
...HAPPILY EVER AFTER!!
TO DO THAT, I HAVE TO SHOW KONOHA AND GINOFORD SUPPORT FOR THEIR MARRIAGE...
GARI
GARI (SCRIBBLE)
GARI
GARI
GARI
GARI
...APOLOGIZE SINCERELY FOR MY TRANSGRES-SIONS UNTIL NOW...
...AND DISTANCE MYSELF FROM MY DARK HISTORY...!!
TIME TO REWRITE MY WHOLE LIFE!!
THAT WOMAN—WRITE A LETTER TO LADY KONOHA?
WHAT IS SHE THINKING...?
GARI (BITE)
ROYAL CAPITAL
RESIDENCE OF COUNT MAGNOLIA

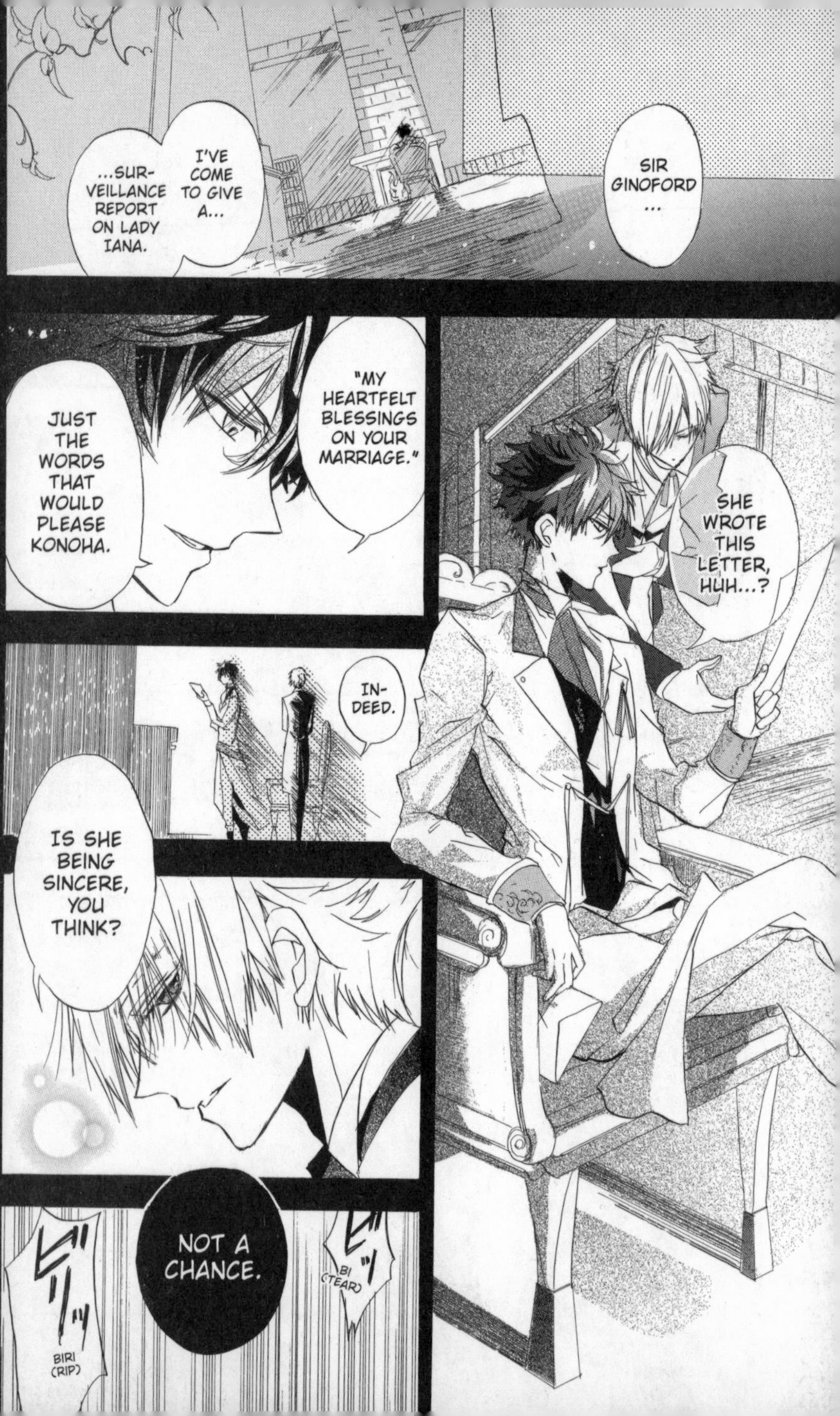
SIR GINOFORD ...
I'VE COME TO GIVE A...
...SUR-VEILLANCE REPORT ON LADY IANA.
SHE WROTE THIS LETTER, HUH...?
"MY HEARTFELT BLESSINGS ON YOUR MARRIAGE."
JUST THE WORDS THAT WOULD PLEASE KONOHA.
IN-DEED.
IS SHE BEING SINCERE, YOU THINK?
BI (TEAR)
NOT A CHANCE.
BIRI (RIP)

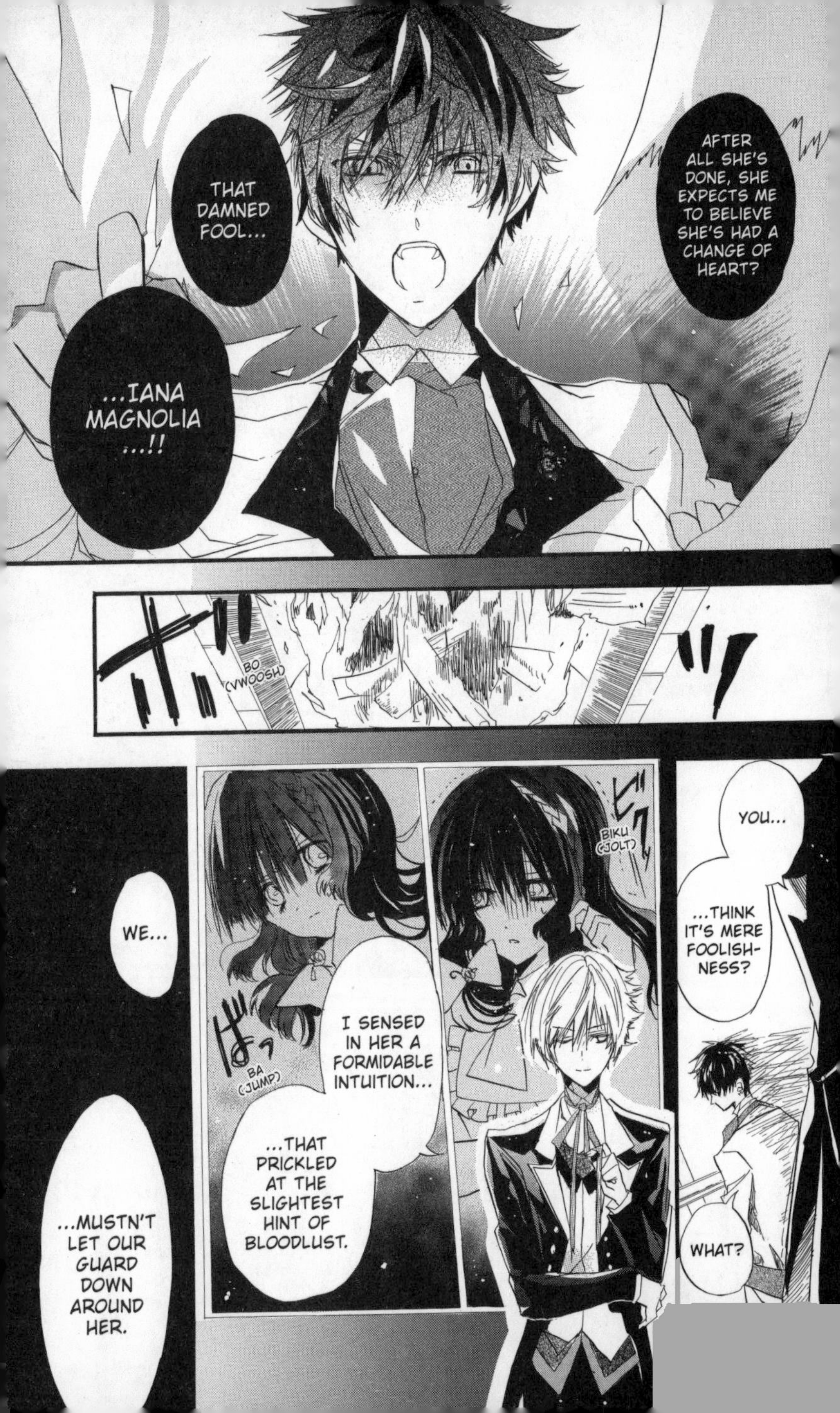
AFTER ALL SHE'S DONE, SHE EXPECTS ME TO BELIEVE SHE'S HAD A CHANGE OF HEART?
THAT DAMNED FOOL...
...IANA MAGNOLIA ...!!
BO (VWOOSH)
YOU...
...THINK IT'S MERE FOOLISHNESS?
WHAT?
BIKU (JOLT)
BA (JUMP)
I SENSED IN HER A FORMIDABLE INTUITION...
...THAT PRICKLED AT THE SLIGHTEST HINT OF BLOODLUST.
WE...
...MUSTN'T LET OUR GUARD DOWN AROUND HER.

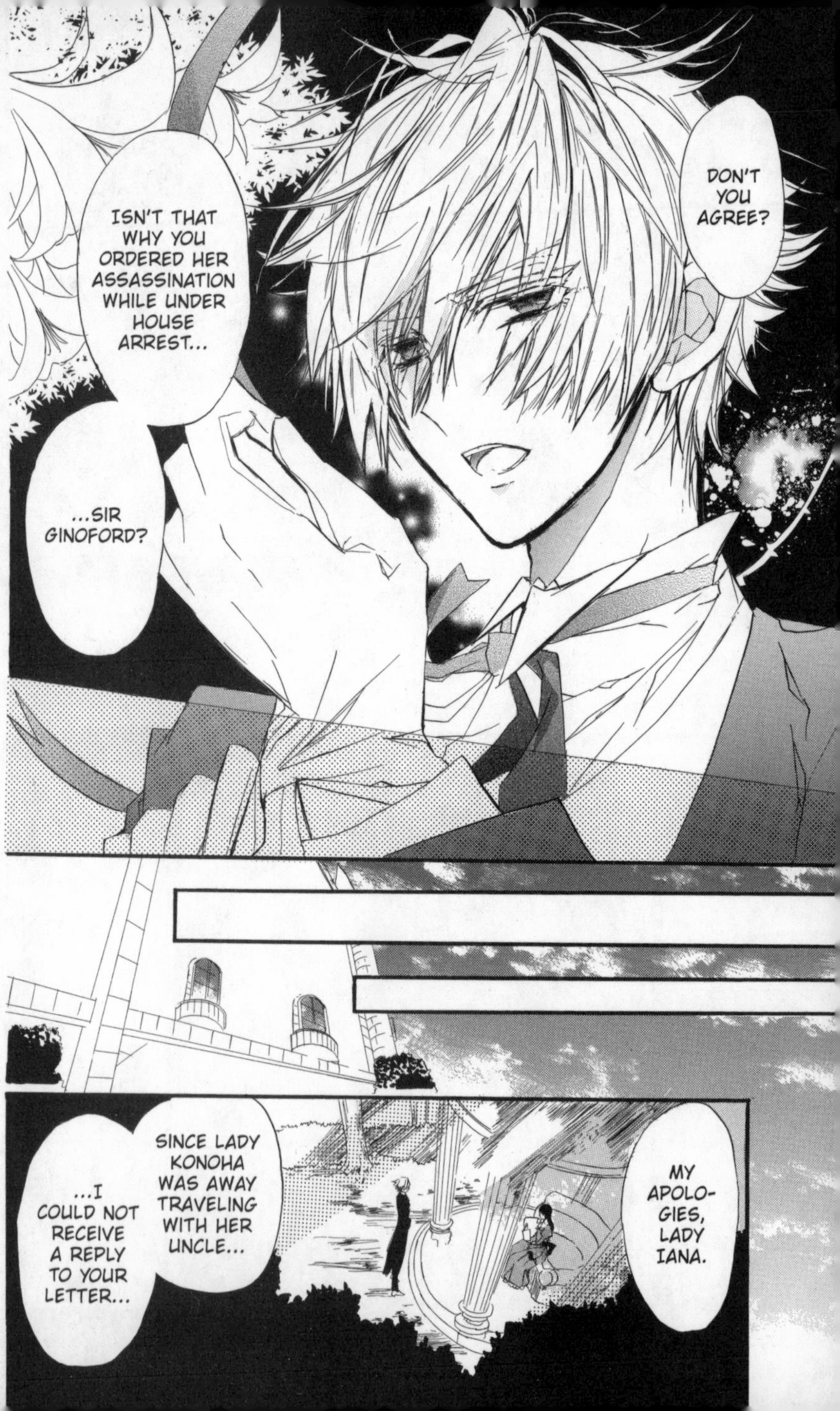
DON'T YOU AGREE?
ISN'T THAT WHY YOU ORDERED HER ASSASSINATION WHILE UNDER HOUSE ARREST...
...SIR GINOFORD?
MY APOLOGIES, LADY IANA.
SINCE LADY KONOHA WAS AWAY TRAVELING WITH HER UNCLE...
...I COULD NOT RECEIVE A REPLY TO YOUR LETTER...

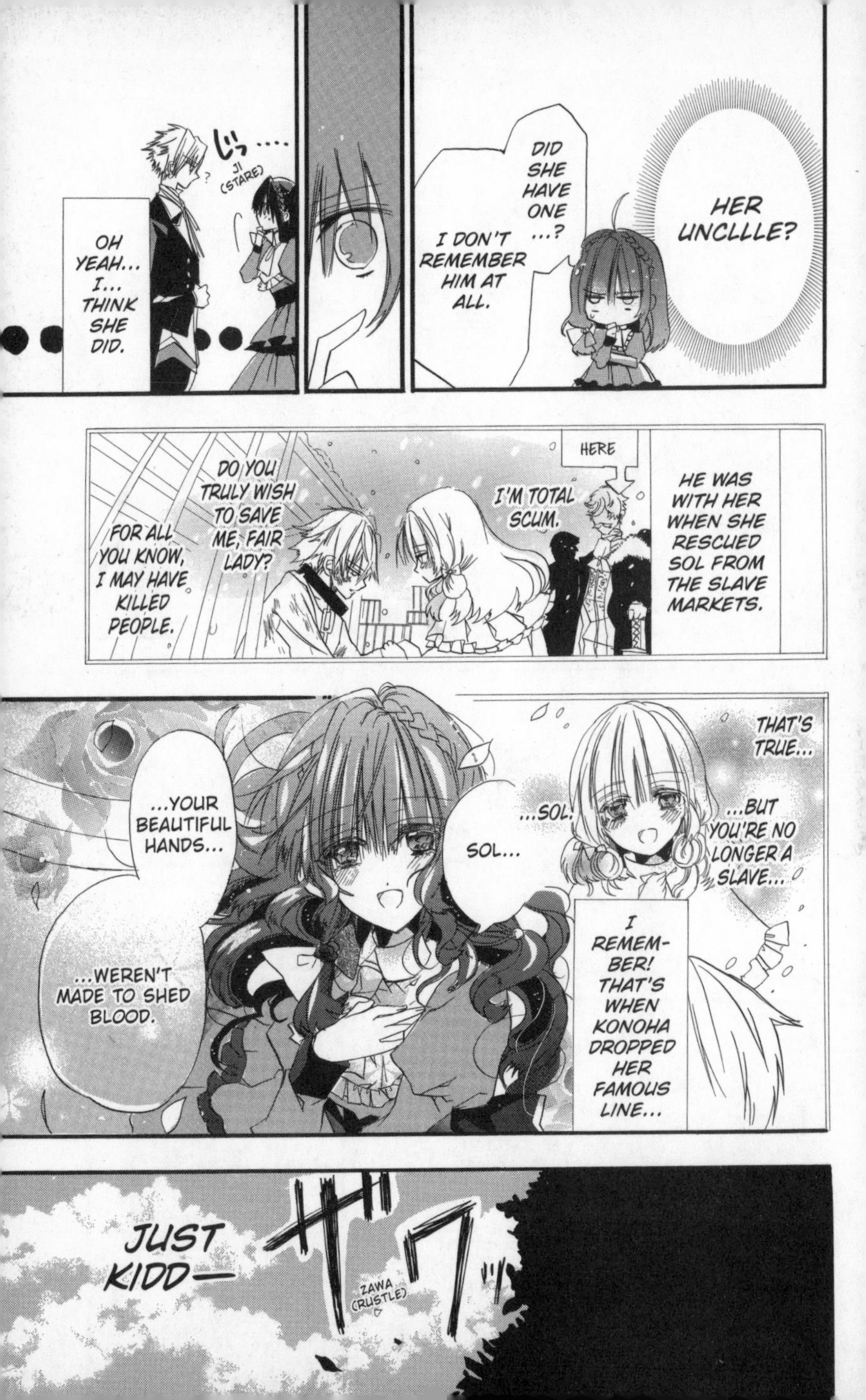
HER UNCLLLE?
DID SHE HAVE ONE ...?
I DON'T REMEMBER HIM AT ALL.
じっ....
JI (STARE)
OH YEAH... I... THINK SHE DID.
HE WAS WITH HER WHEN SHE RESCUED SOL FROM THE SLAVE MARKETS.
HERE
I'M TOTAL SCUM.
DO YOU TRULY WISH TO SAVE ME, FAIR LADY?
FOR ALL YOU KNOW, I MAY HAVE KILLED PEOPLE.
THAT'S TRUE...
...BUT YOU'RE NO LONGER A SLAVE...
...SOL.
I REMEM-BER! THAT'S WHEN KONOHA DROPPED HER FAMOUS LINE...
SOL...
...YOUR BEAUTIFUL HANDS...
...WEREN'T MADE TO SHED BLOOD.
ザワッ
ZAWA (RUSTLE)
JUST KIDD—

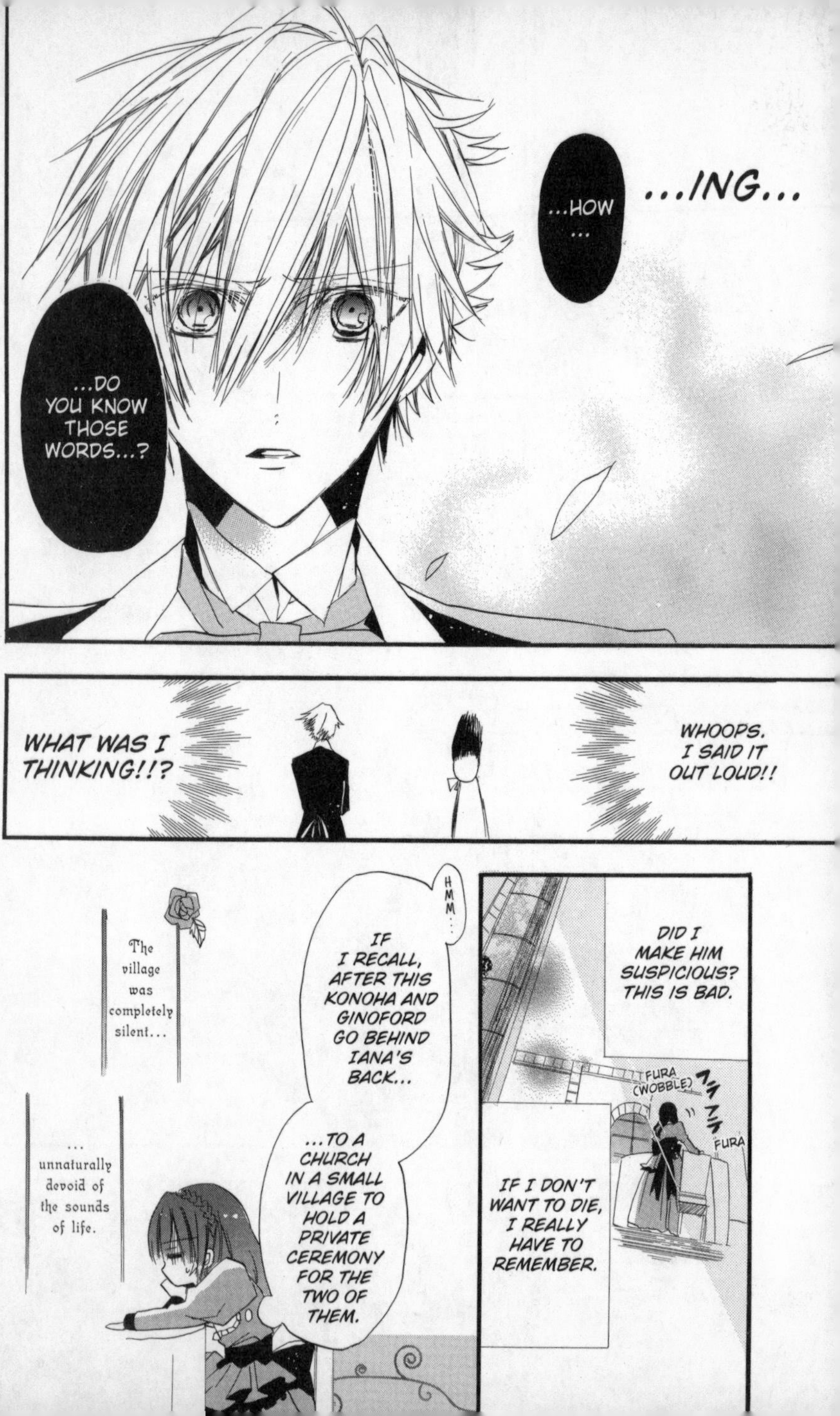
...ING...
...HOW ...
...DO YOU KNOW THOSE WORDS...?
WHOOPS. I SAID IT OUT LOUD!!
WHAT WAS I THINKING!!?
DID I MAKE HIM SUSPICIOUS? THIS IS BAD.
FURA (WOBBLE)
FURA
IF I DON'T WANT TO DIE, I REALLY HAVE TO REMEMBER.
HMM...
IF I RECALL, AFTER THIS KONOHA AND GINOFORD GO BEHIND IANA'S BACK...
...TO A CHURCH IN A SMALL VILLAGE TO HOLD A PRIVATE CEREMONY FOR THE TWO OF THEM.
The village was completely silent...
...unnaturally devoid of the sounds of life.

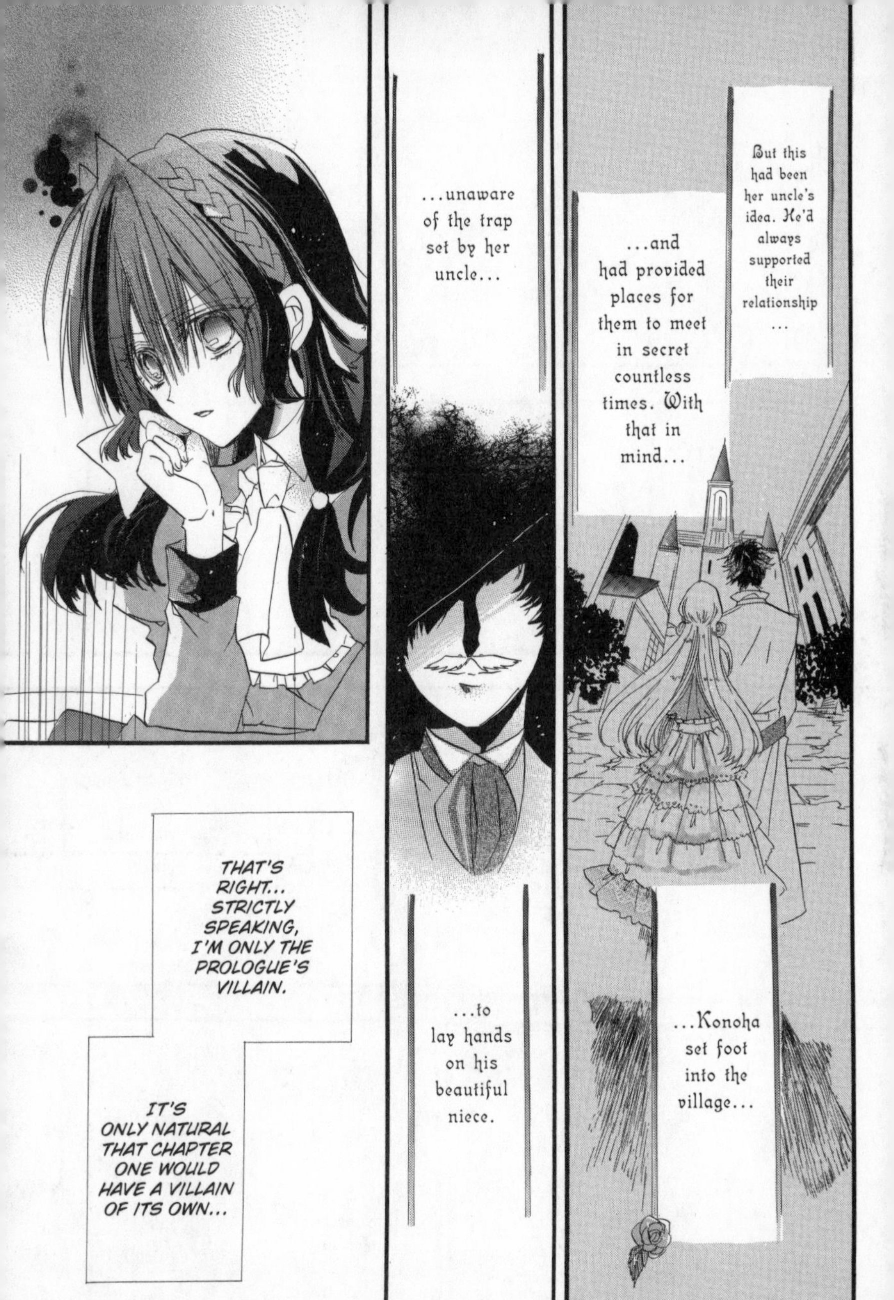
But this had been her uncle's idea. He'd always supported their relationship...
...and had provided places for them to meet in secret countless times. With that in mind...
...Konoha set foot into the village...
...unaware of the trap set by her uncle...
...to lay hands on his beautiful niece.
THAT'S RIGHT... STRICTLY SPEAKING, I'M ONLY THE PROLOGUE'S VILLAIN.
IT'S ONLY NATURAL THAT CHAPTER ONE WOULD HAVE A VILLAIN OF ITS OWN...

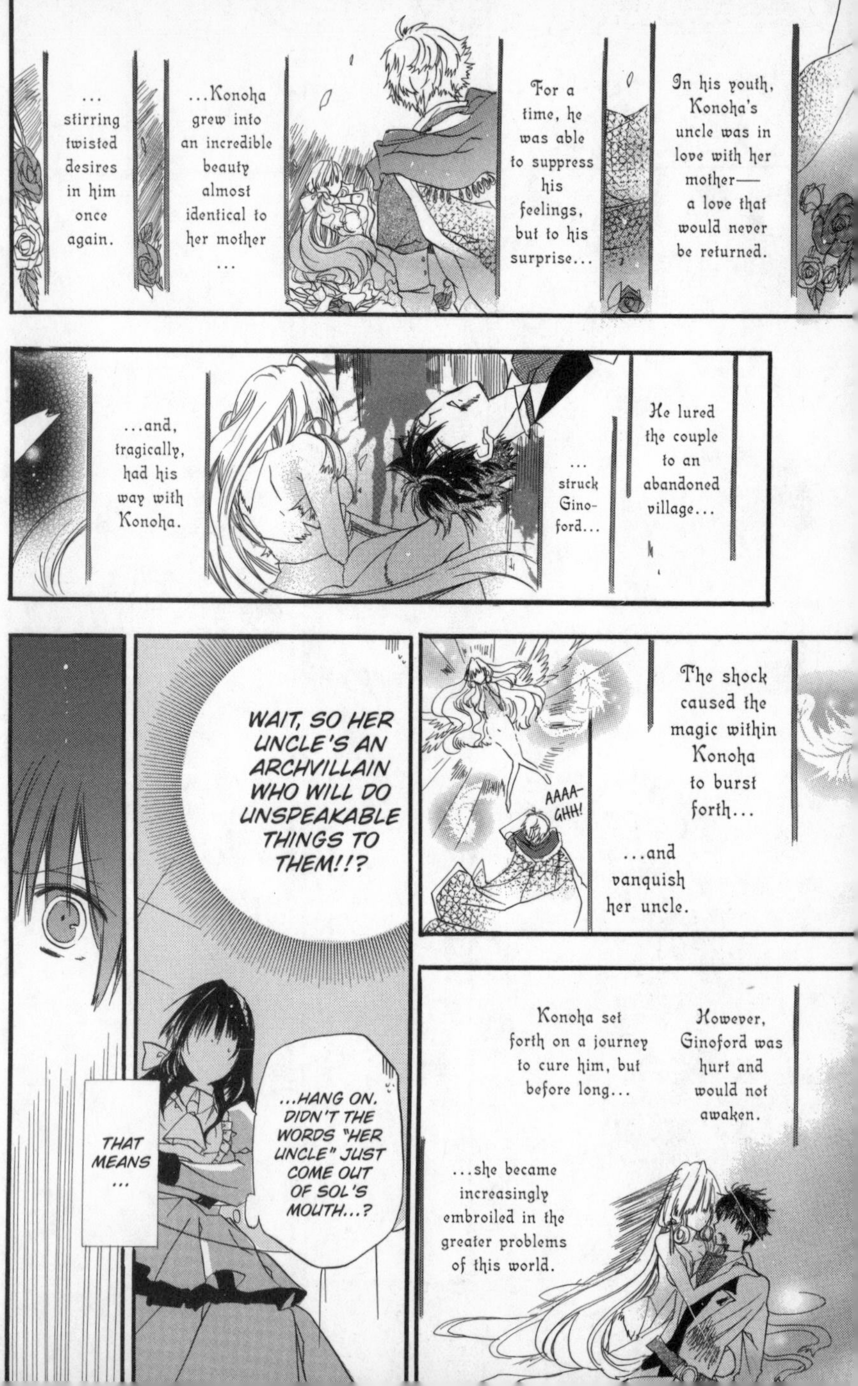
In his youth, Konoha's uncle was in love with her mother— a love that would never be returned.
For a time, he was able to suppress his feelings, but to his surprise...
...Konoha grew into an incredible beauty almost identical to her mother ...
... stirring twisted desires in him once again.
He lured the couple to an abandoned village...
... struck Ginoford...
...and, tragically, had his way with Konoha.
The shock caused the magic within Konoha to burst forth...
AAAA-GHH!
...and vanquish her uncle.
However, Ginoford was hurt and would not awaken.
Konoha set forth on a journey to cure him, but before long...
...she became increasingly embroiled in the greater problems of this world.
WAIT, SO HER UNCLE'S AN ARCHVILLAIN WHO WILL DO UNSPEAKABLE THINGS TO THEM!!?
...HANG ON. DIDN'T THE WORDS "HER UNCLE" JUST COME OUT OF SOL'S MOUTH...?
THAT MEANS ...

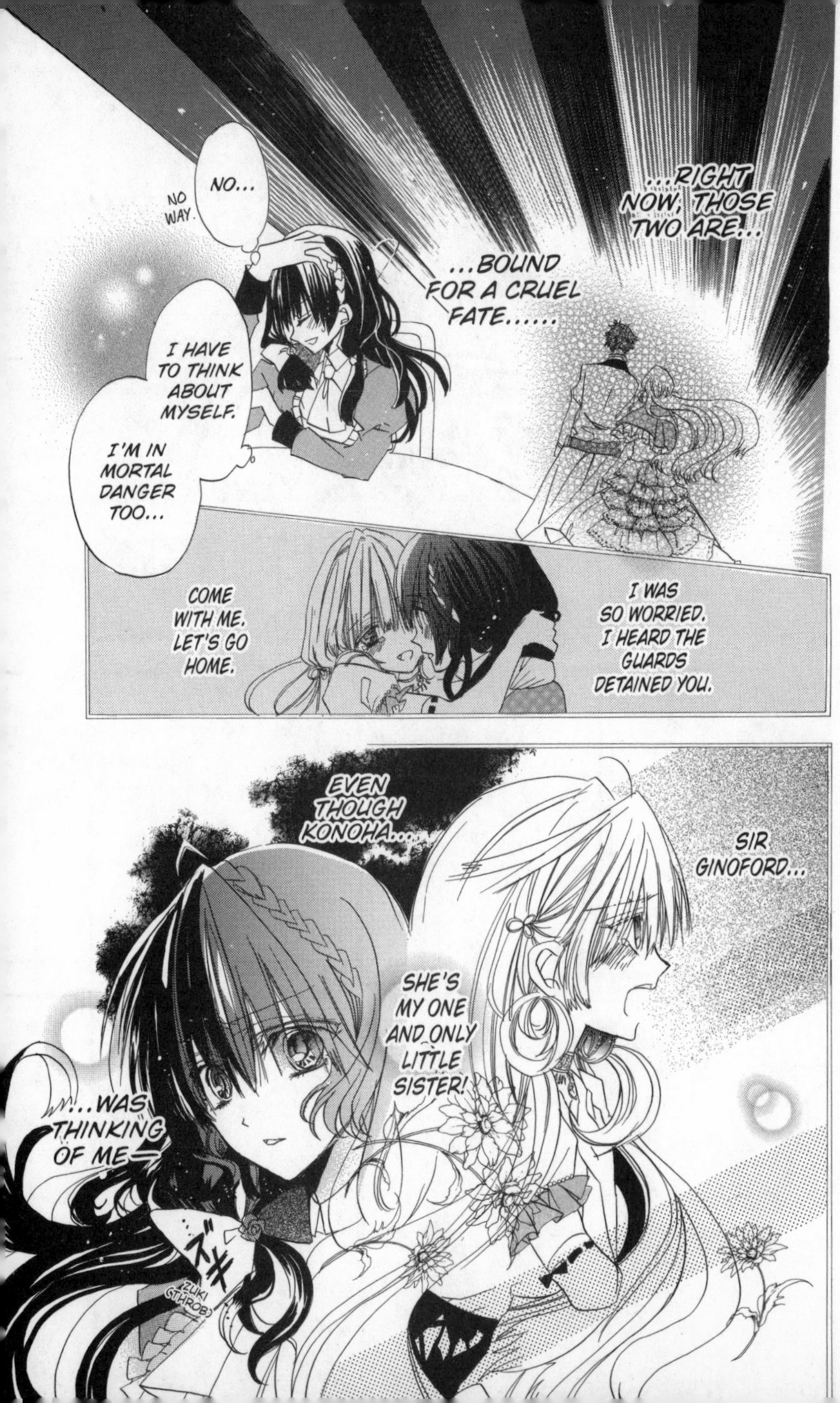
...RIGHT NOW, THOSE TWO ARE...
...BOUND FOR A CRUEL FATE......
NO...
NO WAY.
I HAVE TO THINK ABOUT MYSELF.
I'M IN MORTAL DANGER TOO...
I WAS SO WORRIED. I HEARD THE GUARDS DETAINED YOU.
COME WITH ME. LET'S GO HOME.
SIR GINOFORD...
SHE'S MY ONE AND ONLY LITTLE SISTER!
EVEN THOUGH KONOHA...
...WAS THINKING OF ME—
ズキ
ZUKI (THROB)

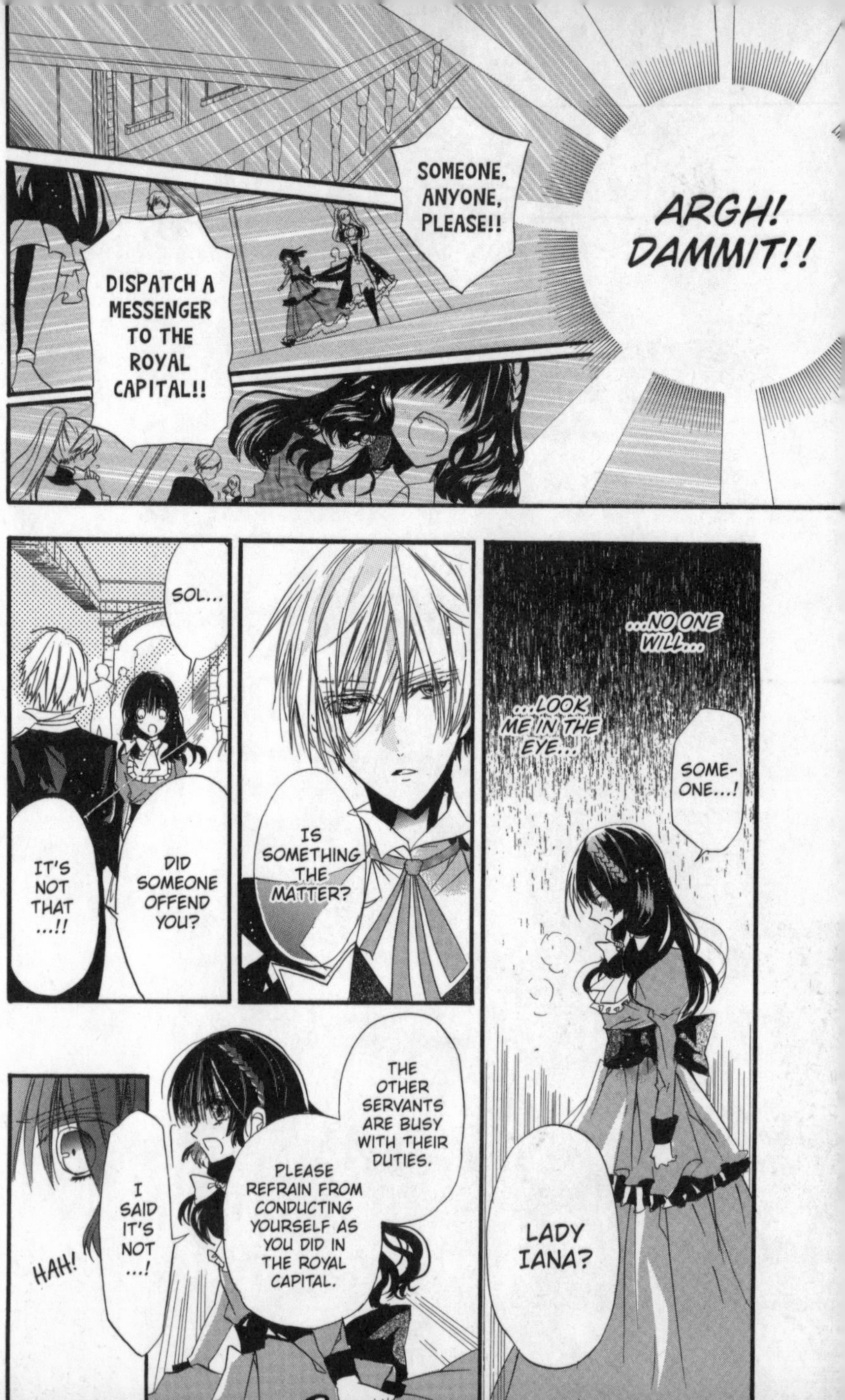
ARGH! DAMMIT!!
SOMEONE, ANYONE, PLEASE!!
DISPATCH A MESSENGER TO THE ROYAL CAPITAL!!
...NO ONE WILL...
...LOOK ME IN THE EYE...
SOME-ONE...!
LADY IANA?
IS SOMETHING THE MATTER?
SOL...
DID SOMEONE OFFEND YOU?
IT'S NOT THAT ...!!
THE OTHER SERVANTS ARE BUSY WITH THEIR DUTIES.
PLEASE REFRAIN FROM CONDUCTING YOURSELF AS YOU DID IN THE ROYAL CAPITAL.
I SAID IT'S NOT ...!
HAH!

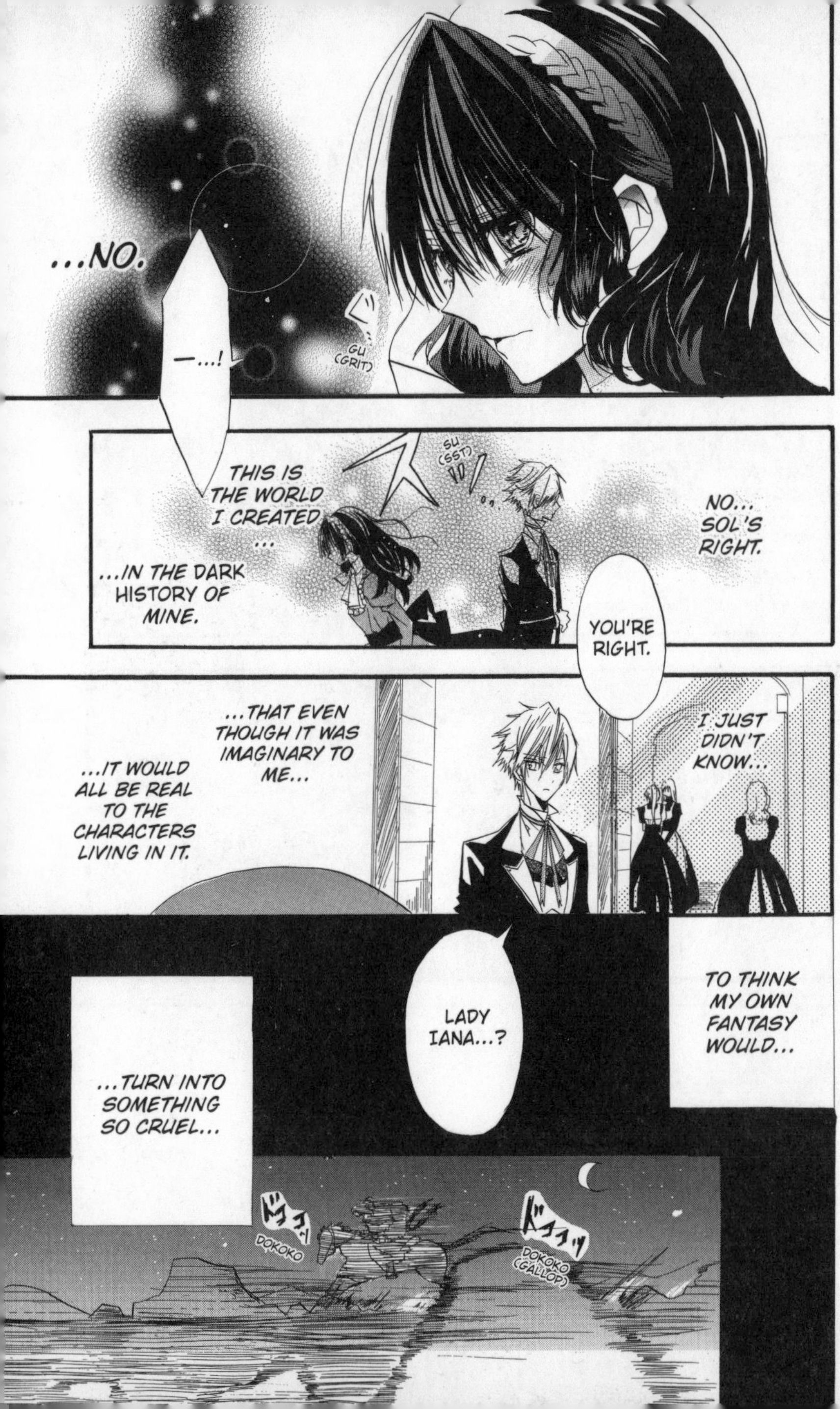
GU (GRIT)
—...!
...NO.
NO... SOL'S RIGHT.
SU (SST)
THIS IS THE WORLD I CREATED ...
...IN THE DARK HISTORY OF MINE.
YOU'RE RIGHT.
I JUST DIDN'T KNOW...
...THAT EVEN THOUGH IT WAS IMAGINARY TO ME...
...IT WOULD ALL BE REAL TO THE CHARACTERS LIVING IN IT.
TO THINK MY OWN FANTASY WOULD...
LADY IANA...?
...TURN INTO SOMETHING SO CRUEL...
DOKOKO (GALLOP)
DOKOKO

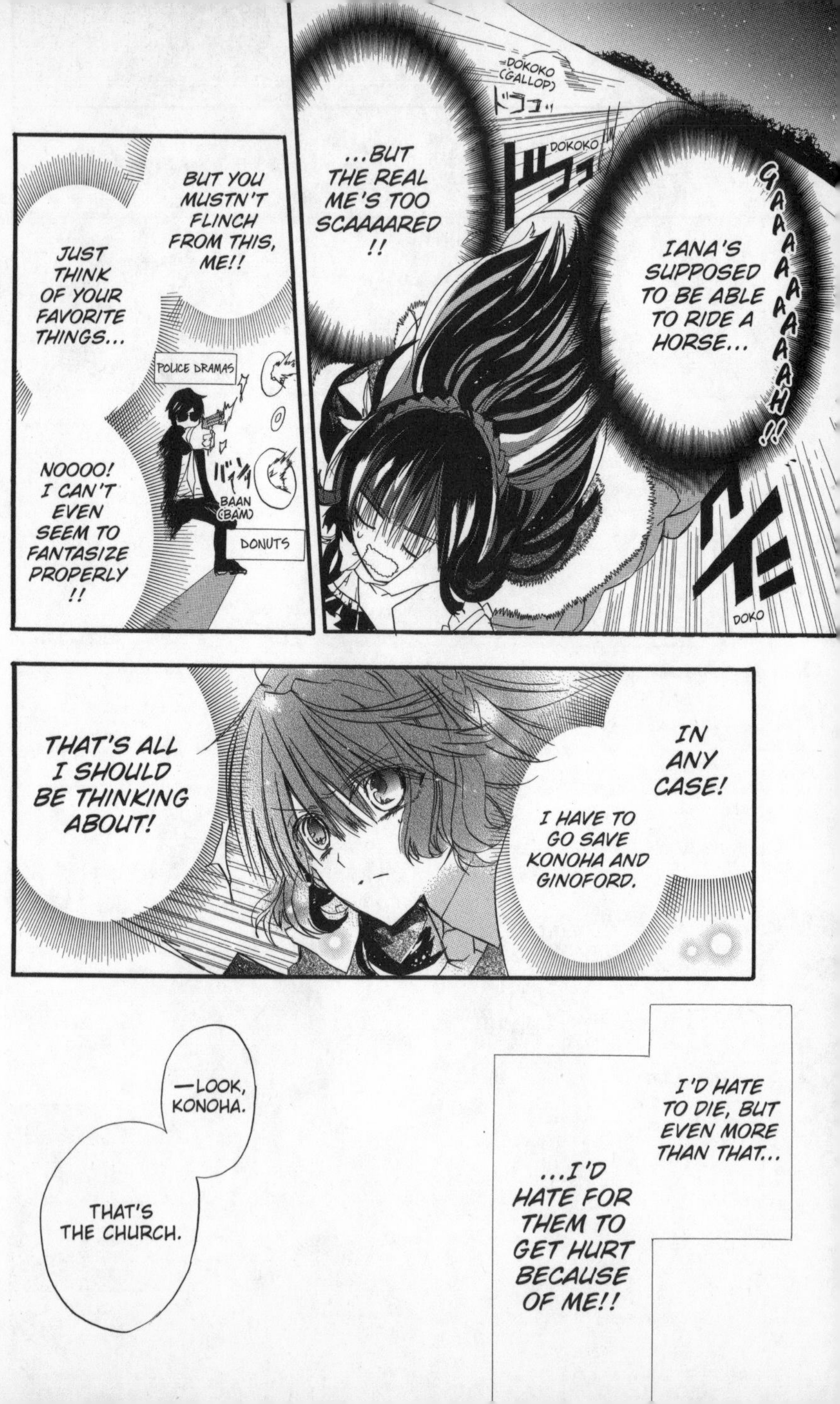
IANA'S SUPPOSED TO BE ABLE TO RIDE A HORSE...
GAAAAAAAAAAH!!
DOKOKO (GALLOP)
...BUT THE REAL ME'S TOO SCAAAARED!!
DOKOKO
DOKO
BUT YOU MUSTN'T FLINCH FROM THIS, ME!!
JUST THINK OF YOUR FAVORITE THINGS...
POLICE DRAMAS
BAAN (BAM)
DONUTS
NOOOO! I CAN'T EVEN SEEM TO FANTASIZE PROPERLY!!
IN ANY CASE!
I HAVE TO GO SAVE KONOHA AND GINOFORD.
THAT'S ALL I SHOULD BE THINKING ABOUT!
I'D HATE TO DIE, BUT EVEN MORE THAN THAT...
...I'D HATE FOR THEM TO GET HURT BECAUSE OF ME!!
—LOOK, KONOHA.
THAT'S THE CHURCH.

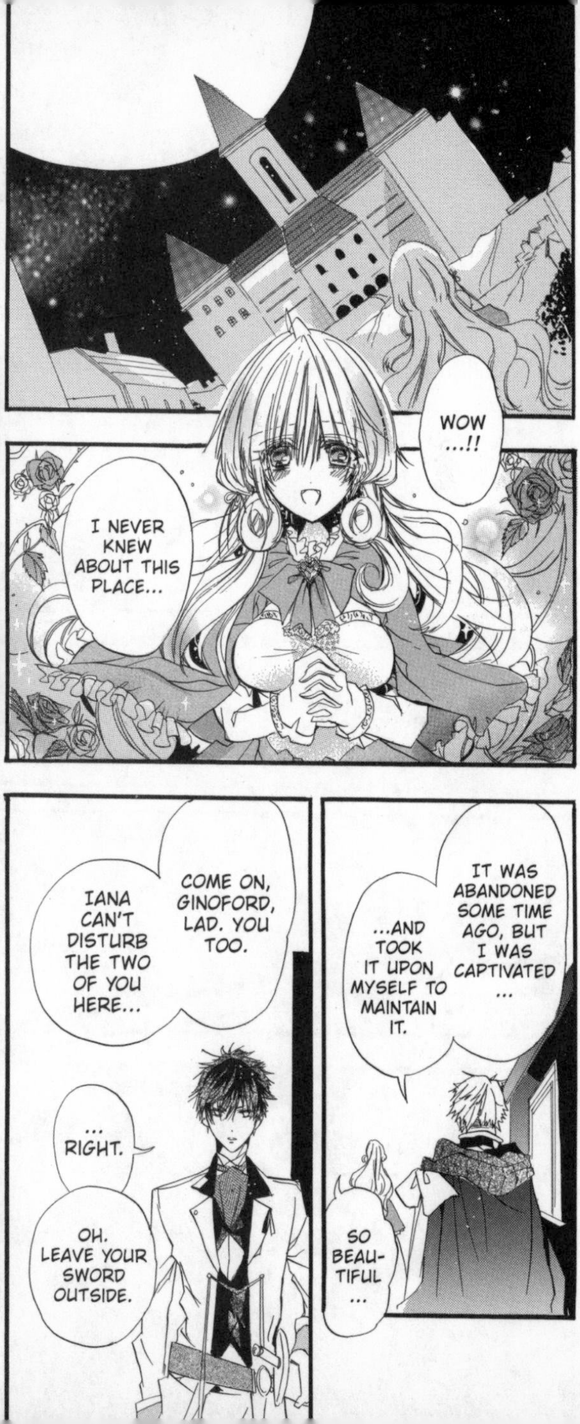
WOW ...!!
I NEVER KNEW ABOUT THIS PLACE...
IT WAS ABANDONED SOME TIME AGO, BUT I WAS CAPTIVATED...
...AND TOOK IT UPON MYSELF TO MAINTAIN IT.
SO BEAU-TIFUL...
COME ON, GINOFORD, LAD. YOU TOO.
IANA CAN'T DISTURB THE TWO OF YOU HERE...
...RIGHT.
OH. LEAVE YOUR SWORD OUTSIDE.

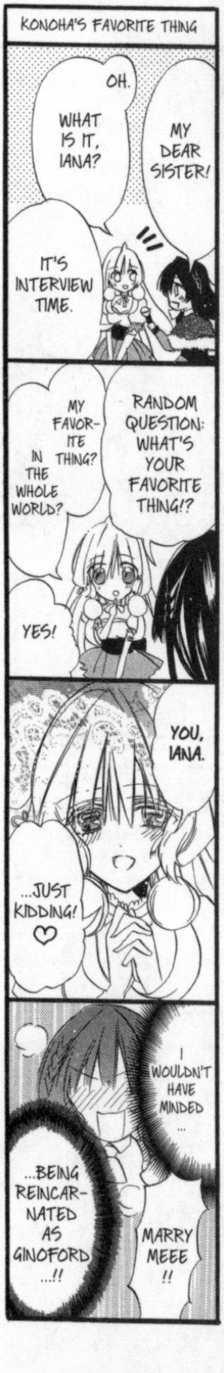
KONOHA'S FAVORITE THING
MY DEAR SISTER!
OH. WHAT IS IT, IANA?
IT'S INTERVIEW TIME.
RANDOM QUESTION: WHAT'S YOUR FAVORITE THING!?
MY FAVOR-ITE THING? IN THE WHOLE WORLD?
YES!
YOU, IANA.
...JUST KIDDING! ♡
I WOULDN'T HAVE MINDED...
...BEING REINCAR-NATED AS GINOFORD...!!
MARRY MEEE!!

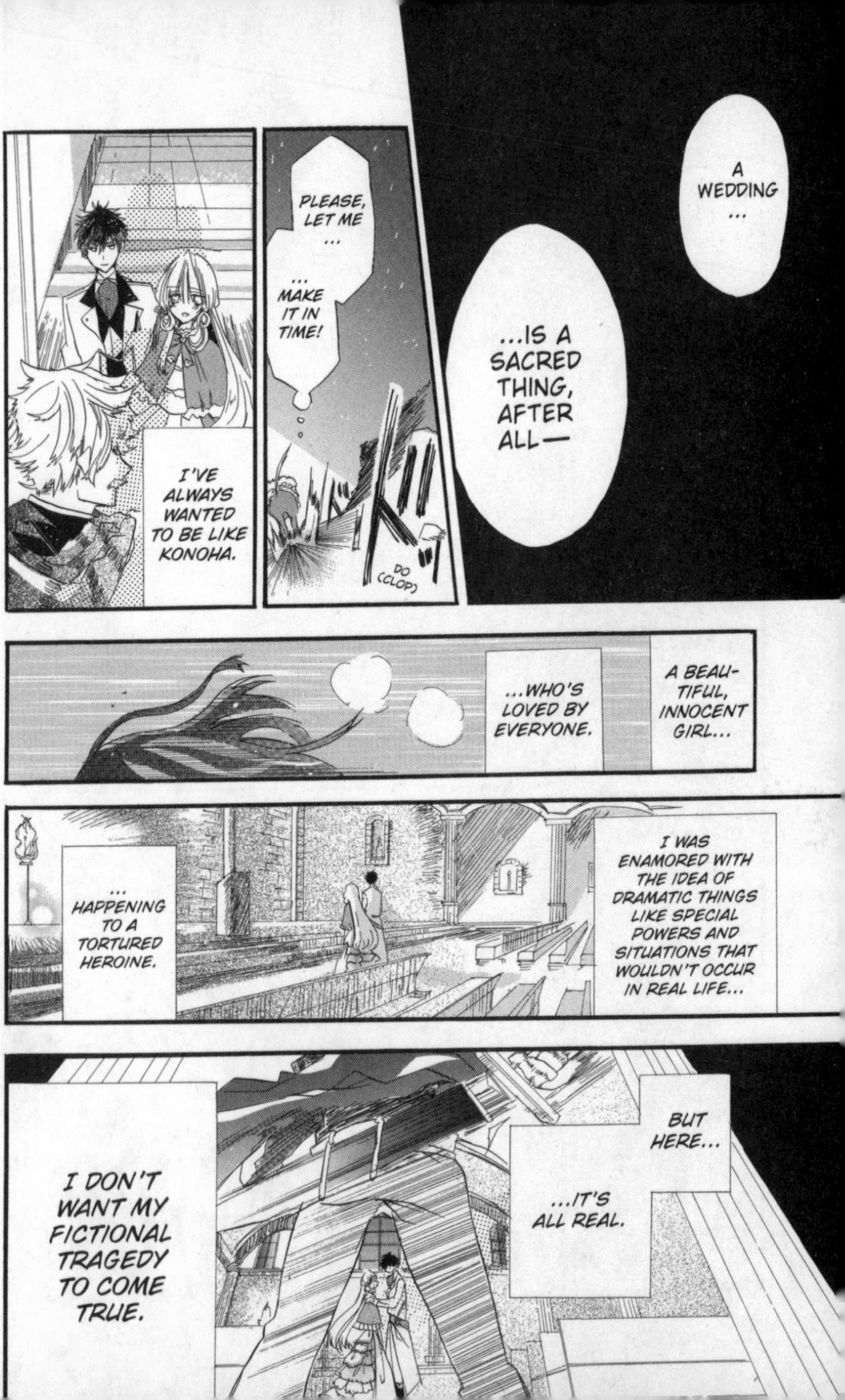
A WEDDING ...
...IS A SACRED THING, AFTER ALL—
PLEASE, LET ME ...
... MAKE IT IN TIME!
DO (CLOP)
I'VE ALWAYS WANTED TO BE LIKE KONOHA.
A BEAU-TIFUL, INNOCENT GIRL...
...WHO'S LOVED BY EVERYONE.
I WAS ENAMORED WITH THE IDEA OF DRAMATIC THINGS LIKE SPECIAL POWERS AND SITUATIONS THAT WOULDN'T OCCUR IN REAL LIFE...
... HAPPENING TO A TORTURED HEROINE.
BUT HERE...
...IT'S ALL REAL.
I DON'T WANT MY FICTIONAL TRAGEDY TO COME TRUE.

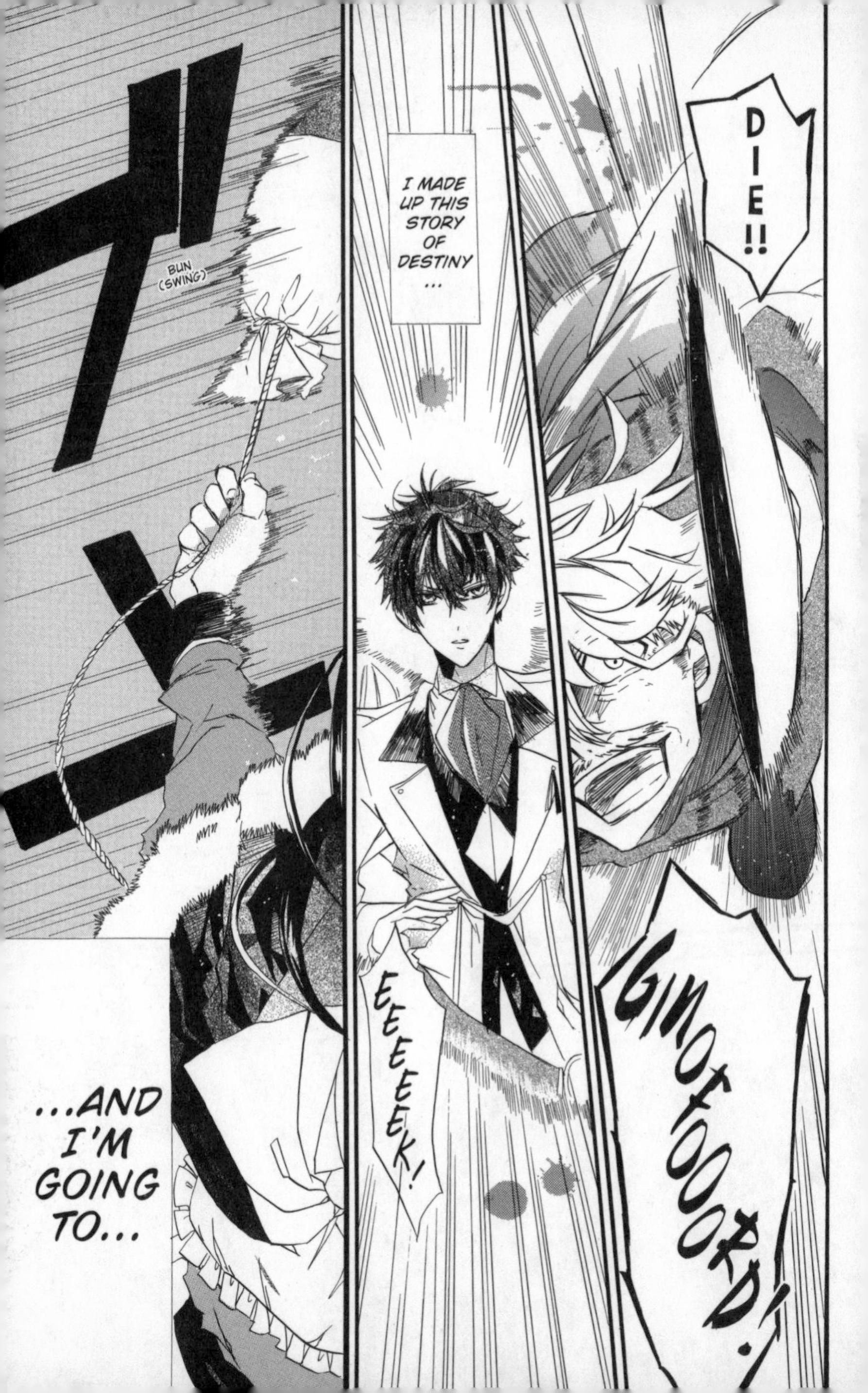
DIE!!
GINOTOOORD!
I MADE UP THIS STORY OF DESTINY...
EEEEEEK!
BUN (SWING)
...AND I'M GOING TO...

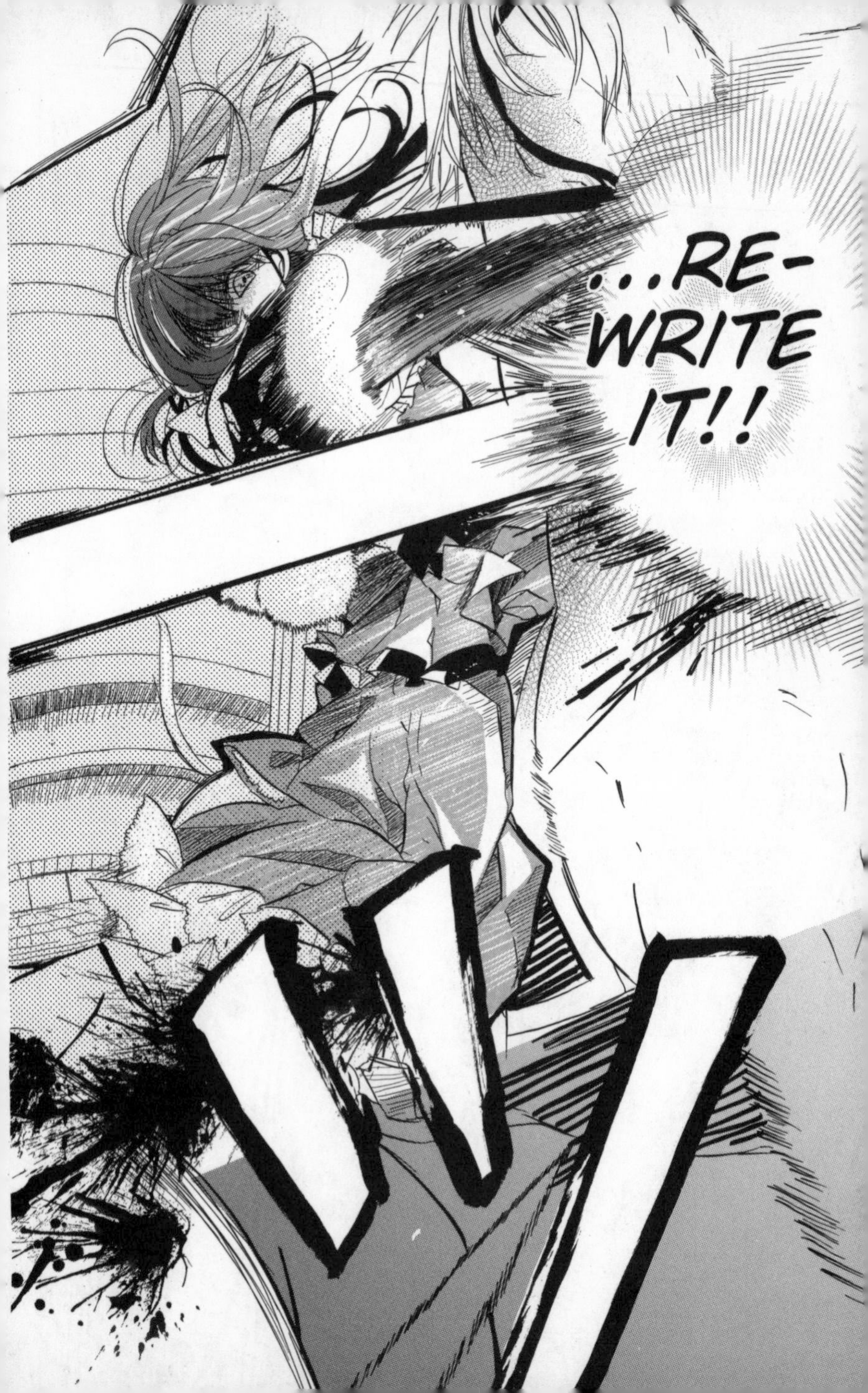
...RE-WRITE IT!!

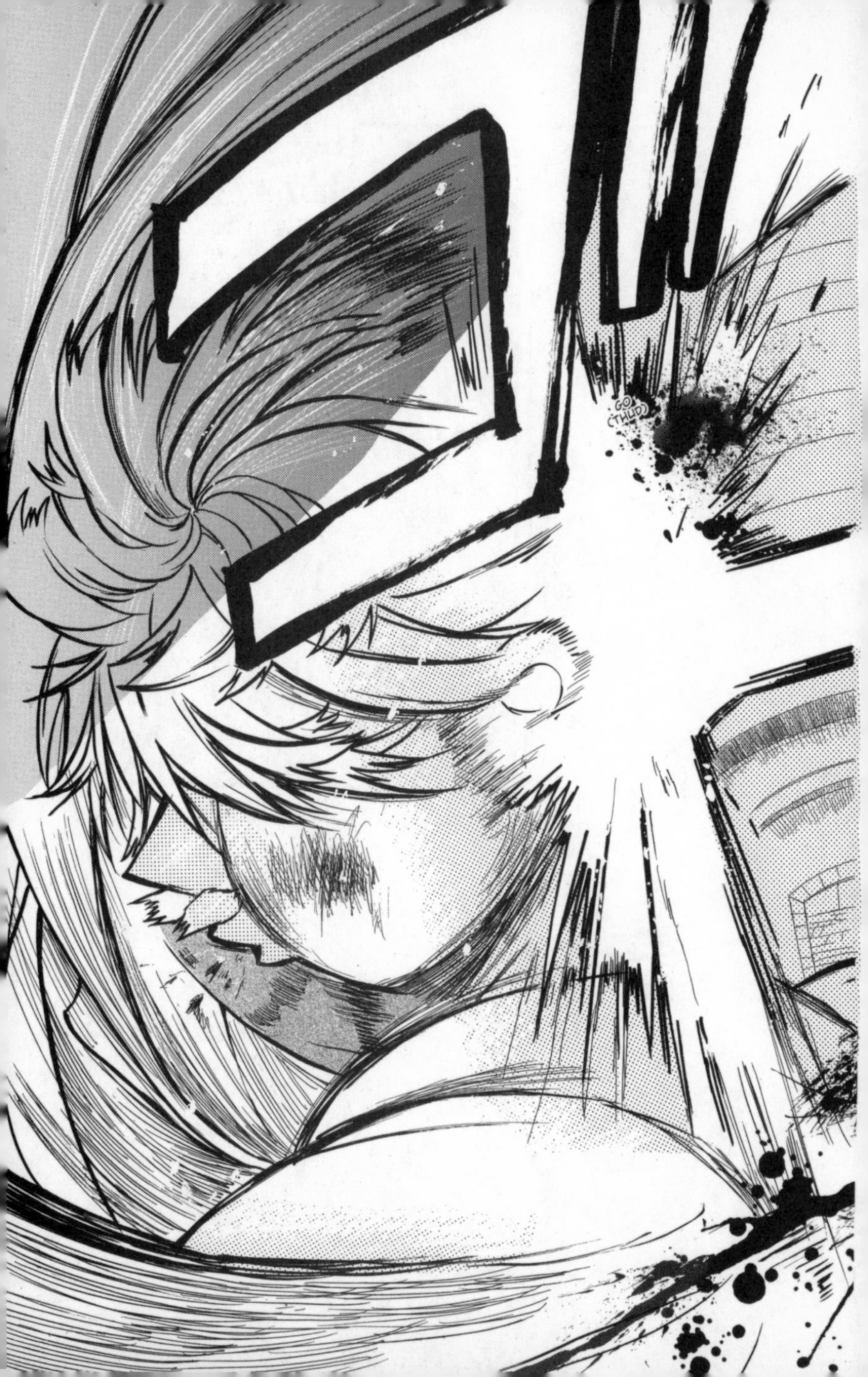
GO
(THUD)

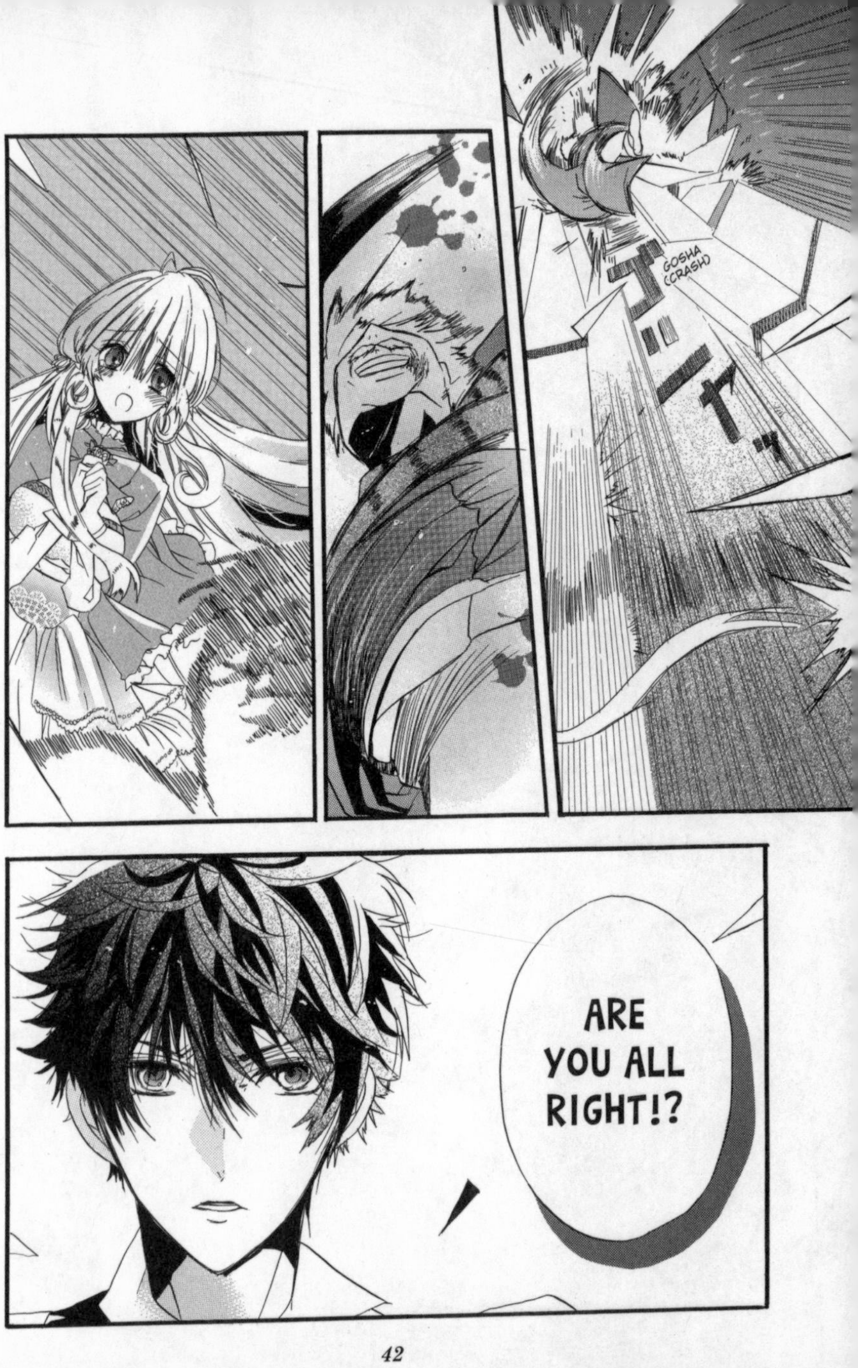
GOSHA (CRASH)
ARE YOU ALL RIGHT!?

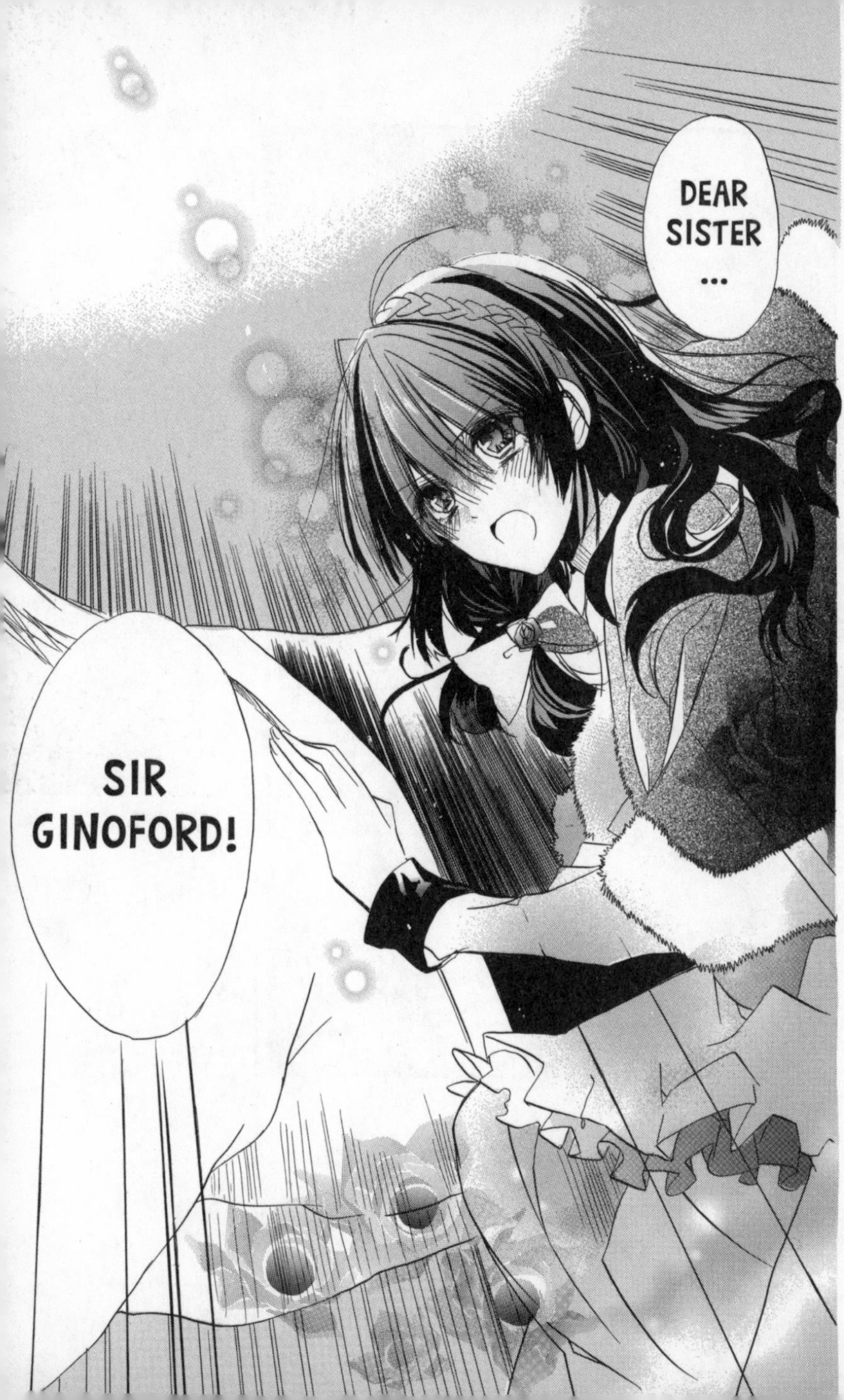
DEAR SISTER ...
SIR GINOFORD!

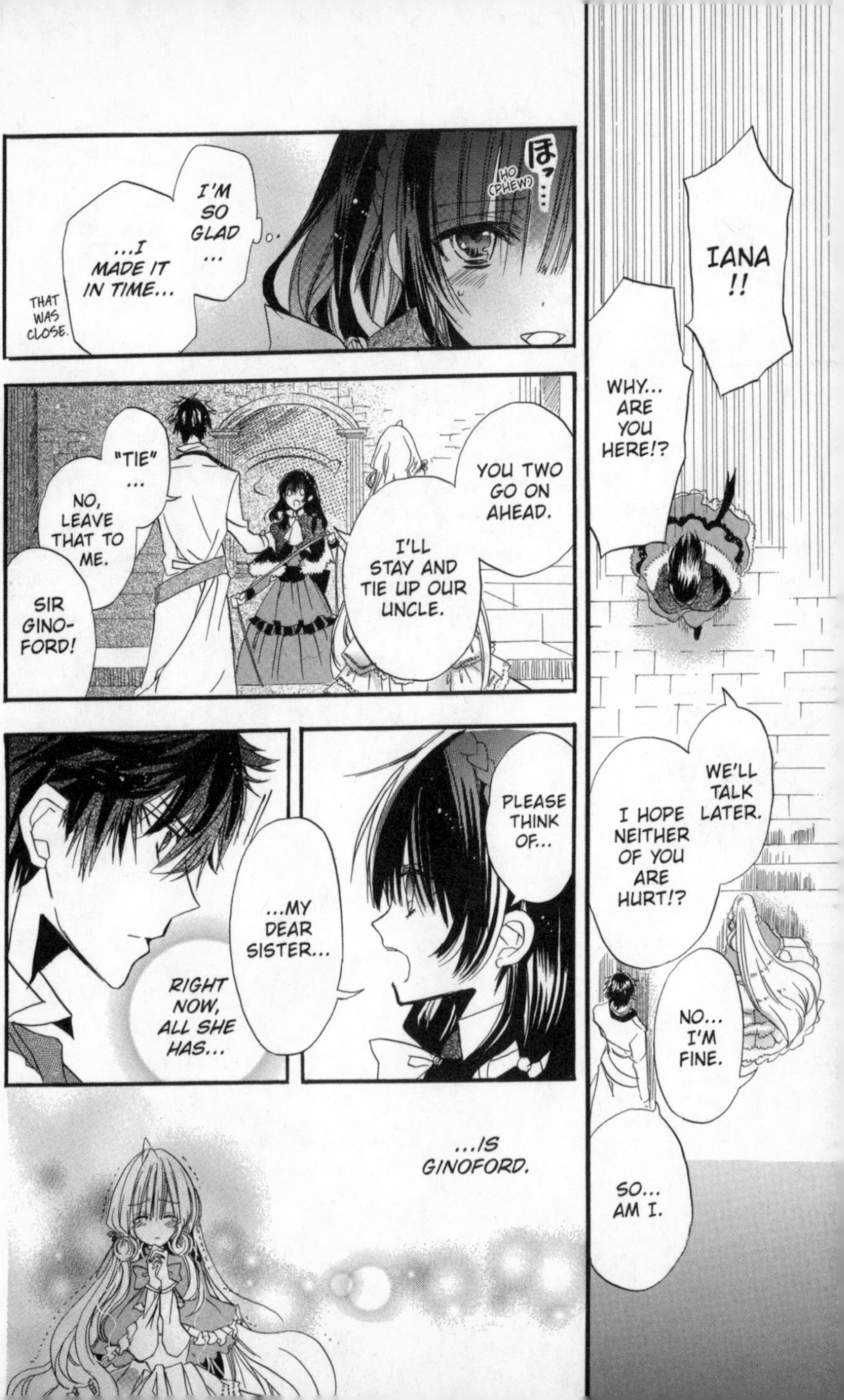
IANA!!
WHY... ARE YOU HERE!?
WE'LL TALK LATER.
I HOPE NEITHER OF YOU ARE HURT!?
NO... I'M FINE.
SO... AM I.
ほっ…
HO (PHEW)
I'M SO GLAD...
...I MADE IT IN TIME...
THAT WAS CLOSE.
YOU TWO GO ON AHEAD.
I'LL STAY AND TIE UP OUR UNCLE.
"TIE"...
NO, LEAVE THAT TO ME.
SIR GINOFORD!
PLEASE THINK OF...
...MY DEAR SISTER...
RIGHT NOW, ALL SHE HAS...
...IS GINOFORD.

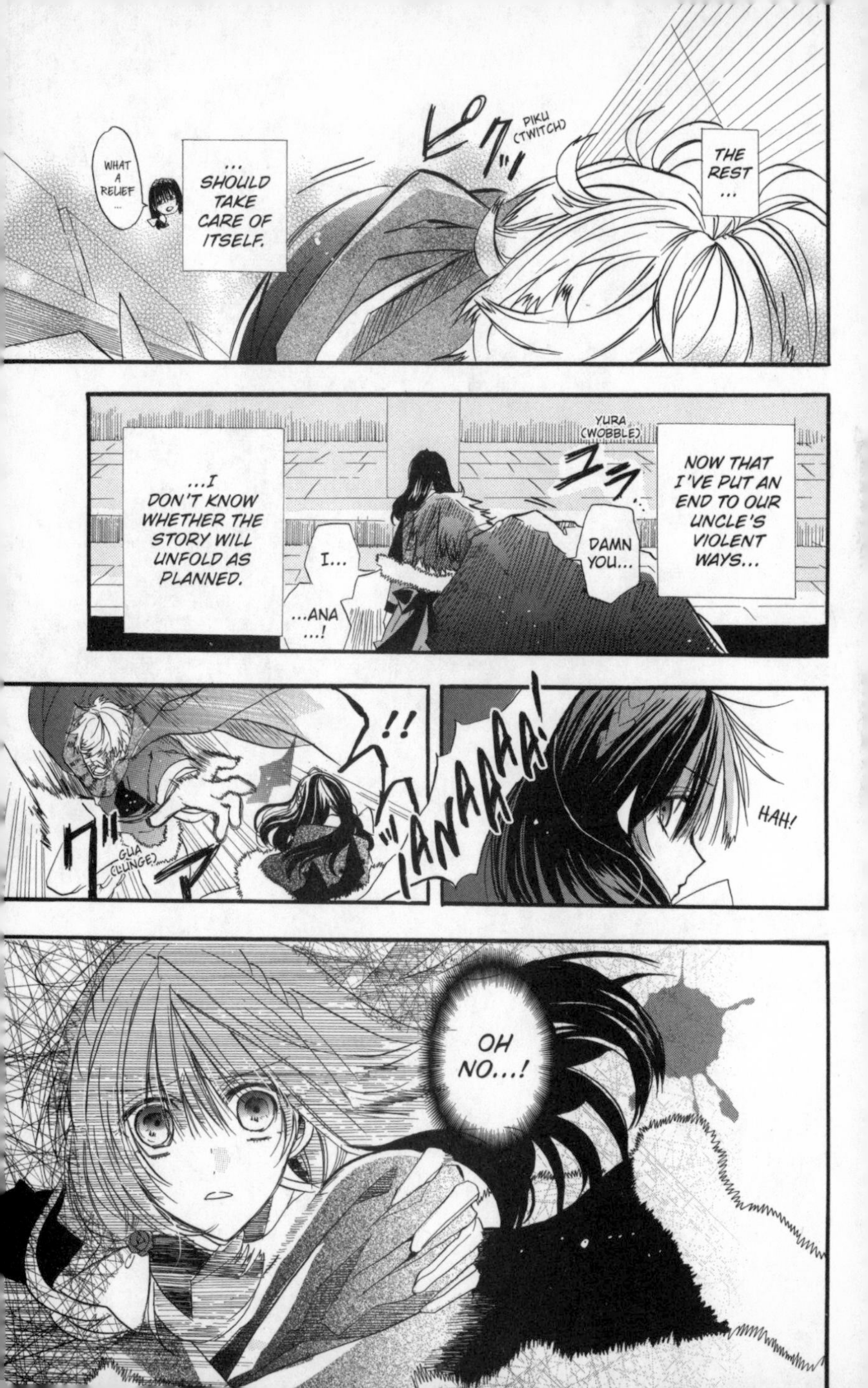
THE REST...
PIKU (TWITCH)
...SHOULD TAKE CARE OF ITSELF.
WHAT A RELIEF...
NOW THAT I'VE PUT AN END TO OUR UNCLE'S VIOLENT WAYS...
YURA (WOBBLE)
DAMN YOU...
I...
...ANA...!
...I DON'T KNOW WHETHER THE STORY WILL UNFOLD AS PLANNED.
HAH!
ANAAAA!
!!
GUA (LUNGE)
OH NO...!

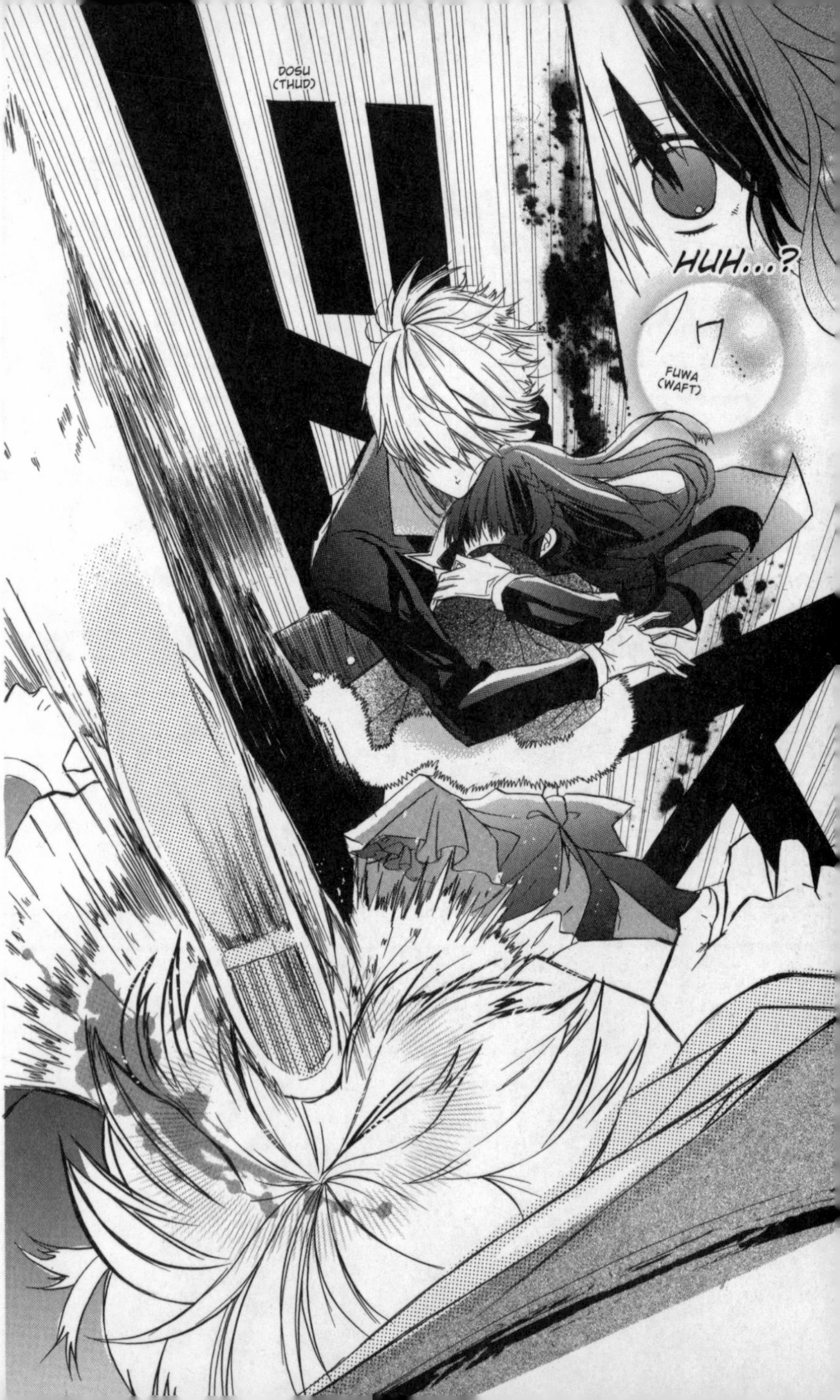
HUH...?
フワ
FUWA (WAFT)
DOSU (THUD)

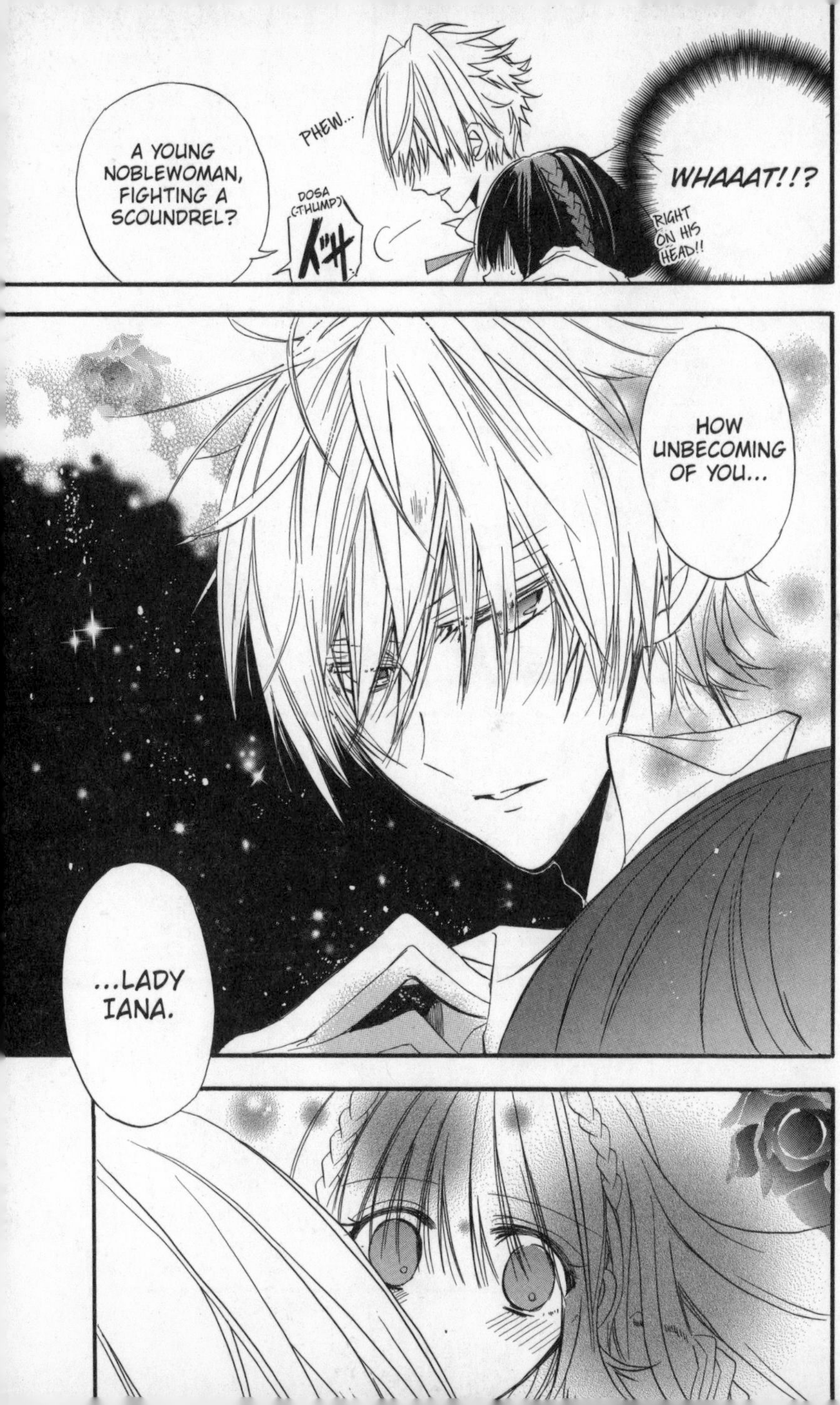
WHAAAT!!?
RIGHT ON HIS HEAD!!
PHEW...
DOSA (THUMP)
A YOUNG NOBLEWOMAN, FIGHTING A SCOUNDREL?
HOW UNBECOMING OF YOU...
...LADY IANA.

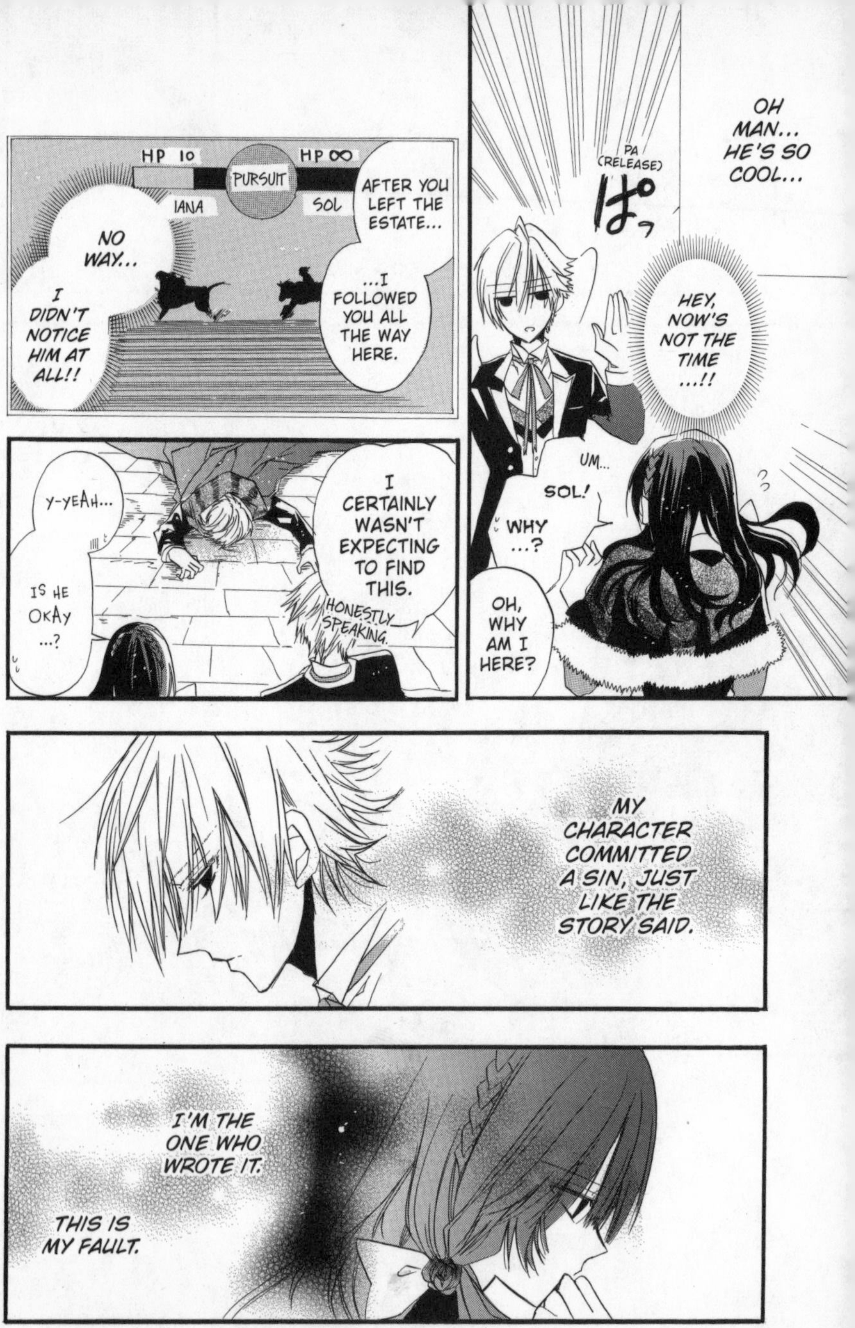
OH MAN... HE'S SO COOL...
PA (RELEASE)
ぱっ
HEY, NOW'S NOT THE TIME ...!!
UM... SOL!
WHY ...?
OH, WHY AM I HERE?
HP 10
HP ∞
PURSUIT
IANA
SOL
AFTER YOU LEFT THE ESTATE...
...I FOLLOWED YOU ALL THE WAY HERE.
NO WAY...
I DIDN'T NOTICE HIM AT ALL!!
I CERTAINLY WASN'T EXPECTING TO FIND THIS.
HONESTLY SPEAKING.
Y-YEAH...
IS HE OKAY ...?
MY CHARACTER COMMITTED A SIN, JUST LIKE THE STORY SAID.
I'M THE ONE WHO WROTE IT.
THIS IS MY FAULT.

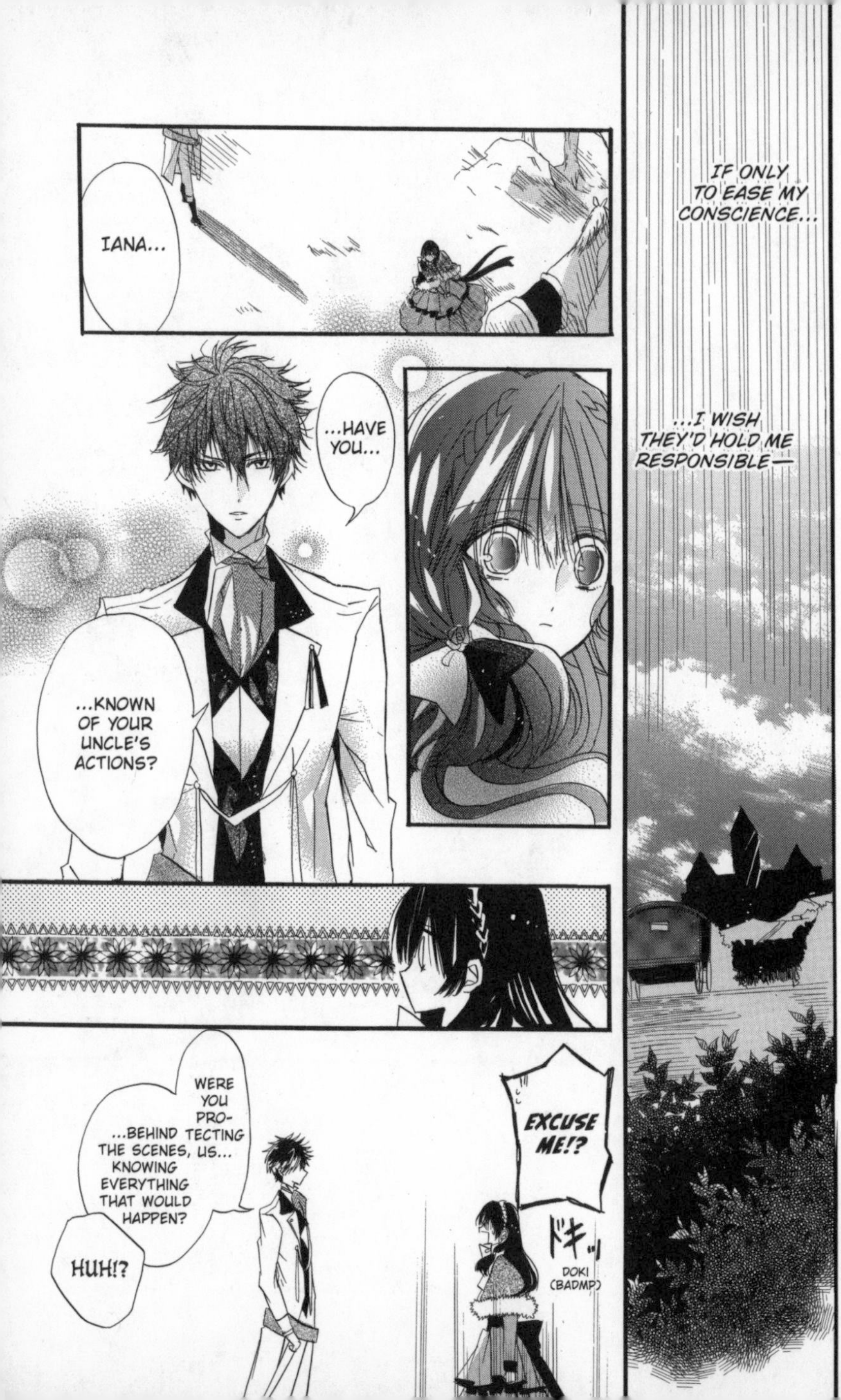
IF ONLY TO EASE MY CONSCIENCE...
...I WISH THEY'D HOLD ME RESPONSIBLE—
IANA...
...HAVE YOU...
...KNOWN OF YOUR UNCLE'S ACTIONS?
ドキッ
DOKI (BADMP)
EXCUSE ME!?
WERE YOU PRO-TECTING US...
...BEHIND THE SCENES, KNOWING EVERYTHING THAT WOULD HAPPEN?
HUH!?

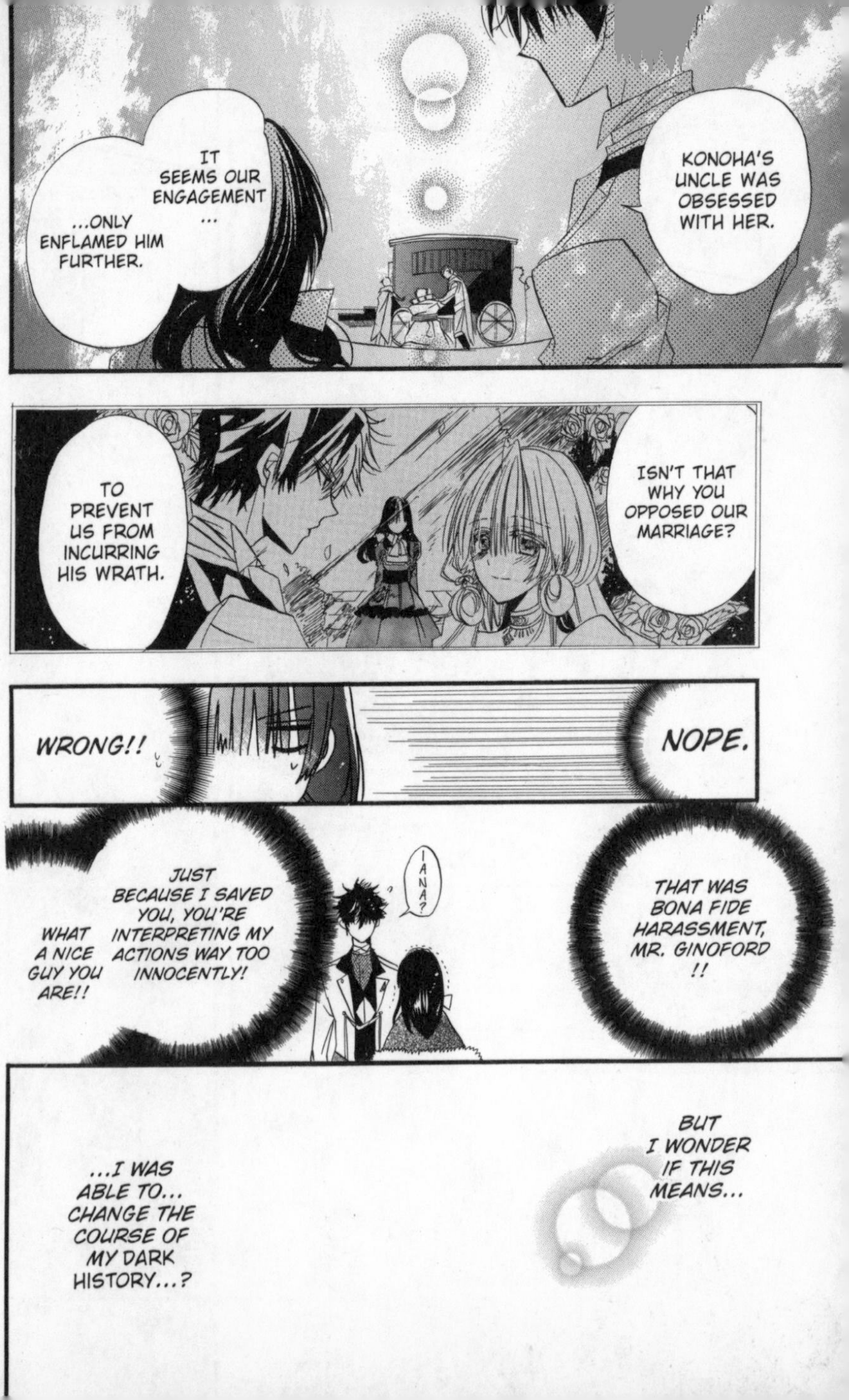
KONOHA'S UNCLE WAS OBSESSED WITH HER.
IT SEEMS OUR ENGAGEMENT ...
...ONLY ENFLAMED HIM FURTHER.
ISN'T THAT WHY YOU OPPOSED OUR MARRIAGE?
TO PREVENT US FROM INCURRING HIS WRATH.
NOPE.
WRONG!!
THAT WAS BONA FIDE HARASSMENT, MR. GINOFORD !!
IANA?
JUST BECAUSE I SAVED YOU, YOU'RE INTERPRETING MY ACTIONS WAY TOO INNOCENTLY!
WHAT A NICE GUY YOU ARE!!
BUT I WONDER IF THIS MEANS...
...I WAS ABLE TO... CHANGE THE COURSE OF MY DARK HISTORY...?

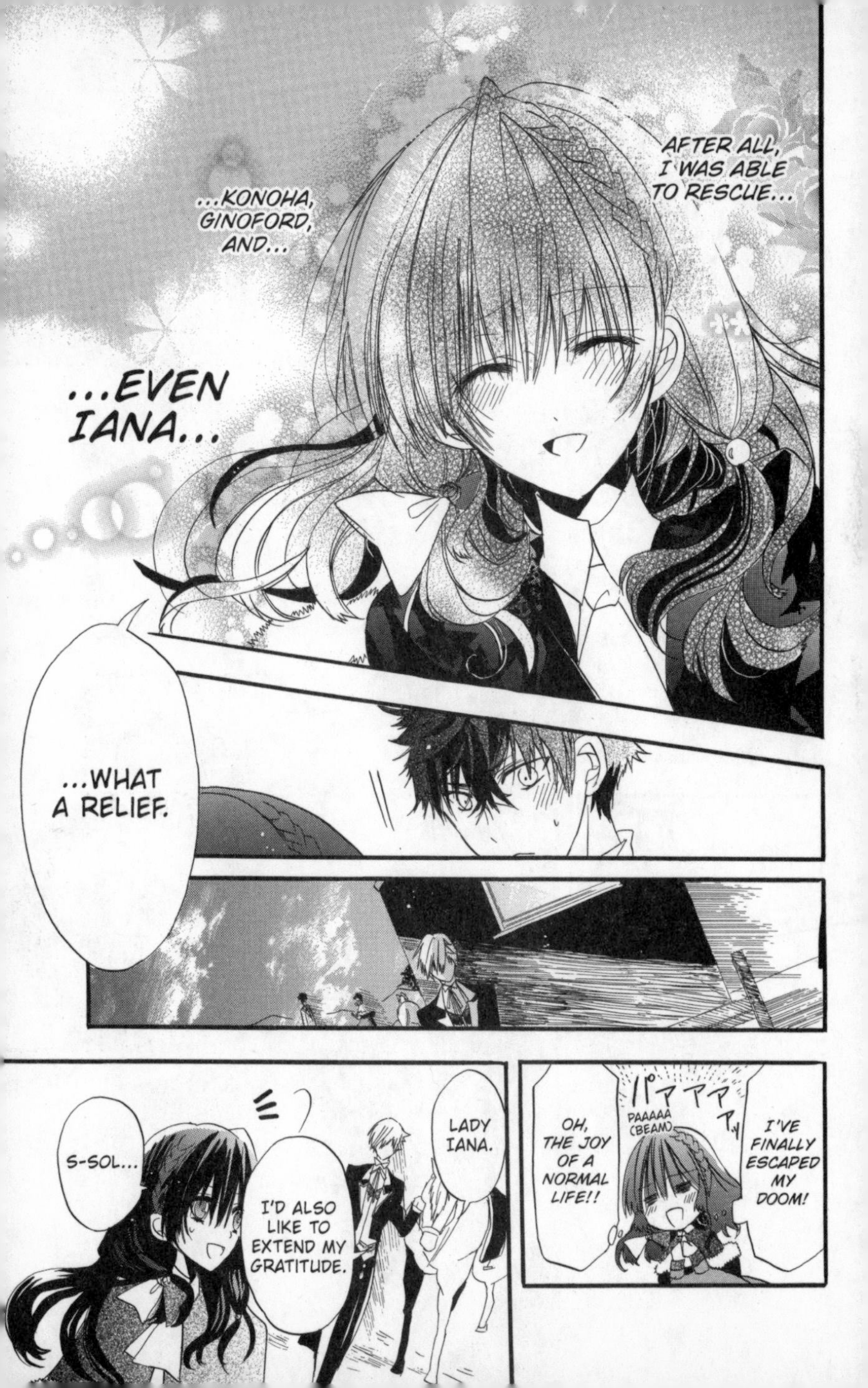
AFTER ALL, I WAS ABLE TO RESCUE...
...KONOHA, GINOFORD, AND...
...EVEN IANA...
...WHAT A RELIEF.
I'VE FINALLY ESCAPED MY DOOM!
パアアアア
PAAAAA (BEAM)
OH, THE JOY OF A NORMAL LIFE!!
LADY IANA.
I'D ALSO LIKE TO EXTEND MY GRATITUDE.
S-SOL...

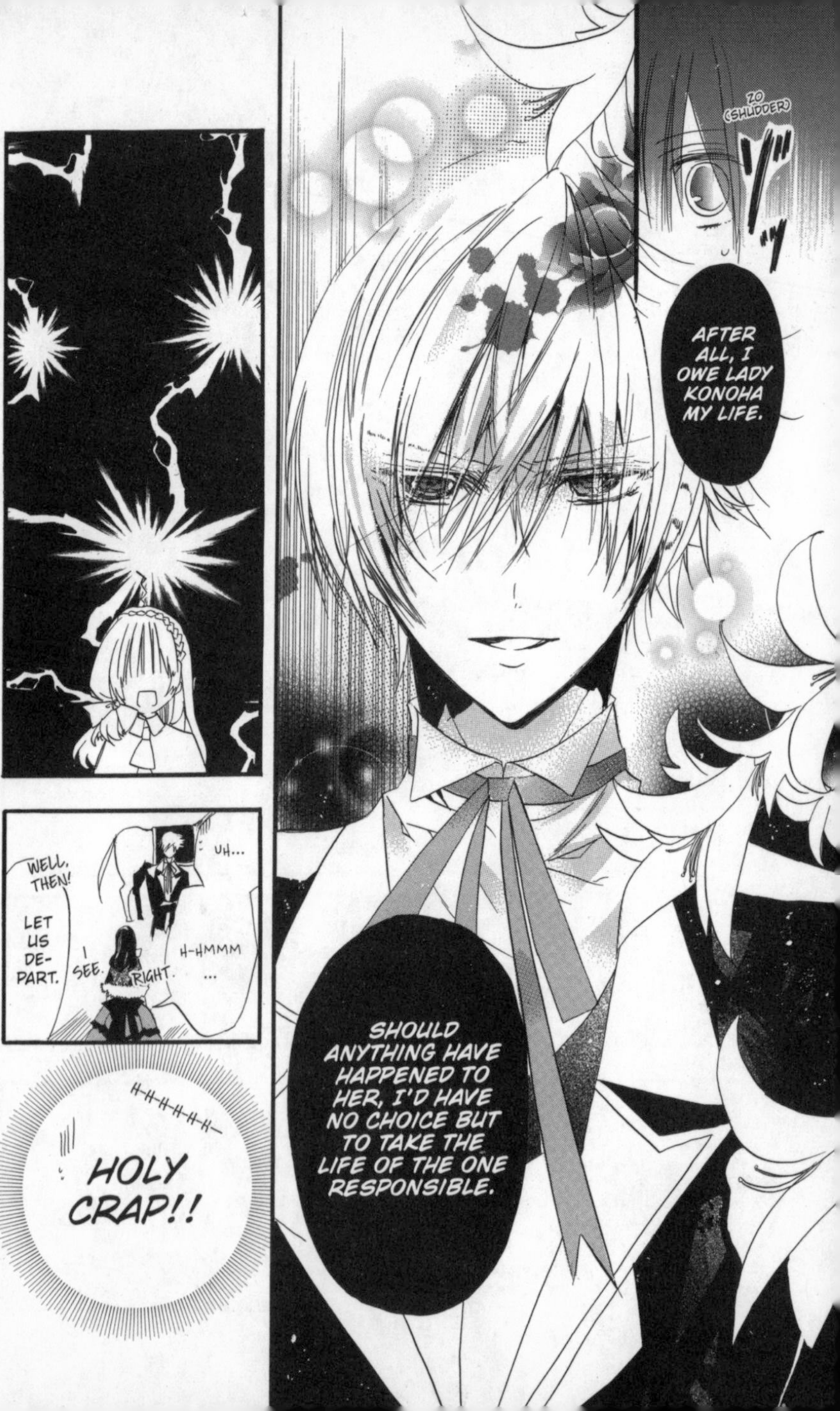
ZO (SHUDDER)
AFTER ALL, I OWE LADY KONOHA MY LIFE.
SHOULD ANYTHING HAVE HAPPENED TO HER, I'D HAVE NO CHOICE BUT TO TAKE THE LIFE OF THE ONE RESPONSIBLE.
UH...
WELL, THEN!
H-HMMM ...
RIGHT.
I SEE.
LET US DE-PART.
H-H-H-H-H-H-
HOLY CRAP!!

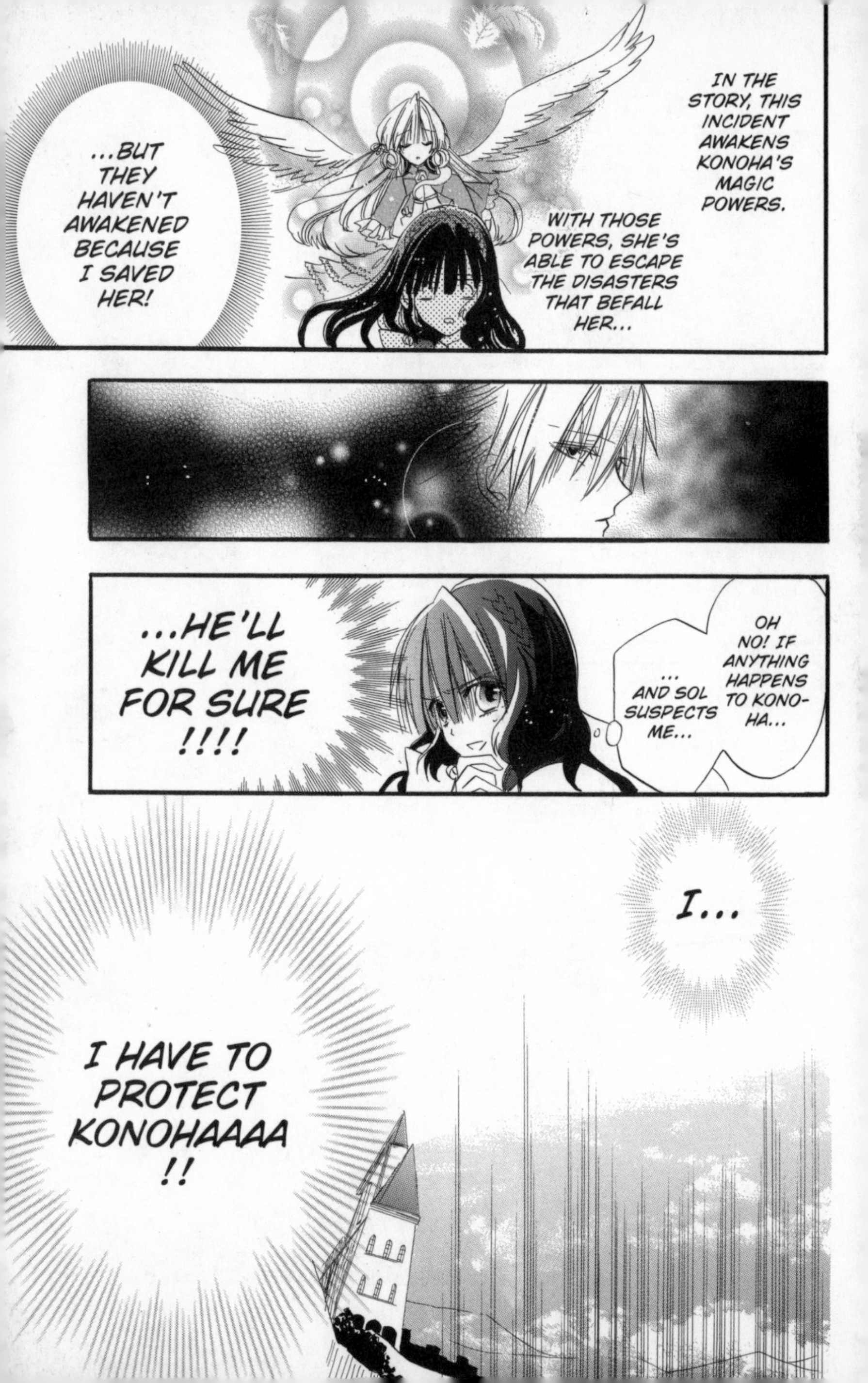
IN THE STORY, THIS INCIDENT AWAKENS KONOHA'S MAGIC POWERS.
WITH THOSE POWERS, SHE'S ABLE TO ESCAPE THE DISASTERS THAT BEFALL HER...
...BUT THEY HAVEN'T AWAKENED BECAUSE I SAVED HER!
OH NO! IF ANYTHING HAPPENS TO KONO-HA...
...AND SOL SUSPECTS ME...
...HE'LL KILL ME FOR SURE!!!!
I...
I HAVE TO PROTECT KONOHAAAA!!

THE DARK HISTORY OF THE REINCARNATED VILLAINESS ②

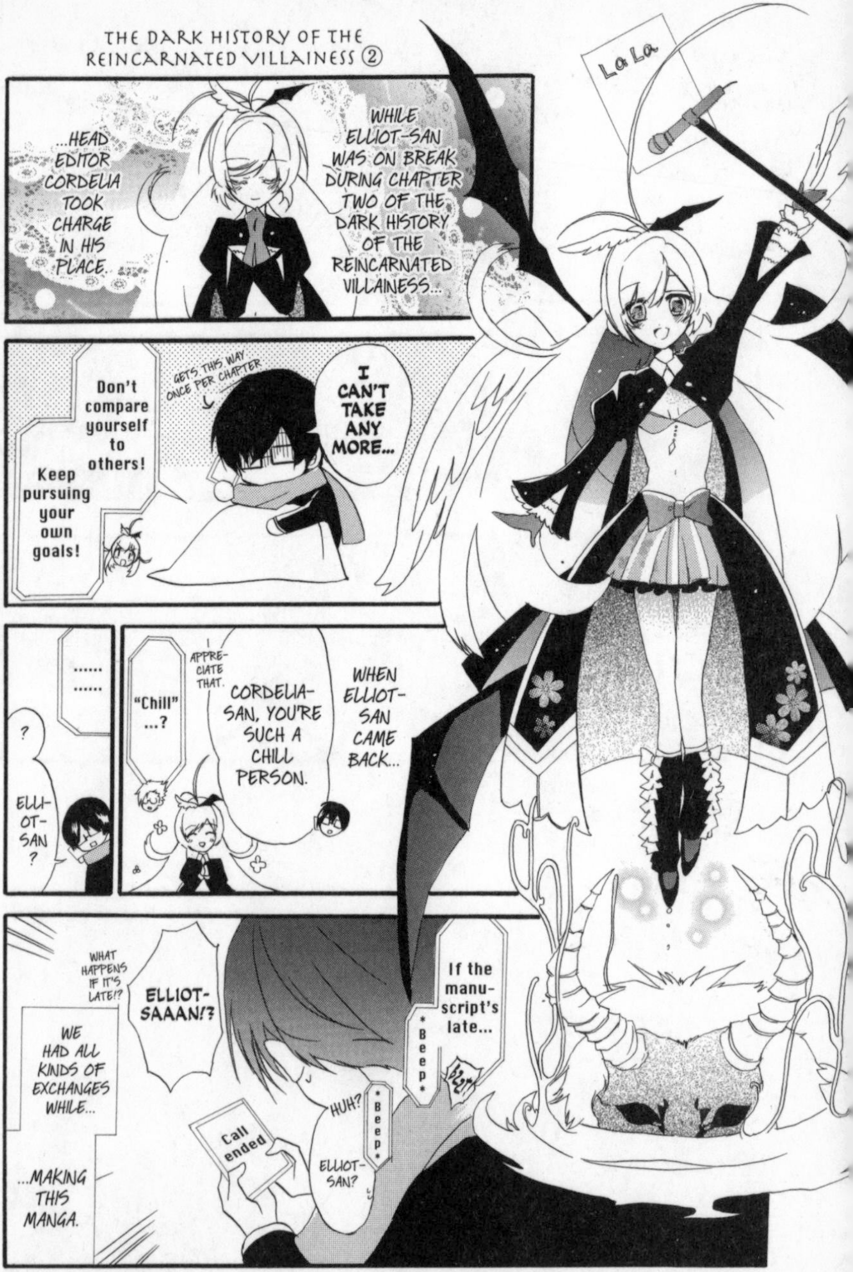
LaLa
WHILE ELLIOT-SAN WAS ON BREAK DURING CHAPTER TWO OF THE DARK HISTORY OF THE REINCARNATED VILLAINESS...
...HEAD EDITOR CORDELIA TOOK CHARGE IN HIS PLACE.
I CAN'T TAKE ANY MORE...
GETS THIS WAY ONCE PER CHAPTER
Don't compare yourself to others!
Keep pursuing your own goals!
WHEN ELLIOT-SAN CAME BACK...
CORDELIA-SAN, YOU'RE SUCH A CHILL PERSON.
I APPRECIATE THAT.
“Chill” ...?
......
......
?
ELLIOT-SAN ?
If the manuscript's late...
Beep
WHAT HAPPENS IF IT'S LATE!?
ELLIOT-SAAAN!?
HUH?
Beep
ELLIOT-SAN?
Call ended
WE HAD ALL KINDS OF EXCHANGES WHILE...
...MAKING THIS MANGA.

DEATH FLAG 2

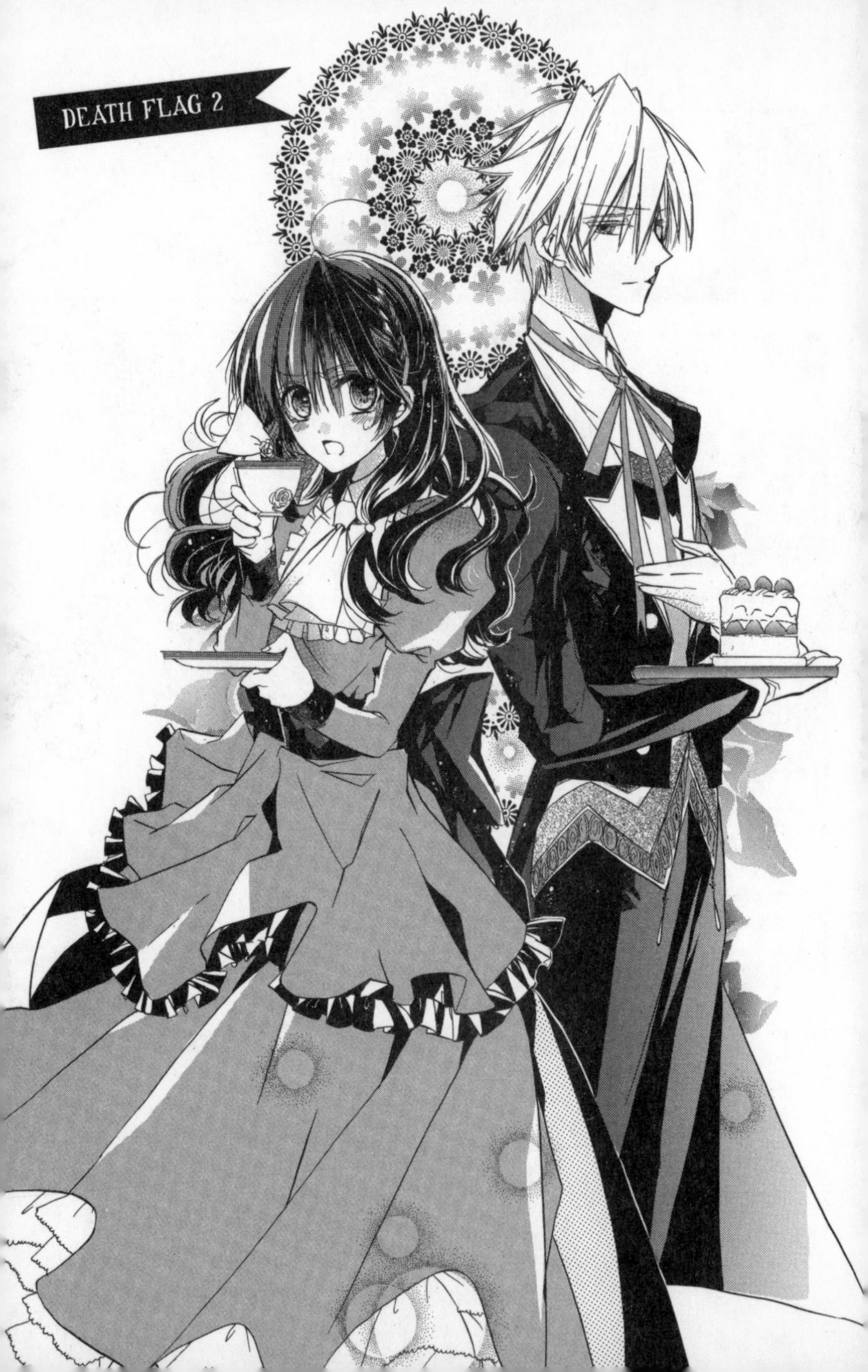

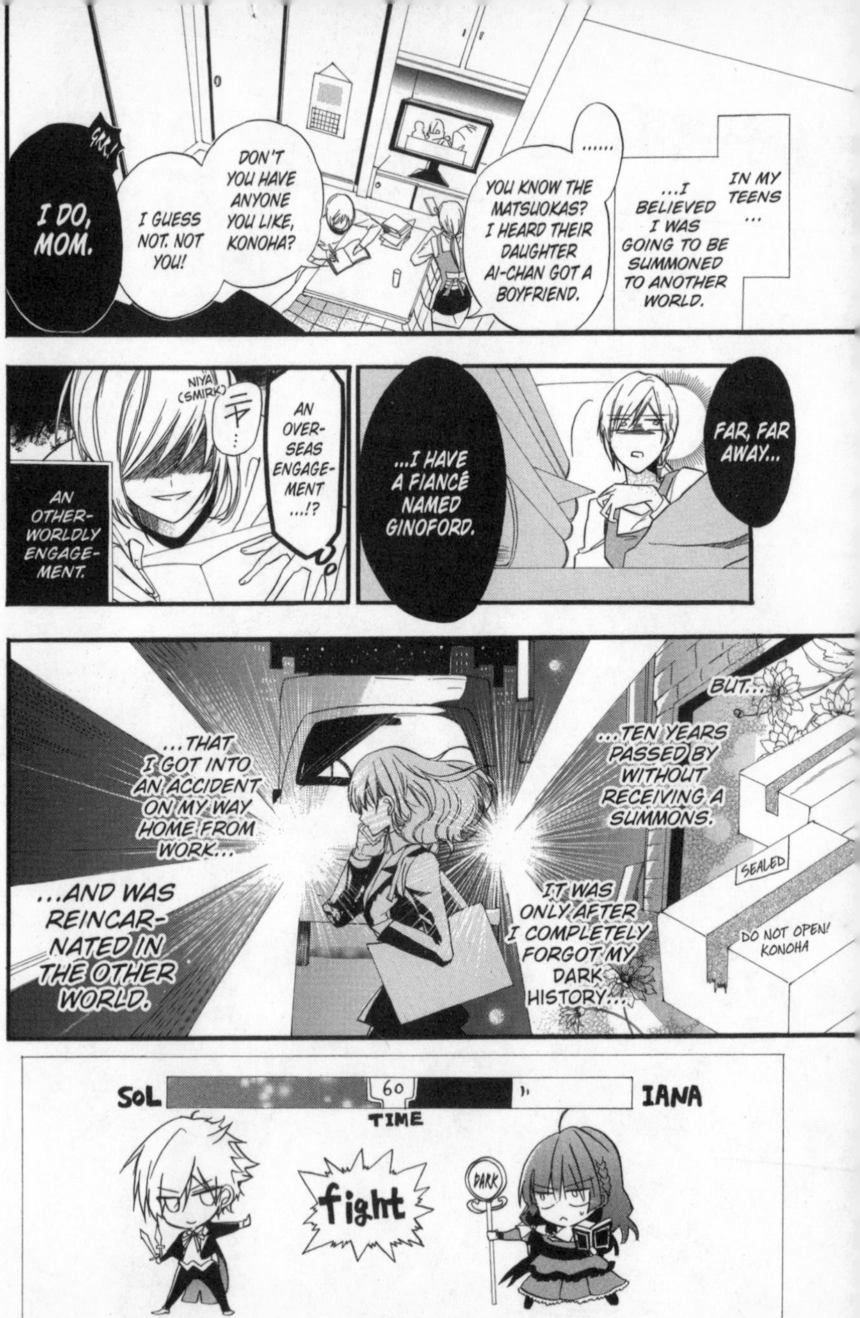
IN MY TEENS...
...I BELIEVED I WAS GOING TO BE SUMMONED TO ANOTHER WORLD.
......
YOU KNOW THE MATSUOKAS? I HEARD THEIR DAUGHTER AI-CHAN GOT A BOYFRIEND.
DON'T YOU HAVE ANYONE YOU LIKE, KONOHA?
I GUESS NOT. NOT YOU!
GRR!
I DO, MOM.
FAR, FAR AWAY...
...I HAVE A FIANCÉ NAMED GINOFORD.
AN OVERSEAS ENGAGEMENT...!?
NIYA (SMIRK)
AN OTHERWORLDLY ENGAGEMENT.
BUT...
...TEN YEARS PASSED BY WITHOUT RECEIVING A SUMMONS.
SEALED
DO NOT OPEN! KONOHA
IT WAS ONLY AFTER I COMPLETELY FORGOT MY DARK HISTORY...
...THAT I GOT INTO AN ACCIDENT ON MY WAY HOME FROM WORK...
...AND WAS REINCARNATED IN THE OTHER WORLD.
SOL
60
TIME
IANA
fight
DARK

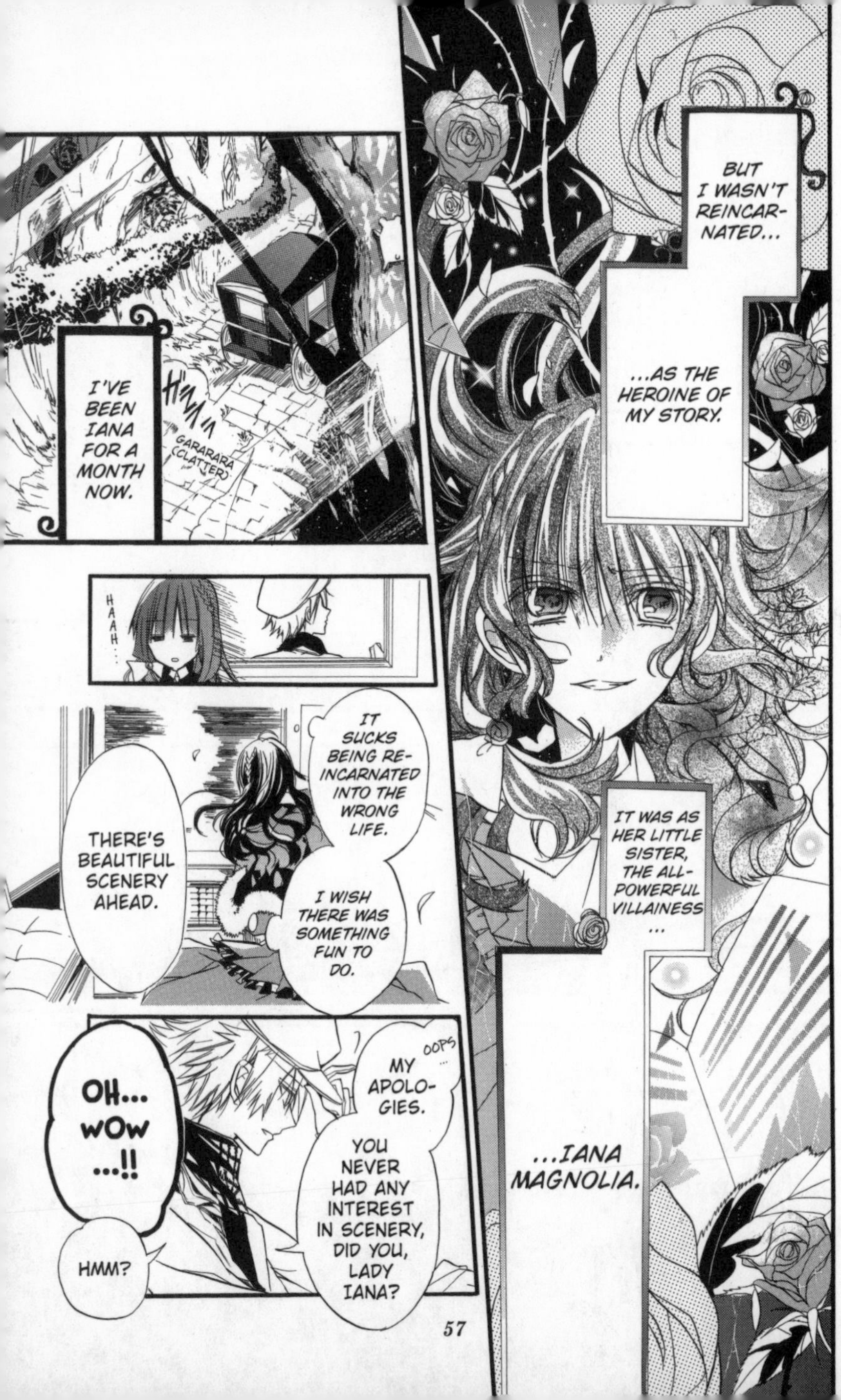
BUT I WASN'T REINCARNATED...
...AS THE HEROINE OF MY STORY.
IT WAS AS HER LITTLE SISTER, THE ALL-POWERFUL VILLAINESS ...
...IANA MAGNOLIA.
GARARARA (CLATTER)
I'VE BEEN IANA FOR A MONTH NOW.
HAAAH...
IT SUCKS BEING REINCARNATED INTO THE WRONG LIFE.
I WISH THERE WAS SOMETHING FUN TO DO.
THERE'S BEAUTIFUL SCENERY AHEAD.
OOPS...
MY APOLOGIES.
YOU NEVER HAD ANY INTEREST IN SCENERY, DID YOU, LADY IANA?
OH... WOW ...!!
HMM?

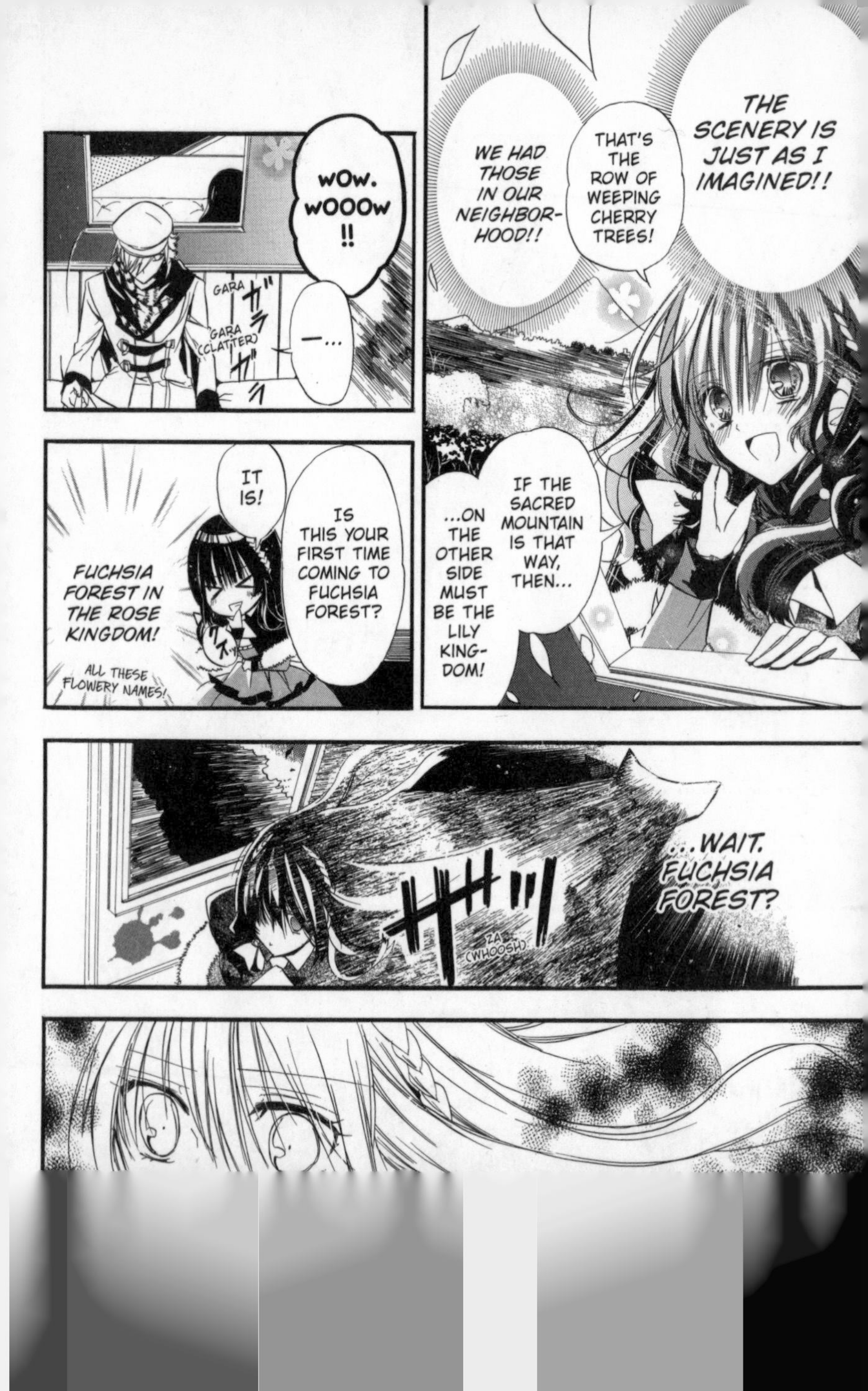

THE SCENERY IS JUST AS I IMAGINED!!
THAT'S THE ROW OF WEEPING CHERRY TREES!
WE HAD THOSE IN OUR NEIGHBOR-HOOD!!
IF THE SACRED MOUNTAIN IS THAT WAY, THEN...
...ON THE OTHER SIDE MUST BE THE LILY KING-DOM!
wOw. wOOOw!!
—...
GARA GARA (CLATTER)
IS THIS YOUR FIRST TIME COMING TO FUCHSIA FOREST?
IT IS!
FUCHSIA FOREST IN THE ROSE KINGDOM!
ALL THESE FLOWERY NAMES!
...WAIT. FUCHSIA FOREST?
ZA (WHOOSH)

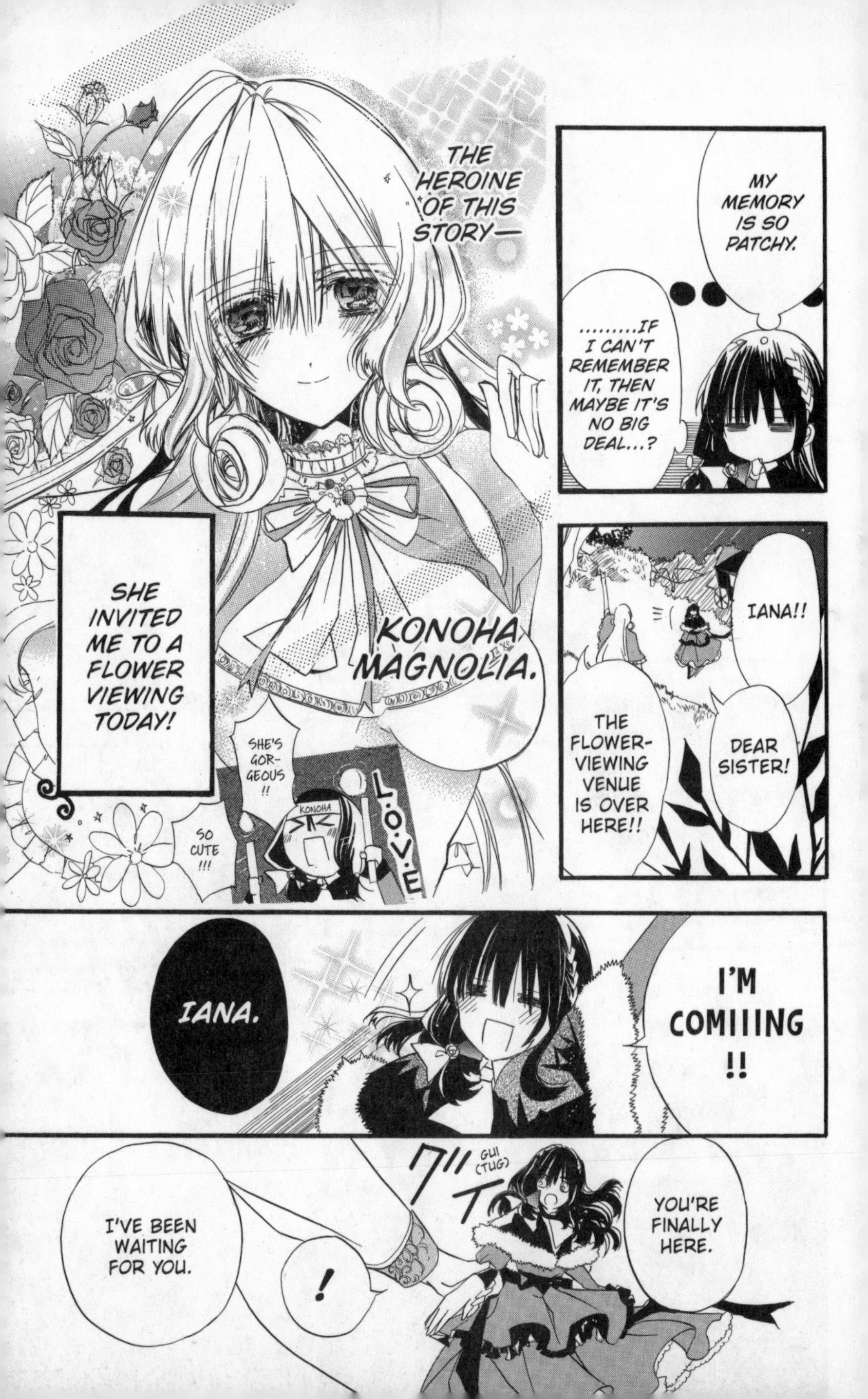

MY MEMORY IS SO PATCHY.
........IF I CAN'T REMEMBER IT, THEN MAYBE IT'S NO BIG DEAL...?
IANA!!
DEAR SISTER!
THE FLOWER-VIEWING VENUE IS OVER HERE!!
THE HEROINE OF THIS STORY—
KONOHA MAGNOLIA.
SHE INVITED ME TO A FLOWER VIEWING TODAY!
SHE'S GORGEOUS !!
KONOHA
L.O.V.E
SO CUTE !!!
I'M COMIIING !!
IANA.
YOU'RE FINALLY HERE.
GUI (TUG)
I'VE BEEN WAITING FOR YOU.
!

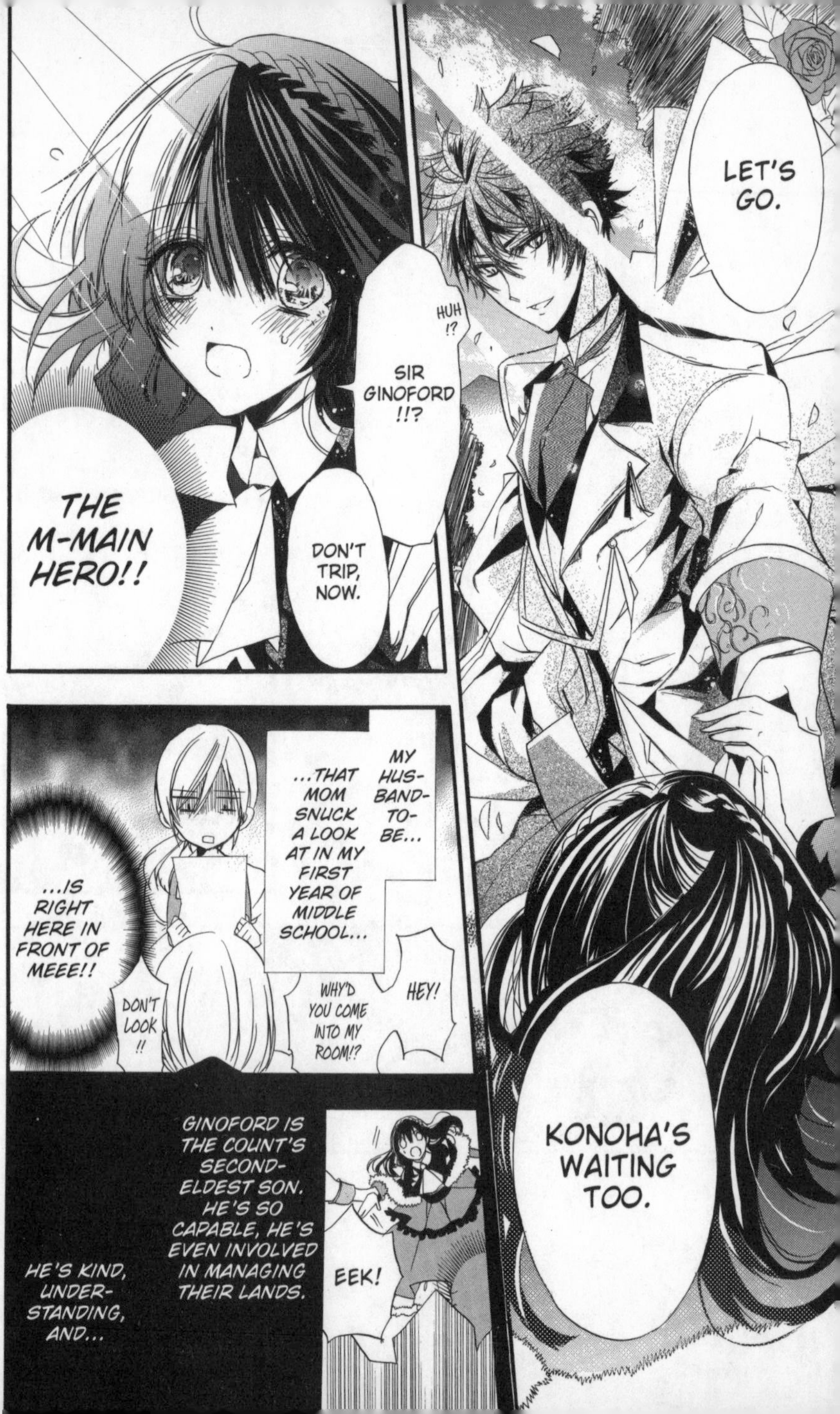
LET'S GO.
KONOHA'S WAITING TOO.
HUH!?
SIR GINOFORD!!?
DON'T TRIP, NOW.
THE M-MAIN HERO!!
MY HUS-BAND-TO-BE...
...THAT MOM SNUCK A LOOK AT IN MY FIRST YEAR OF MIDDLE SCHOOL...
...IS RIGHT HERE IN FRONT OF MEEE!!
HEY!
WHY'D YOU COME INTO MY ROOM!?
DON'T LOOK!!
EEK!
GINOFORD IS THE COUNT'S SECOND-ELDEST SON. HE'S SO CAPABLE, HE'S EVEN INVOLVED IN MANAGING THEIR LANDS.
HE'S KIND, UNDER-STANDING, AND...

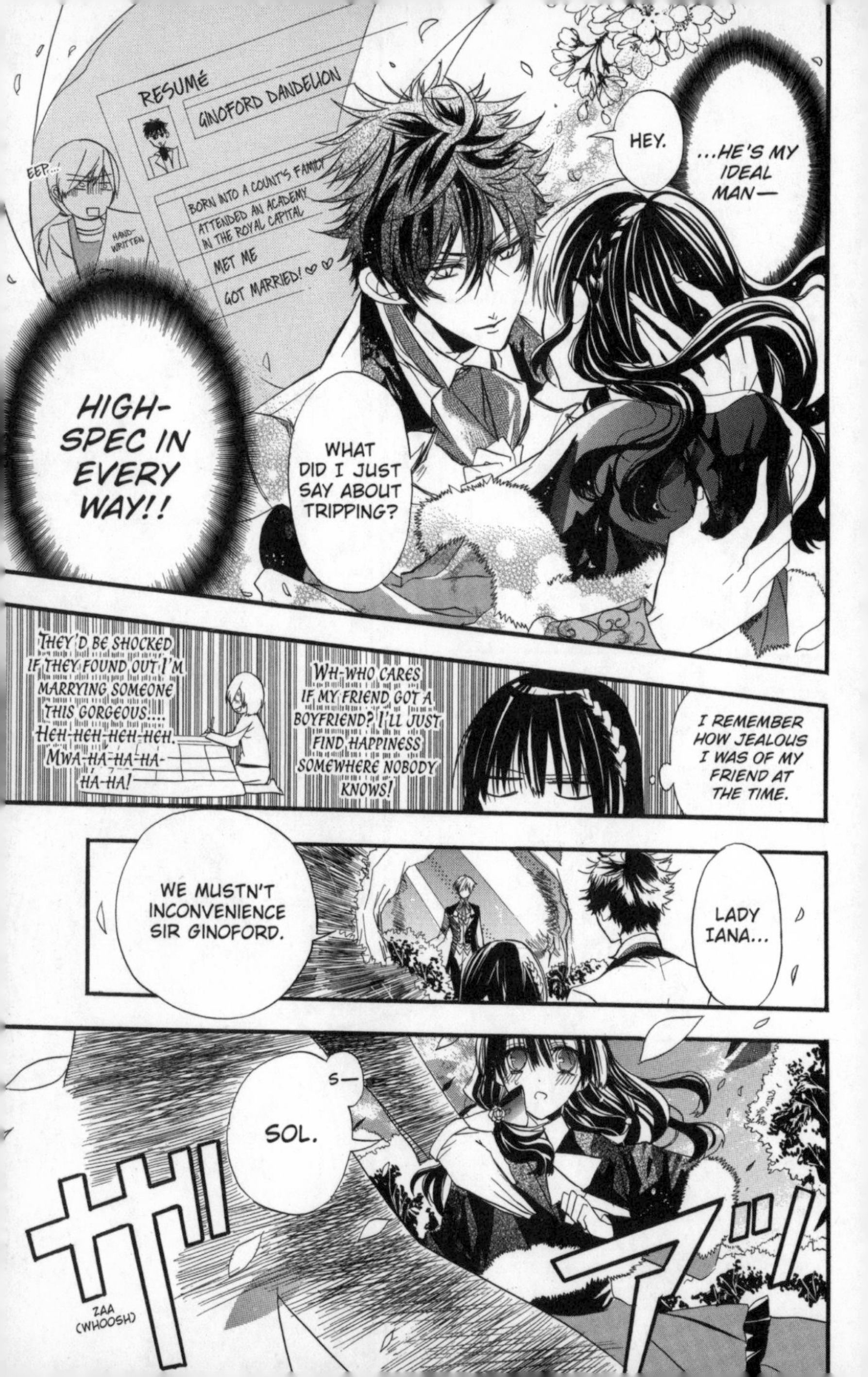
...HE'S MY IDEAL MAN—
HEY.
RESUMÉ
GINOFORD DANDELION
BORN INTO A COUNT'S FAMILY
ATTENDED AN ACADEMY IN THE ROYAL CAPITAL
MET ME
GOT MARRIED! ♡♡
HAND-WRITTEN
EEP...
WHAT DID I JUST SAY ABOUT TRIPPING?
HIGH-SPEC IN EVERY WAY!!
I REMEMBER HOW JEALOUS I WAS OF MY FRIEND AT THE TIME.
WH-WHO CARES IF MY FRIEND GOT A BOYFRIEND? I'LL JUST FIND HAPPINESS SOMEWHERE NOBODY KNOWS!
THEY'D BE SHOCKED IF THEY FOUND OUT I'M MARRYING SOMEONE THIS GORGEOUS.... HEH-HEH-HEH-HEH. MWA-HA-HA-HA-HA-HA!
LADY IANA...
WE MUSTN'T INCONVENIENCE SIR GINOFORD.
S—
SOL.
ZAA (WHOOSH)

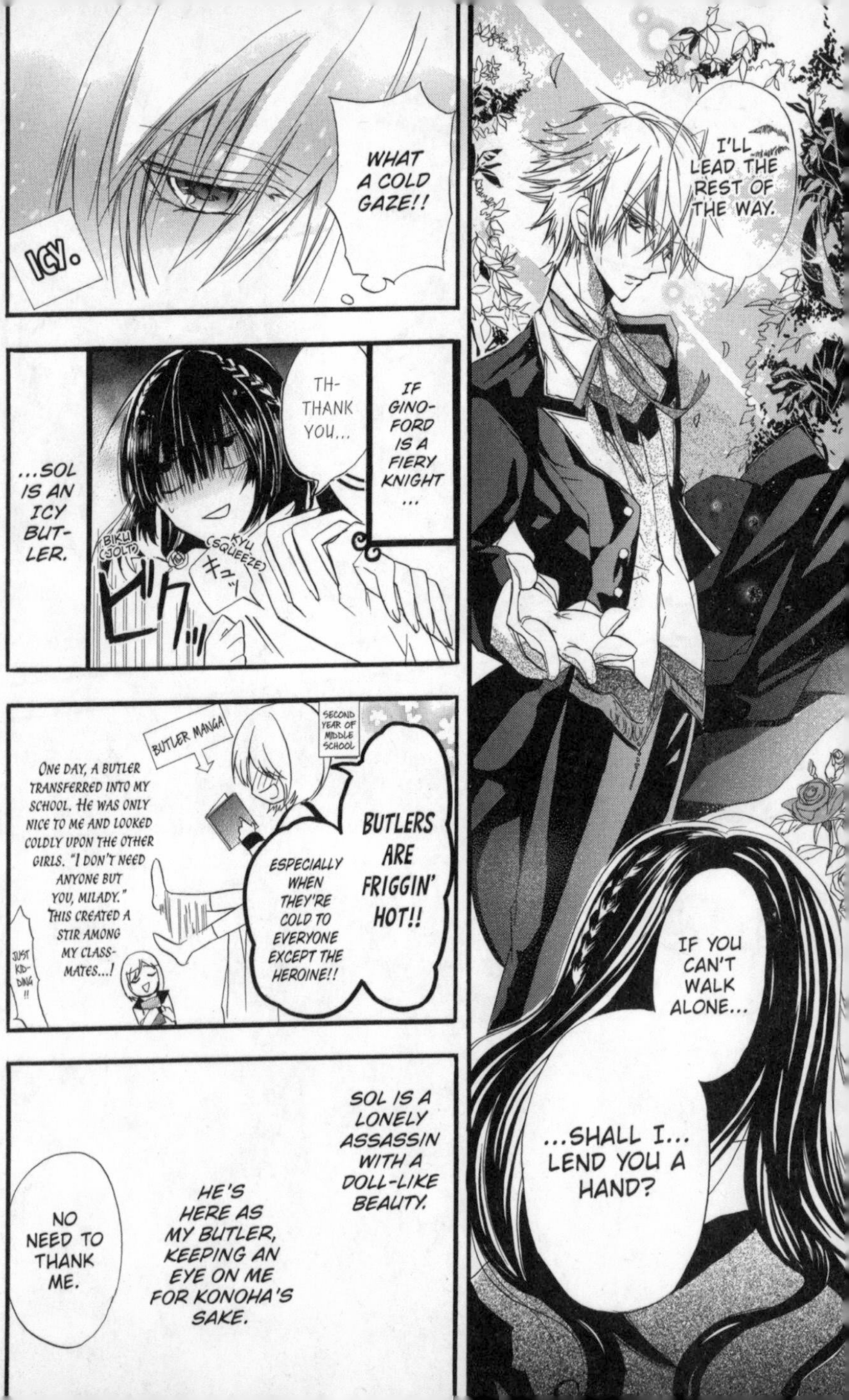

I'LL LEAD THE REST OF THE WAY.
IF YOU CAN'T WALK ALONE...
...SHALL I... LEND YOU A HAND?
WHAT A COLD GAZE!!
ICY.
IF GINO-FORD IS A FIERY KNIGHT...
TH-THANK YOU...
...SOL IS AN ICY BUT-LER.
KYU (SQUEEZE)
BIKU (JOLT)
SECOND YEAR OF MIDDLE SCHOOL
BUTLER MANGA
BUTLERS ARE FRIGGIN' HOT!!
ESPECIALLY WHEN THEY'RE COLD TO EVERYONE EXCEPT THE HEROINE!!
ONE DAY, A BUTLER TRANSFERRED INTO MY SCHOOL. HE WAS ONLY NICE TO ME AND LOOKED COLDLY UPON THE OTHER GIRLS. "I DON'T NEED ANYONE BUT YOU, MILADY." THIS CREATED A STIR AMONG MY CLASS-MATES...!
JUST KID-DING!!
SOL IS A LONELY ASSASSIN WITH A DOLL-LIKE BEAUTY.
HE'S HERE AS MY BUTLER, KEEPING AN EYE ON ME FOR KONOHA'S SAKE.
NO NEED TO THANK ME.

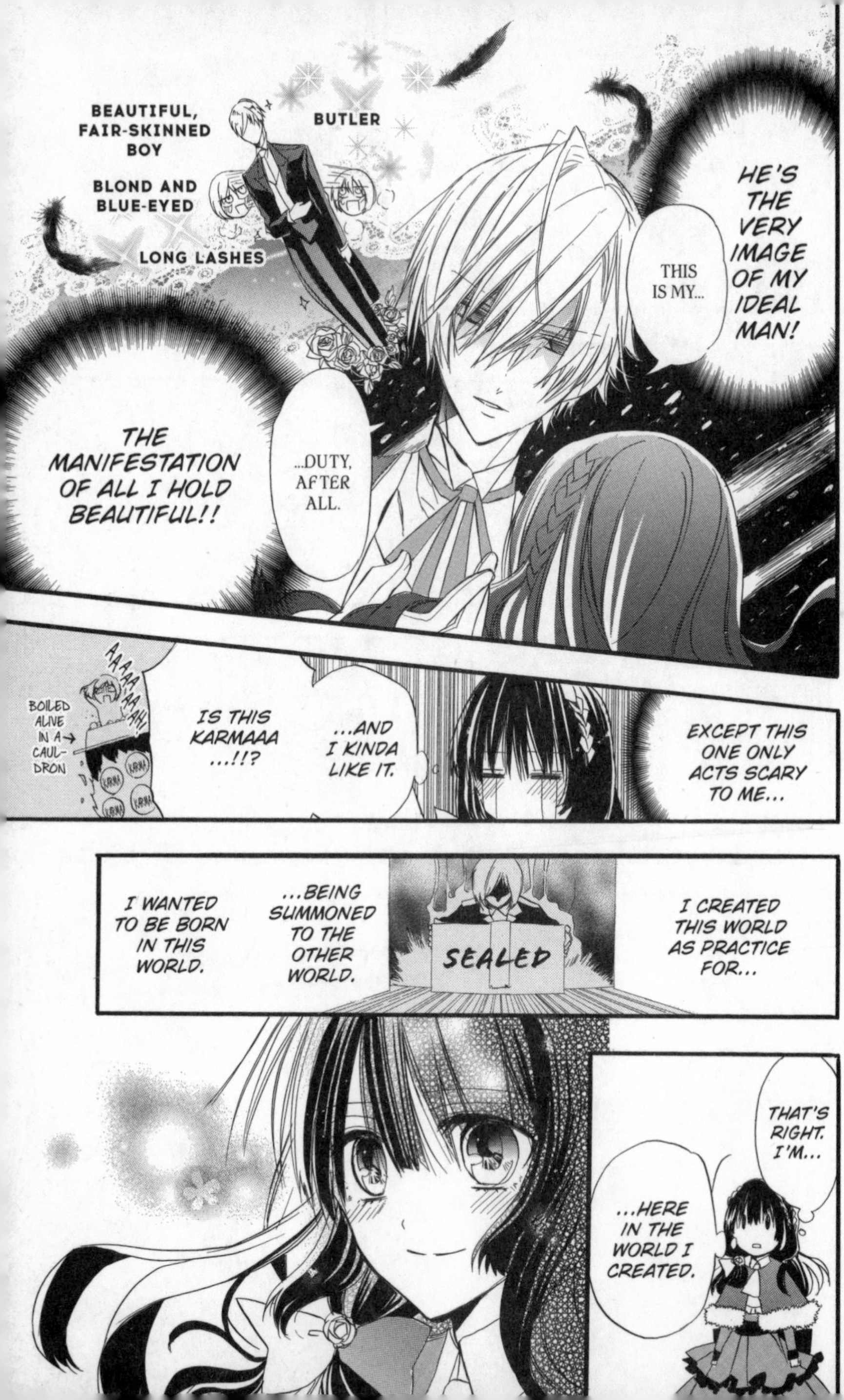
HE'S THE VERY IMAGE OF MY IDEAL MAN!
THIS IS MY...
...DUTY, AFTER ALL.
THE MANIFESTATION OF ALL I HOLD BEAUTIFUL!!
BUTLER
BEAUTIFUL, FAIR-SKINNED BOY
BLOND AND BLUE-EYED
LONG LASHES
EXCEPT THIS ONE ONLY ACTS SCARY TO ME...
...AND I KINDA LIKE IT.
IS THIS KARMAAA ...!!?
AAAAAAAH!
BOILED ALIVE IN A CAULDRON
KARMA
KARMA
KARMA
KARMA
I CREATED THIS WORLD AS PRACTICE FOR...
SEALED
...BEING SUMMONED TO THE OTHER WORLD.
I WANTED TO BE BORN IN THIS WORLD.
THAT'S RIGHT. I'M...
...HERE IN THE WORLD I CREATED.

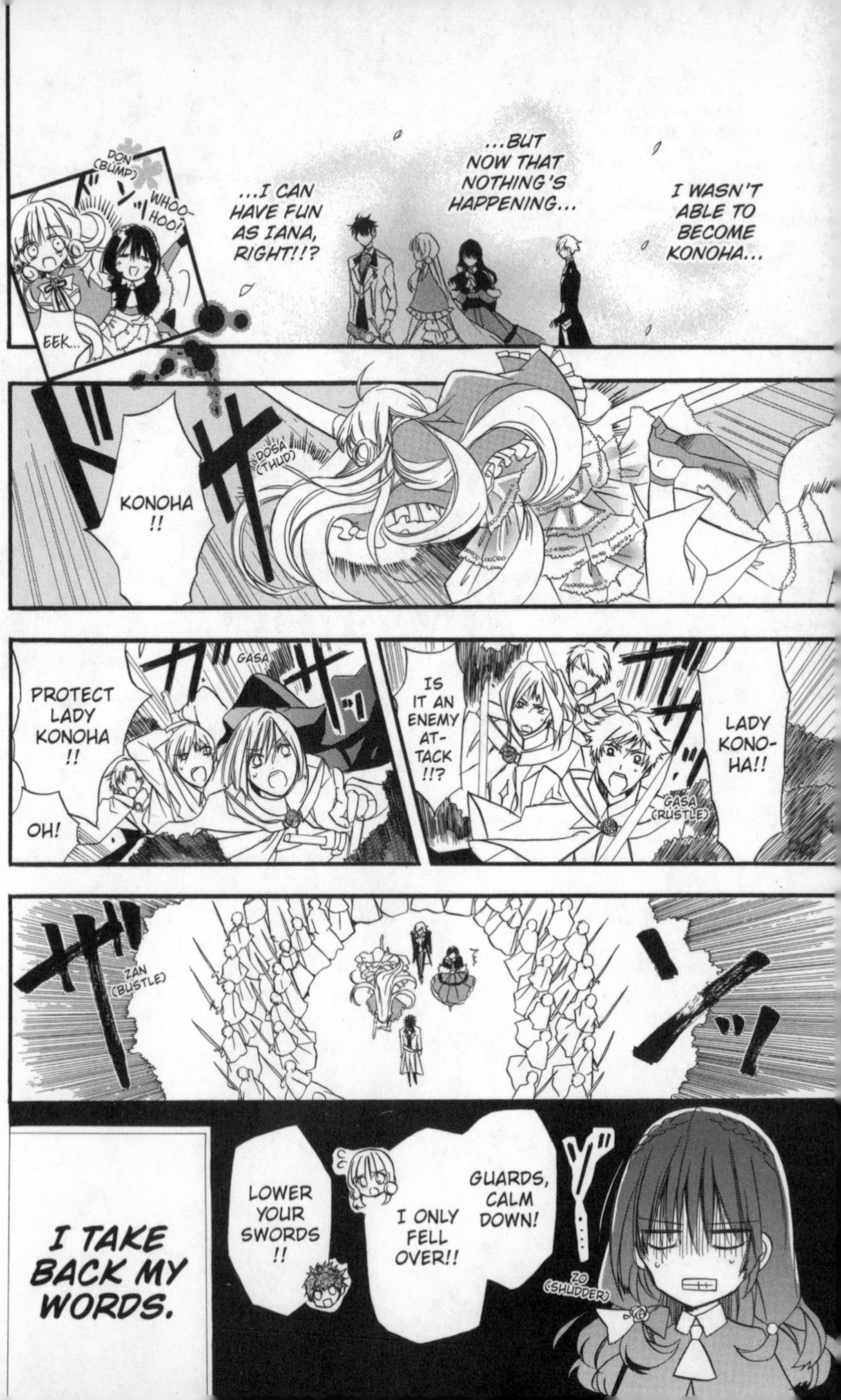
I WASN'T ABLE TO BECOME KONOHA...
...BUT NOW THAT NOTHING'S HAPPENING...
...I CAN HAVE FUN AS IANA, RIGHT!!?
WHOO-HOO?
DON (BUMP)
EEK...
DOSA (THUD)
KONOHA!!
LADY KONOHA!!
GASA (RUSTLE)
IS IT AN ENEMY ATTACK!!?
GASA
PROTECT LADY KONOHA!!
OH!
ZAN (BUSTLE)
ZO (SHUDDER)
GUARDS, CALM DOWN!
I ONLY FELL OVER!!
LOWER YOUR SWORDS!!
I TAKE BACK MY WORDS.

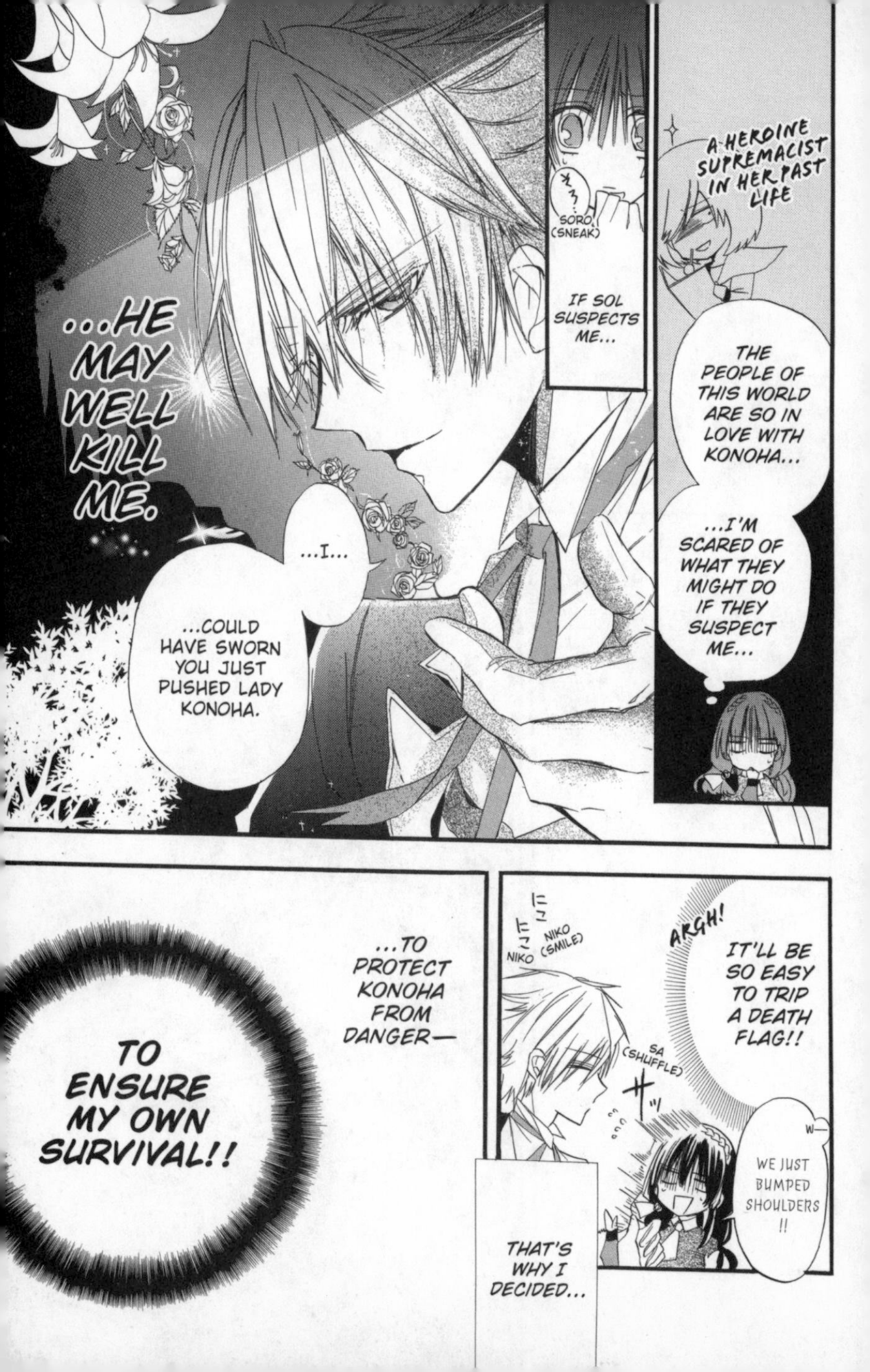

A HEROINE SUPREMACIST IN HER PAST LIFE
THE PEOPLE OF THIS WORLD ARE SO IN LOVE WITH KONOHA...
...I'M SCARED OF WHAT THEY MIGHT DO IF THEY SUSPECT ME...
SORO (SNEAK)
IF SOL SUSPECTS ME...
...I...
...COULD HAVE SWORN YOU JUST PUSHED LADY KONOHA.
...HE MAY WELL KILL ME.
ARGH!
IT'LL BE SO EASY TO TRIP A DEATH FLAG!!
NIKO NIKO (SMILE)
SA (SHUFFLE)
W—
WE JUST BUMPED SHOULDERS !!
THAT'S WHY I DECIDED...
...TO PROTECT KONOHA FROM DANGER—
TO ENSURE MY OWN SURVIVAL!!

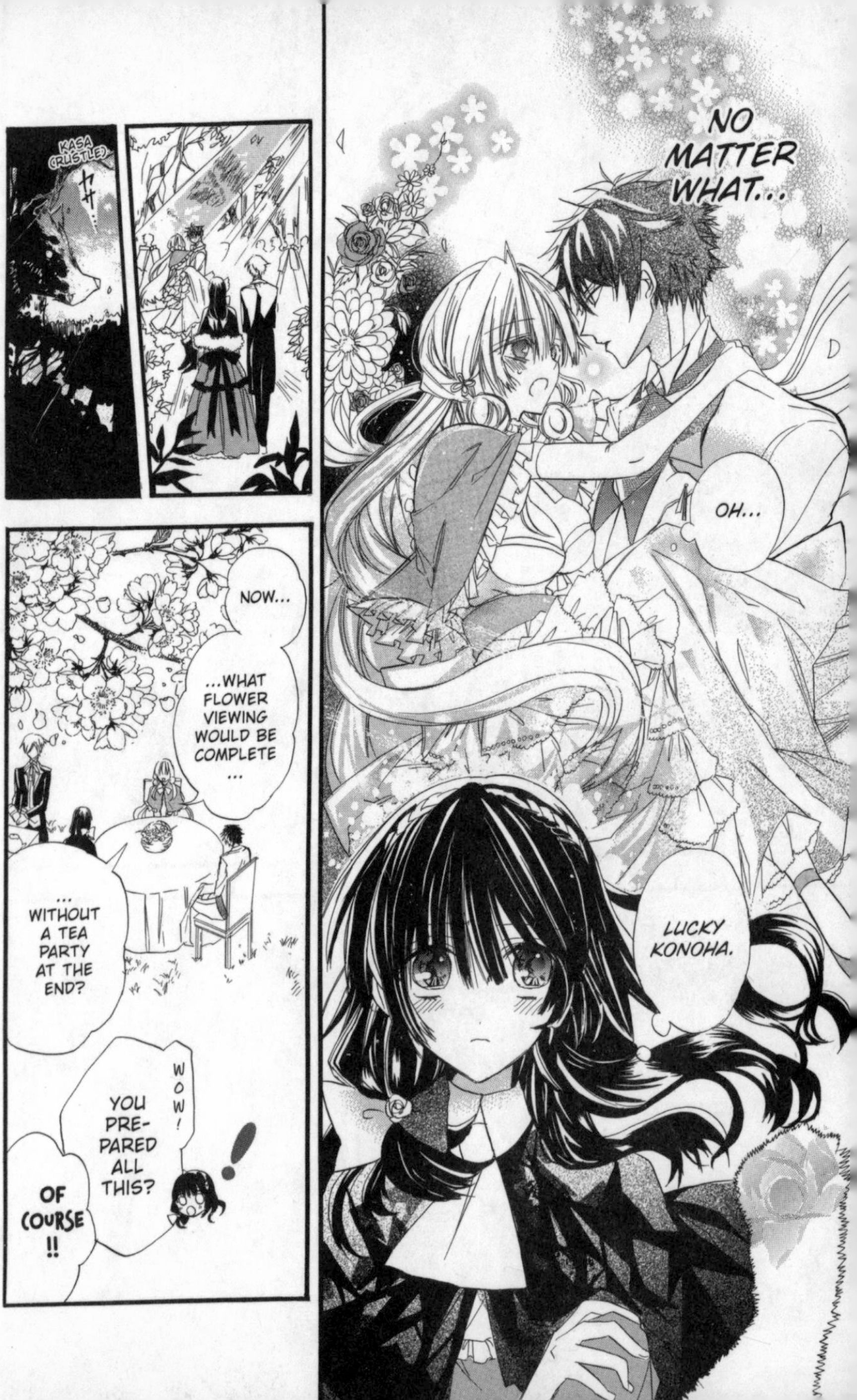
NO MATTER WHAT...
OH...
LUCKY KONOHA.
KASA (RUSTLE)
NOW...
...WHAT FLOWER VIEWING WOULD BE COMPLETE ...
...WITHOUT A TEA PARTY AT THE END?
WOW!
YOU PRE-PARED ALL THIS?
OF COURSE!!

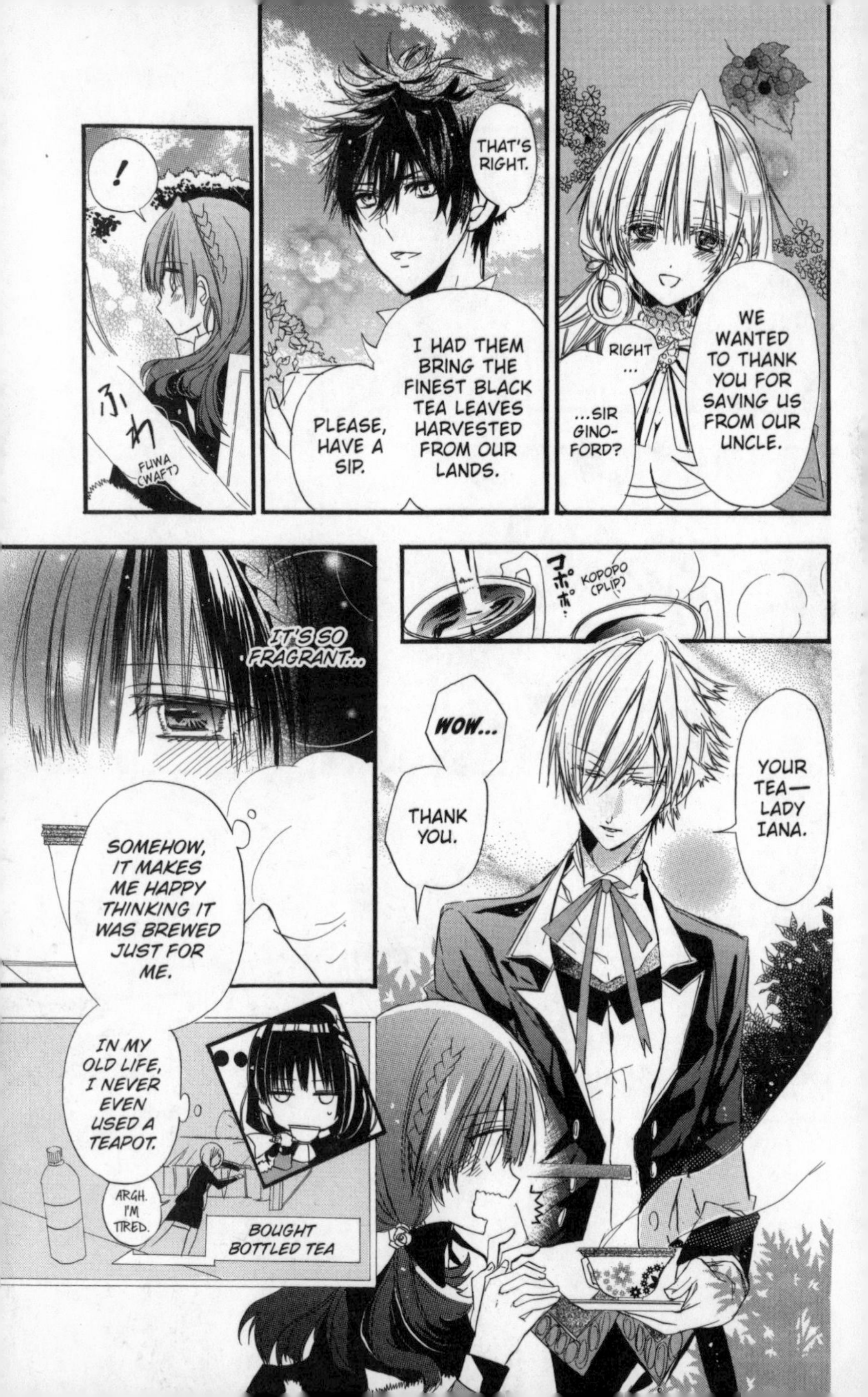
WE WANTED TO THANK YOU FOR SAVING US FROM OUR UNCLE.
RIGHT ...
...SIR GINO-FORD?
THAT'S RIGHT.
I HAD THEM BRING THE FINEST BLACK TEA LEAVES HARVESTED FROM OUR LANDS.
PLEASE, HAVE A SIP.
!
ふわ
FUWA (WAFT)
コポポ
KOPOPO (PLIP)
YOUR TEA—LADY IANA.
WOW...
THANK YOU.
IT'S SO FRAGRANT...
SOMEHOW, IT MAKES ME HAPPY THINKING IT WAS BREWED JUST FOR ME.
IN MY OLD LIFE, I NEVER EVEN USED A TEAPOT.
ARGH. I'M TIRED.
BOUGHT BOTTLED TEA

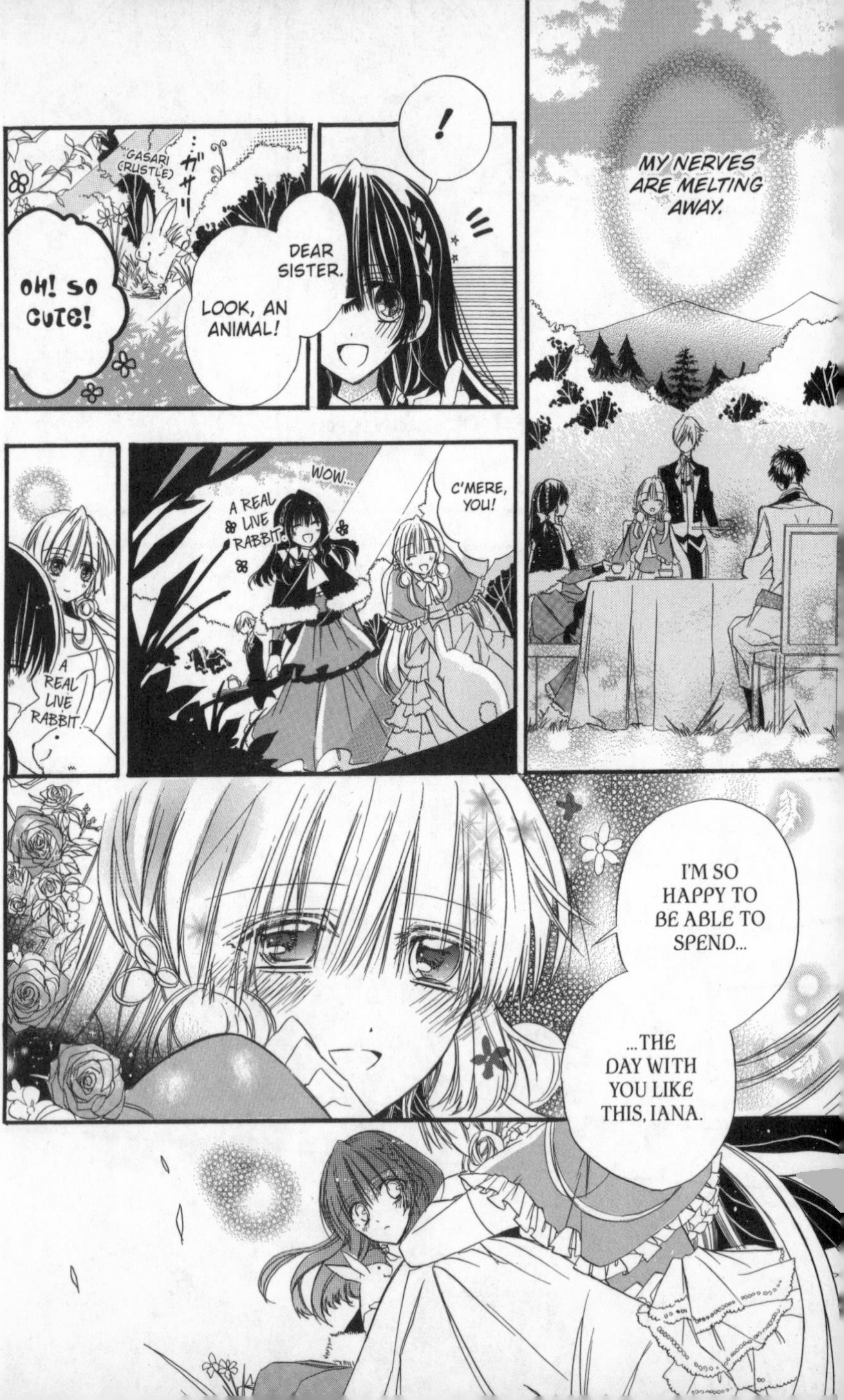
MY NERVES ARE MELTING AWAY.
!
DEAR SISTER.
LOOK, AN ANIMAL!
GASARI (RUSTLE)
ガサリ
OH! SO CUTE!
C'MERE, YOU!
WOW...
A REAL LIVE RABBIT.
A REAL LIVE RABBIT.
I'M SO HAPPY TO BE ABLE TO SPEND...
...THE DAY WITH YOU LIKE THIS, IANA.

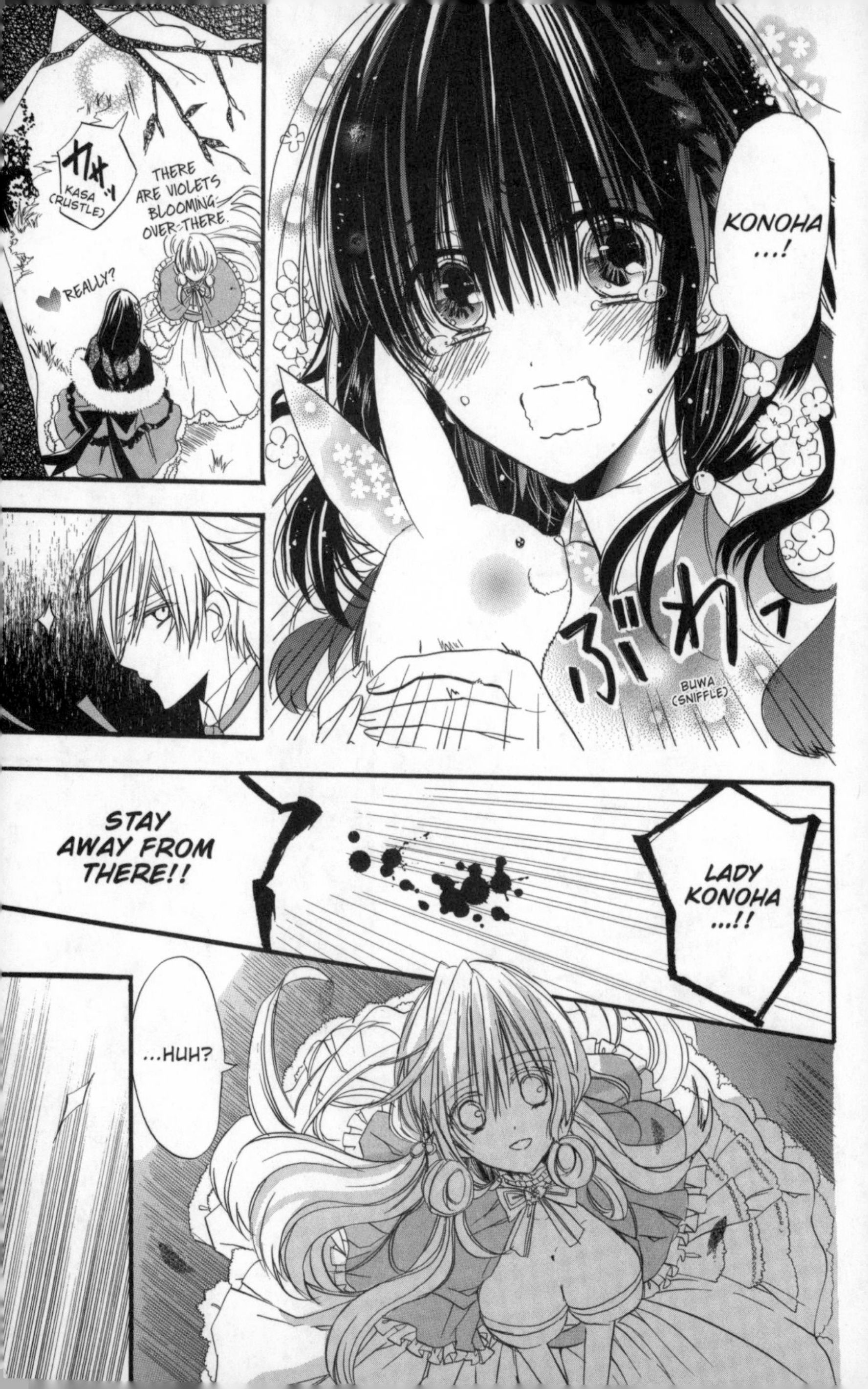
KONOHA ...!
ぶわ
BUWA (SNIFFLE)
カサッ
KASA (RUSTLE)
THERE ARE VIOLETS BLOOMING OVER THERE.
REALLY?
LADY KONOHA ...!!
STAY AWAY FROM THERE!!
...HUH?

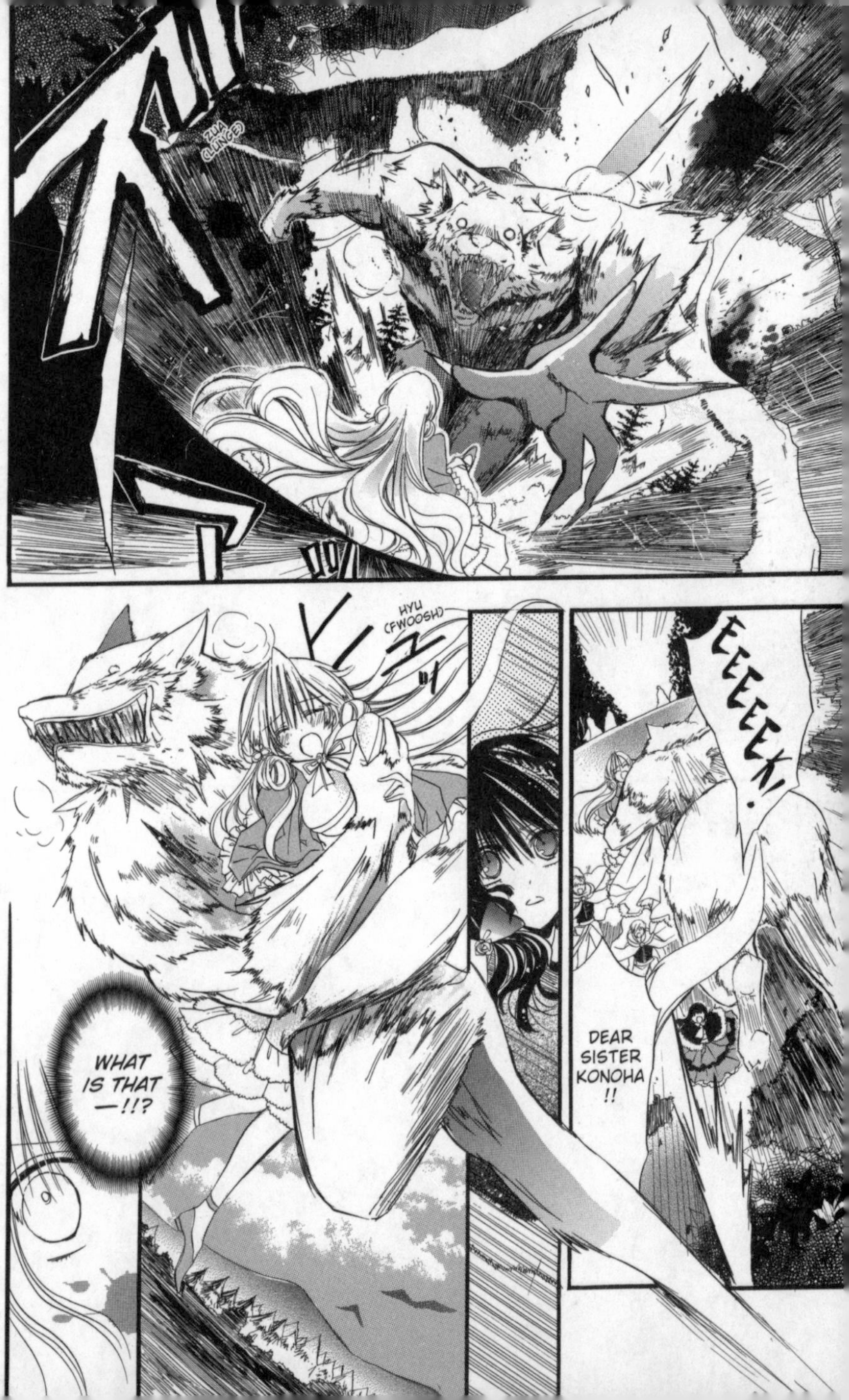
ZUA (LUNGE)
EEEEEK!
DEAR SISTER KONOHA!!
HYU (FWOOSH)
WHAT IS THAT—!!?

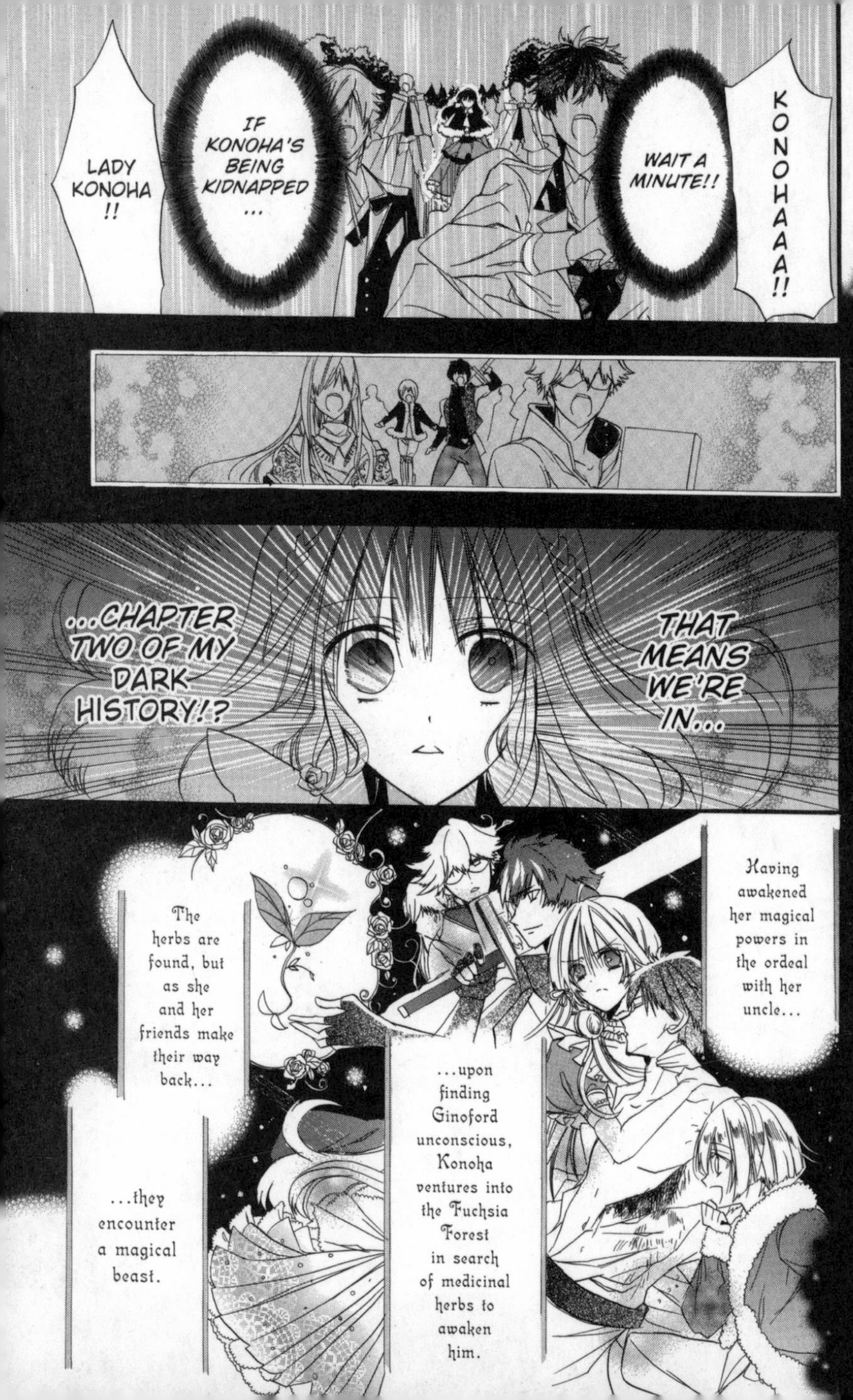
KONOHAAAA!!
WAIT A MINUTE!!
IF KONOHA'S BEING KIDNAPPED...
LADY KONOHA!!
THAT MEANS WE'RE IN...
...CHAPTER TWO OF MY DARK HISTORY!?
Having awakened her magical powers in the ordeal with her uncle...
...upon finding Ginoford unconscious, Konoha ventures into the Fuchsia Forest in search of medicinal herbs to awaken him.
The herbs are found, but as she and her friends make their way back...
...they encounter a magical beast.

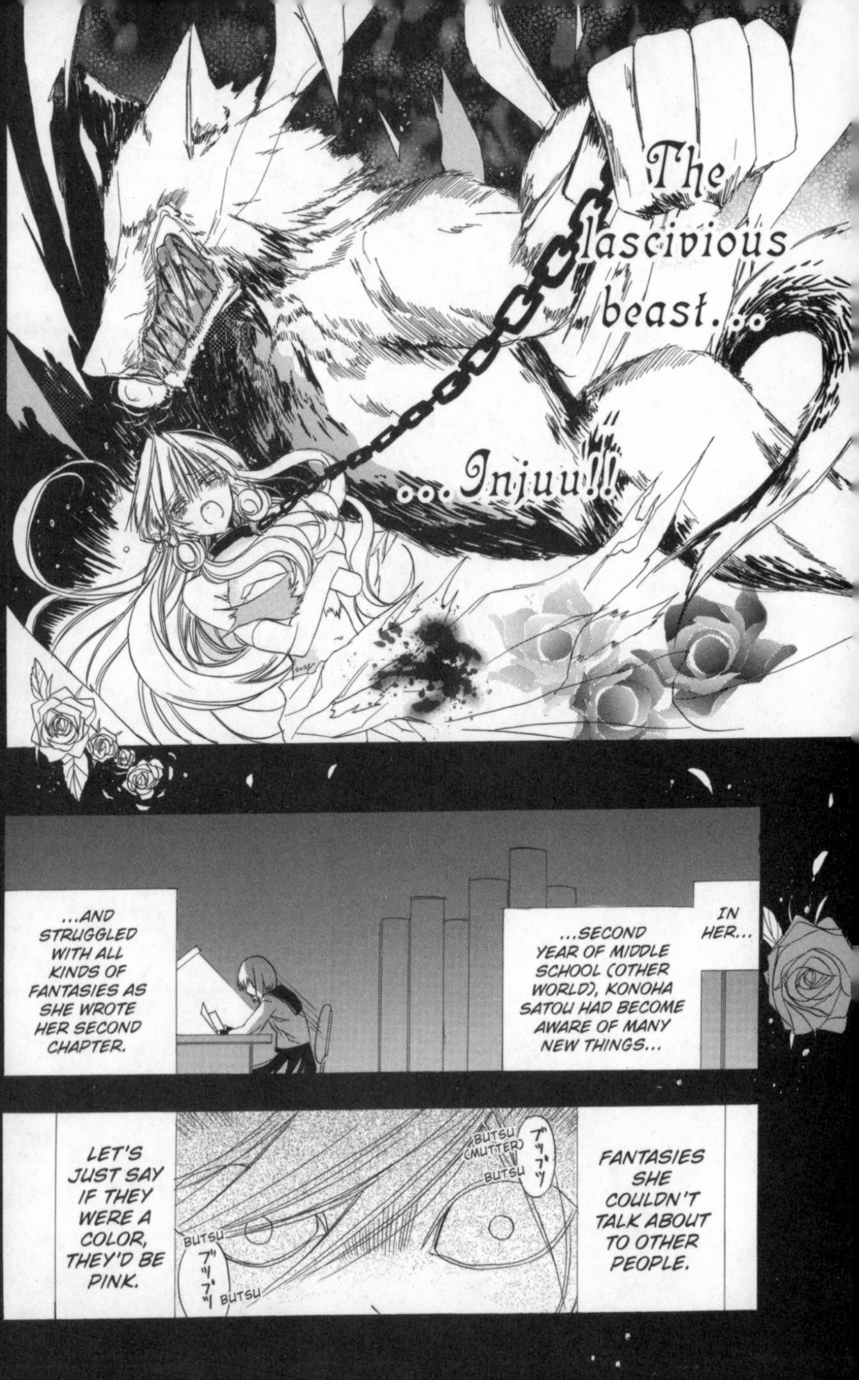
The lascivious beast...
...Injuu!!
IN HER...
...SECOND YEAR OF MIDDLE SCHOOL (OTHER WORLD), KONOHA SATOU HAD BECOME AWARE OF MANY NEW THINGS...
...AND STRUGGLED WITH ALL KINDS OF FANTASIES AS SHE WROTE HER SECOND CHAPTER.
FANTASIES SHE COULDN'T TALK ABOUT TO OTHER PEOPLE.
ブツブツ
BUTSU (MUTTER) BUTSU
ブツブツ
BUTSU BUTSU
LET'S JUST SAY IF THEY WERE A COLOR, THEY'D BE PINK.

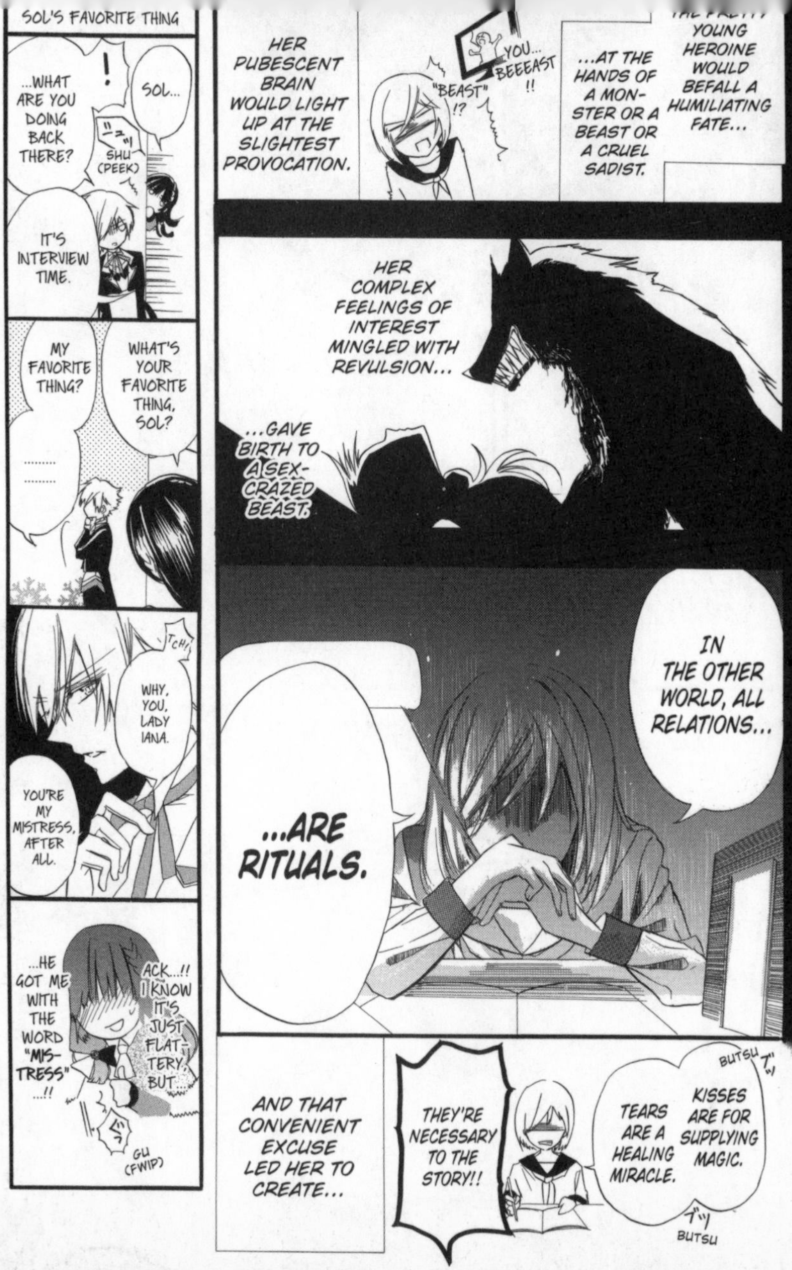
YOUNG HEROINE WOULD BEFALL A HUMILIATING FATE...
...AT THE HANDS OF A MONSTER OR A BEAST OR A CRUEL SADIST.
YOU... BEEEAST !!
"BEAST" !?
HER PUBESCENT BRAIN WOULD LIGHT UP AT THE SLIGHTEST PROVOCATION.
HER COMPLEX FEELINGS OF INTEREST MINGLED WITH REVULSION...
...GAVE BIRTH TO A SEX-CRAZED BEAST.
IN THE OTHER WORLD, ALL RELATIONS...
...ARE RITUALS.
BUTSU
KISSES ARE FOR SUPPLYING MAGIC.
TEARS ARE A HEALING MIRACLE.
BUTSU
THEY'RE NECESSARY TO THE STORY!!
AND THAT CONVENIENT EXCUSE LED HER TO CREATE...
SOL'S FAVORITE THING
!
SOL...
...WHAT ARE YOU DOING BACK THERE?
SHU (PEEK)
IT'S INTERVIEW TIME.
WHAT'S YOUR FAVORITE THING, SOL?
MY FAVORITE THING?
....
....
TCH!
WHY, YOU, LADY IANA.
YOU'RE MY MISTRESS, AFTER ALL.
ACK...!! I KNOW IT'S JUST FLATTERY, BUT...
...HE GOT ME WITH THE WORD "MISTRESS"...!!
GU (FWIP)

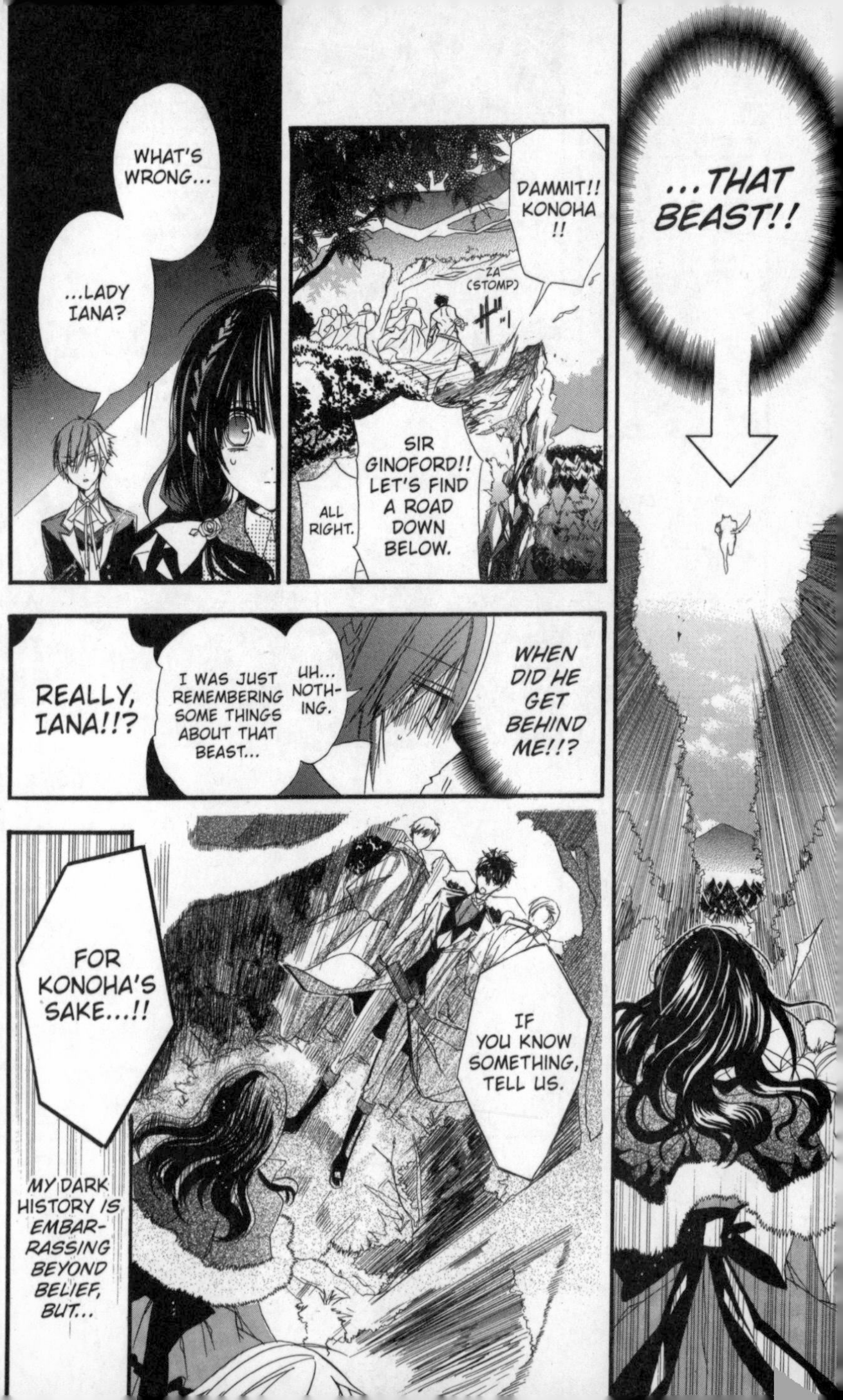
DAMMIT!! KONOHA!!
ZA (STOMP)
SIR GINOFORD!! LET'S FIND A ROAD DOWN BELOW.
ALL RIGHT.
WHAT'S WRONG...
...LADY IANA?
WHEN DID HE GET BEHIND ME!!?
UH... NOTHING.
I WAS JUST REMEMBERING SOME THINGS ABOUT THAT BEAST...
REALLY, IANA!!?
IF YOU KNOW SOMETHING, TELL US.
FOR KONOHA'S SAKE...!!
MY DARK HISTORY IS EMBARRASSING BEYOND BELIEF, BUT...
...THAT BEAST!!

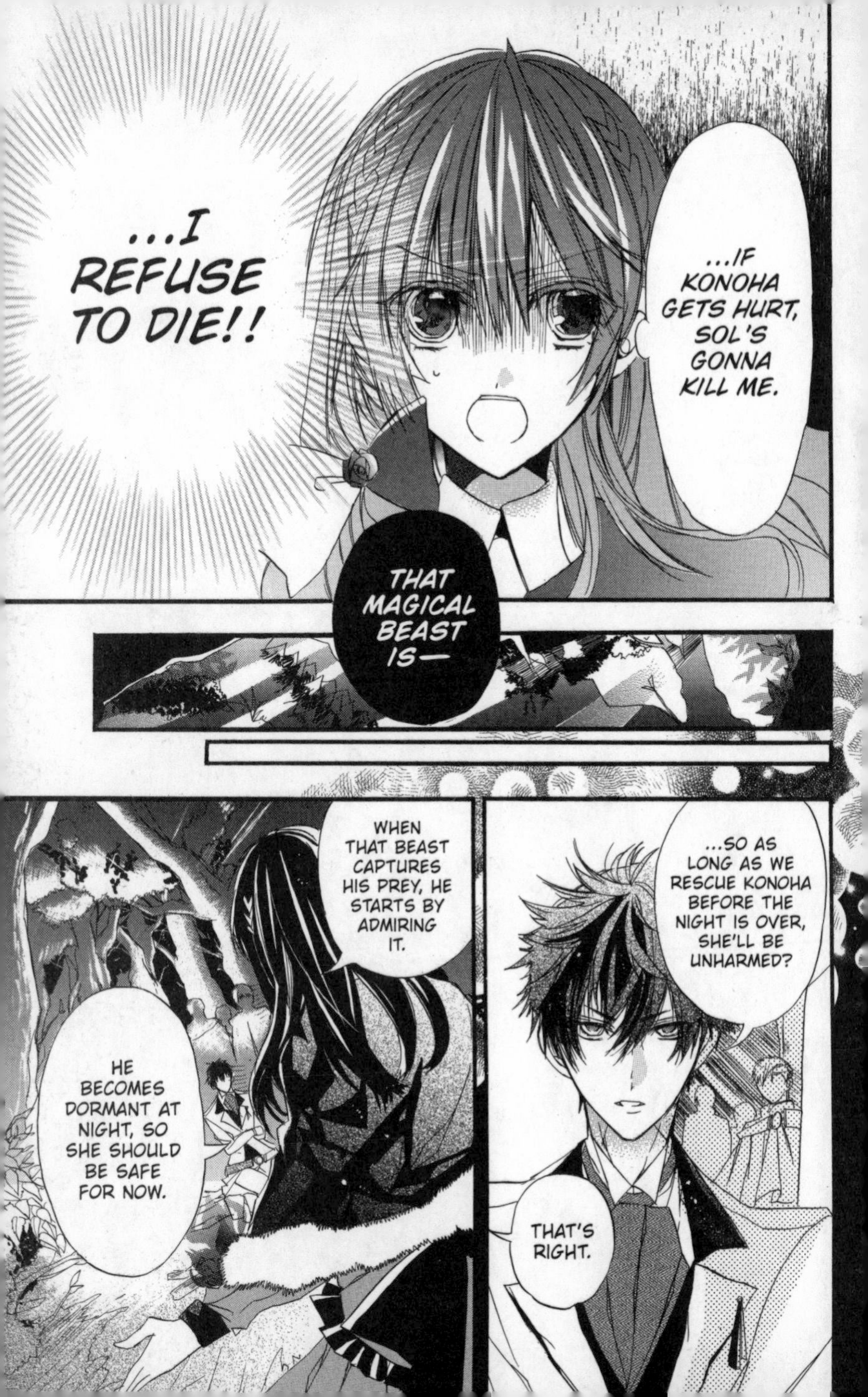
...IF KONOHA GETS HURT, SOL'S GONNA KILL ME.
...I REFUSE TO DIE!!
THAT MAGICAL BEAST IS—
...SO AS LONG AS WE RESCUE KONOHA BEFORE THE NIGHT IS OVER, SHE'LL BE UNHARMED?
THAT'S RIGHT.
WHEN THAT BEAST CAPTURES HIS PREY, HE STARTS BY ADMIRING IT.
HE BECOMES DORMANT AT NIGHT, SO SHE SHOULD BE SAFE FOR NOW.

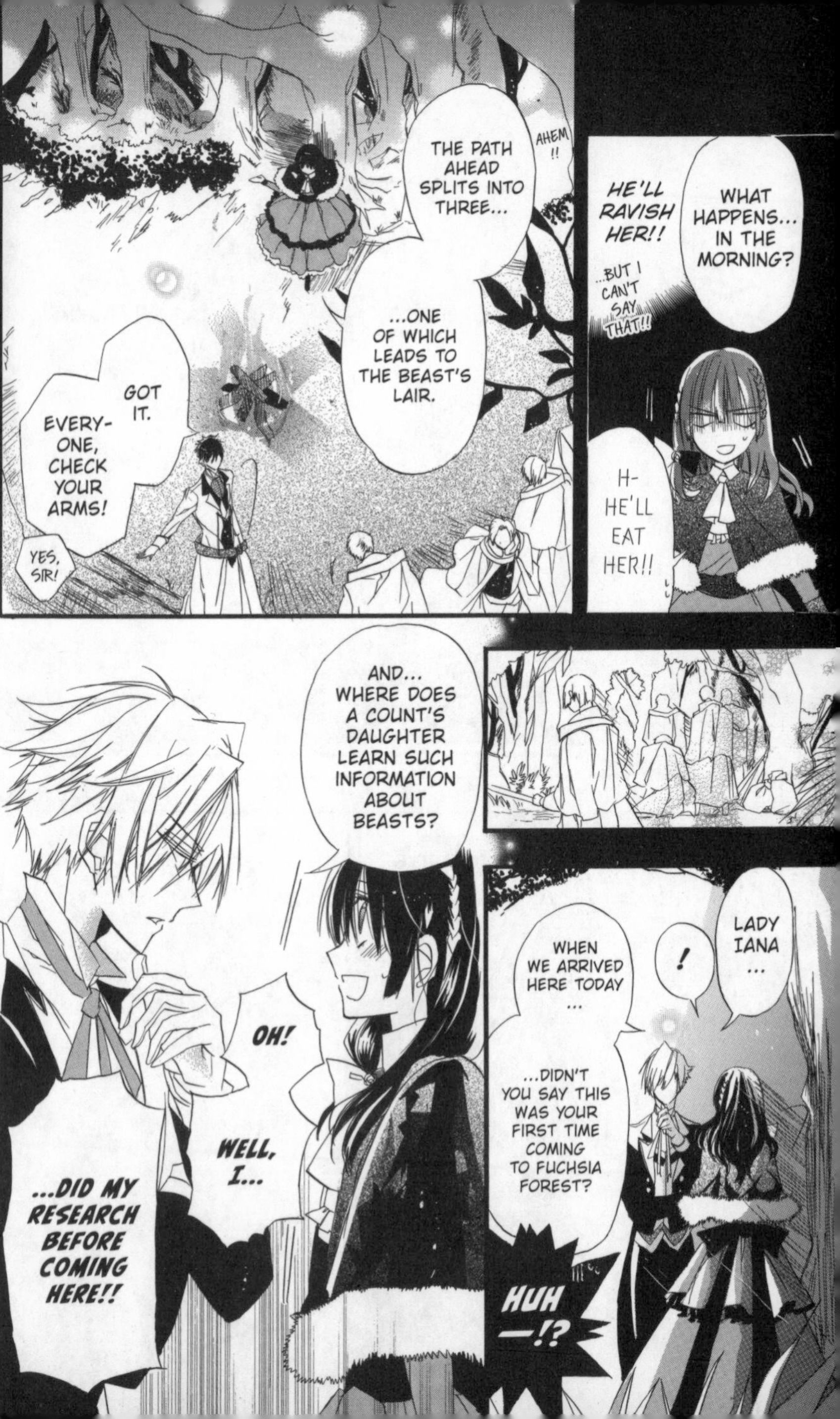
WHAT HAPPENS... IN THE MORNING?
HE'LL RAVISH HER!!
...BUT I CAN'T SAY THAT!!
H-HE'LL EAT HER!!
AHEM!!
THE PATH AHEAD SPLITS INTO THREE...
...ONE OF WHICH LEADS TO THE BEAST'S LAIR.
GOT IT.
EVERY-ONE, CHECK YOUR ARMS!
YES, SIR!
LADY IANA...
!
WHEN WE ARRIVED HERE TODAY...
...DIDN'T YOU SAY THIS WAS YOUR FIRST TIME COMING TO FUCHSIA FOREST?
HUH—!?
AND... WHERE DOES A COUNT'S DAUGHTER LEARN SUCH INFORMATION ABOUT BEASTS?
OH!
WELL, I...
...DID MY RESEARCH BEFORE COMING HERE!!

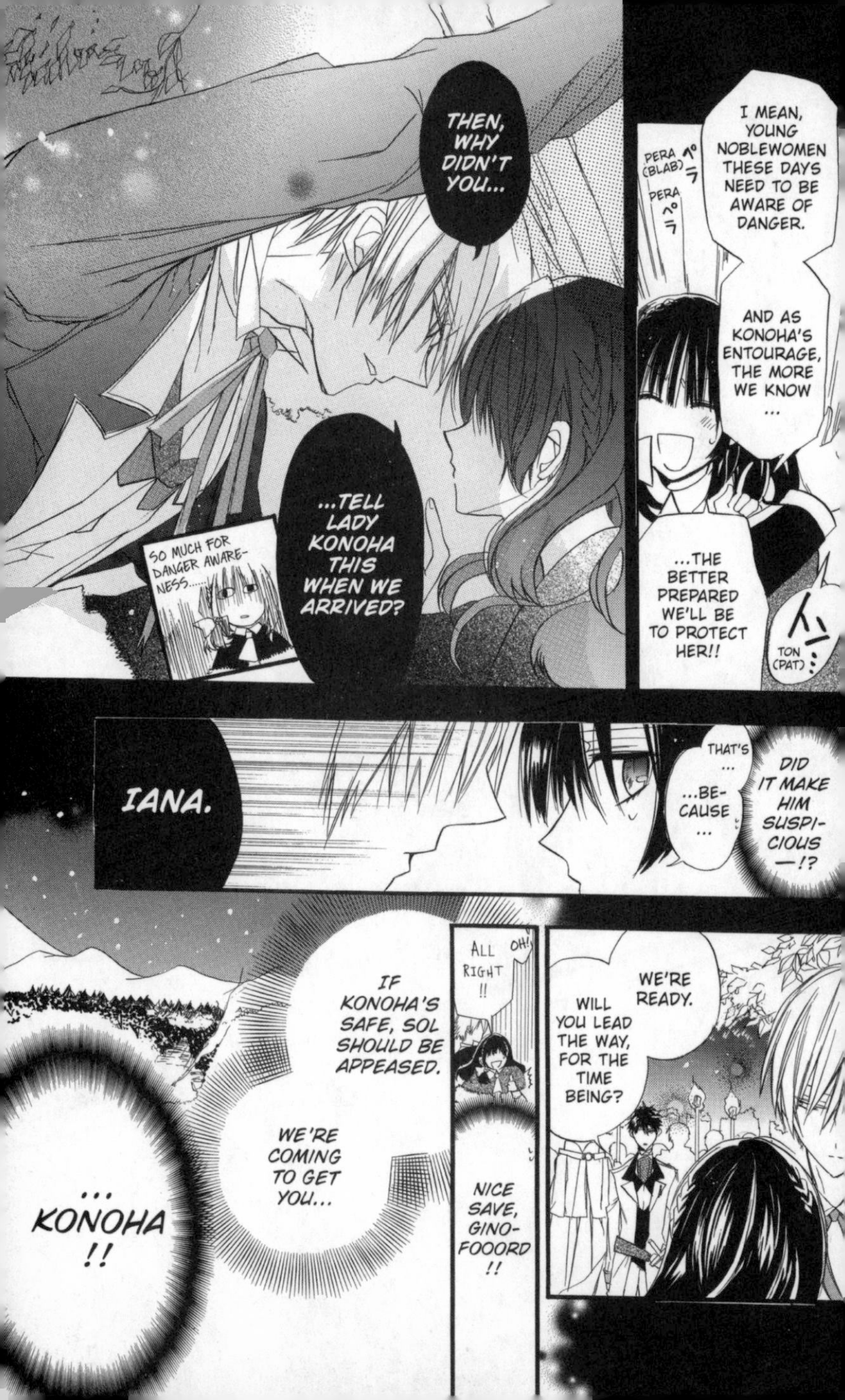
I MEAN, YOUNG NOBLEWOMEN THESE DAYS NEED TO BE AWARE OF DANGER.
PERA (BLAB) PERA
AND AS KONOHA'S ENTOURAGE, THE MORE WE KNOW ...
...THE BETTER PREPARED WE'LL BE TO PROTECT HER!!
TON (PAT)
THEN, WHY DIDN'T YOU...
...TELL LADY KONOHA THIS WHEN WE ARRIVED?
SO MUCH FOR DANGER AWARENESS......
DID IT MAKE HIM SUSPICIOUS—!?
THAT'S ... ...BECAUSE ...
IANA.
WE'RE READY.
WILL YOU LEAD THE WAY, FOR THE TIME BEING?
OH!
ALL RIGHT!!
NICE SAVE, GINOFOOORD!!
IF KONOHA'S SAFE, SOL SHOULD BE APPEASED.
WE'RE COMING TO GET YOU...
...KONOHA!!

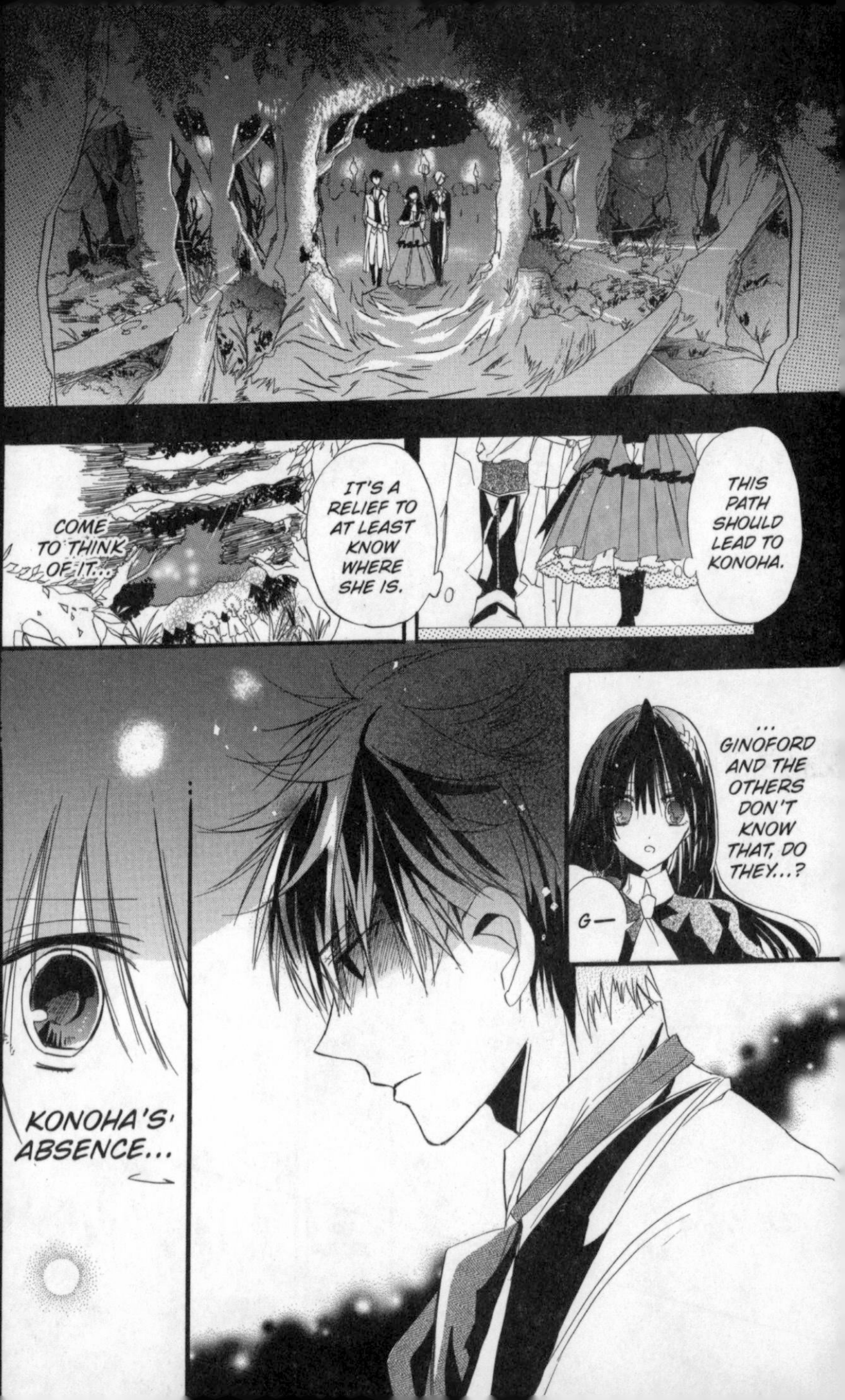
THIS PATH SHOULD LEAD TO KONOHA.
IT'S A RELIEF TO AT LEAST KNOW WHERE SHE IS.
COME TO THINK OF IT...
...GINOFORD AND THE OTHERS DON'T KNOW THAT, DO THEY...?
G—
KONOHA'S ABSENCE...

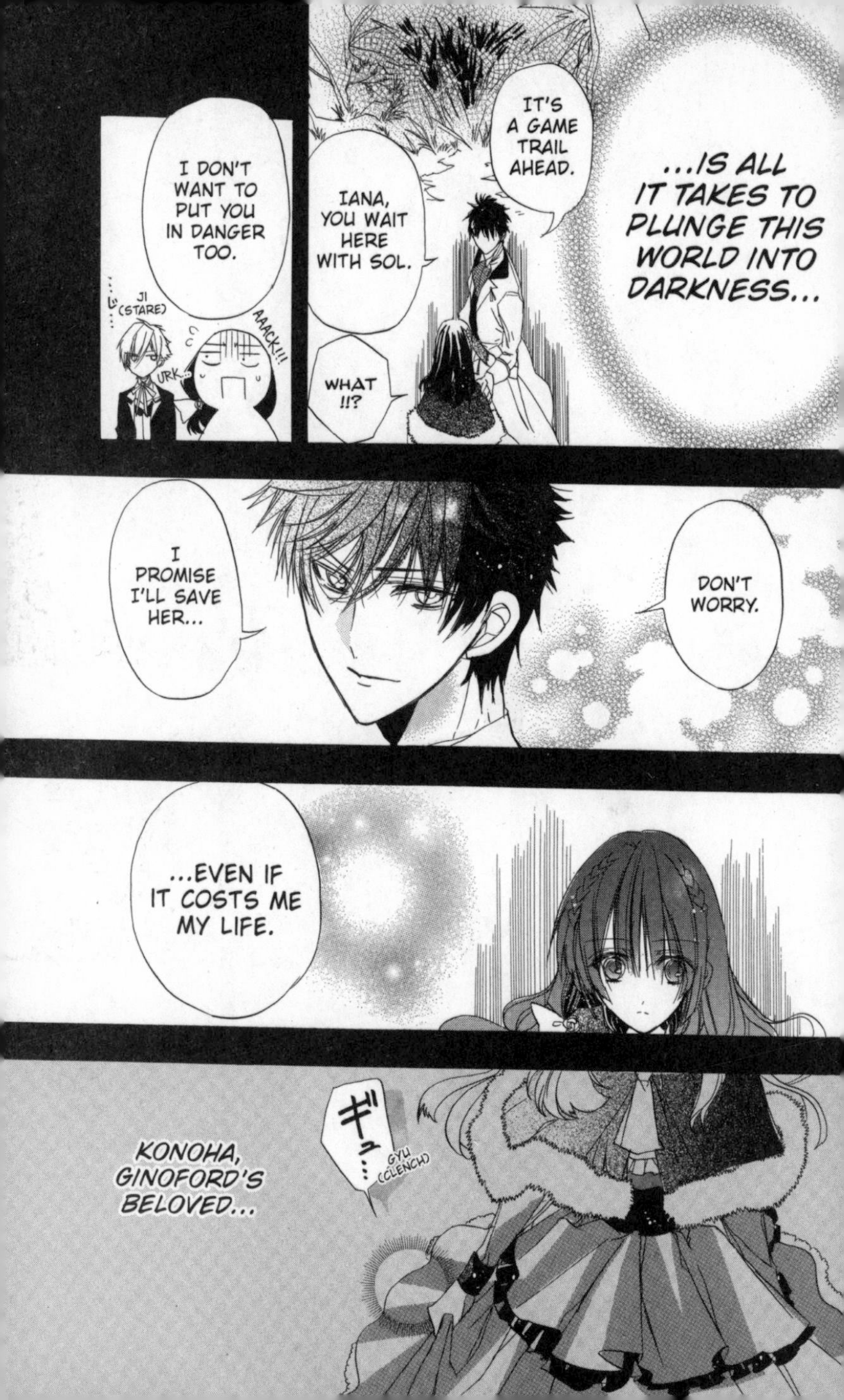
...IS ALL IT TAKES TO PLUNGE THIS WORLD INTO DARKNESS...
IT'S A GAME TRAIL AHEAD.
IANA, YOU WAIT HERE WITH SOL.
WHAT !!?
I DON'T WANT TO PUT YOU IN DANGER TOO.
AAACK!!!
JI (STARE)
URK...
DON'T WORRY.
I PROMISE I'LL SAVE HER...
...EVEN IF IT COSTS ME MY LIFE.
ギュ…
GYU (CLENCH)
KONOHA, GINOFORD'S BELOVED...

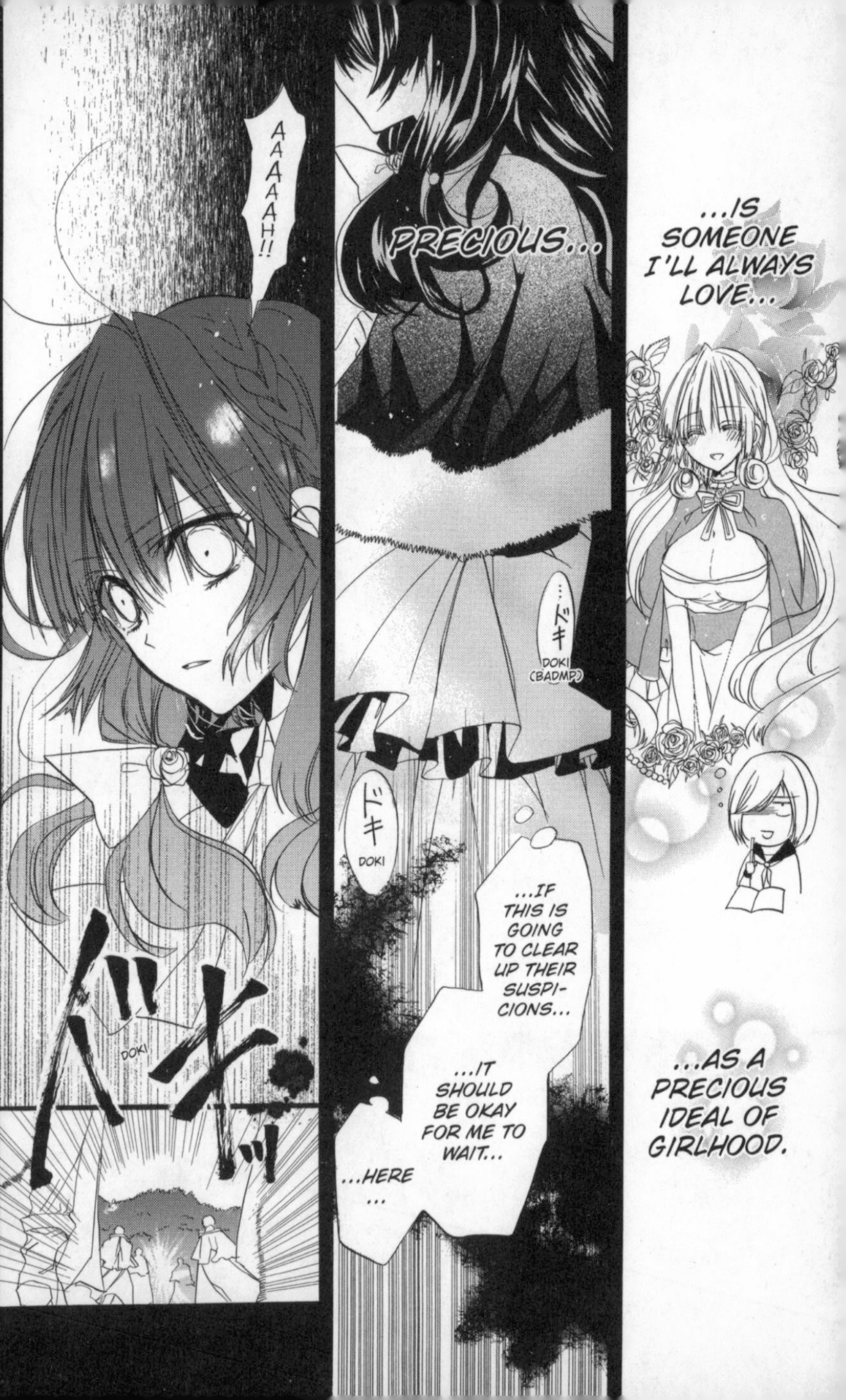
...IS SOMEONE I'LL ALWAYS LOVE...
...AS A PRECIOUS IDEAL OF GIRLHOOD.
PRECIOUS...
...ドキ
DOKI (BADMP)
ドキ
DOKI
...IF THIS IS GOING TO CLEAR UP THEIR SUSPICIONS...
...IT SHOULD BE OKAY FOR ME TO WAIT...
...HERE ...
AAAAAAH!!
DOKI

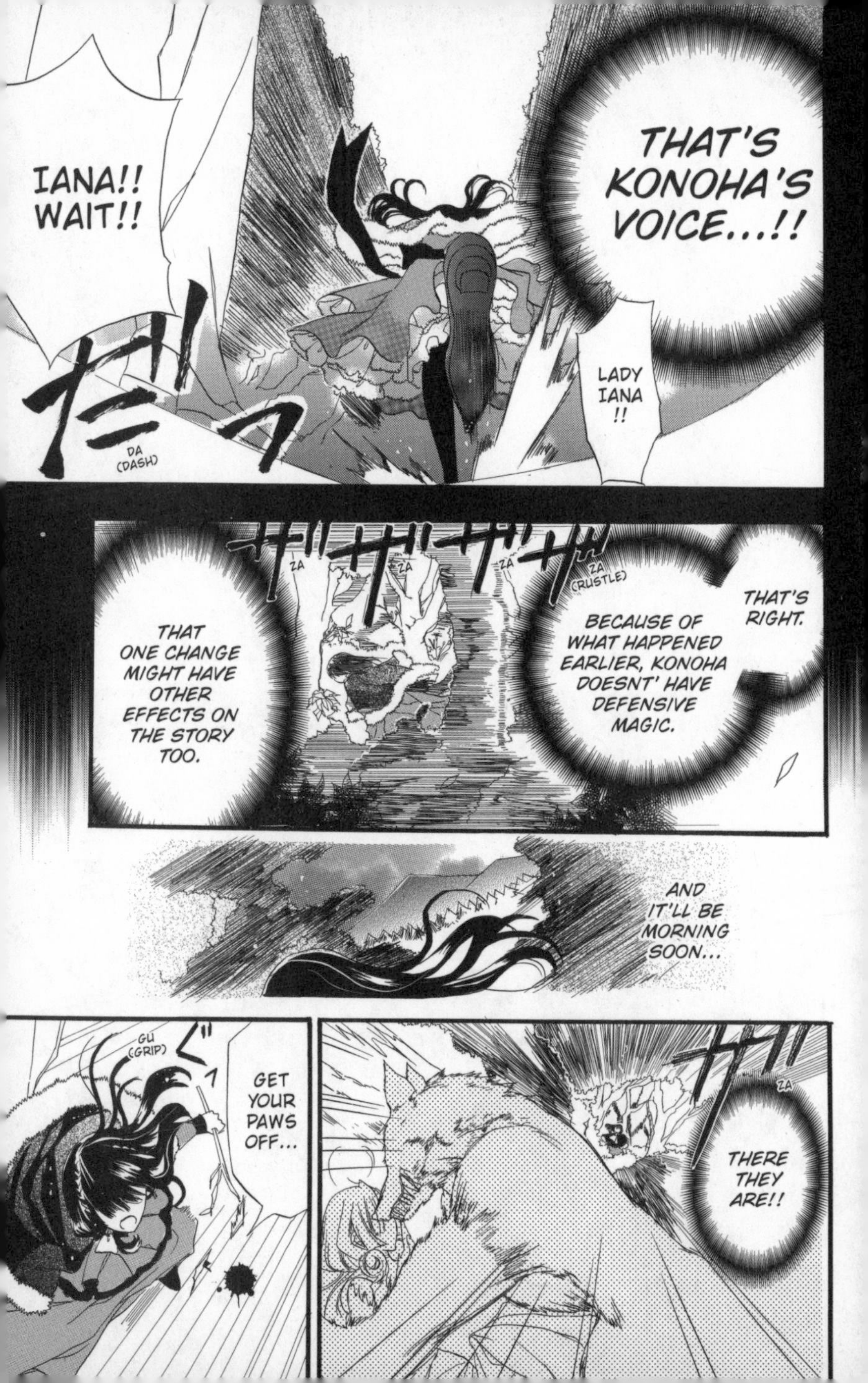
THAT'S KONOHA'S VOICE...!!
LADY IANA !!
IANA!! WAIT!!
DA (DASH)
ZA
ZA
ZA
ZA (RUSTLE)
THAT'S RIGHT.
BECAUSE OF WHAT HAPPENED EARLIER, KONOHA DOESNT' HAVE DEFENSIVE MAGIC.
THAT ONE CHANGE MIGHT HAVE OTHER EFFECTS ON THE STORY TOO.
AND IT'LL BE MORNING SOON...
ZA
THERE THEY ARE!!
GU (GRIP)
GET YOUR PAWS OFF...

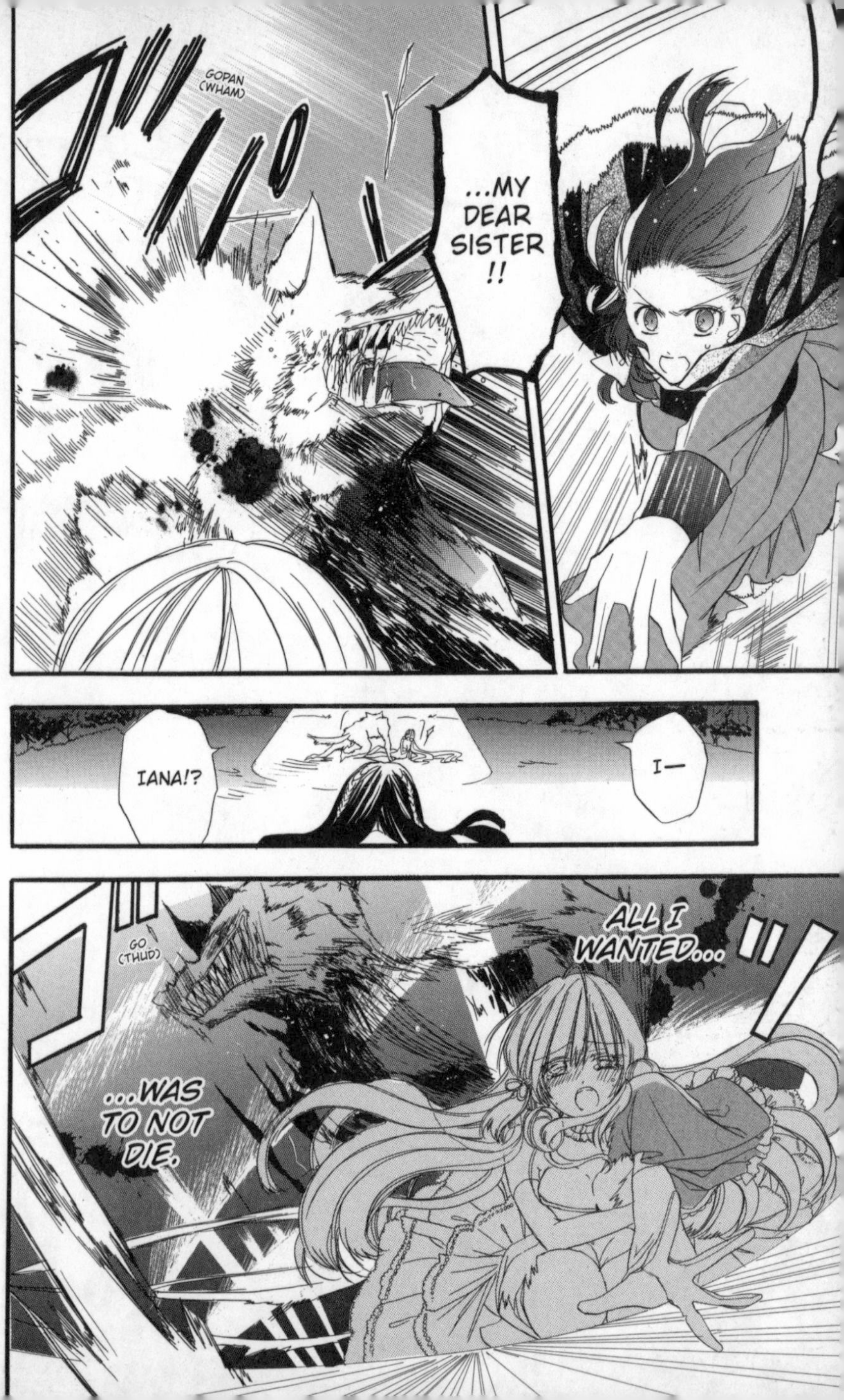
...MY DEAR SISTER!!
GOPAN (WHAM)
I—
IANA!?
ALL I WANTED...
GO (THUD)
...WAS TO NOT DIE.

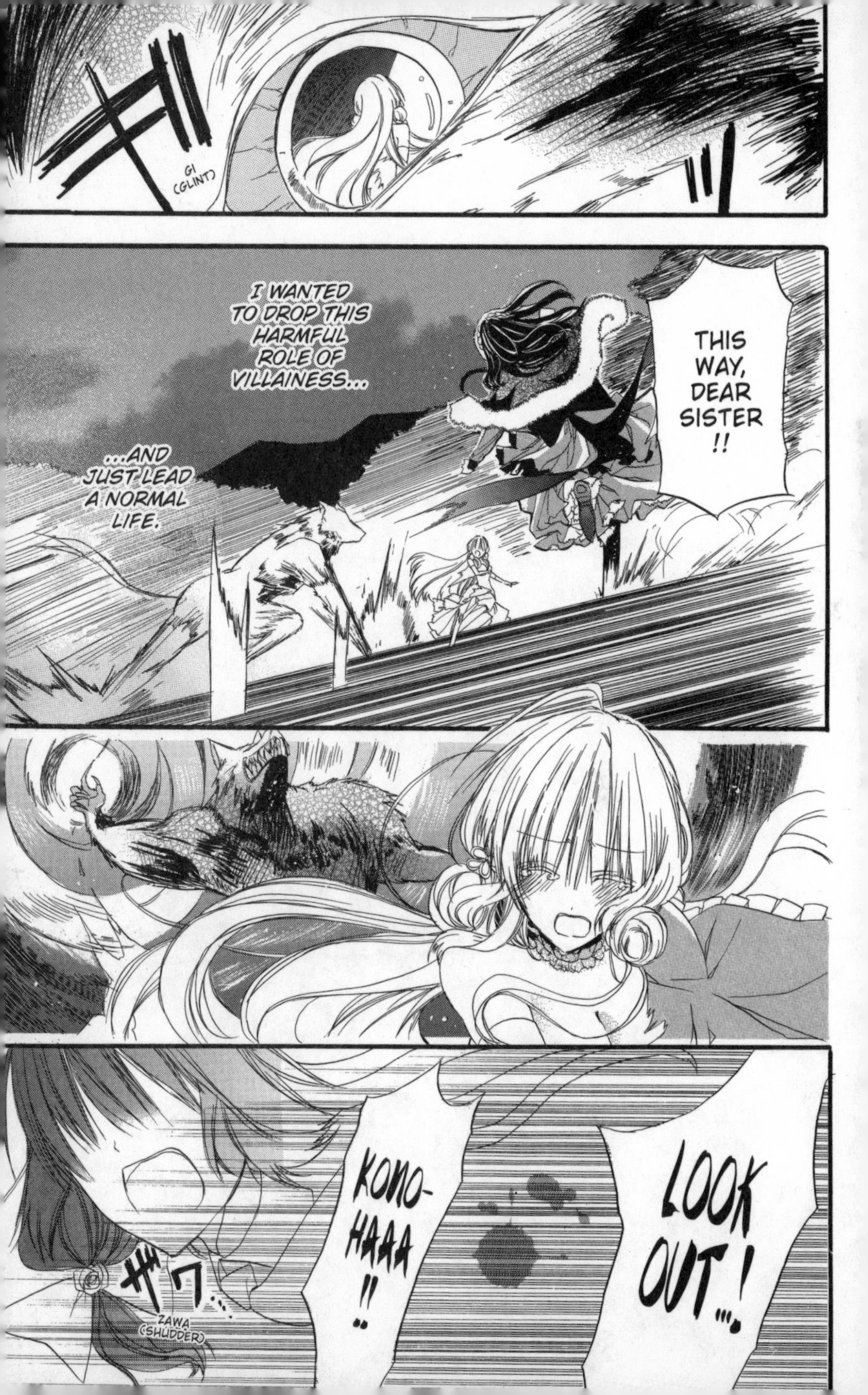
GI
(GLINT)
THIS WAY, DEAR SISTER !!
I WANTED TO DROP THIS HARMFUL ROLE OF VILLAINESS...
...AND JUST LEAD A NORMAL LIFE.
LOOK OUT...!
KONO-HAAA !!
ZAWA
(SHUDDER)

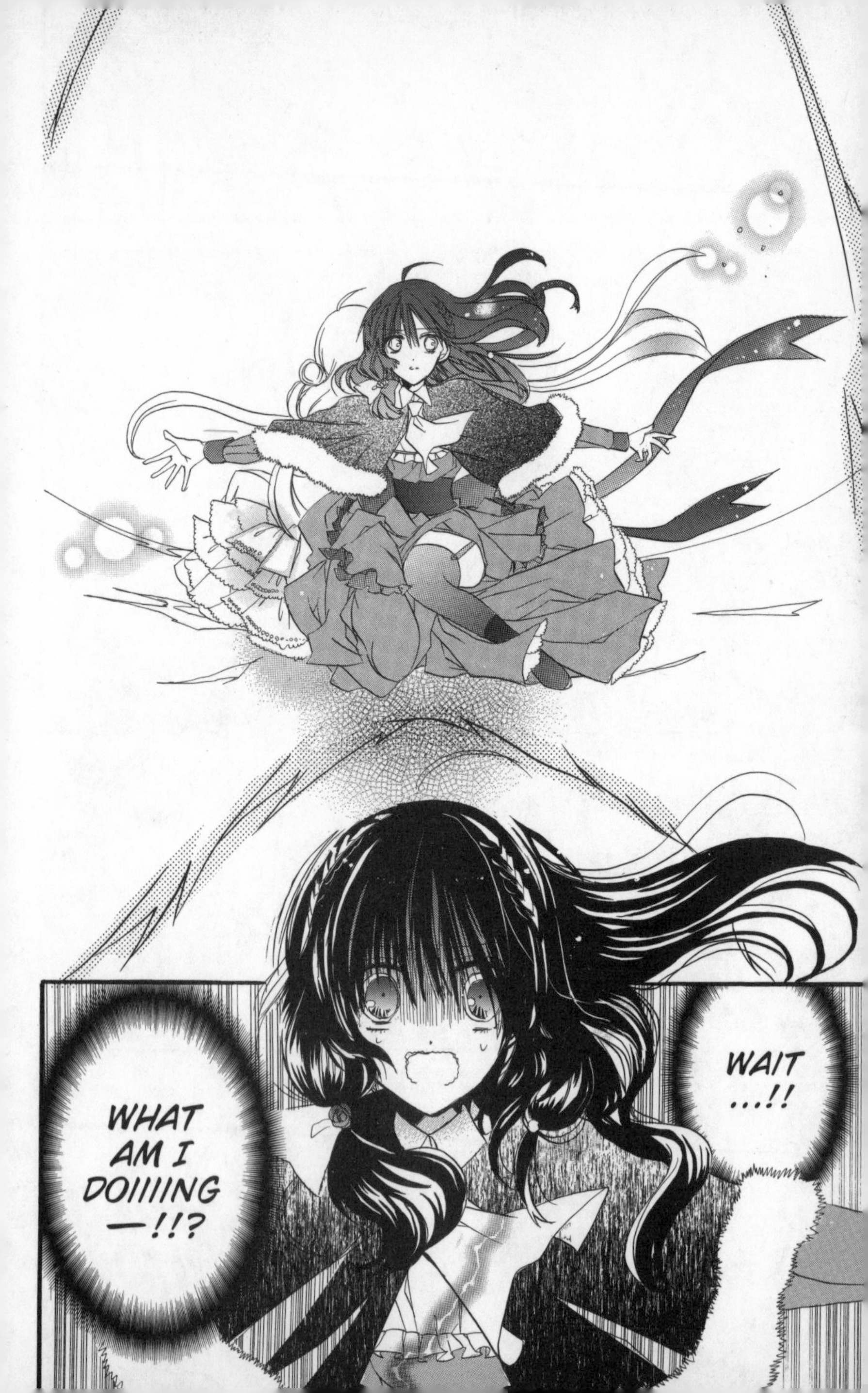
WAIT ...!!
WHAT AM I DOIIIIING —!!?

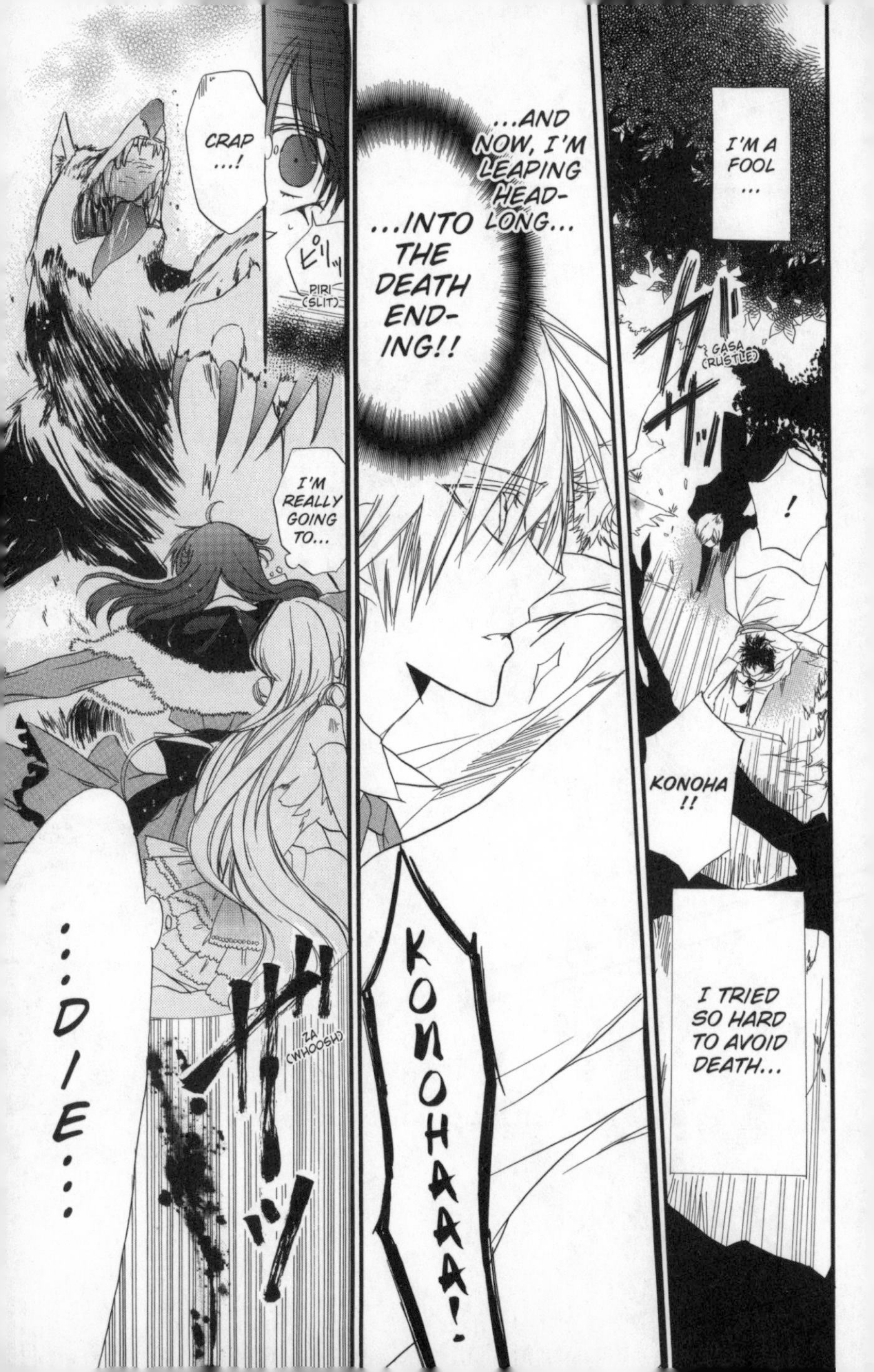
I'M A FOOL ...
GASA (RUSTLE)
!
KONOHA !!
I TRIED SO HARD TO AVOID DEATH...
...AND NOW, I'M LEAPING HEAD-LONG...
...INTO THE DEATH END-ING!!
KONOHAAAA!
CRAP ...!
ピリッ
PIRI (SLIT)
I'M REALLY GOING TO...
...DIE...
ZA (WHOOSH)

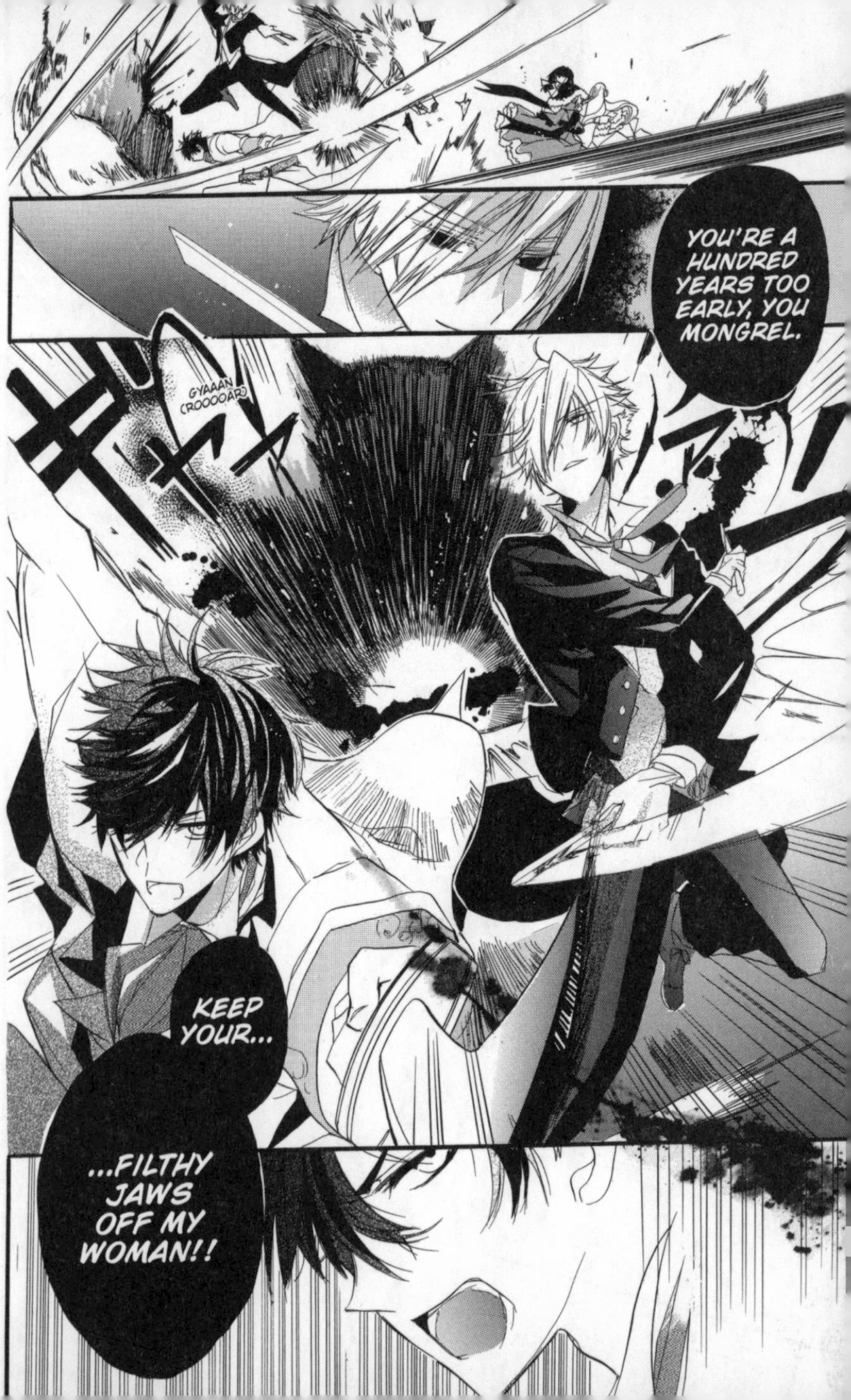
YOU'RE A HUNDRED YEARS TOO EARLY, YOU MONGREL.
GYAAAN (ROOOOAR)
KEEP YOUR...
...FILTHY JAWS OFF MY WOMAN!!

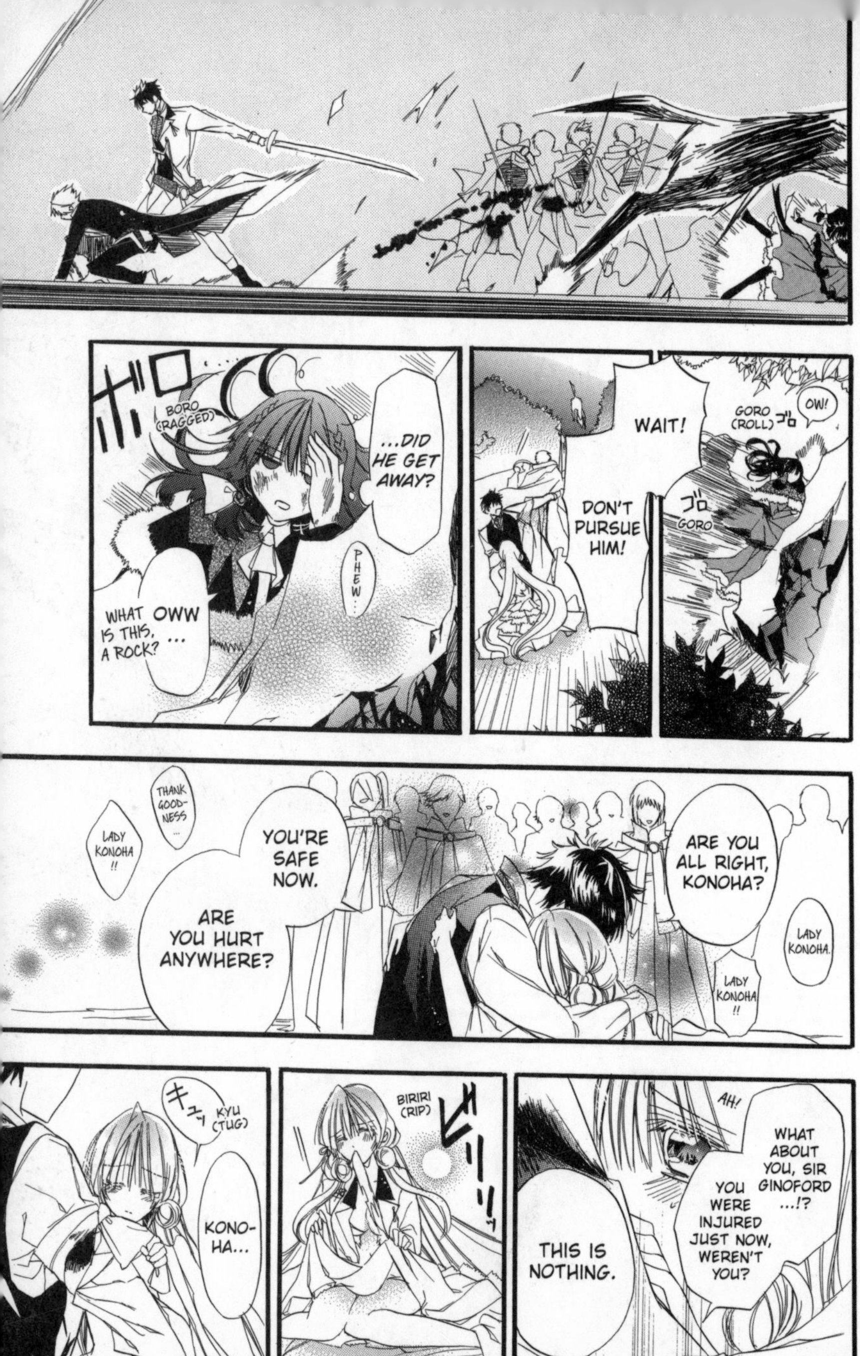
GORO (ROLL) ゴロ
OW!
ゴロ GORO
WAIT!
DON'T PURSUE HIM!
ボロ BORO (RAGGED)
...DID HE GET AWAY?
PHEW...
OWW...
WHAT IS THIS, A ROCK?
ARE YOU ALL RIGHT, KONOHA?
LADY KONOHA.
LADY KONOHA!!
YOU'RE SAFE NOW.
ARE YOU HURT ANYWHERE?
THANK GOODNESS...
LADY KONOHA!!
AH!
WHAT ABOUT YOU, SIR GINOFORD ...!?
YOU WERE INJURED JUST NOW, WEREN'T YOU?
THIS IS NOTHING.
BIRIRI (RIP) ビリリ!!
キュッ KYU (TUG)
KONO-HA...

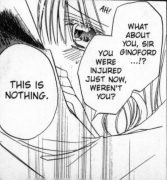

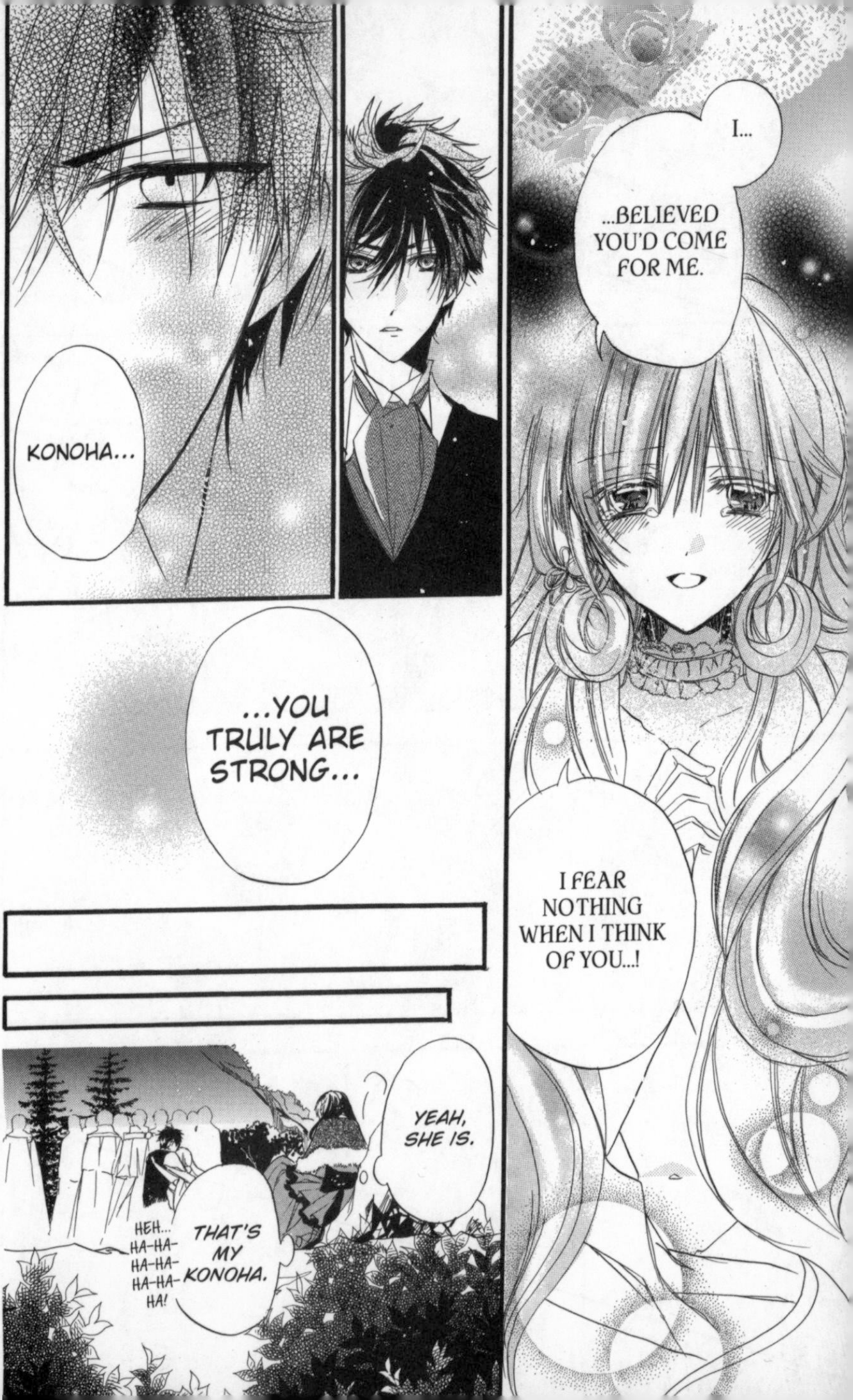
I...
...BELIEVED YOU'D COME FOR ME.
I FEAR NOTHING WHEN I THINK OF YOU...!
KONOHA...
...YOU TRULY ARE STRONG...
YEAH, SHE IS.
THAT'S MY KONOHA.
HEH... HA-HA-HA-HA-HA-HA-HA!

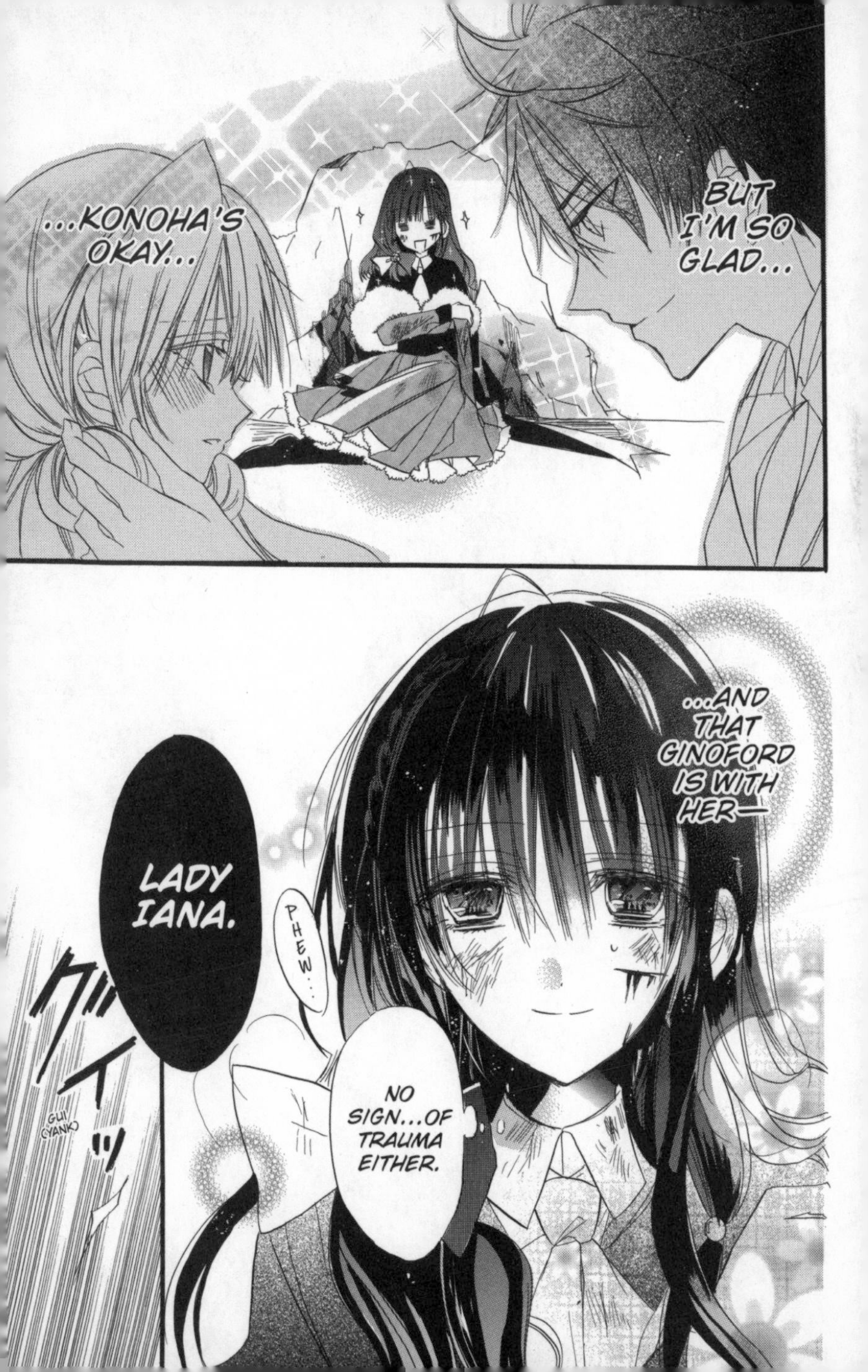
BUT I'M SO GLAD...
...KONOHA'S OKAY...
...AND THAT GINOFORD IS WITH HER—
PHEW...
NO SIGN...OF TRAUMA EITHER.
LADY IANA.
GUI (YANK)

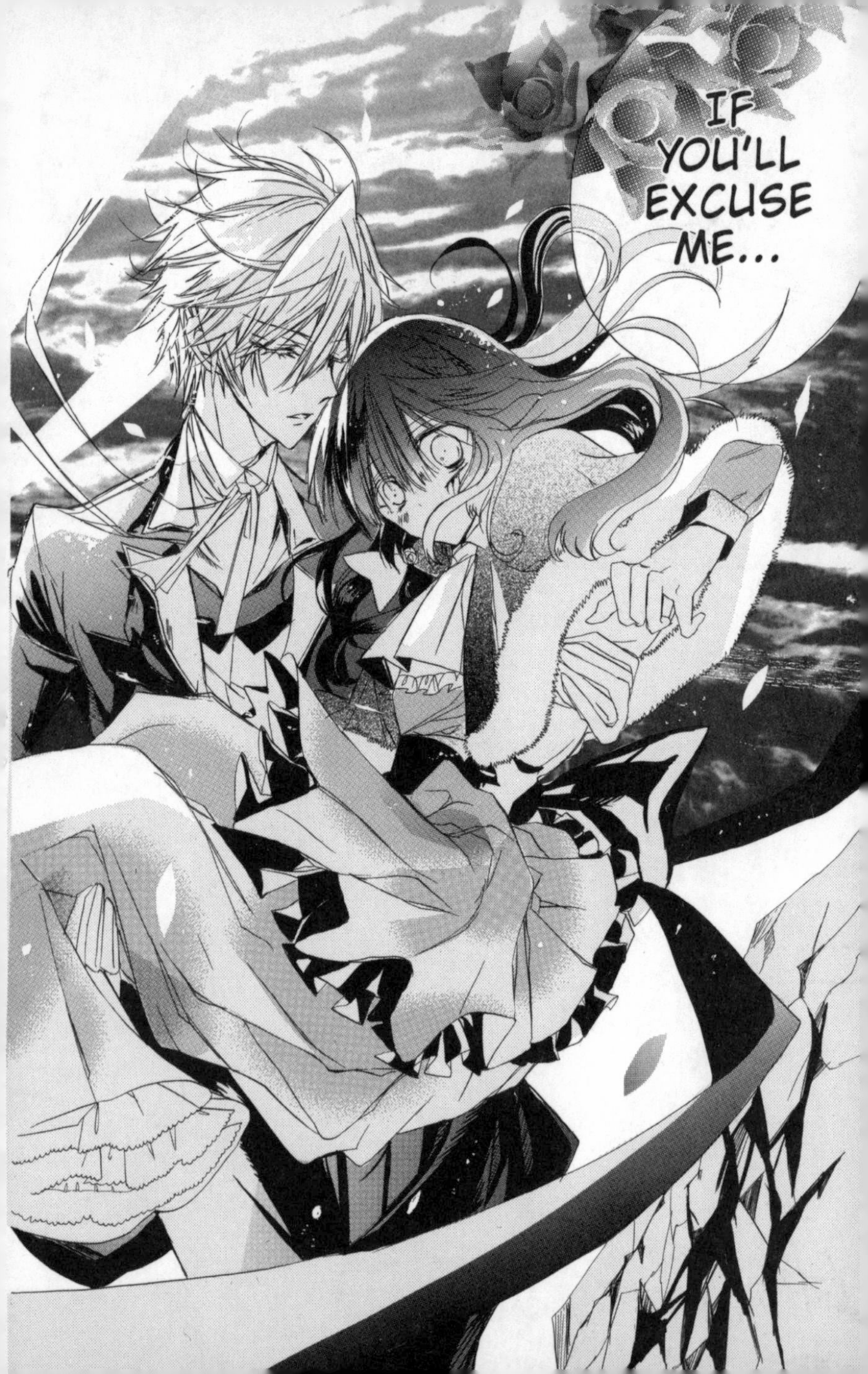
IF YOU'LL EXCUSE ME...

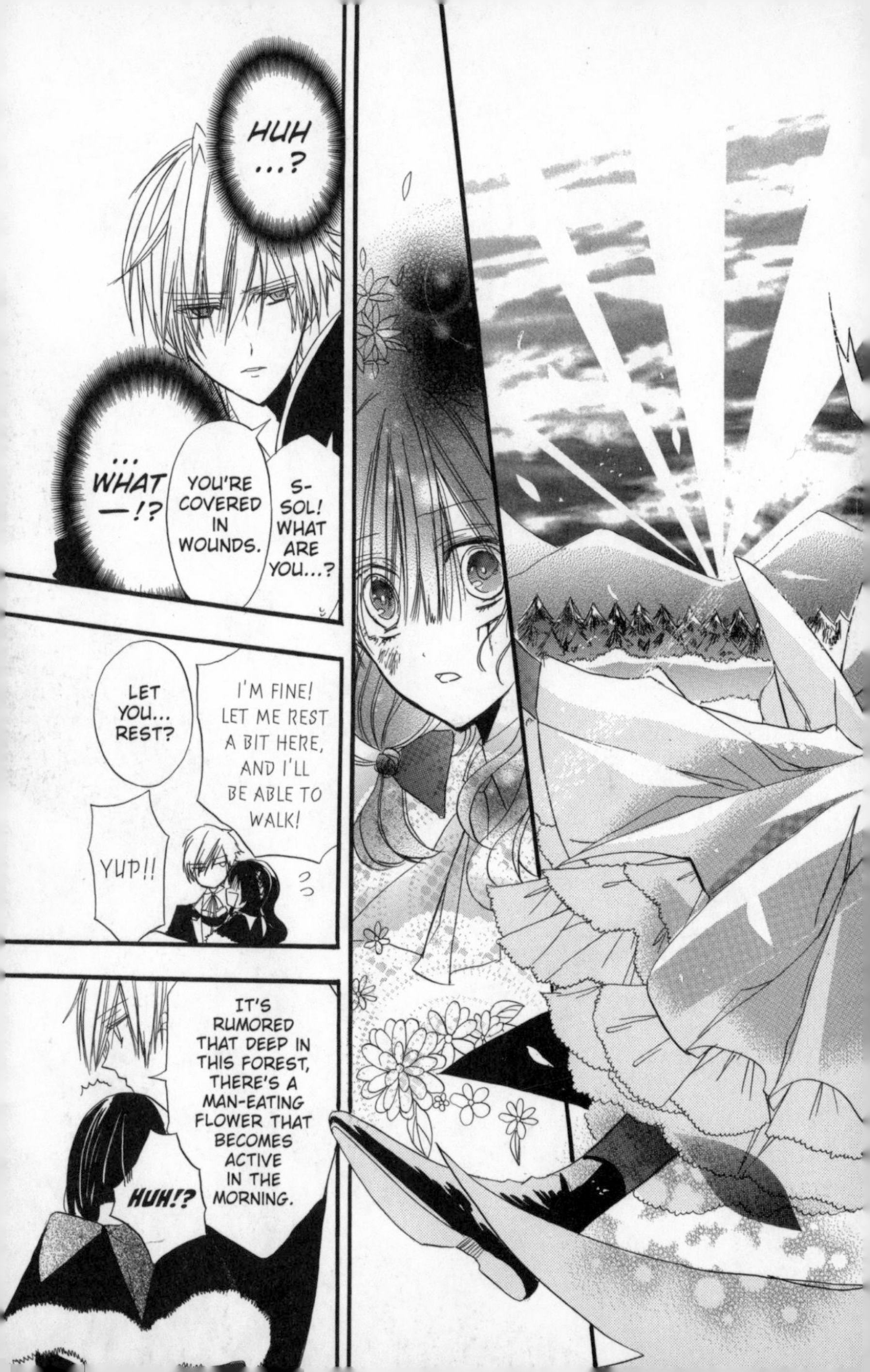
HUH ...?
S-SOL! WHAT ARE YOU...?
YOU'RE COVERED IN WOUNDS.
... WHAT—!?
I'M FINE! LET ME REST A BIT HERE, AND I'LL BE ABLE TO WALK!
LET YOU... REST?
YUP!!
IT'S RUMORED THAT DEEP IN THIS FOREST, THERE'S A MAN-EATING FLOWER THAT BECOMES ACTIVE IN THE MORNING.
HUH!?

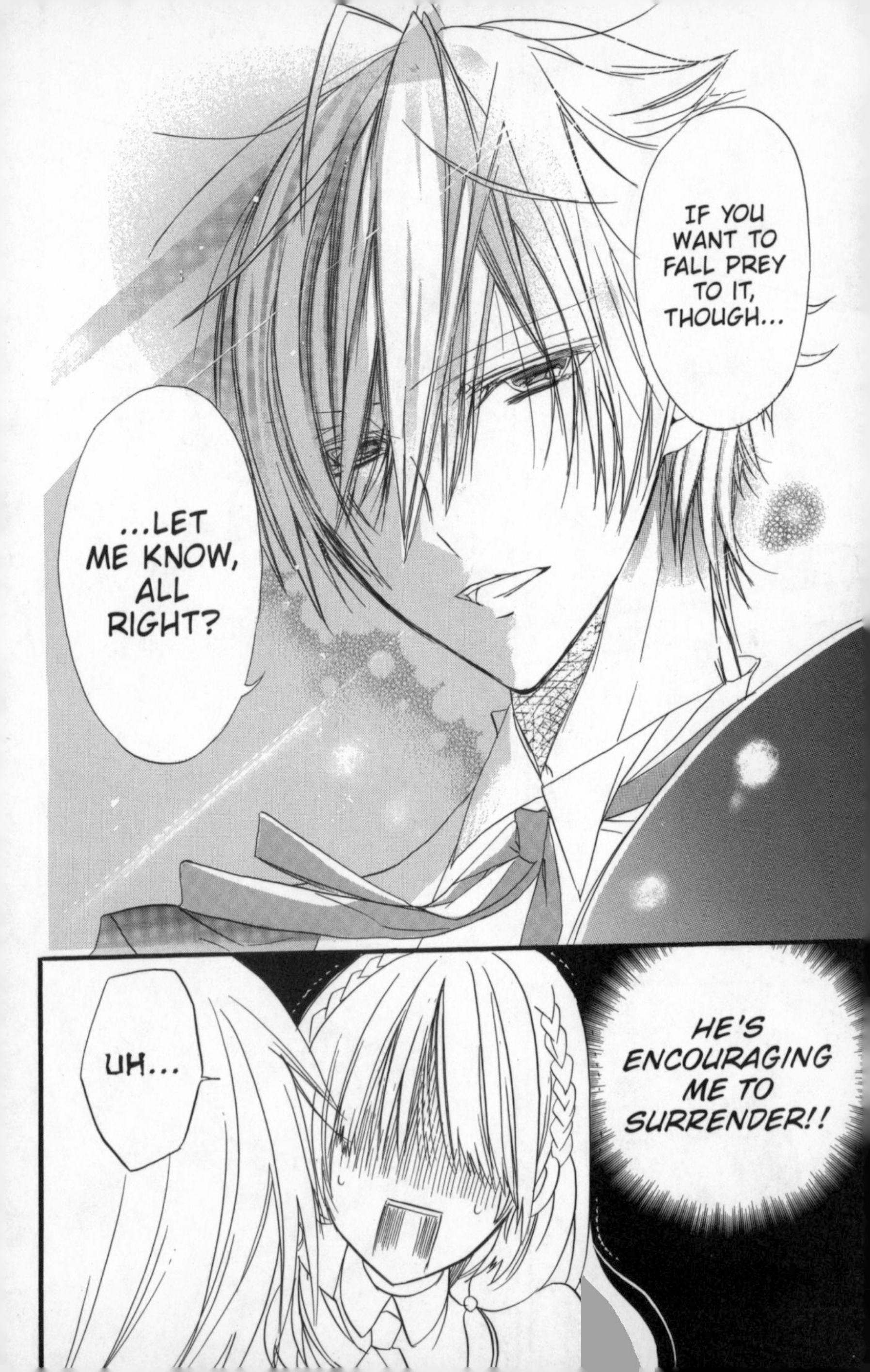
IF YOU WANT TO FALL PREY TO IT, THOUGH...
...LET ME KNOW, ALL RIGHT?
HE'S ENCOURAGING ME TO SURRENDER!!
UH...

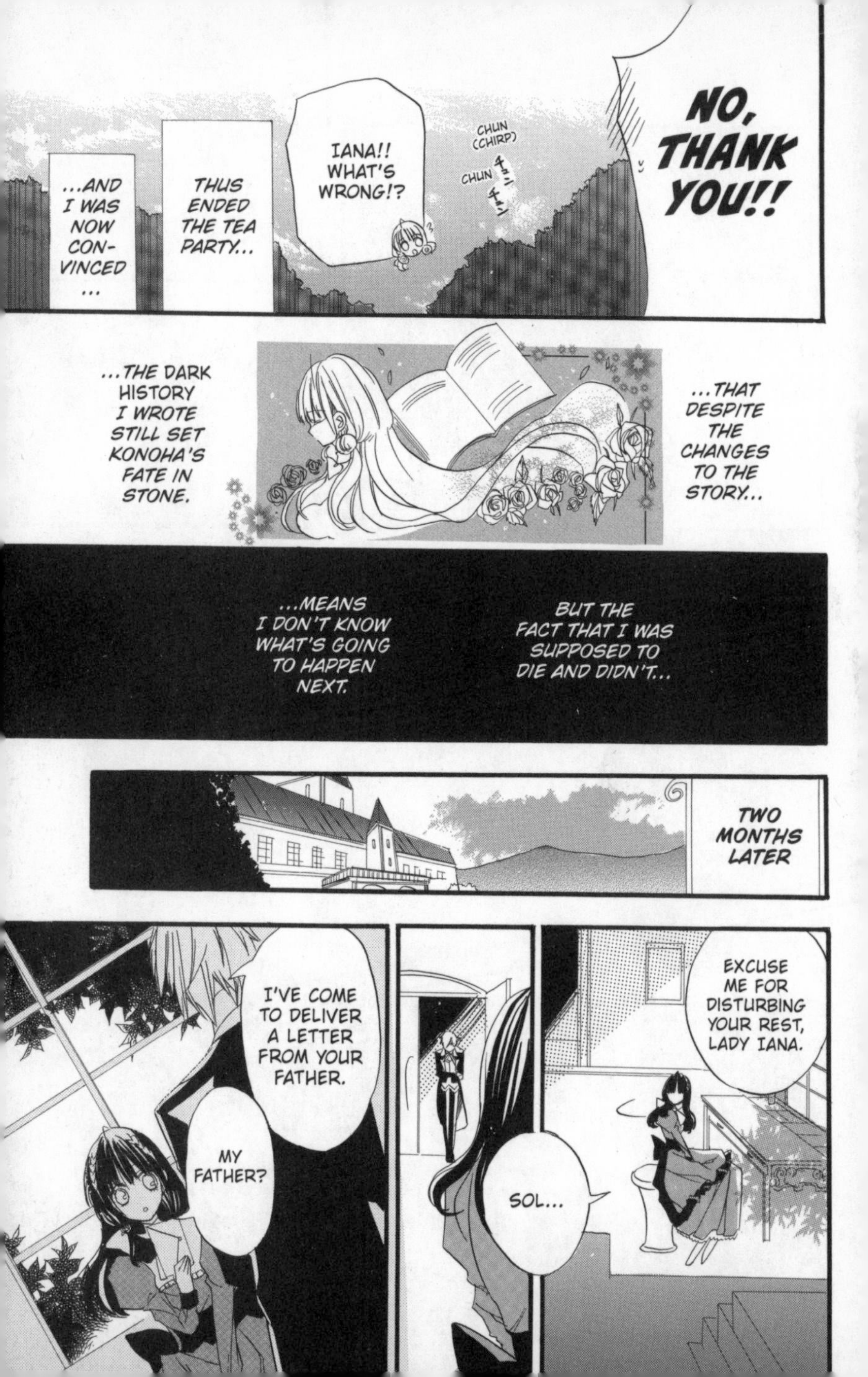
NO, THANK YOU!!
IANA!! WHAT'S WRONG!?
CHUN (CHIRP)
CHUN
THUS ENDED THE TEA PARTY...
...AND I WAS NOW CON-VINCED...
...THAT DESPITE THE CHANGES TO THE STORY...
...THE DARK HISTORY I WROTE STILL SET KONOHA'S FATE IN STONE.
BUT THE FACT THAT I WAS SUPPOSED TO DIE AND DIDN'T...
...MEANS I DON'T KNOW WHAT'S GOING TO HAPPEN NEXT.
TWO MONTHS LATER
EXCUSE ME FOR DISTURBING YOUR REST, LADY IANA.
SOL...
I'VE COME TO DELIVER A LETTER FROM YOUR FATHER.
MY FATHER?

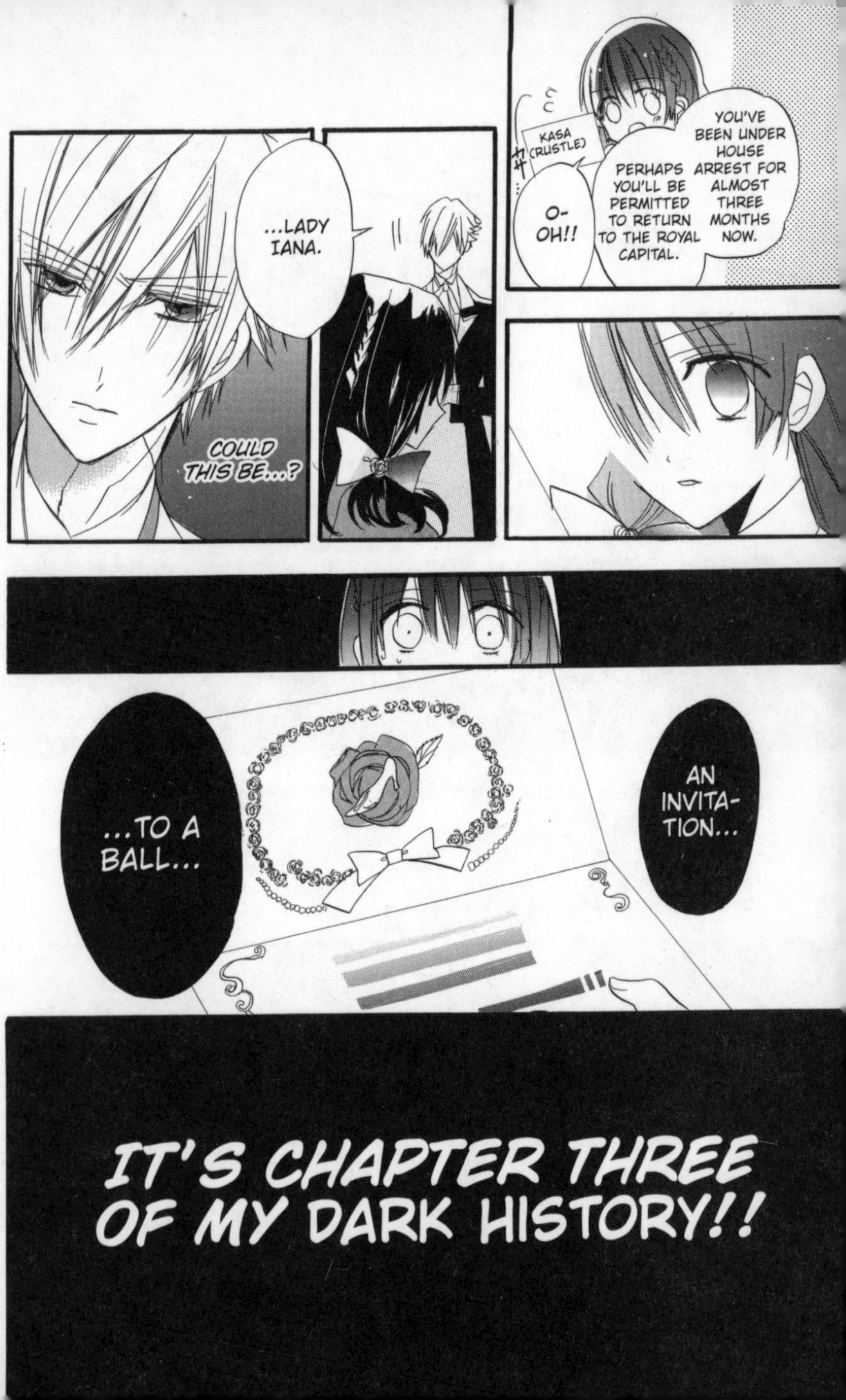
YOU'VE BEEN UNDER HOUSE ARREST FOR ALMOST THREE MONTHS NOW.
PERHAPS YOU'LL BE PERMITTED TO RETURN TO THE ROYAL CAPITAL.
KASA (RUSTLE)
O-OH!!
...LADY IANA.
COULD THIS BE...?
AN INVITATION...
...TO A BALL...
IT'S CHAPTER THREE OF MY DARK HISTORY!!

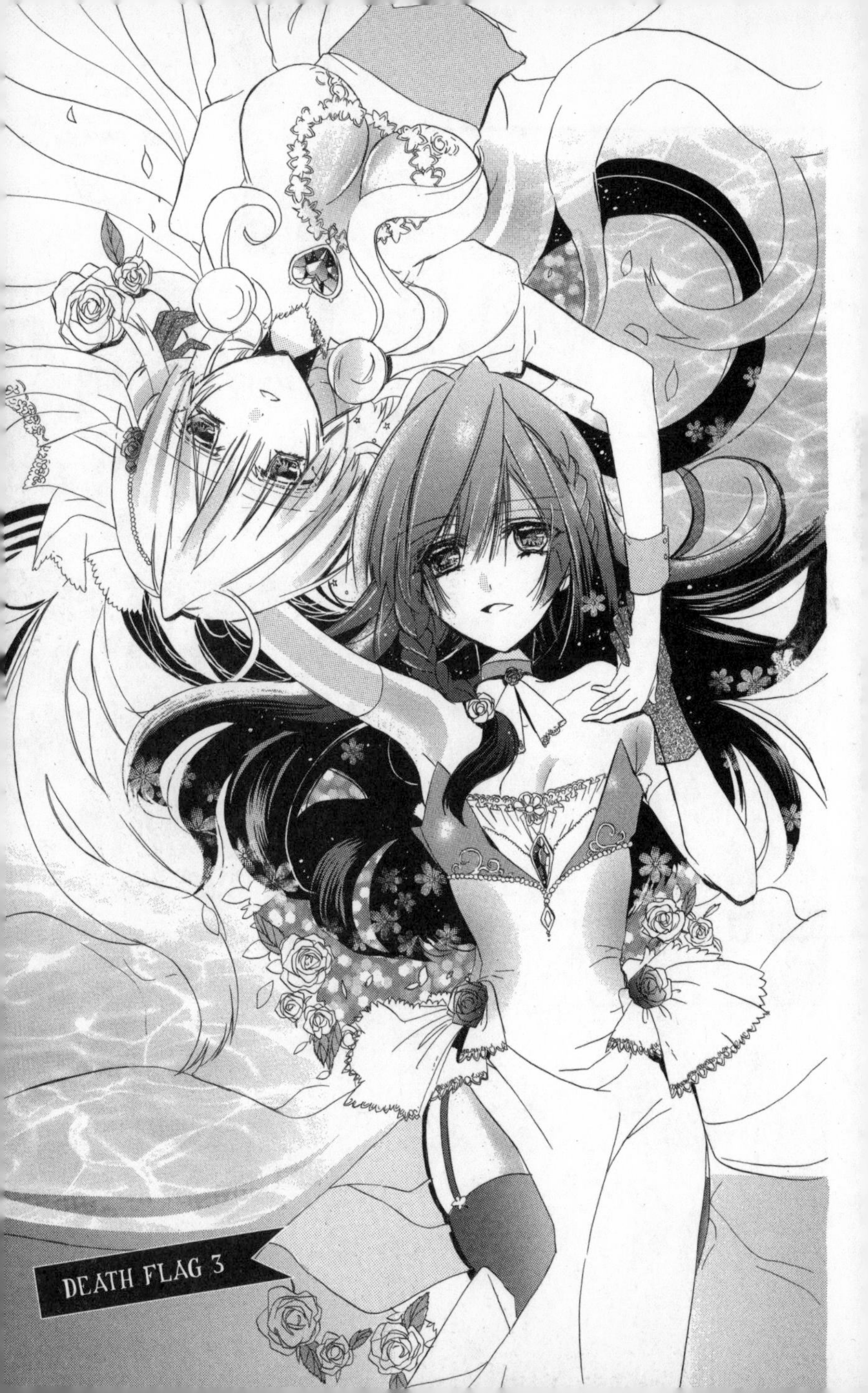
DEATH FLAG 3

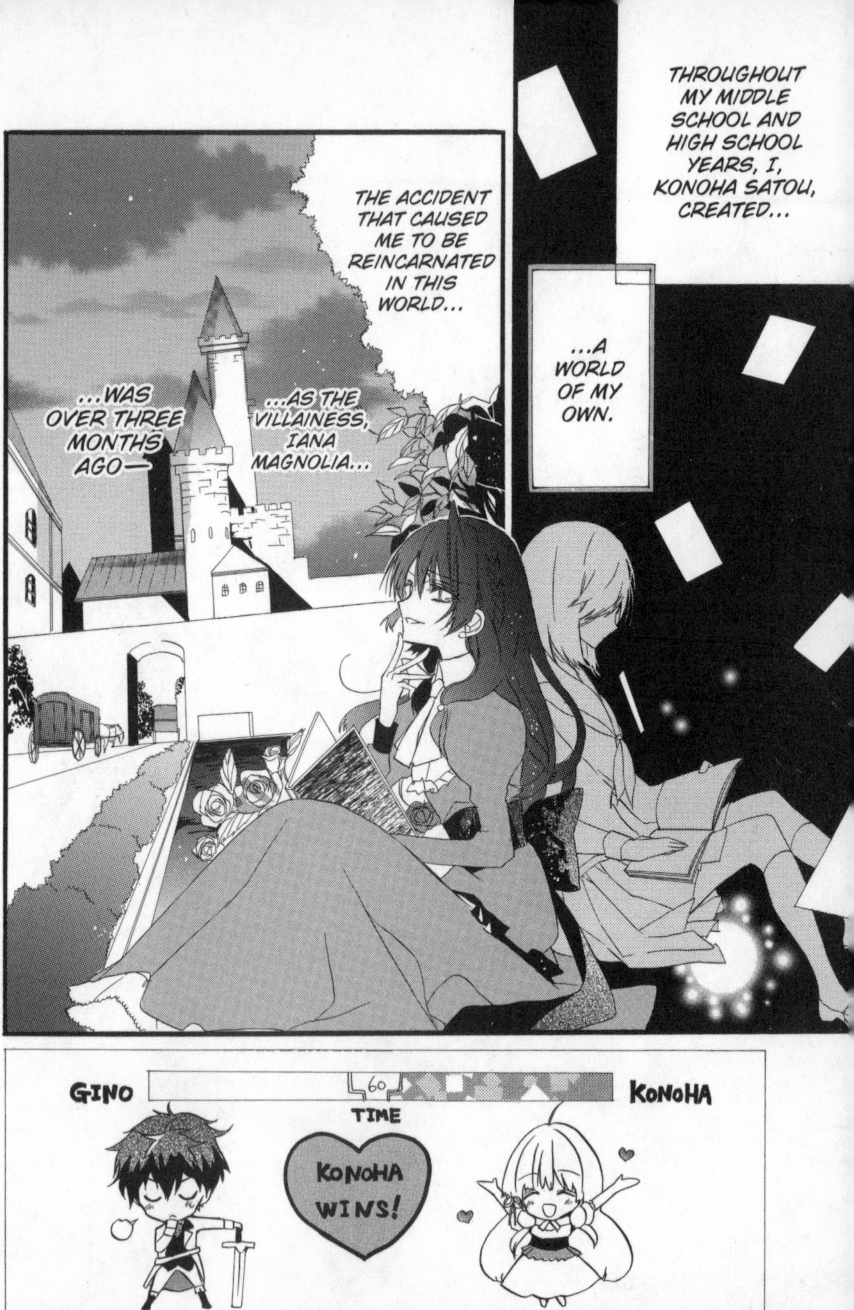
THROUGHOUT MY MIDDLE SCHOOL AND HIGH SCHOOL YEARS, I, KONOHA SATOU, CREATED...
...A WORLD OF MY OWN.
THE ACCIDENT THAT CAUSED ME TO BE REINCARNATED IN THIS WORLD...
...AS THE VILLAINESS, IANA MAGNOLIA...
...WAS OVER THREE MONTHS AGO—
KONOHA
60
TIME
GINO
KONOHA WINS!

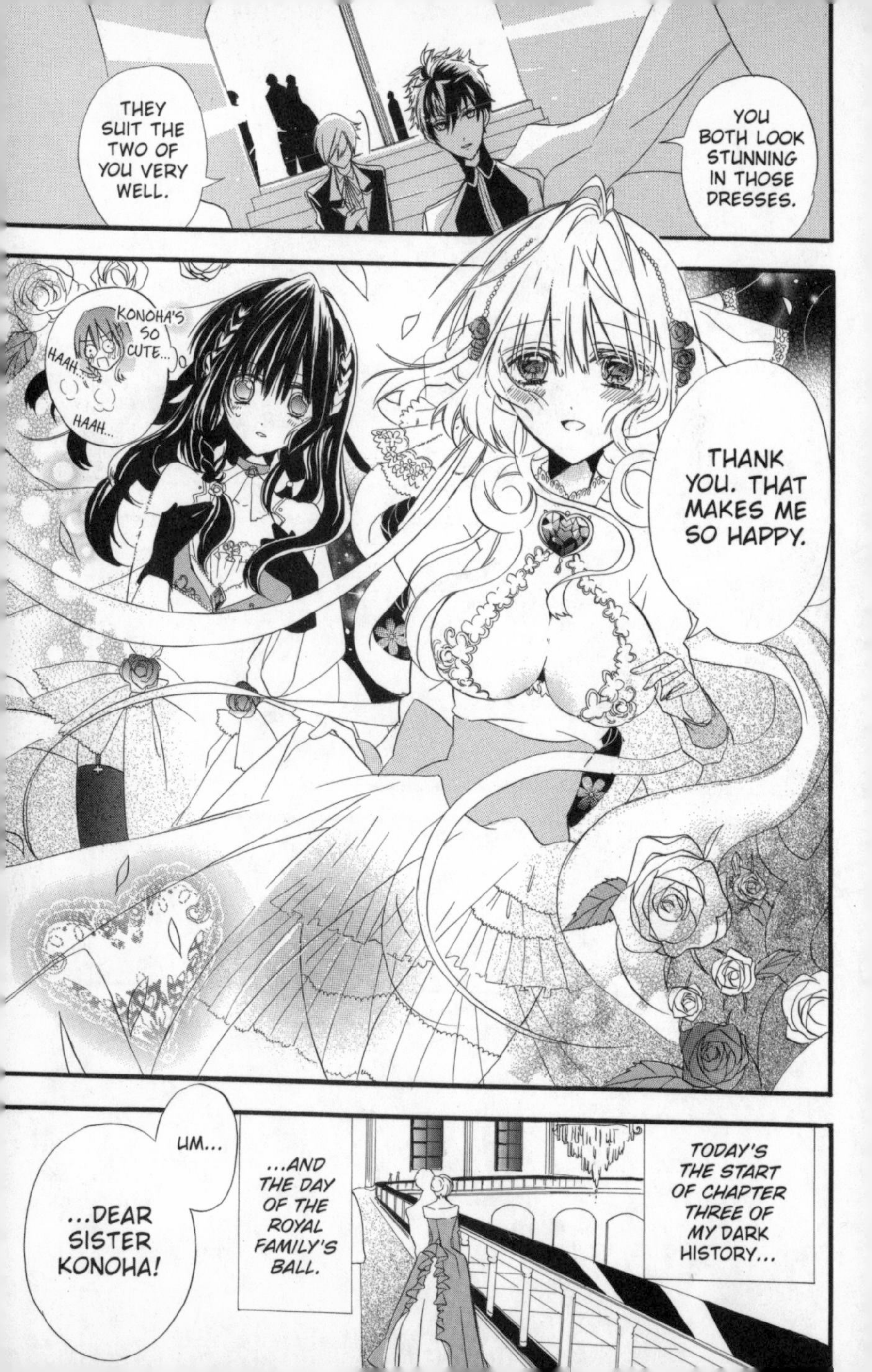
YOU BOTH LOOK STUNNING IN THOSE DRESSES.
THEY SUIT THE TWO OF YOU VERY WELL.
THANK YOU. THAT MAKES ME SO HAPPY.
KONOHA'S SO CUTE...
HAAH... HAAH...
TODAY'S THE START OF CHAPTER THREE OF MY DARK HISTORY...
...AND THE DAY OF THE ROYAL FAMILY'S BALL.
UM...
...DEAR SISTER KONOHA!

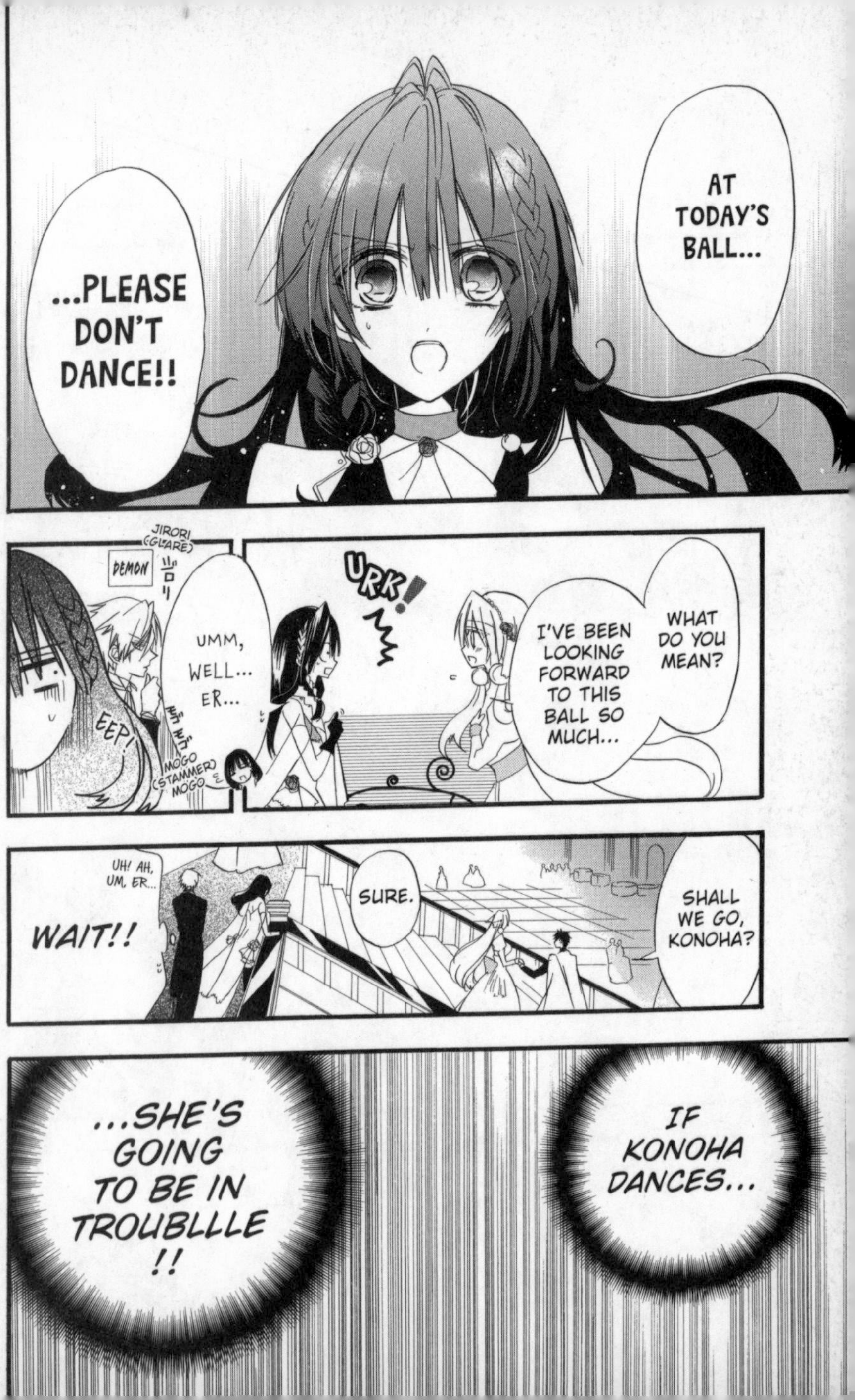
AT TODAY'S BALL...
...PLEASE DON'T DANCE!!
WHAT DO YOU MEAN?
I'VE BEEN LOOKING FORWARD TO THIS BALL SO MUCH...
URK!
JIRORI (GLARE)
DEMON
UMM, WELL... ER...
EEP!
MOGO (STAMMER) MOGO
SHALL WE GO, KONOHA?
SURE.
UH! AH, UM, ER...
WAIT!!
IF KONOHA DANCES...
...SHE'S GOING TO BE IN TROUBLLLE!!

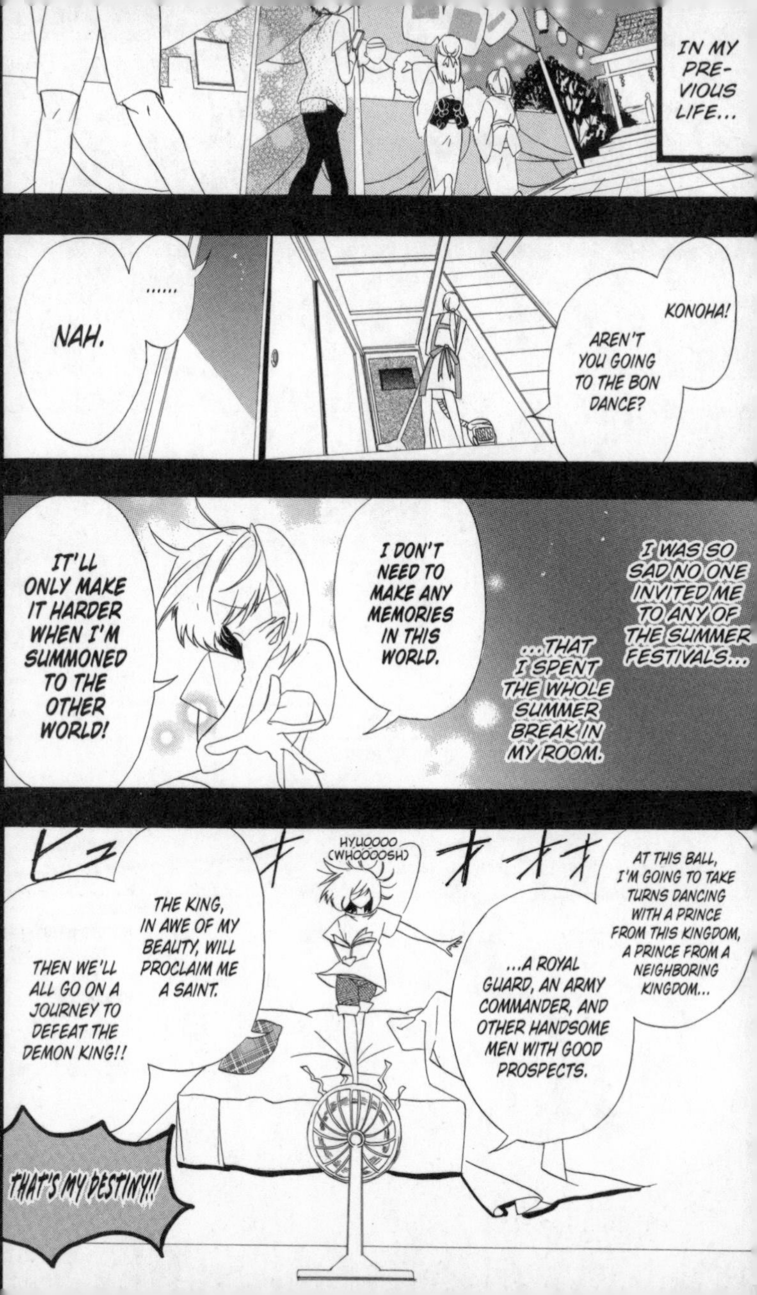
IN MY PRE-VIOUS LIFE...
KONOHA!
AREN'T YOU GOING TO THE BON DANCE?
......
NAH.
I WAS SO SAD NO ONE INVITED ME TO ANY OF THE SUMMER FESTIVALS...
...THAT I SPENT THE WHOLE SUMMER BREAK IN MY ROOM.
I DON'T NEED TO MAKE ANY MEMORIES IN THIS WORLD.
IT'LL ONLY MAKE IT HARDER WHEN I'M SUMMONED TO THE OTHER WORLD!
AT THIS BALL, I'M GOING TO TAKE TURNS DANCING WITH A PRINCE FROM THIS KINGDOM, A PRINCE FROM A NEIGHBORING KINGDOM...
...A ROYAL GUARD, AN ARMY COMMANDER, AND OTHER HANDSOME MEN WITH GOOD PROSPECTS.
HYUOOOO (WHOOOOSH)
THE KING, IN AWE OF MY BEAUTY, WILL PROCLAIM ME A SAINT.
THEN WE'LL ALL GO ON A JOURNEY TO DEFEAT THE DEMON KING!!
THAT'S MY DESTINY!!

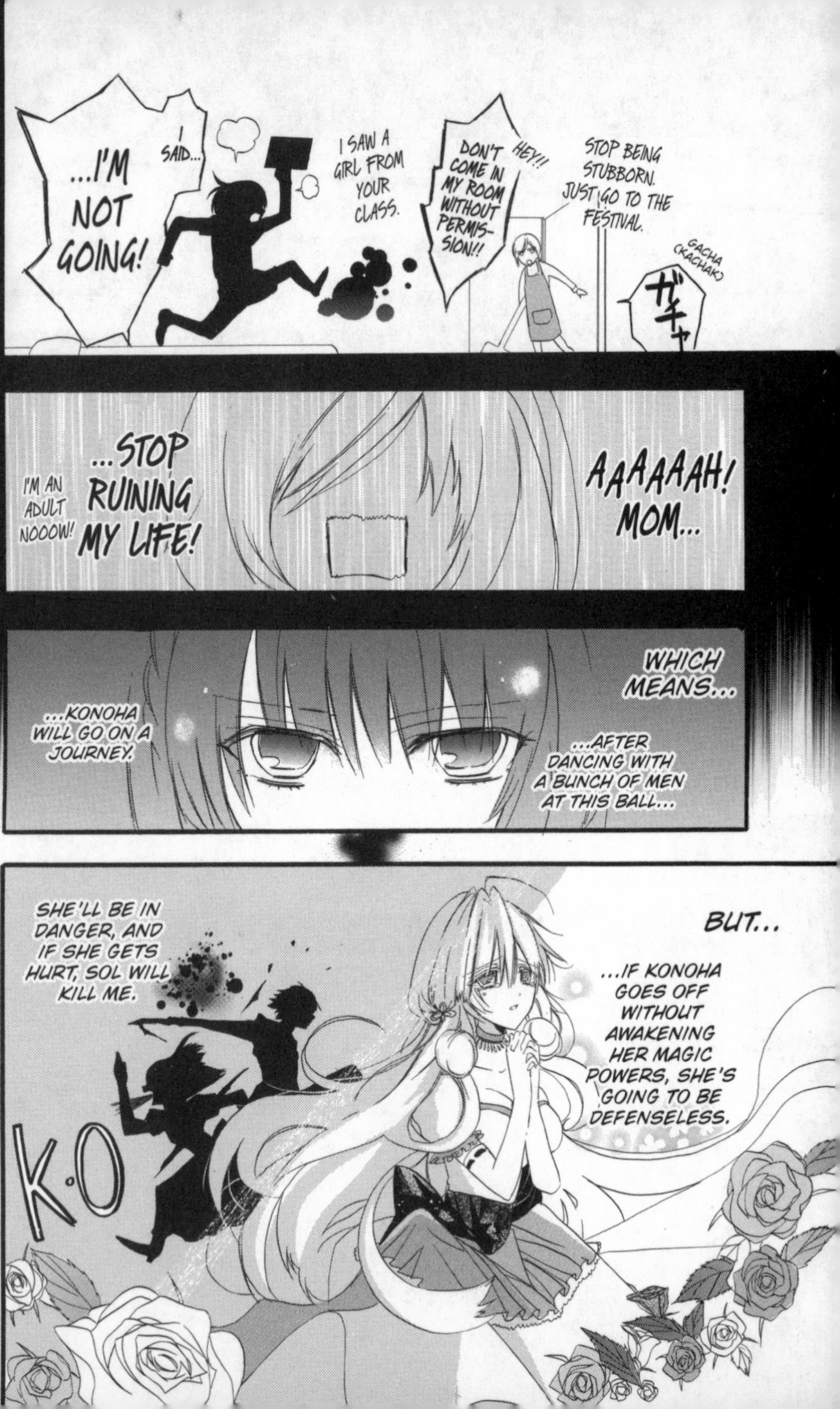
GACHA (KACHAK)
ガチャ
STOP BEING STUBBORN. JUST GO TO THE FESTIVAL.
HEY!!
DON'T COME IN MY ROOM WITHOUT PERMIS-SION!!
I SAW A GIRL FROM YOUR CLASS.
I SAID...
...I'M NOT GOING!
AAAAAAH! MOM...
...STOP RUINING MY LIFE!
I'M AN ADULT NOOOW!
WHICH MEANS...
...AFTER DANCING WITH A BUNCH OF MEN AT THIS BALL...
...KONOHA WILL GO ON A JOURNEY.
BUT...
...IF KONOHA GOES OFF WITHOUT AWAKENING HER MAGIC POWERS, SHE'S GOING TO BE DEFENSELESS.
SHE'LL BE IN DANGER, AND IF SHE GETS HURT, SOL WILL KILL ME.
K.O

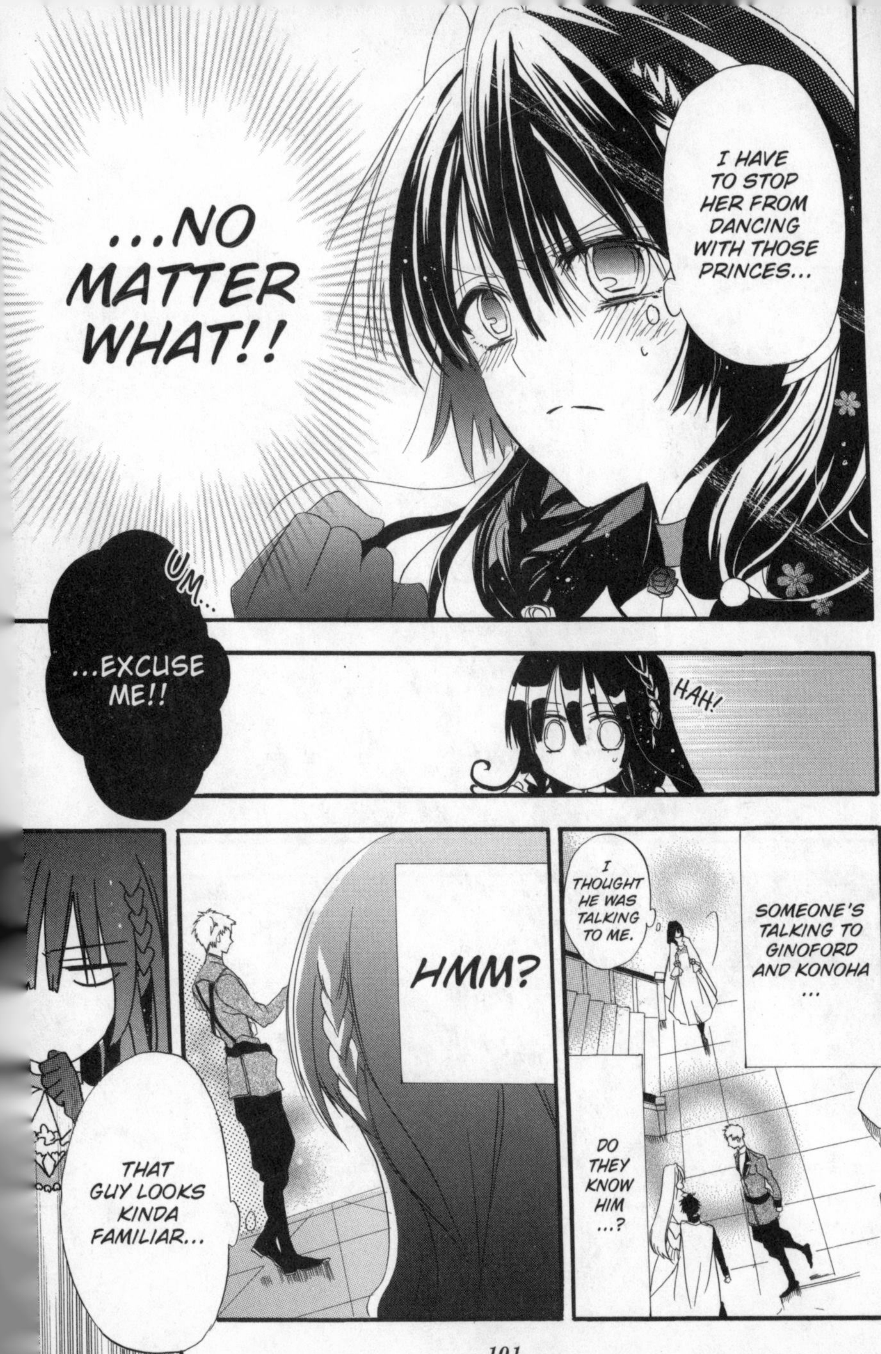
I HAVE TO STOP HER FROM DANCING WITH THOSE PRINCES...
...NO MATTER WHAT!!
UM...
...EXCUSE ME!!
HAH!
SOMEONE'S TALKING TO GINOFORD AND KONOHA...
I THOUGHT HE WAS TALKING TO ME.
DO THEY KNOW HIM...?
HMM?
THAT GUY LOOKS KINDA FAMILIAR...

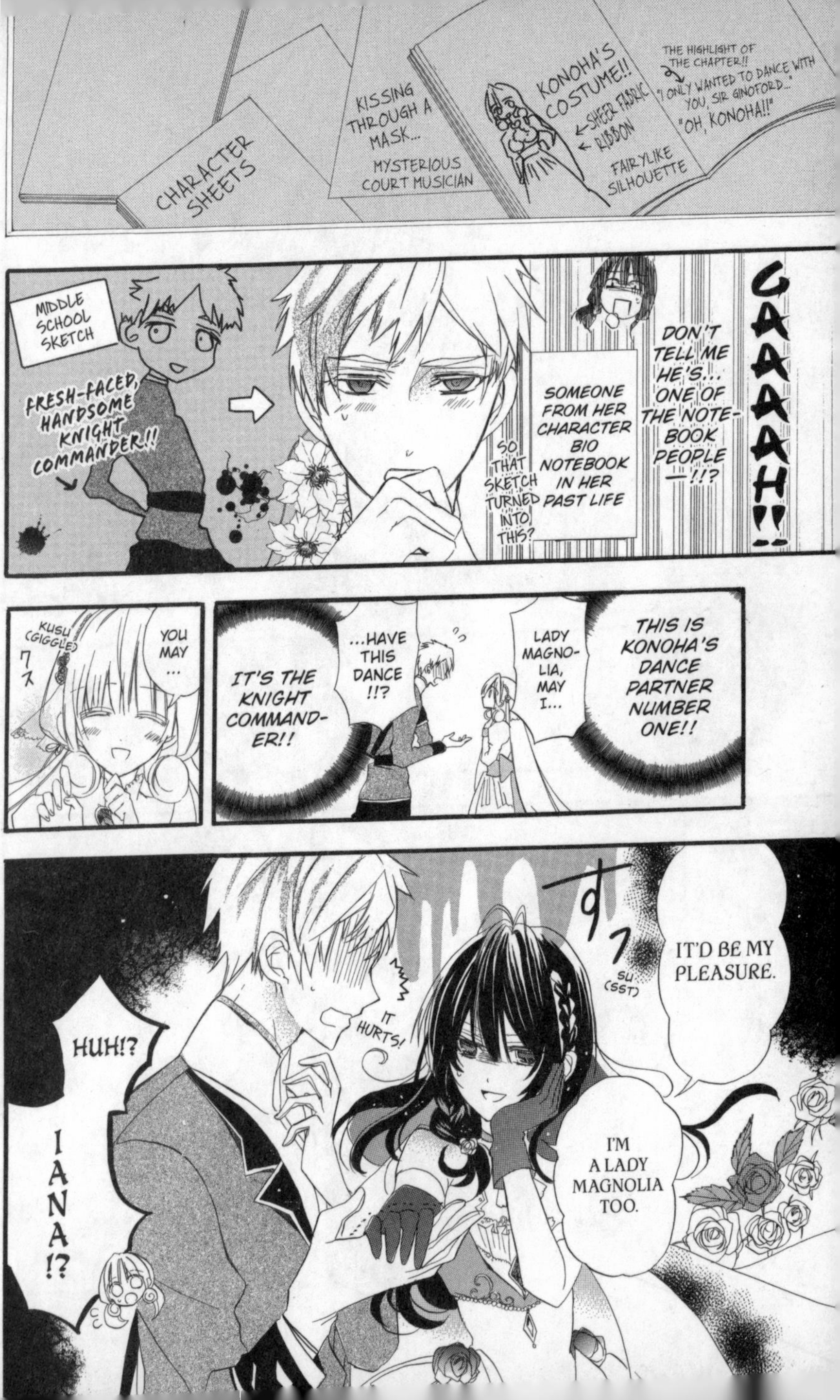
THE HIGHLIGHT OF THE CHAPTER!!
"I ONLY WANTED TO DANCE WITH YOU, SIR GINOFORD..."
"OH, KONOHA!!"
KONOHA'S COSTUME!!
SHEER FABRIC
RIBBON
FAIRYLIKE SILHOUETTE
KISSING THROUGH A MASK...
MYSTERIOUS COURT MUSICIAN
CHARACTER SHEETS
GAAAAAH!!
DON'T TELL ME HE'S... ONE OF THE NOTEBOOK PEOPLE—!!?
SOMEONE FROM HER CHARACTER BIO NOTEBOOK IN HER PAST LIFE
SO THAT SKETCH TURNED INTO THIS?
MIDDLE SCHOOL SKETCH
FRESH-FACED, HANDSOME KNIGHT COMMANDER!!
THIS IS KONOHA'S DANCE PARTNER NUMBER ONE!!
LADY MAGNOLIA, MAY I...
...HAVE THIS DANCE!!?
IT'S THE KNIGHT COMMANDER!!
YOU MAY...
KUSU (GIGGLE)
IT'D BE MY PLEASURE.
SU (SST)
I'M A LADY MAGNOLIA TOO.
IT HURTS!
HUH!?
IANA!?

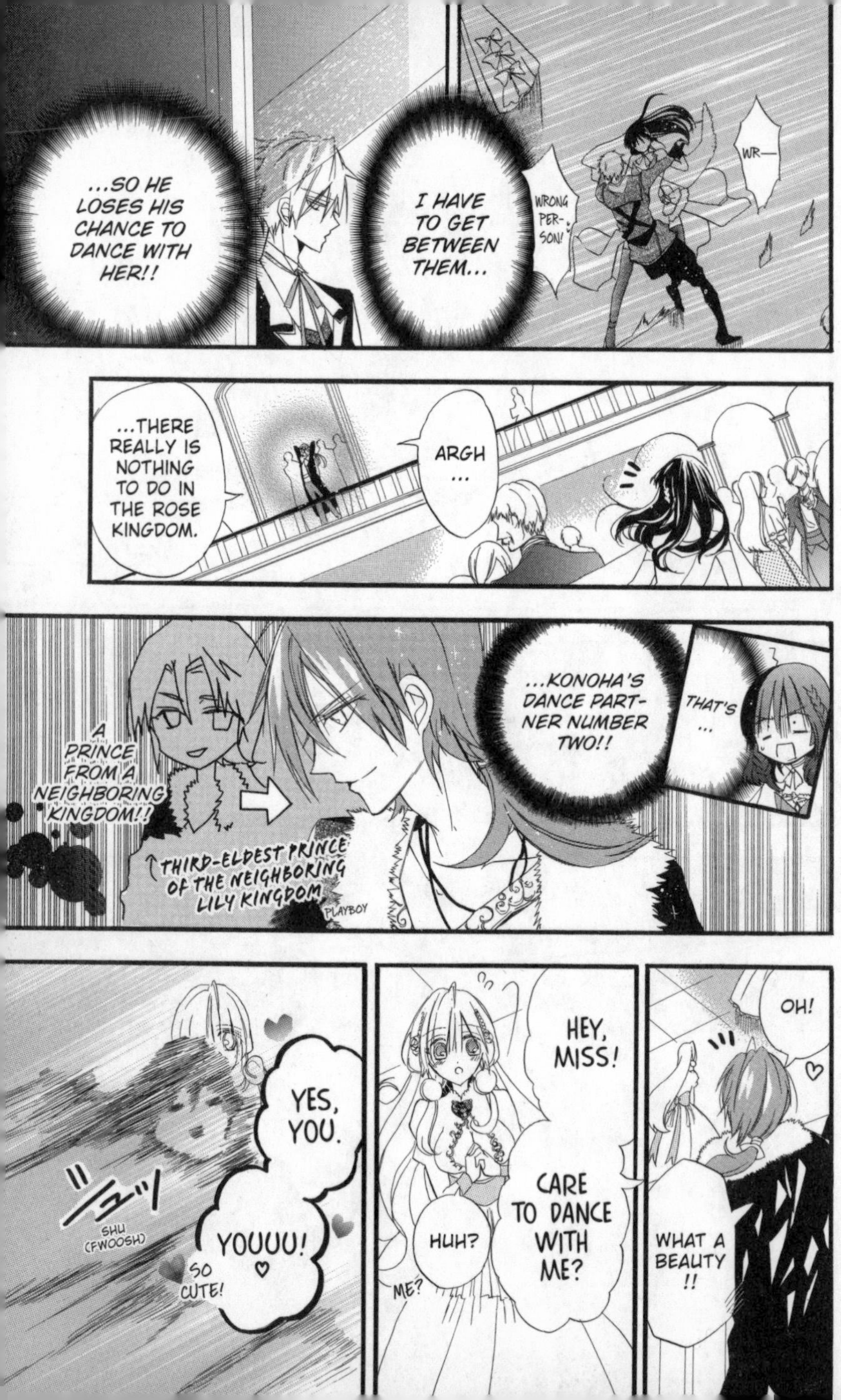
WR—
WRONG PER-SON!
I HAVE TO GET BETWEEN THEM...
...SO HE LOSES HIS CHANCE TO DANCE WITH HER!!
ARGH ...
...THERE REALLY IS NOTHING TO DO IN THE ROSE KINGDOM.
THAT'S ...
...KONOHA'S DANCE PARTNER NUMBER TWO!!
A PRINCE FROM A NEIGHBORING KINGDOM!!
THIRD-ELDEST PRINCE OF THE NEIGHBORING LILY KINGDOM
PLAYBOY
OH!
WHAT A BEAUTY !!
HEY, MISS!
CARE TO DANCE WITH ME?
HUH?
ME?
YES, YOU.
YOUUU!
SO CUTE!
シュッ
SHU (FWOOSH)

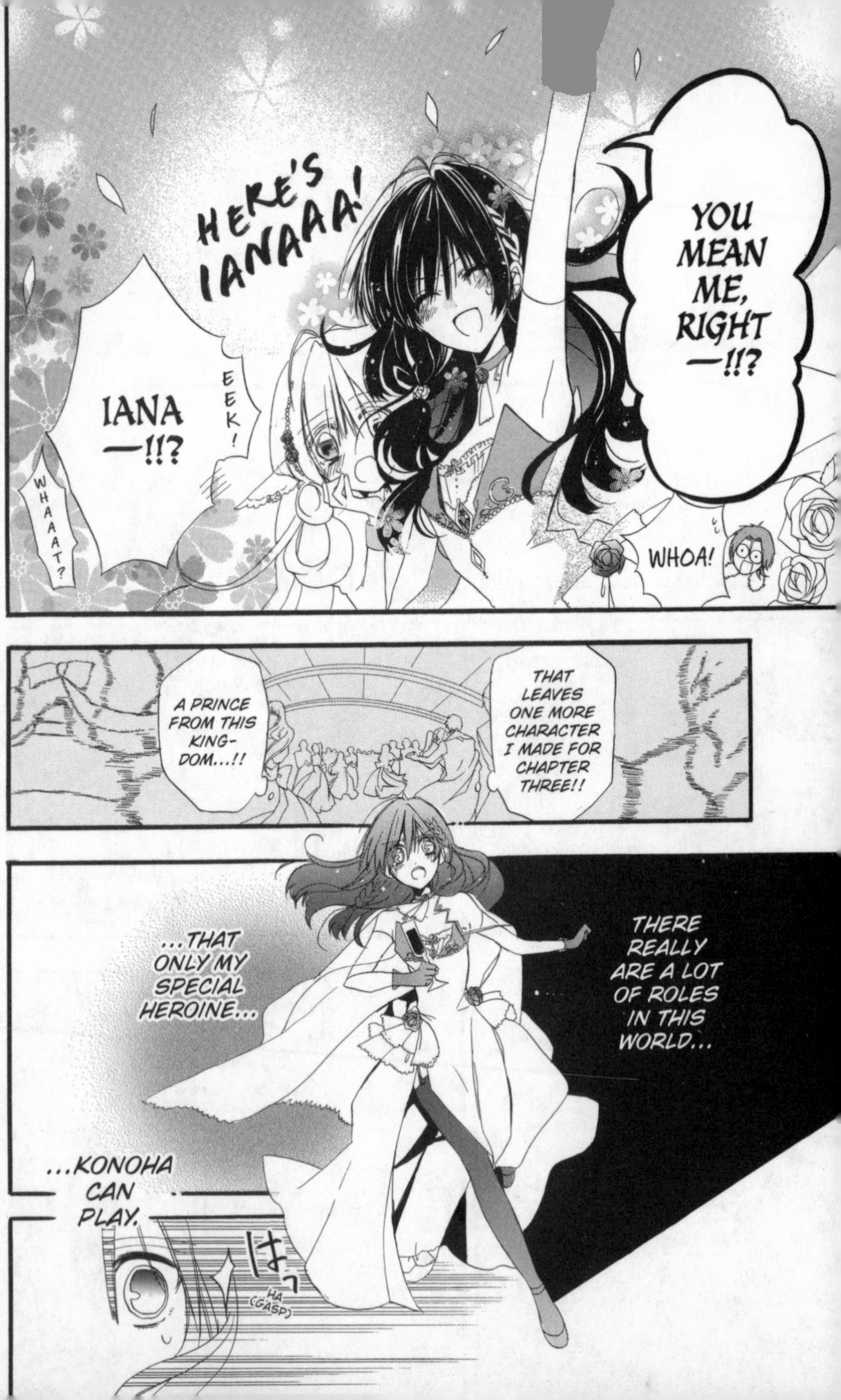
YOU MEAN ME, RIGHT—!!?
HERE'S IANAAA!
WHOA!
EEK!
IANA—!!?
WHAAAT?
THAT LEAVES ONE MORE CHARACTER I MADE FOR CHAPTER THREE!!
A PRINCE FROM THIS KING-DOM...!!
THERE REALLY ARE A LOT OF ROLES IN THIS WORLD...
...THAT ONLY MY SPECIAL HEROINE...
...KONOHA CAN PLAY.
はっ
HA (GASP)

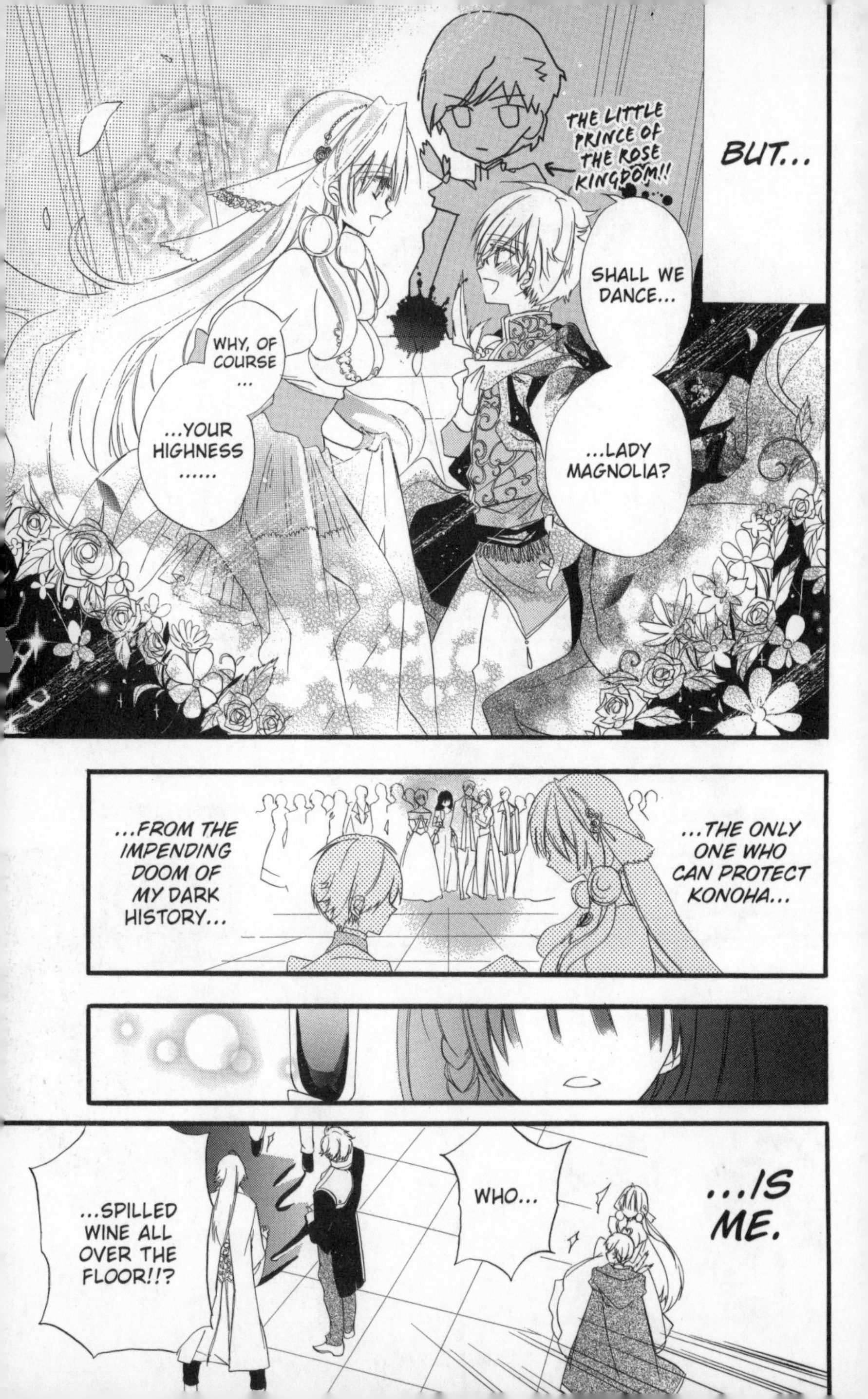

BUT...
THE LITTLE PRINCE OF THE ROSE KINGDOM!!
SHALL WE DANCE...
...LADY MAGNOLIA?
WHY, OF COURSE ...
...YOUR HIGHNESS ......
...THE ONLY ONE WHO CAN PROTECT KONOHA...
...FROM THE IMPENDING DOOM OF MY DARK HISTORY...
...IS ME.
WHO...
...SPILLED WINE ALL OVER THE FLOOR!!?

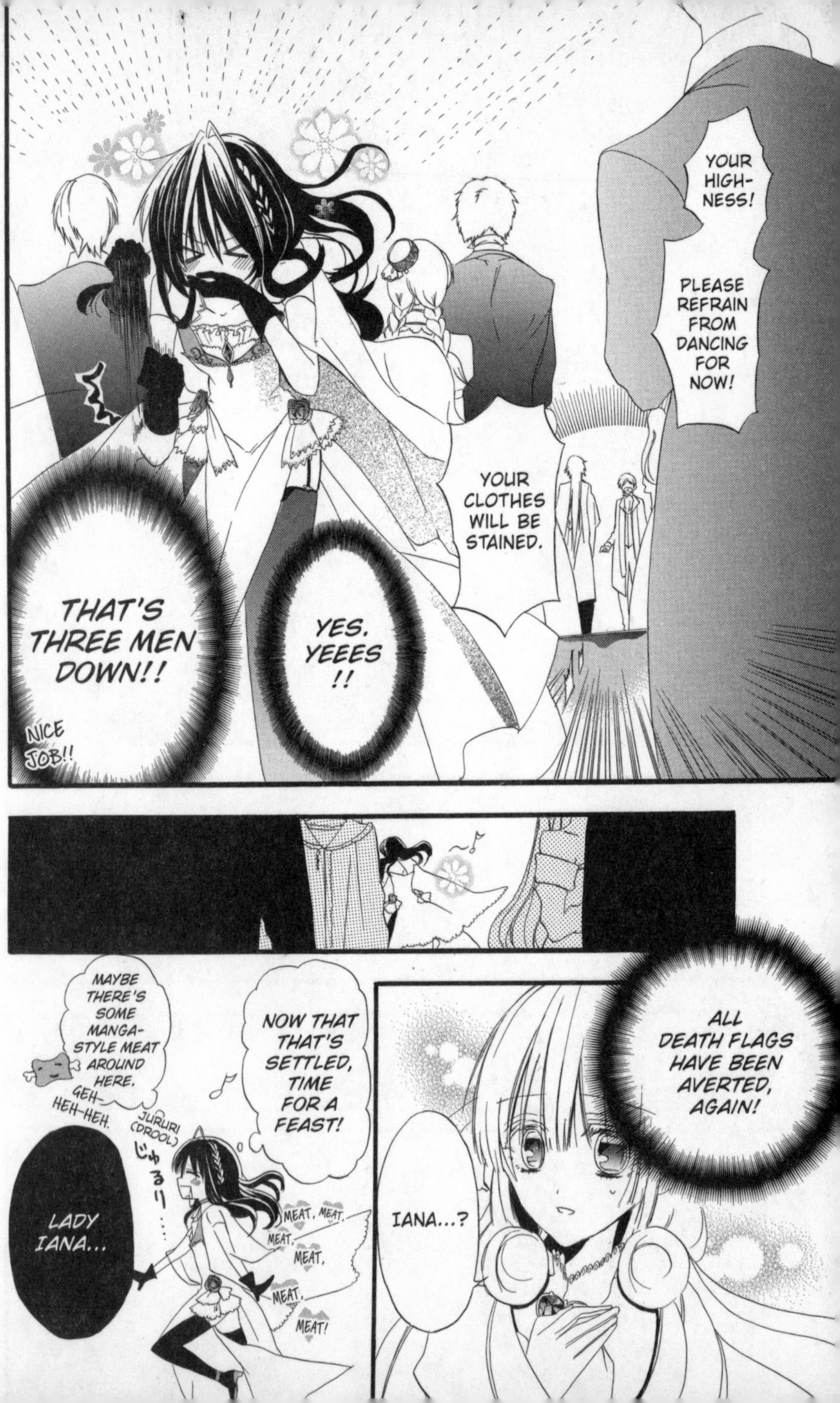
YOUR HIGH-NESS!
PLEASE REFRAIN FROM DANCING FOR NOW!
YOUR CLOTHES WILL BE STAINED.
YES. YEEES!!
THAT'S THREE MEN DOWN!!
NICE JOB!!
ALL DEATH FLAGS HAVE BEEN AVERTED, AGAIN!
IANA...?
NOW THAT THAT'S SETTLED, TIME FOR A FEAST!
MAYBE THERE'S SOME MANGA-STYLE MEAT AROUND HERE.
GEH-HEH-HEH.
JURURI (DROOL)
じゅるり…
MEAT, MEAT.
MEAT,
MEAT,
MEAT,
MEAT!
LADY IANA...

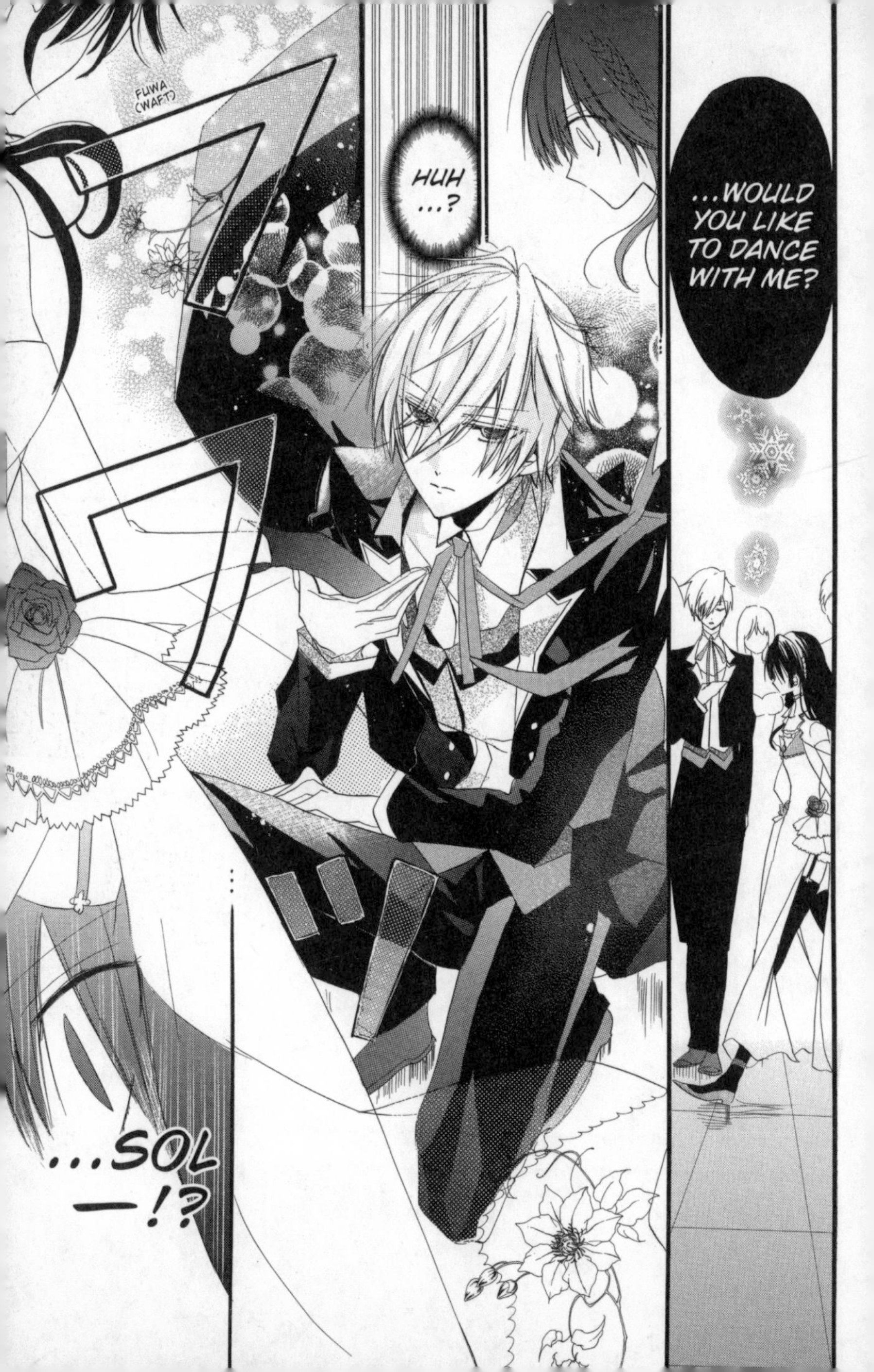
...WOULD YOU LIKE TO DANCE WITH ME?
HUH ...?
FUWA (WAFT)
...SOL —!?

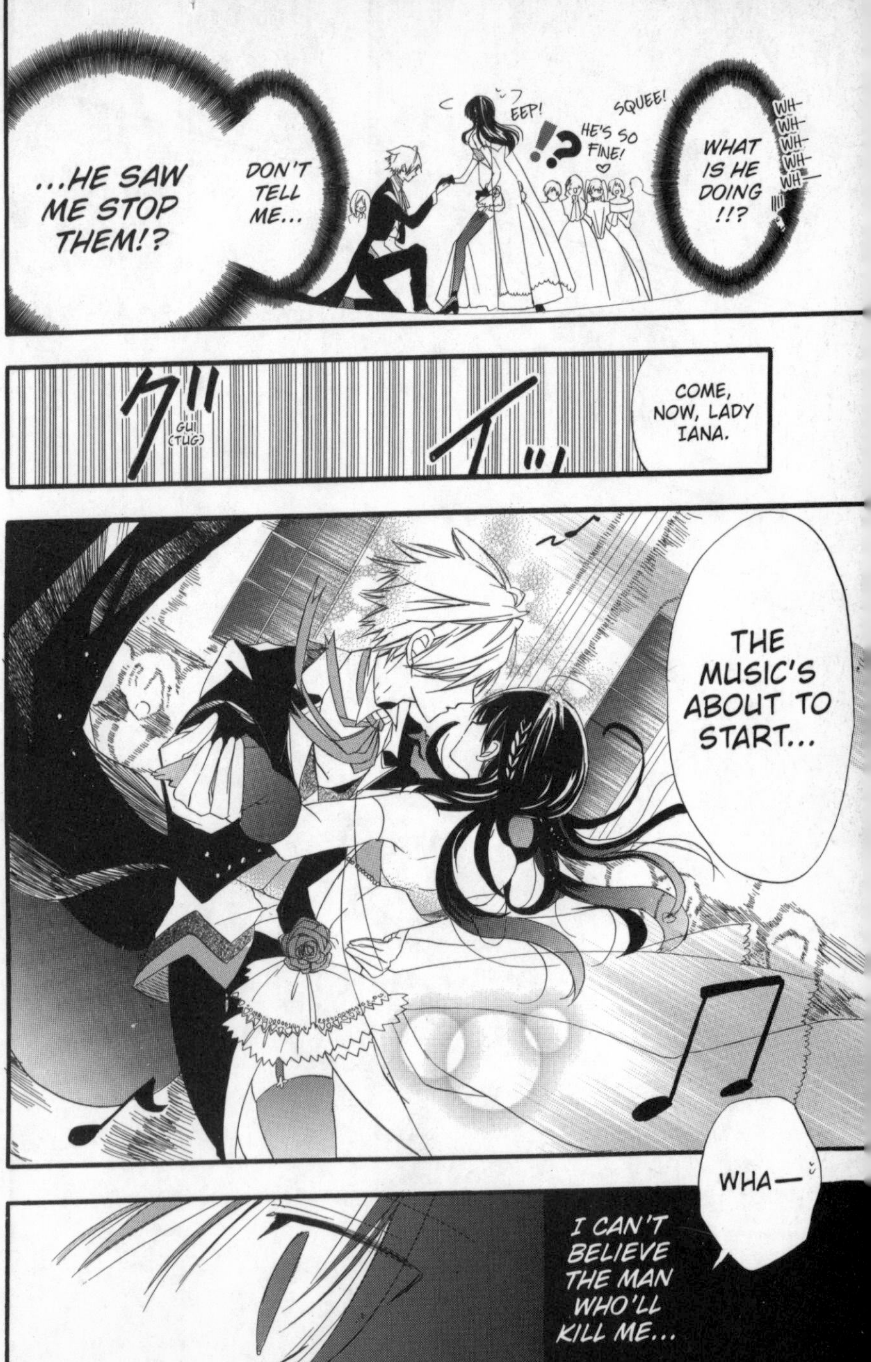
WH-WH-WH-WH-WH-!!!
WHAT IS HE DOING!!?
SQUEE!
HE'S SO FINE!
EEP!
DON'T TELL ME...
...HE SAW ME STOP THEM!?
COME, NOW, LADY IANA.
GUI (TUG)
THE MUSIC'S ABOUT TO START...
WHA—
I CAN'T BELIEVE THE MAN WHO'LL KILL ME...

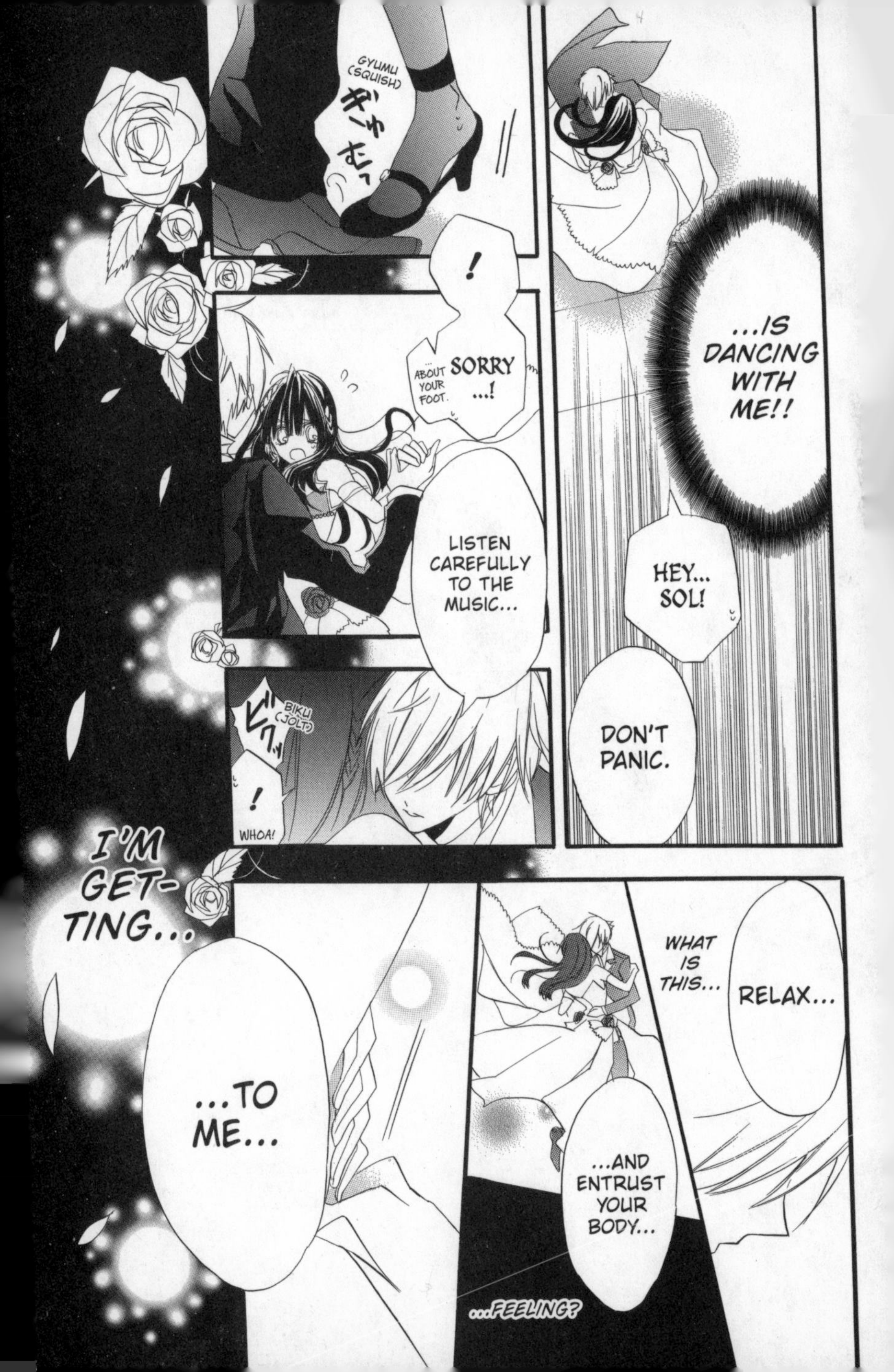
...IS DANCING WITH ME!!
HEY... SOL!
DON'T PANIC.
GYUMU (SQUISH)
ぎゅむっ
!
SORRY ...!
...ABOUT YOUR FOOT.
LISTEN CAREFULLY TO THE MUSIC...
BIKU (JOLT)
!
WHOA!
RELAX...
WHAT IS THIS...
...AND ENTRUST YOUR BODY...
...FEELING?
...TO ME...
I'M GET-TING...

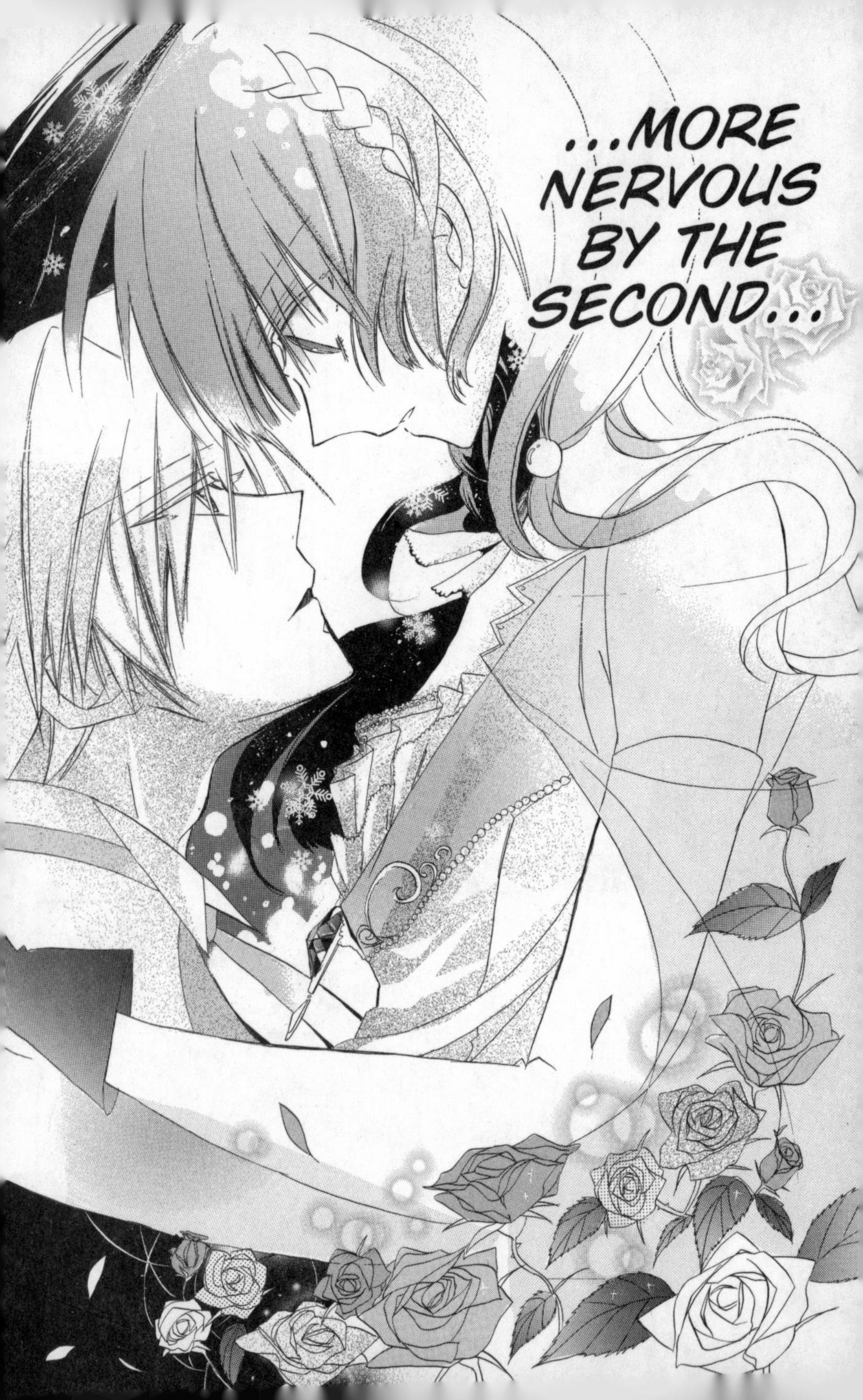
...MORE NERVOUS BY THE SECOND...

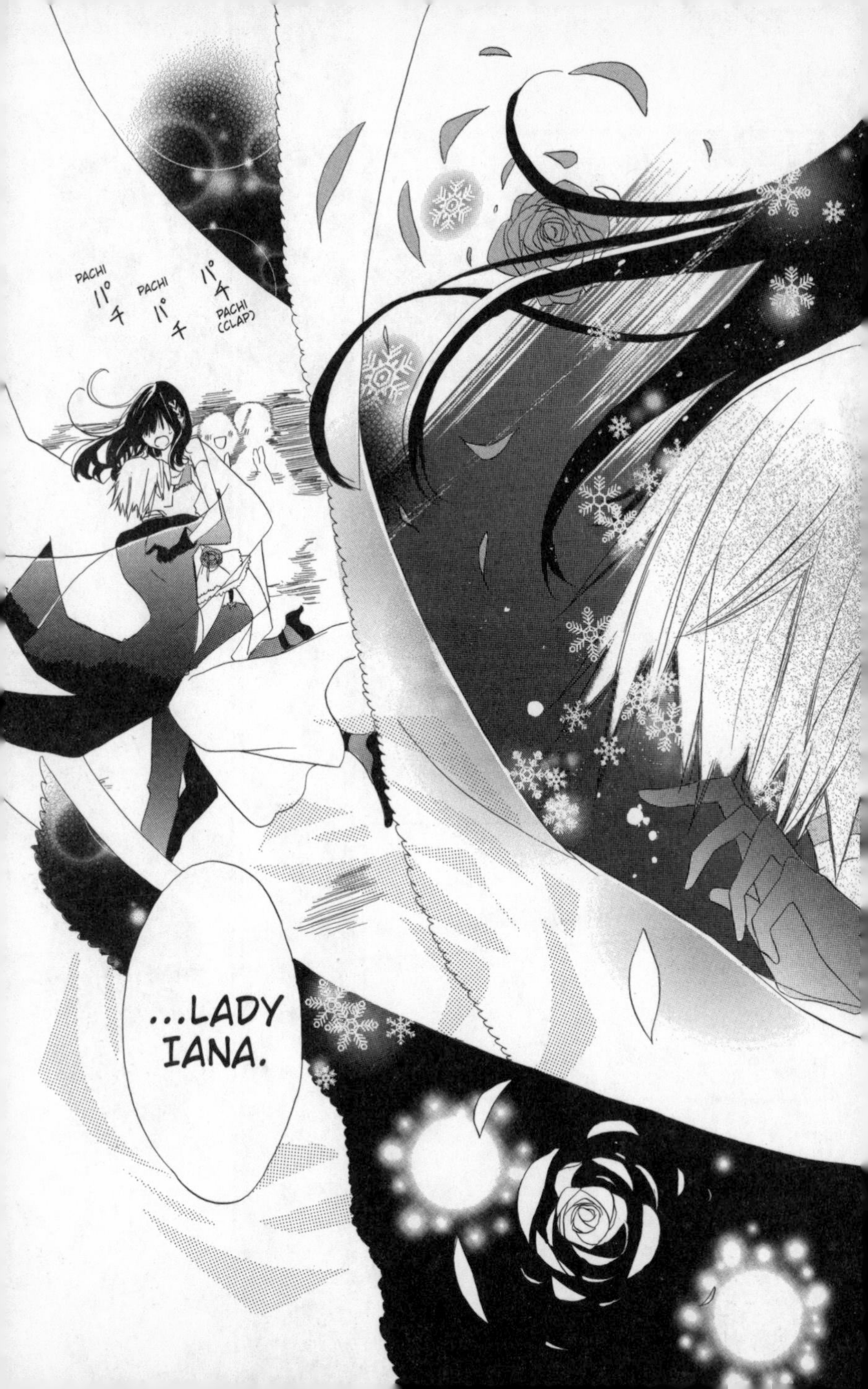
パチ
PACHI (CLAP)
パチ
PACHI
パチ
PACHI
...LADY IANA.

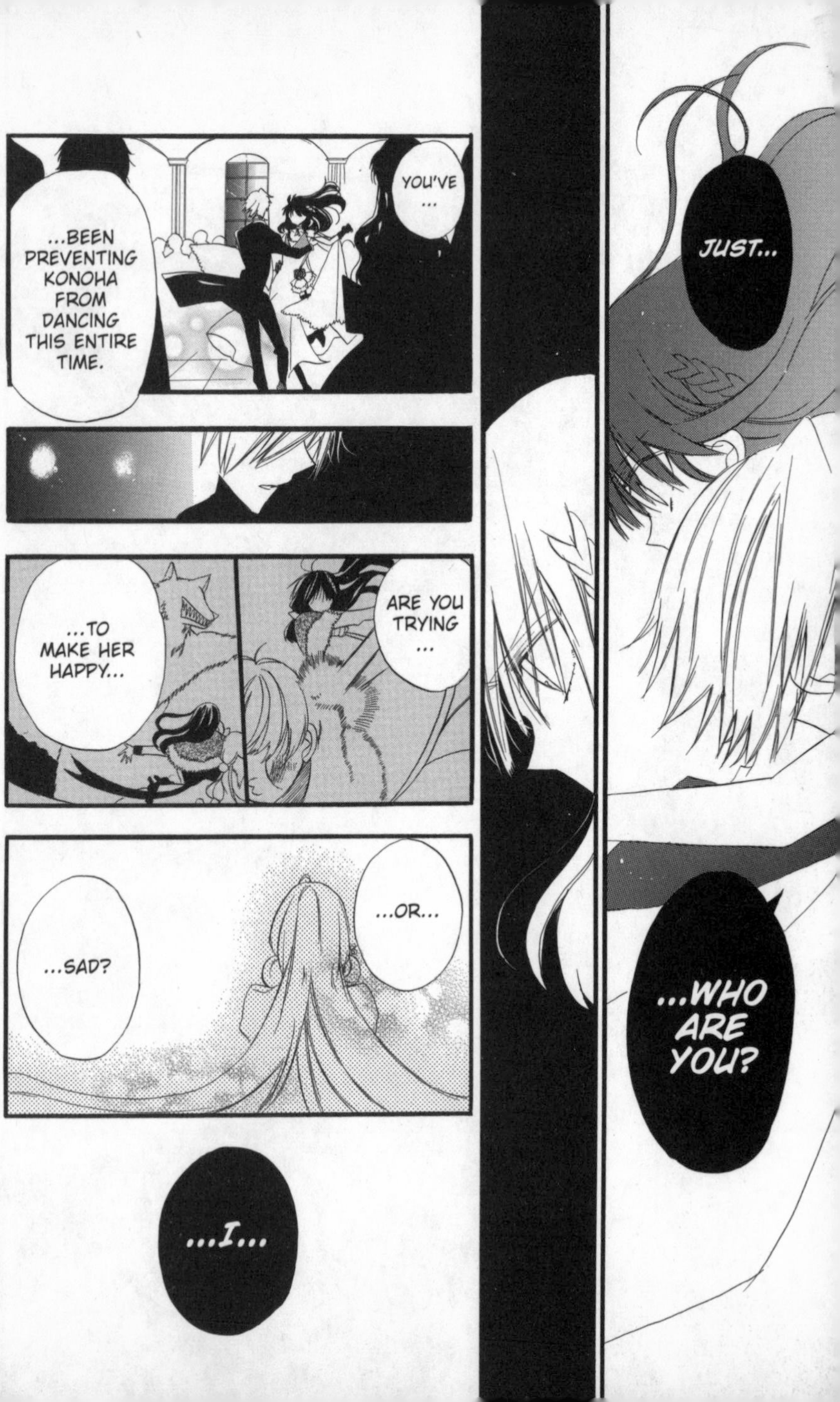
YOU'VE ...
...BEEN PREVENTING KONOHA FROM DANCING THIS ENTIRE TIME.
ARE YOU TRYING ...
...TO MAKE HER HAPPY...
...OR...
...SAD?
...I...
JUST...
...WHO ARE YOU?

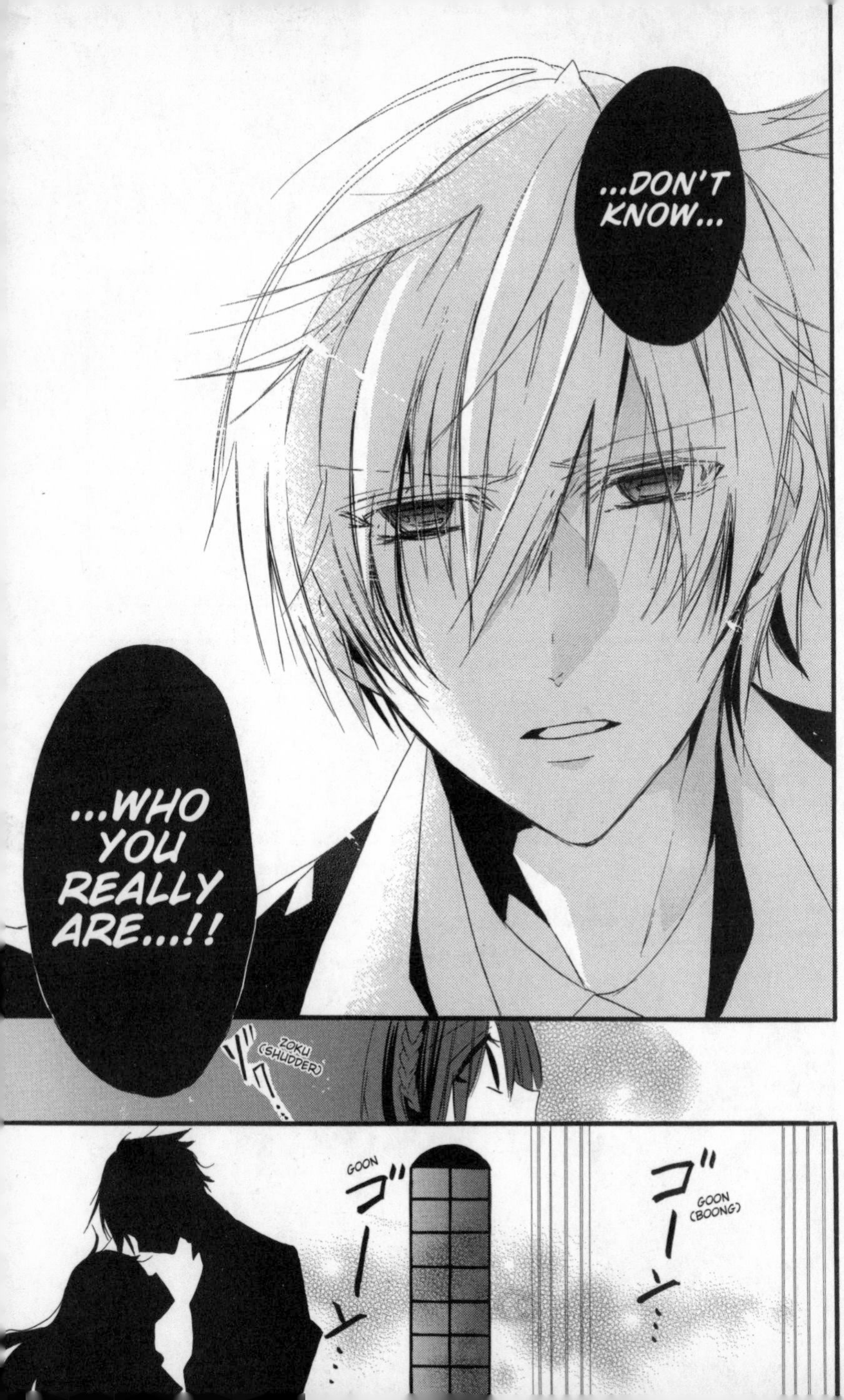
...DON'T KNOW...
...WHO YOU REALLY ARE...!!
ZOKU (SHUDDER)
GOON (BOONG)
GOON

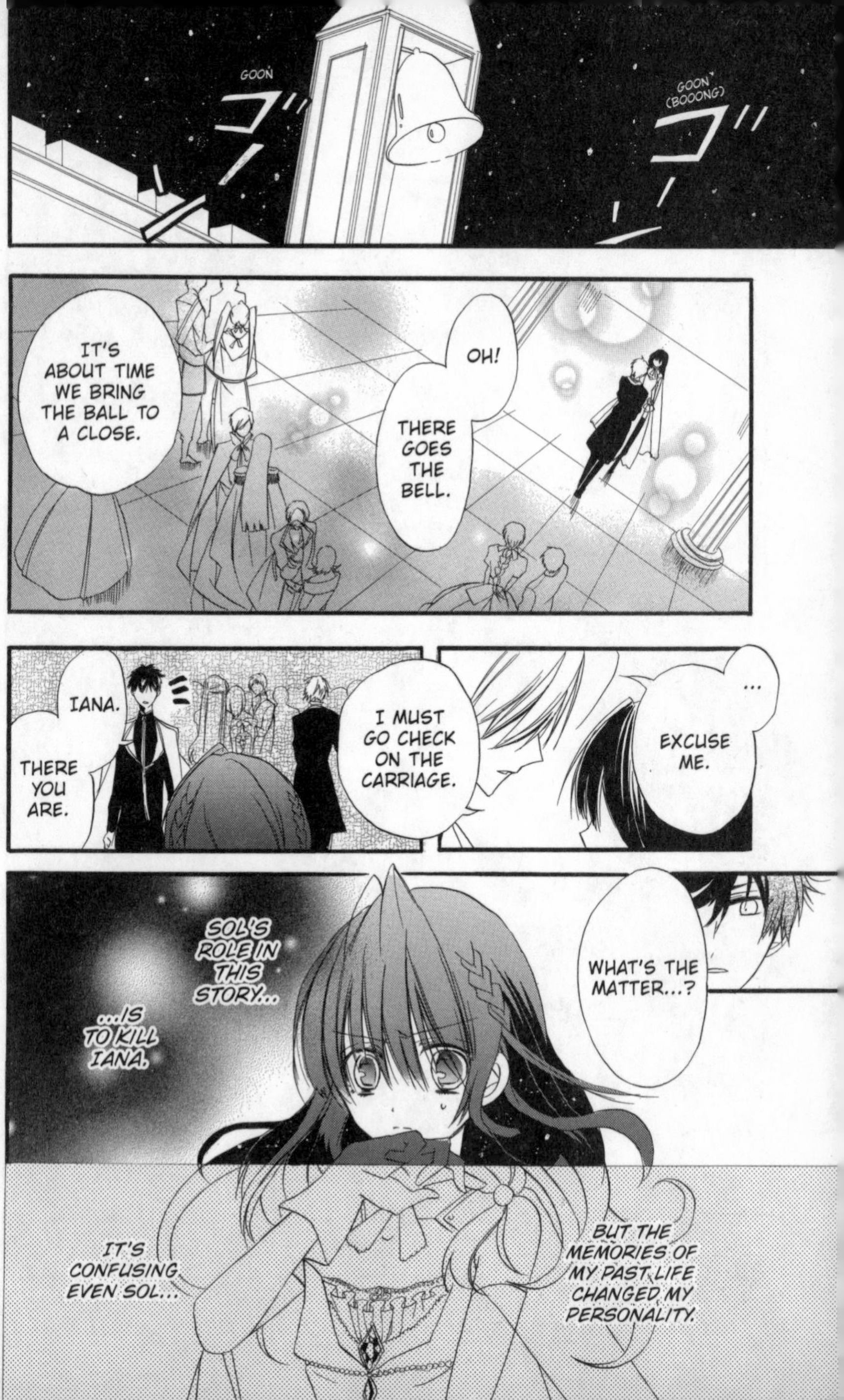
GOON (BOOONG)
GOON
OH!
THERE GOES THE BELL.
IT'S ABOUT TIME WE BRING THE BALL TO A CLOSE.
...
EXCUSE ME.
I MUST GO CHECK ON THE CARRIAGE.
IANA.
THERE YOU ARE.
WHAT'S THE MATTER...?
SOL'S ROLE IN THIS STORY...
...IS TO KILL IANA.
BUT THE MEMORIES OF MY PAST LIFE CHANGED MY PERSONALITY.
IT'S CONFUSING EVEN SOL...

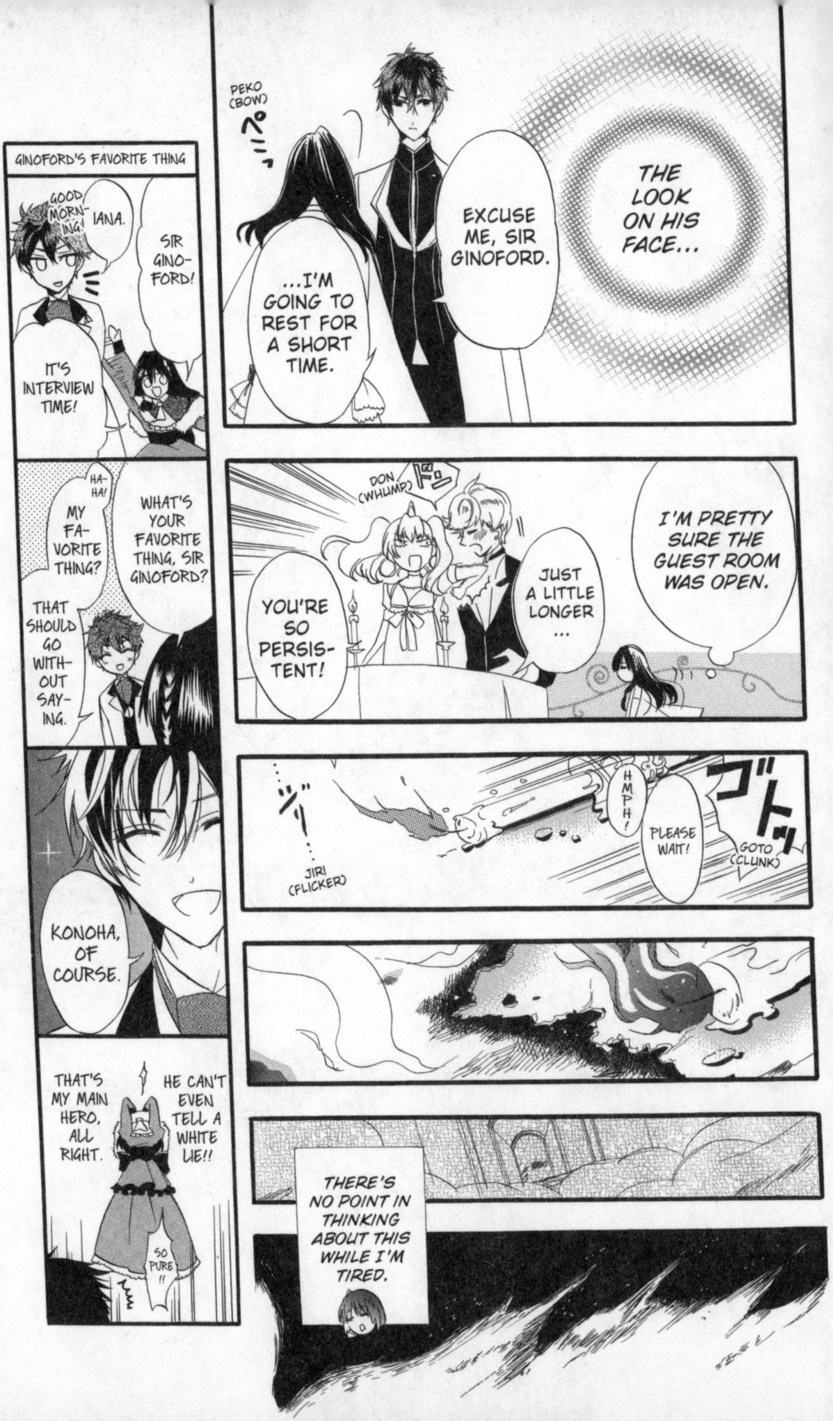
THE LOOK ON HIS FACE...
EXCUSE ME, SIR GINOFORD.
...I'M GOING TO REST FOR A SHORT TIME.
PEKO (BOW)
I'M PRETTY SURE THE GUEST ROOM WAS OPEN.
JUST A LITTLE LONGER ...
DON (WHUMP)
YOU'RE SO PERSISTENT!
GOTO (CLUNK)
PLEASE WAIT!
HMPH!
JIRI (FLICKER)
THERE'S NO POINT IN THINKING ABOUT THIS WHILE I'M TIRED.
GINOFORD'S FAVORITE THING
SIR GINOFORD!
GOOD MORNING!
IANA.
IT'S INTERVIEW TIME!
WHAT'S YOUR FAVORITE THING, SIR GINOFORD?
MY FAVORITE THING?
HA-HA!
THAT SHOULD GO WITHOUT SAYING.
KONOHA, OF COURSE.
HE CAN'T EVEN TELL A WHITE LIE!!
THAT'S MY MAIN HERO, ALL RIGHT.
SO PURE!!

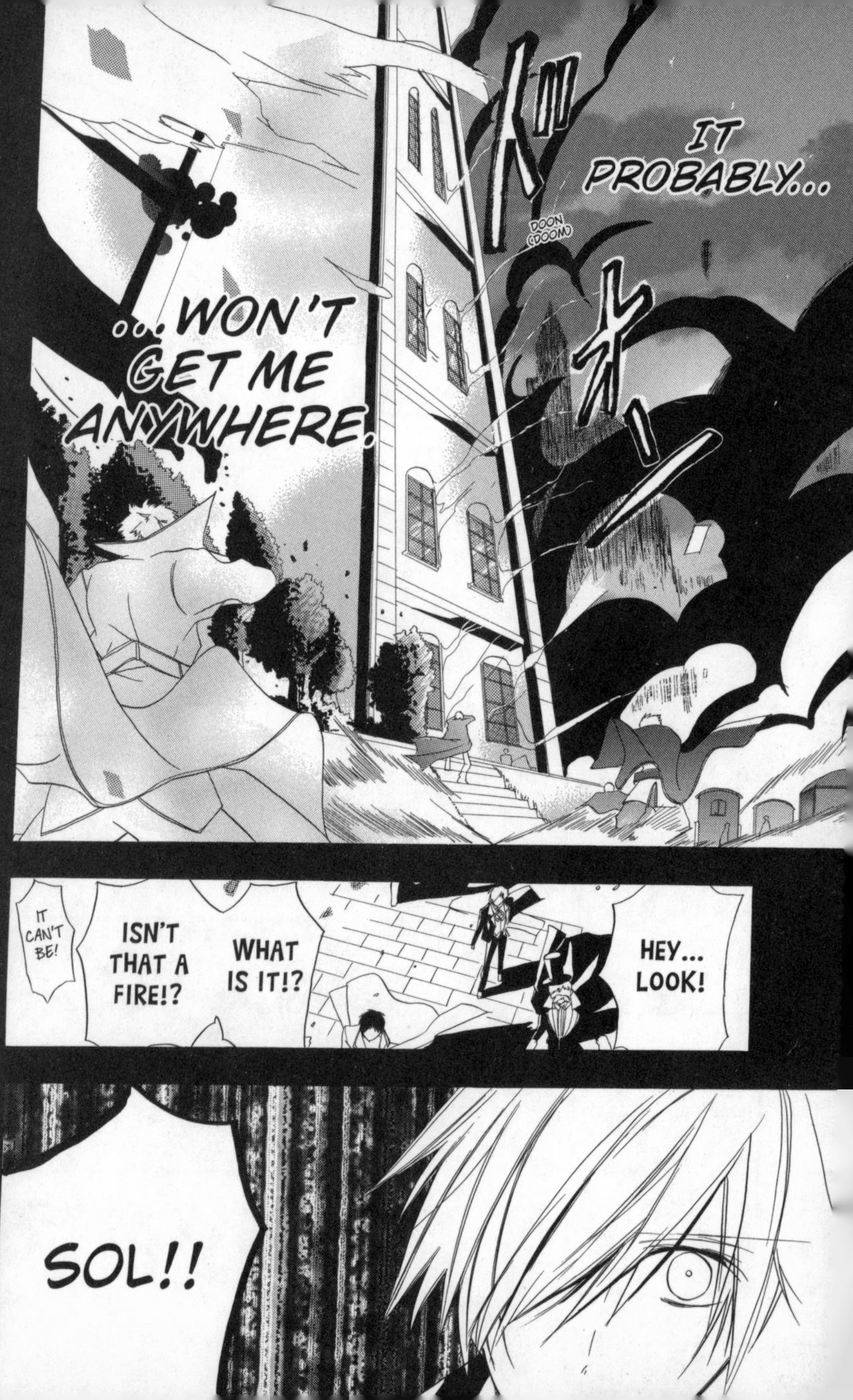

IT PROBABLY...
DOON (DOOM)
...WON'T GET ME ANYWHERE.
HEY... LOOK!
WHAT IS IT!?
ISN'T THAT A FIRE!?
IT CAN'T BE!
SOL!!

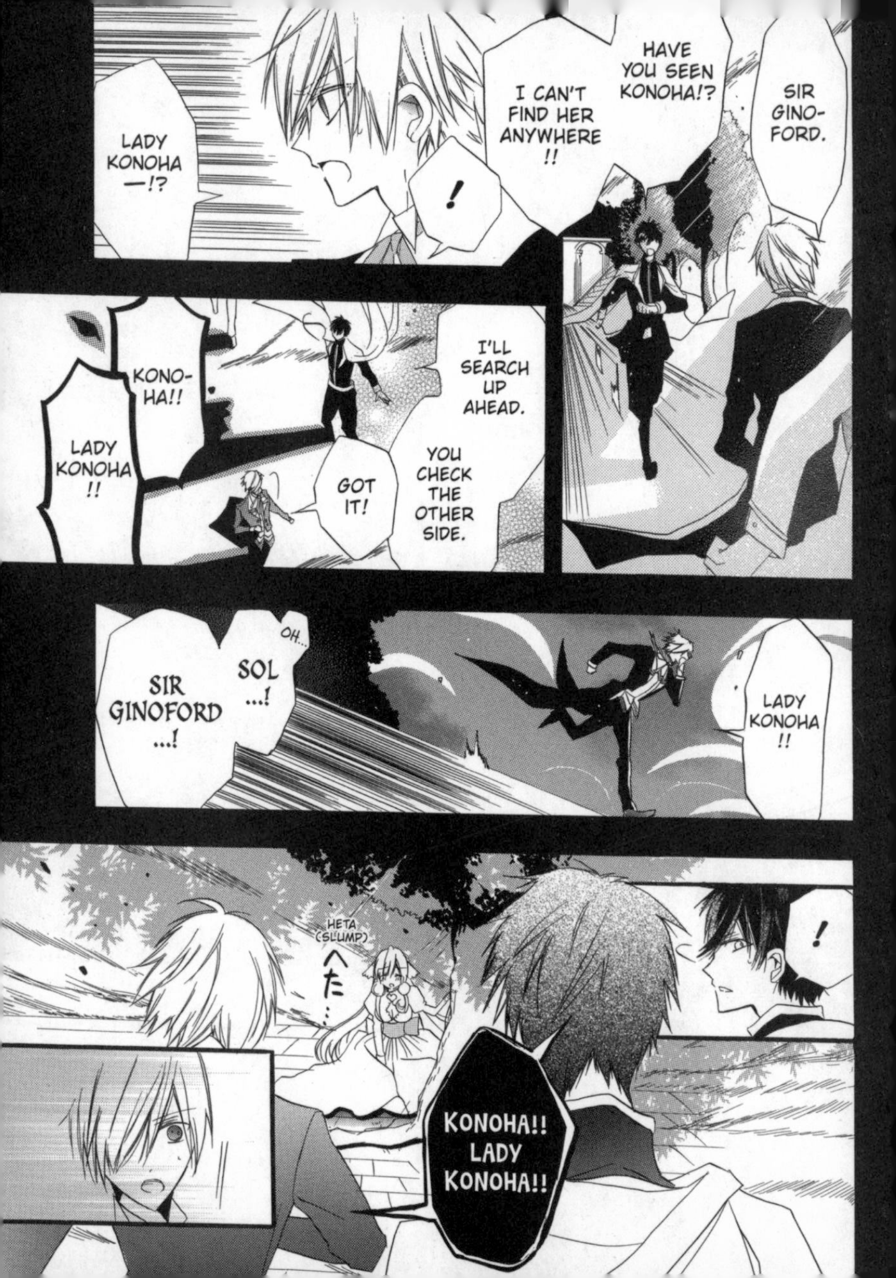
SIR GINOFORD.
HAVE YOU SEEN KONOHA!?
I CAN'T FIND HER ANYWHERE!!
!
LADY KONOHA—!?
I'LL SEARCH UP AHEAD.
YOU CHECK THE OTHER SIDE.
GOT IT!
KONOHA!!
LADY KONOHA!!
LADY KONOHA!!
OH...
SOL...!
SIR GINOFORD...!
!
HETA (SLUMP)
へた…
KONOHA!! LADY KONOHA!!

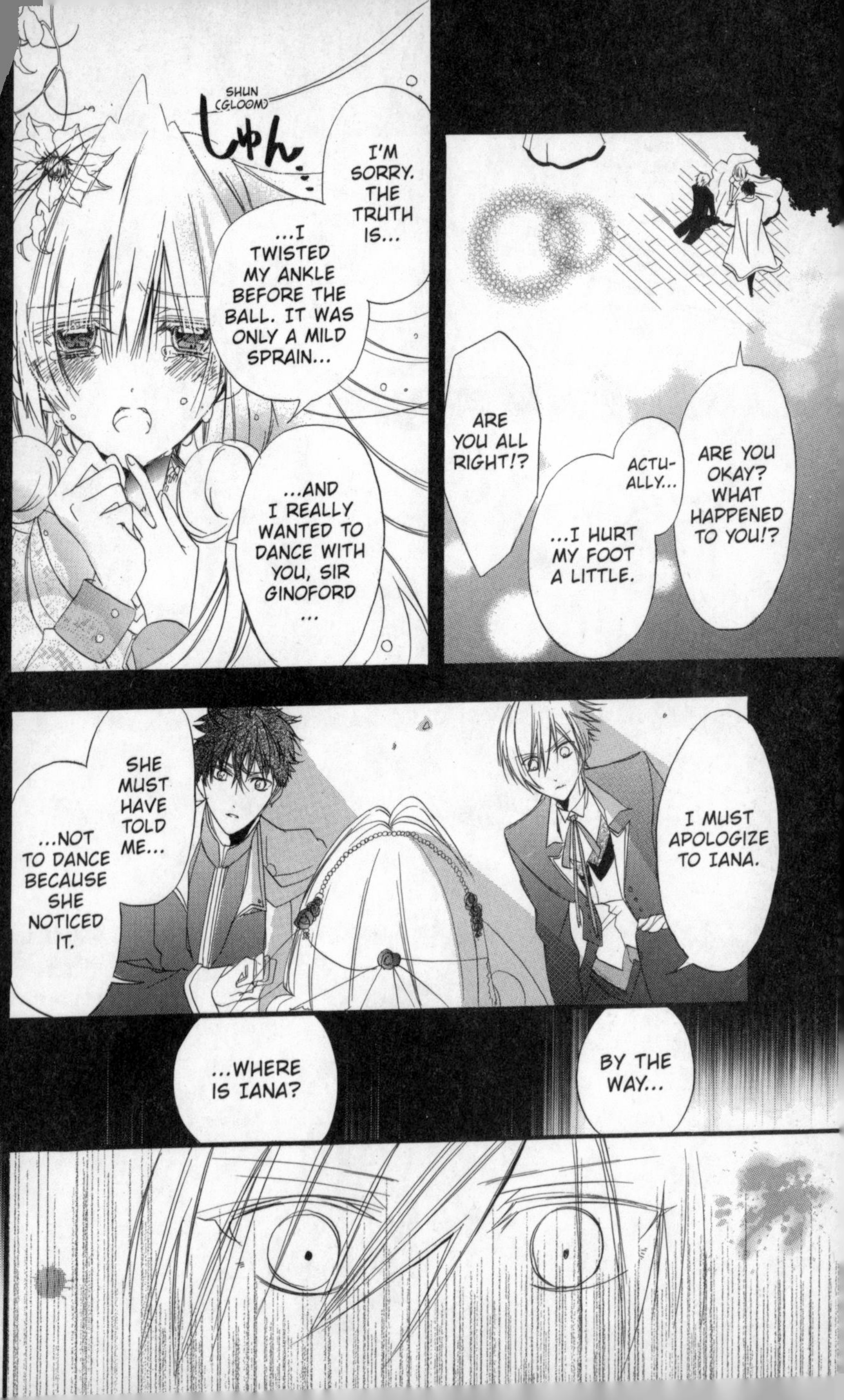
ARE YOU OKAY? WHAT HAPPENED TO YOU!?
ACTU-ALLY...
...I HURT MY FOOT A LITTLE.
ARE YOU ALL RIGHT!?
I'M SORRY. THE TRUTH IS...
しゅん
SHUN (GLOOM)
...I TWISTED MY ANKLE BEFORE THE BALL. IT WAS ONLY A MILD SPRAIN...
...AND I REALLY WANTED TO DANCE WITH YOU, SIR GINOFORD...
I MUST APOLOGIZE TO IANA.
SHE MUST HAVE TOLD ME...
...NOT TO DANCE BECAUSE SHE NOTICED IT.
BY THE WAY...
...WHERE IS IANA?

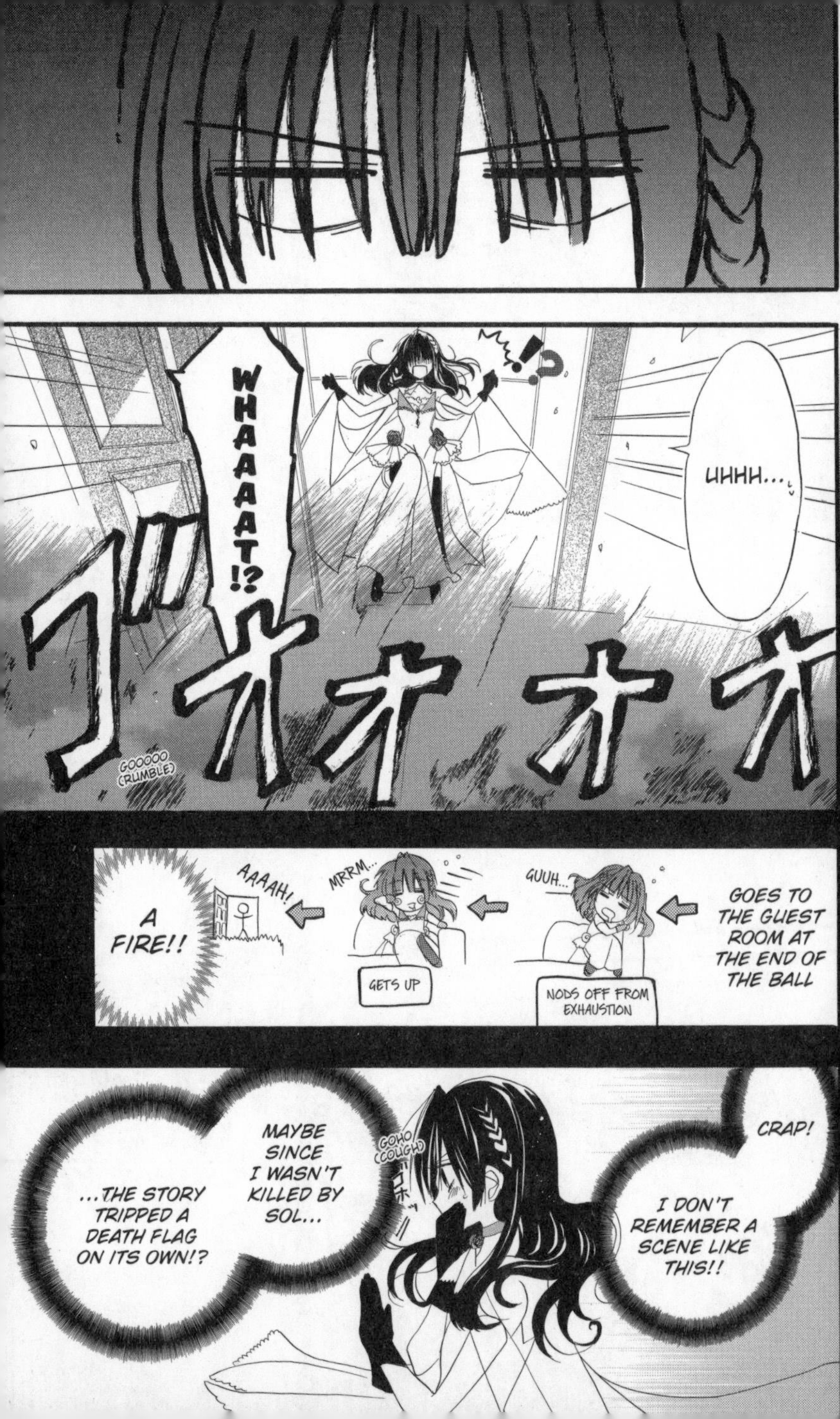
UHHH...
WHAAAAAT!?
ゴオオオ
GOOOOO (RUMBLE)
GOES TO THE GUEST ROOM AT THE END OF THE BALL
GUUH...
NODS OFF FROM EXHAUSTION
MRRM...
GETS UP
AAAAH!
A FIRE!!
CRAP!
I DON'T REMEMBER A SCENE LIKE THIS!!
GOHO (COUGH)
MAYBE SINCE I WASN'T KILLED BY SOL...
...THE STORY TRIPPED A DEATH FLAG ON ITS OWN!?

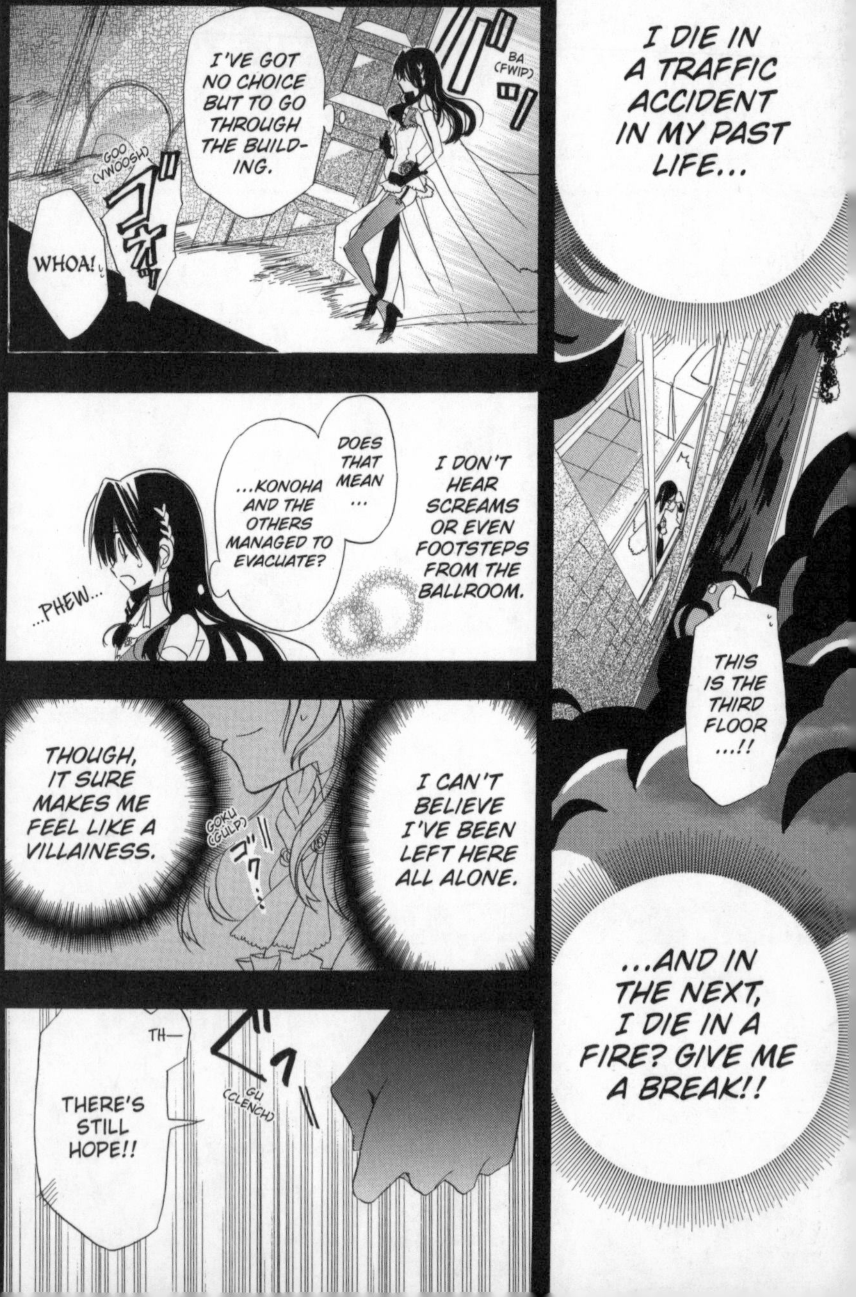
I DIE IN A TRAFFIC ACCIDENT IN MY PAST LIFE...
THIS IS THE THIRD FLOOR ...!!
...AND IN THE NEXT, I DIE IN A FIRE? GIVE ME A BREAK!!
BA (FWIP)
I'VE GOT NO CHOICE BUT TO GO THROUGH THE BUILD-ING.
GOO (VWOOSH)
WHOA!
I DON'T HEAR SCREAMS OR EVEN FOOTSTEPS FROM THE BALLROOM.
DOES THAT MEAN ...
...KONOHA AND THE OTHERS MANAGED TO EVACUATE?
...PHEW...
I CAN'T BELIEVE I'VE BEEN LEFT HERE ALL ALONE.
GOKU (GULP)
THOUGH, IT SURE MAKES ME FEEL LIKE A VILLAINESS.
GU (CLENCH)
TH—
THERE'S STILL HOPE!!

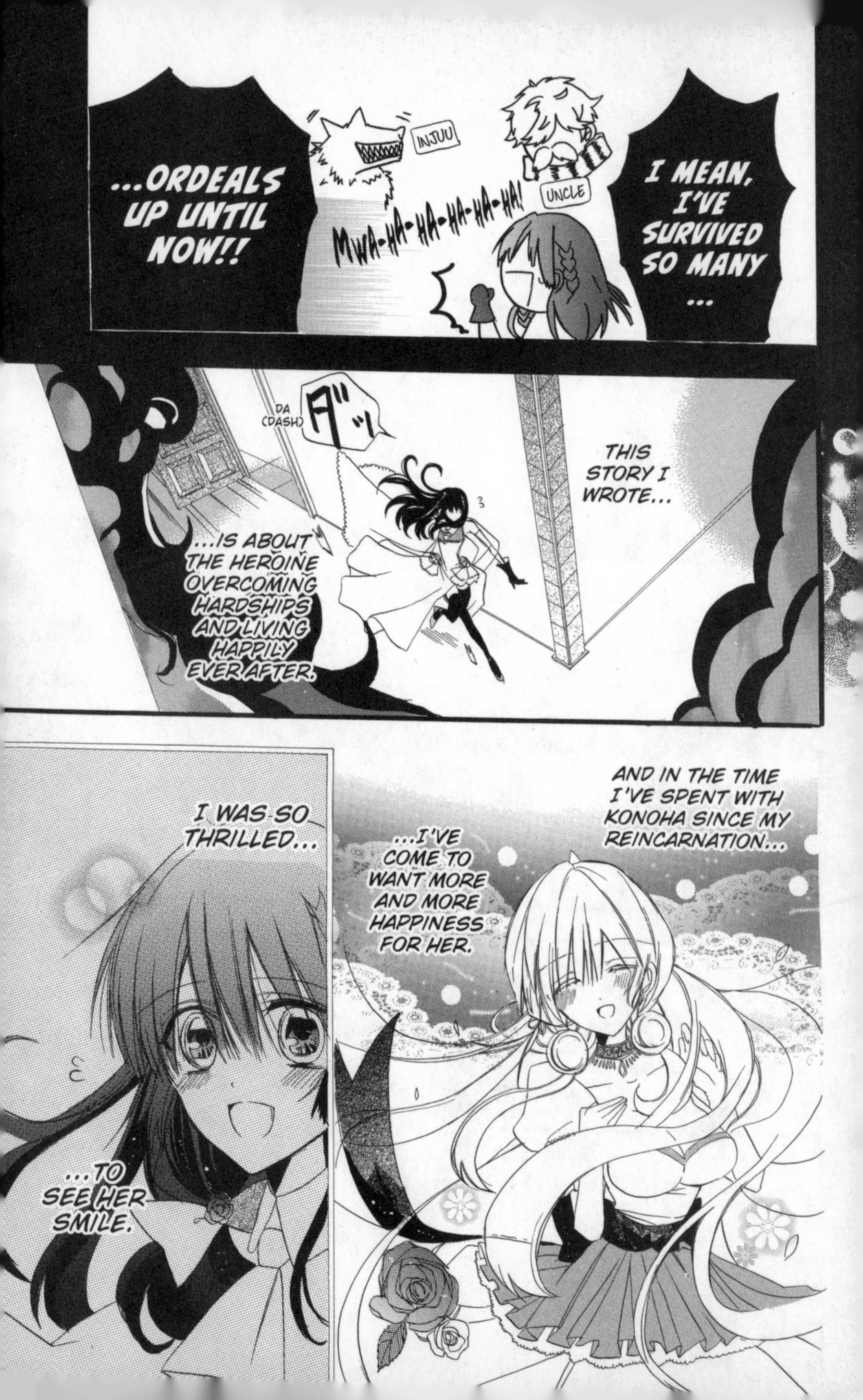
I MEAN, I'VE SURVIVED SO MANY ...
UNCLE
INJUU
MWA-HA-HA-HA-HA-HA-HA!
...ORDEALS UP UNTIL NOW!!
THIS STORY I WROTE...
DA (DASH)
...IS ABOUT THE HEROINE OVERCOMING HARDSHIPS AND LIVING HAPPILY EVER AFTER.
AND IN THE TIME I'VE SPENT WITH KONOHA SINCE MY REINCARNATION...
...I'VE COME TO WANT MORE AND MORE HAPPINESS FOR HER.
I WAS SO THRILLED...
...TO SEE HER SMILE.

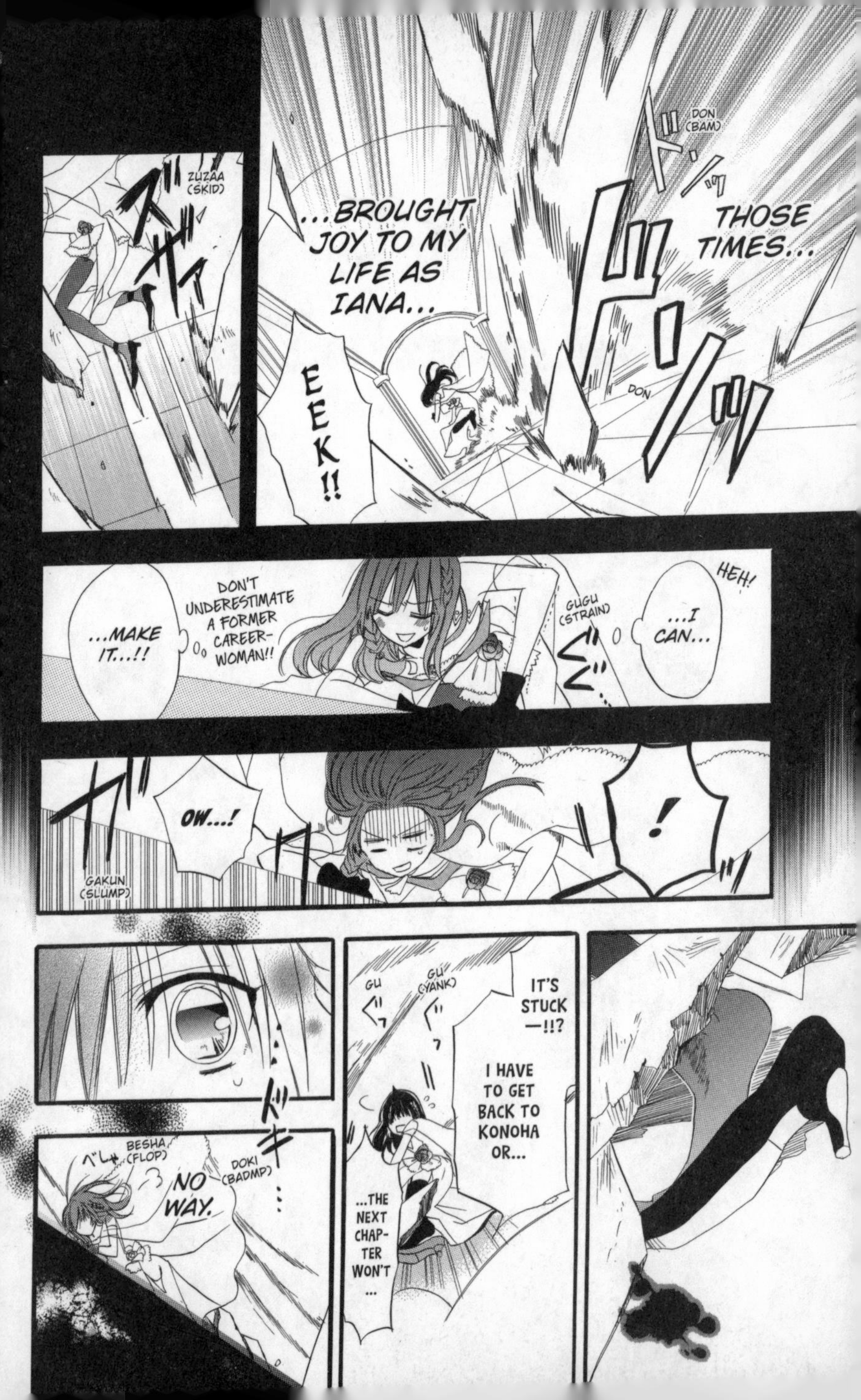
DON (BAM)
THOSE TIMES...
...BROUGHT JOY TO MY LIFE AS IANA...
EEK!!
DON
ZUZAA (SKID)
HEH!
GUGU (STRAIN)
...I CAN...
DON'T UNDERESTIMATE A FORMER CAREER-WOMAN!!
...MAKE IT...!!
!
OW...!
GAKUN (SLUMP)
IT'S STUCK—!!?
GU (YANK)
GU
I HAVE TO GET BACK TO KONOHA OR...
...THE NEXT CHAPTER WON'T ...
DOKI (BADMP)
BESHA (FLOP)
NO WAY.

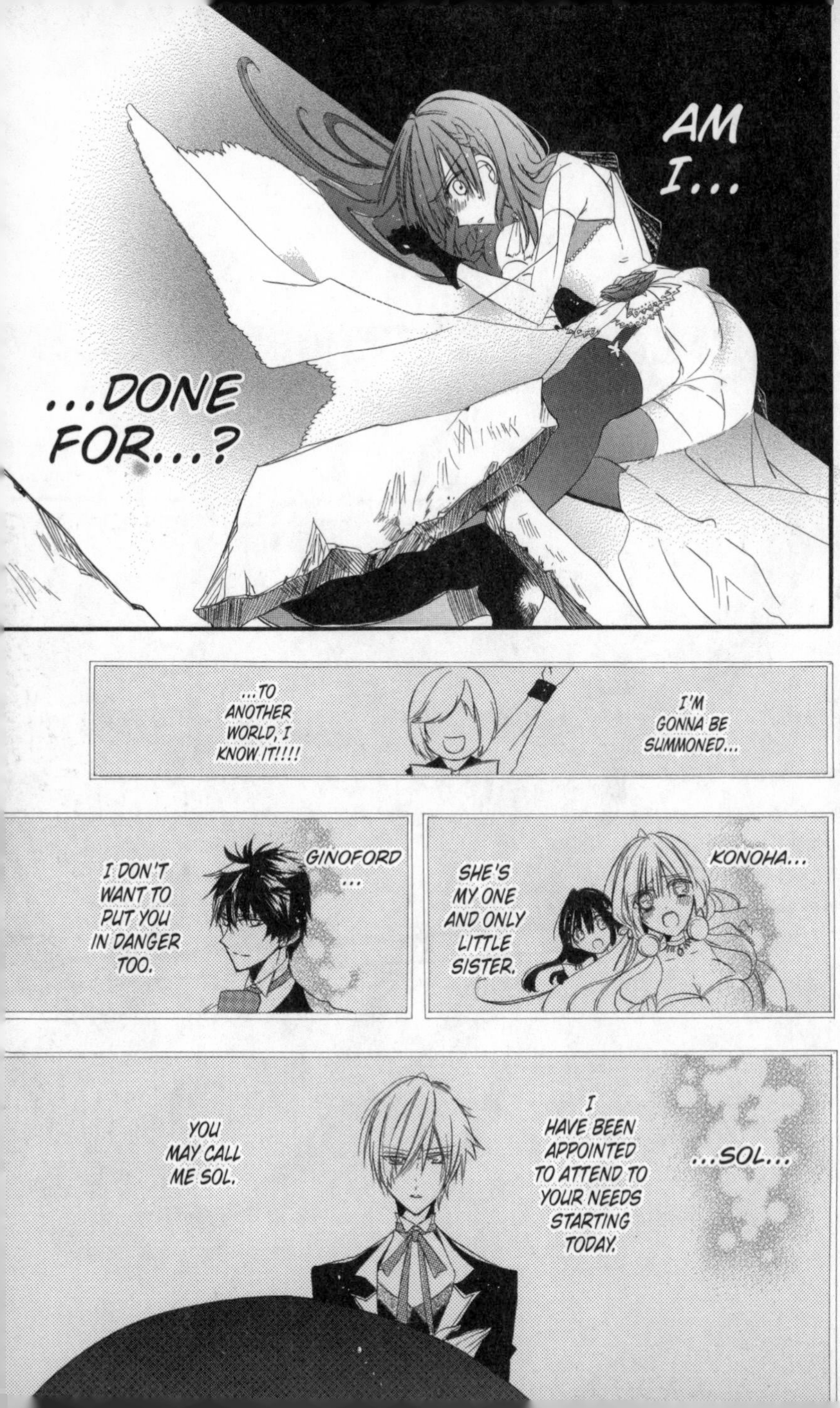
AM I...
...DONE FOR...?
I'M GONNA BE SUMMONED...
...TO ANOTHER WORLD, I KNOW IT!!!!
KONOHA...
SHE'S MY ONE AND ONLY LITTLE SISTER.
GINOFORD...
I DON'T WANT TO PUT YOU IN DANGER TOO.
...SOL...
I HAVE BEEN APPOINTED TO ATTEND TO YOUR NEEDS STARTING TODAY.
YOU MAY CALL ME SOL.

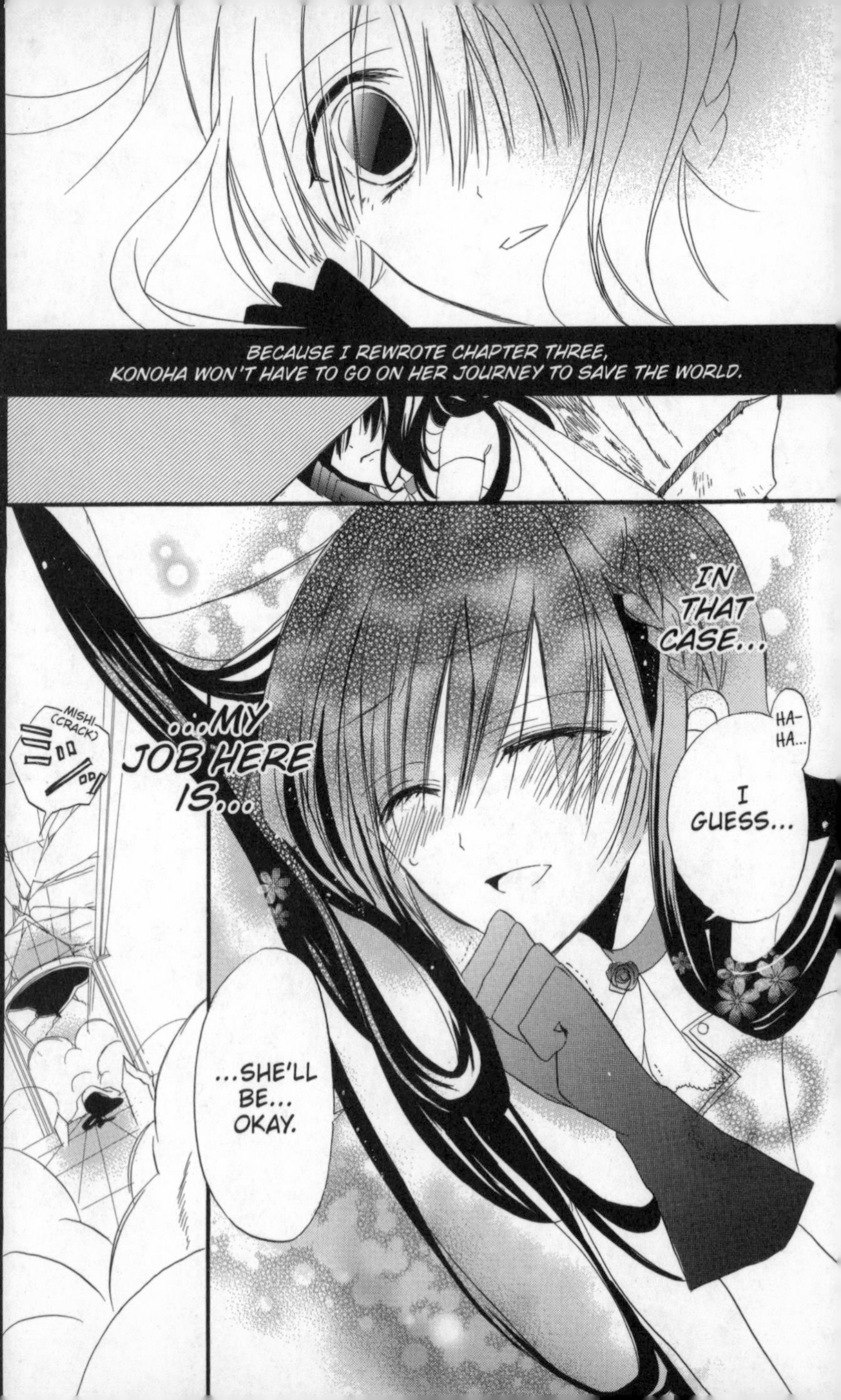
BECAUSE I REWROTE CHAPTER THREE, KONOHA WON'T HAVE TO GO ON HER JOURNEY TO SAVE THE WORLD.
IN THAT CASE...
HA-HA...
I GUESS...
...MY JOB HERE IS...
MISHI (CRACK)
...SHE'LL BE... OKAY.

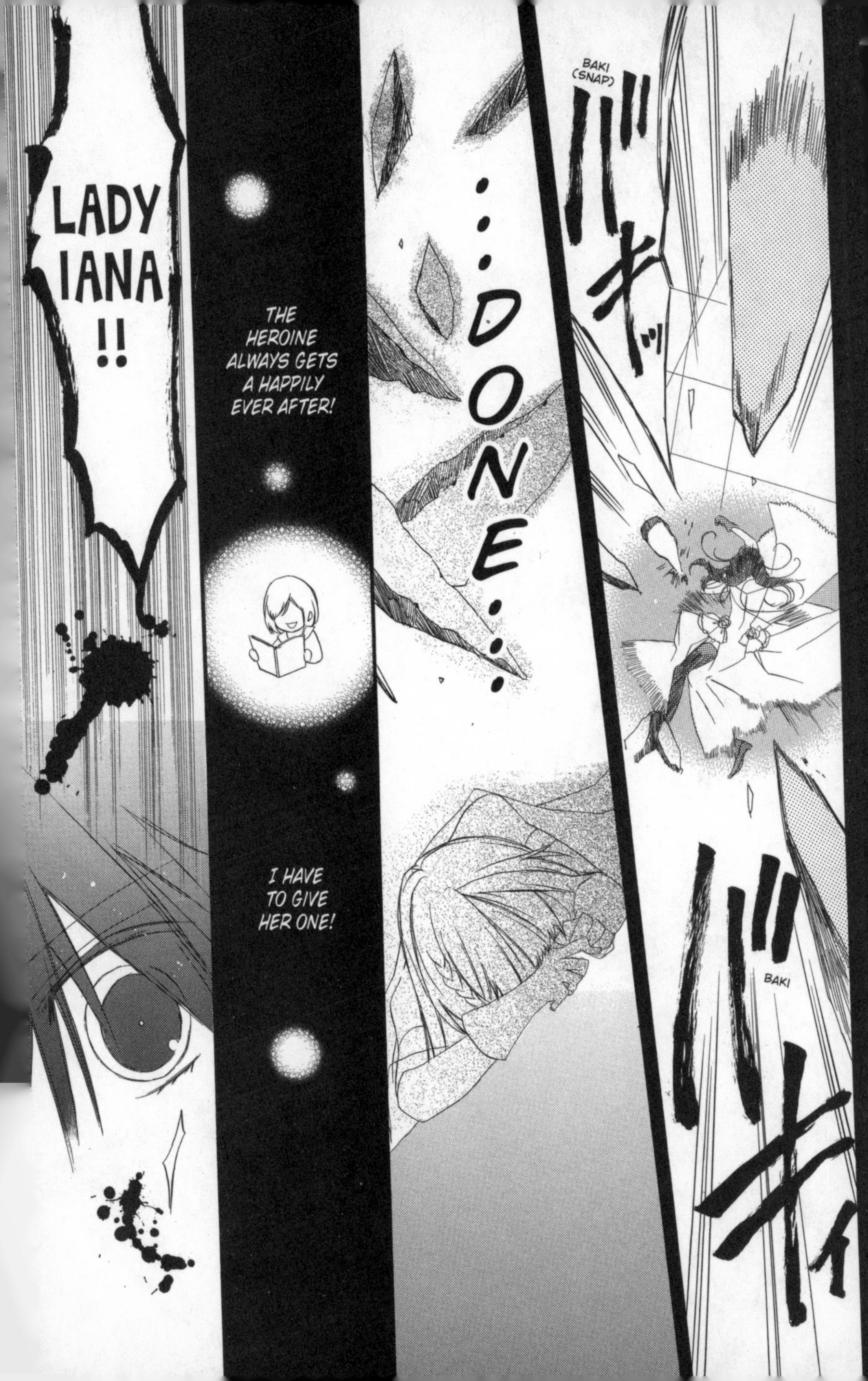
BAKI (SNAP)
バキッ
BAKI
バキィ
...DONE...
THE HEROINE ALWAYS GETS A HAPPILY EVER AFTER!
I HAVE TO GIVE HER ONE!
LADY IANA!!

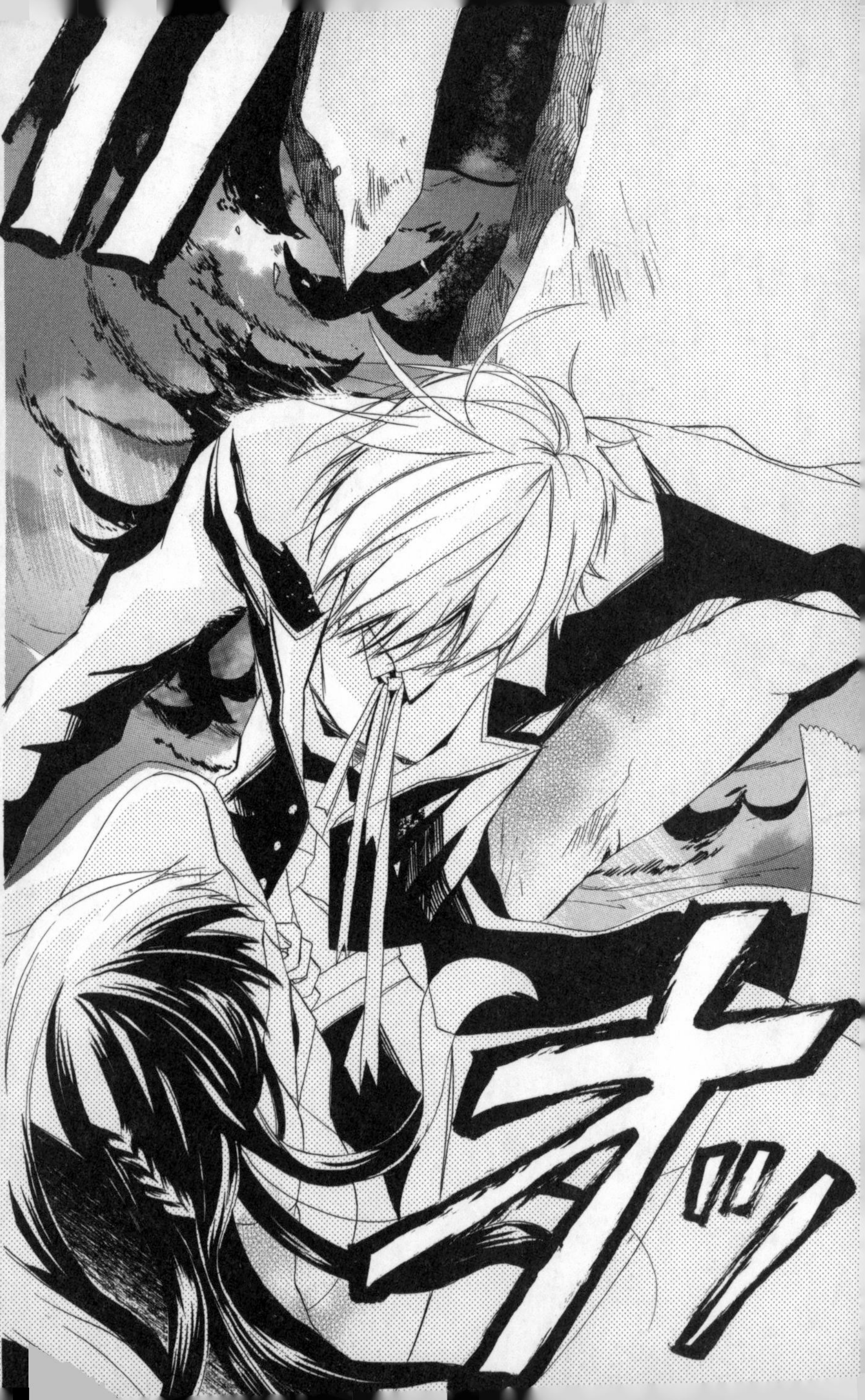
ズッ

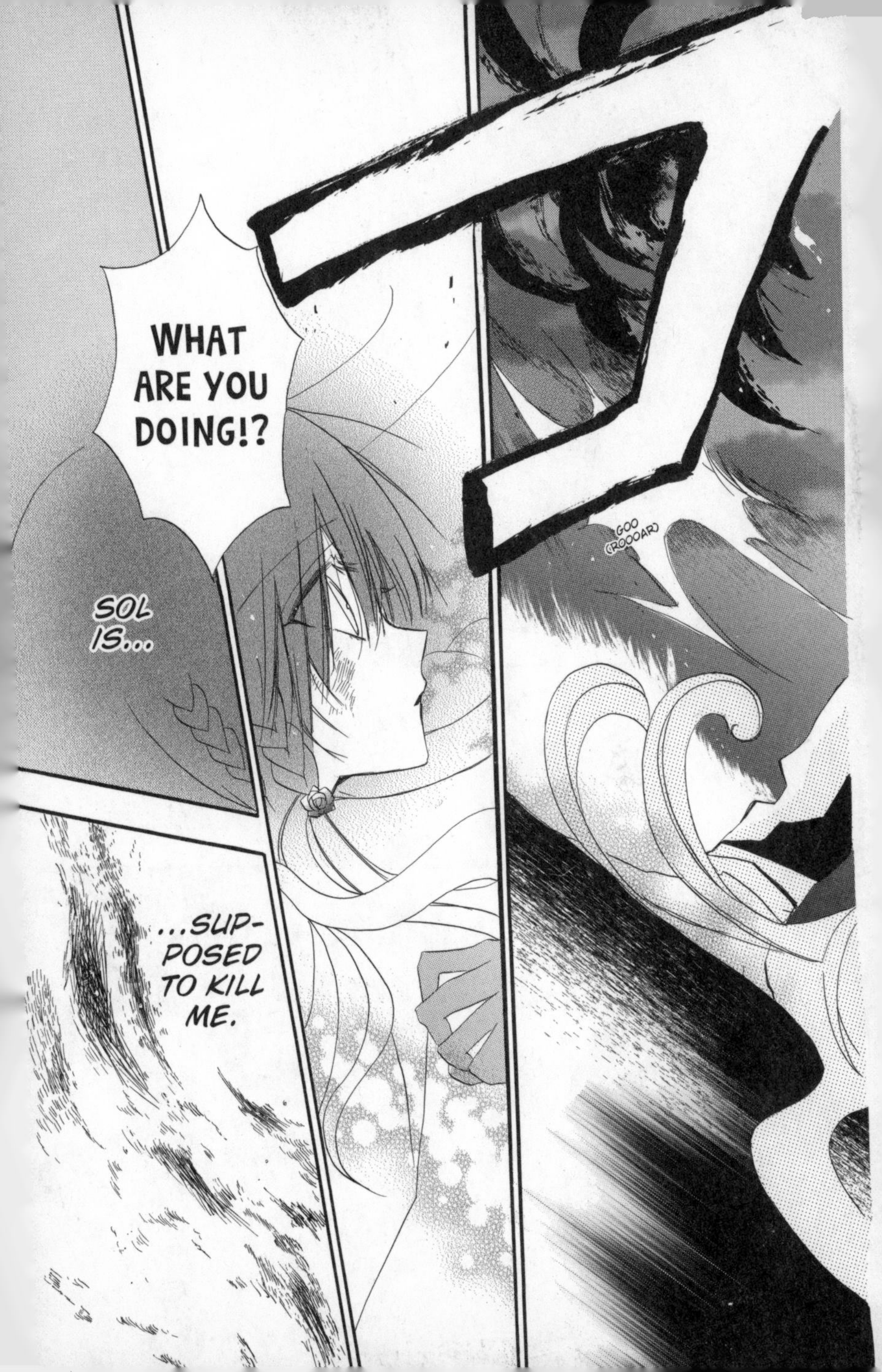
GOO (ROOOAR)
WHAT ARE YOU DOING!?
SOL IS...
...SUP-POSED TO KILL ME.

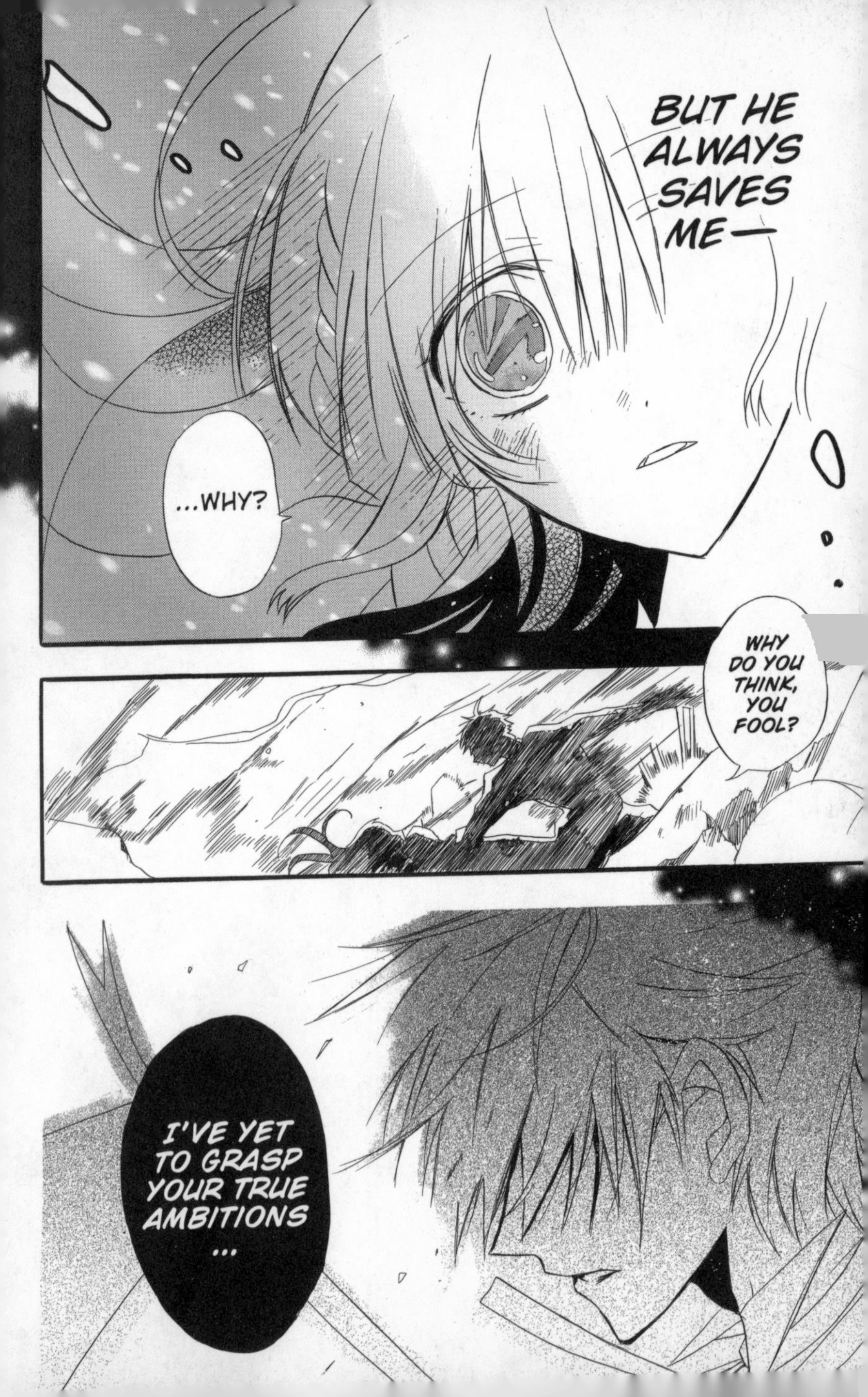
BUT HE ALWAYS SAVES ME—
...WHY?
WHY DO YOU THINK, YOU FOOL?
I'VE YET TO GRASP YOUR TRUE AMBITIONS ...

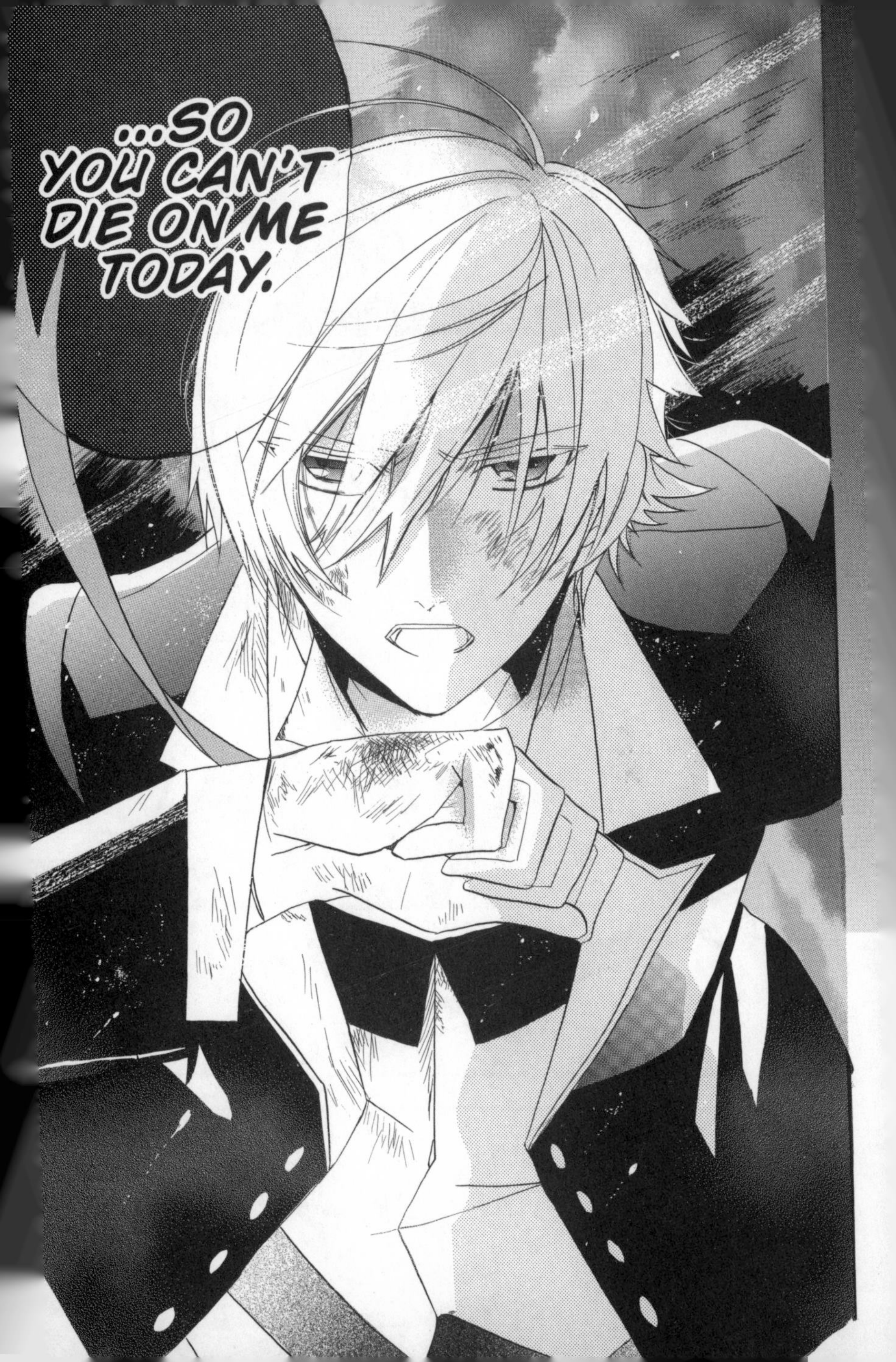
...SO YOU CAN'T DIE ON ME TODAY.

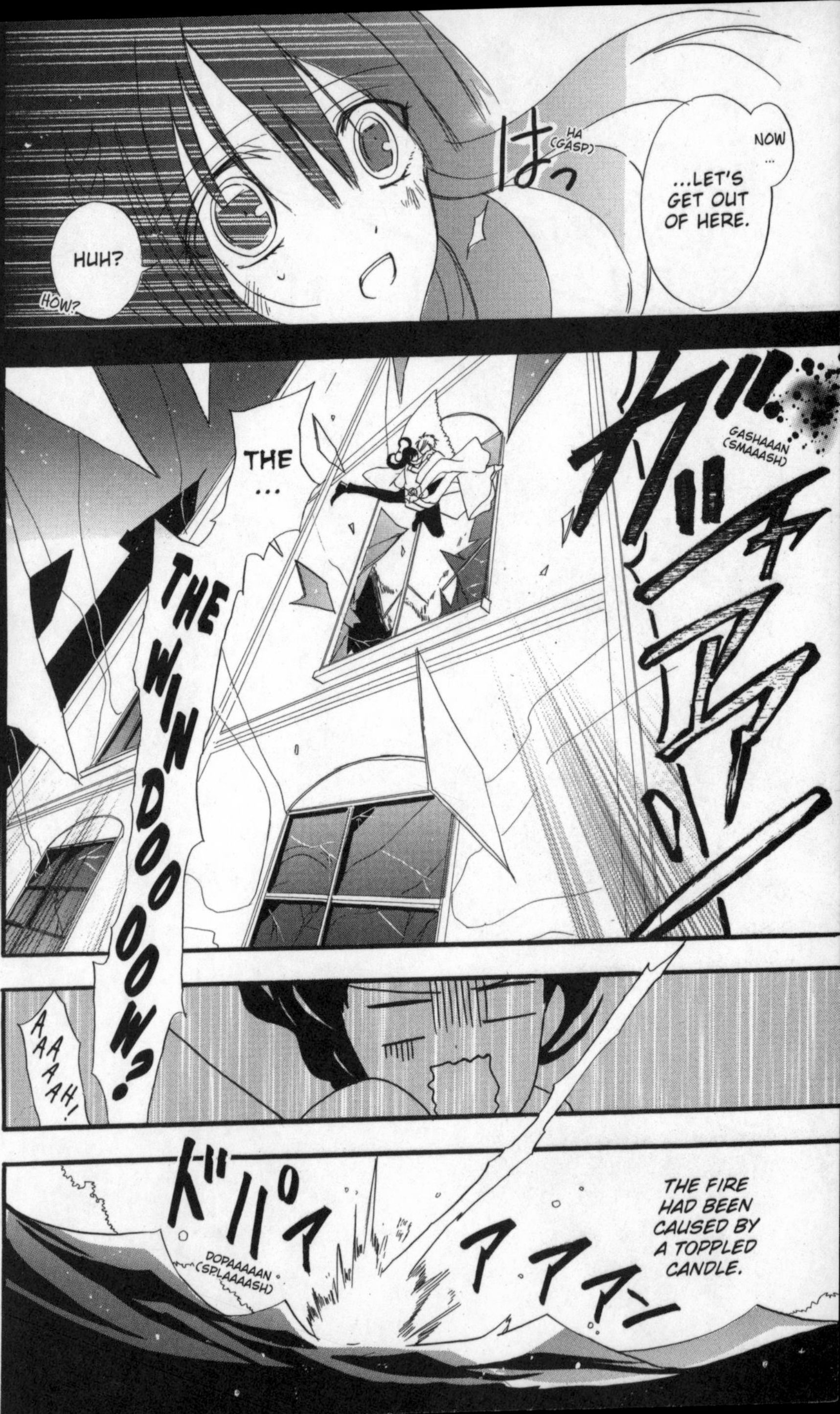
NOW ...
...LET'S GET OUT OF HERE.
HA (GASP)
HUH?
HOW?
GASHAAAN (SMAAASH)
THE ...
THE WINDOOOOOOW?!
AAAAAH!
THE FIRE HAD BEEN CAUSED BY A TOPPLED CANDLE.
DOPAAAAAN (SPLAAAASH)

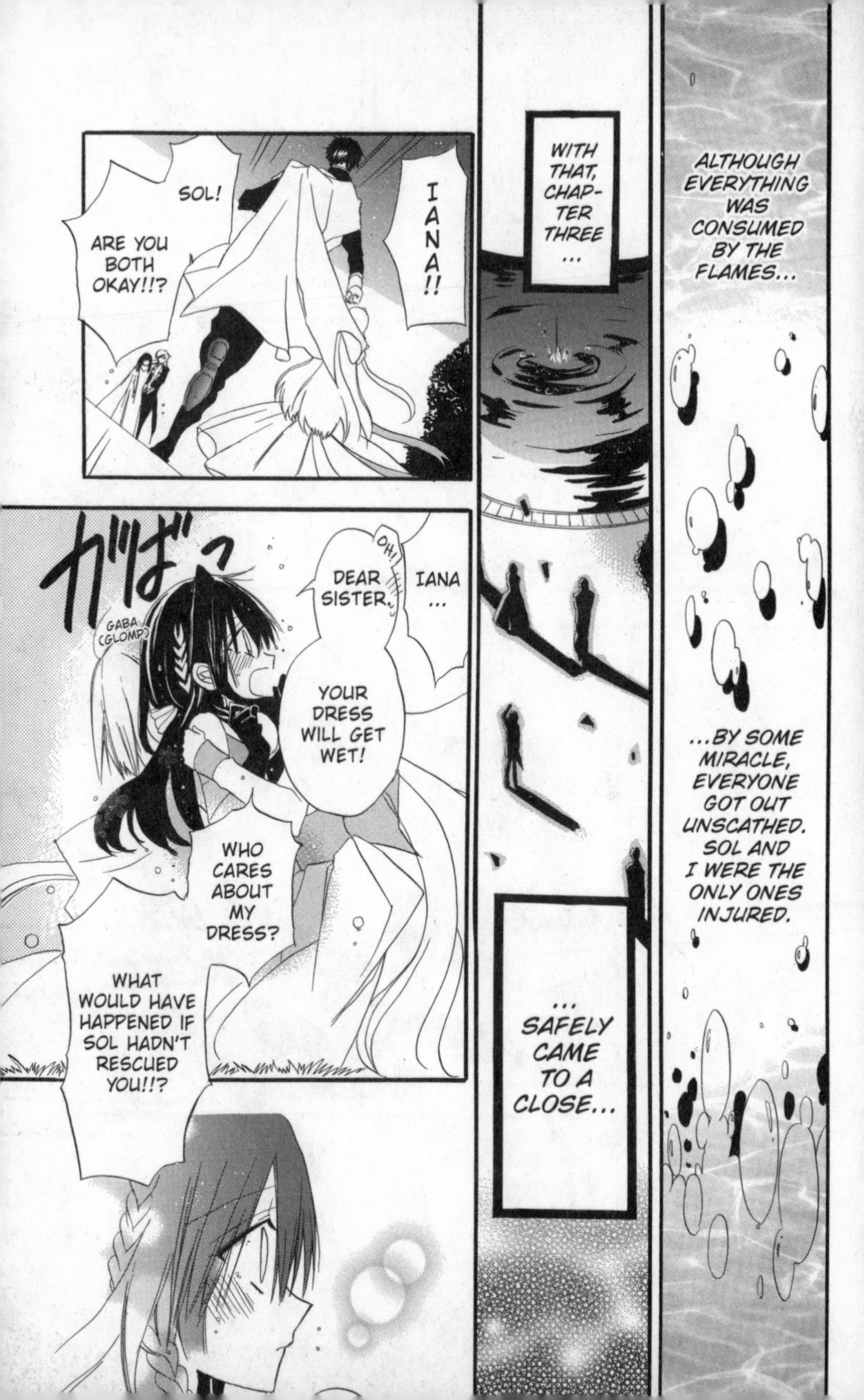
ALTHOUGH EVERYTHING WAS CONSUMED BY THE FLAMES...
...BY SOME MIRACLE, EVERYONE GOT OUT UNSCATHED. SOL AND I WERE THE ONLY ONES INJURED.
WITH THAT, CHAPTER THREE...
...SAFELY CAME TO A CLOSE...
IANA!!
SOL!
ARE YOU BOTH OKAY!!?
OH!
IANA...
DEAR SISTER...
がばっ
GABA (GLOMP)
YOUR DRESS WILL GET WET!
WHO CARES ABOUT MY DRESS?
WHAT WOULD HAVE HAPPENED IF SOL HADN'T RESCUED YOU!!?

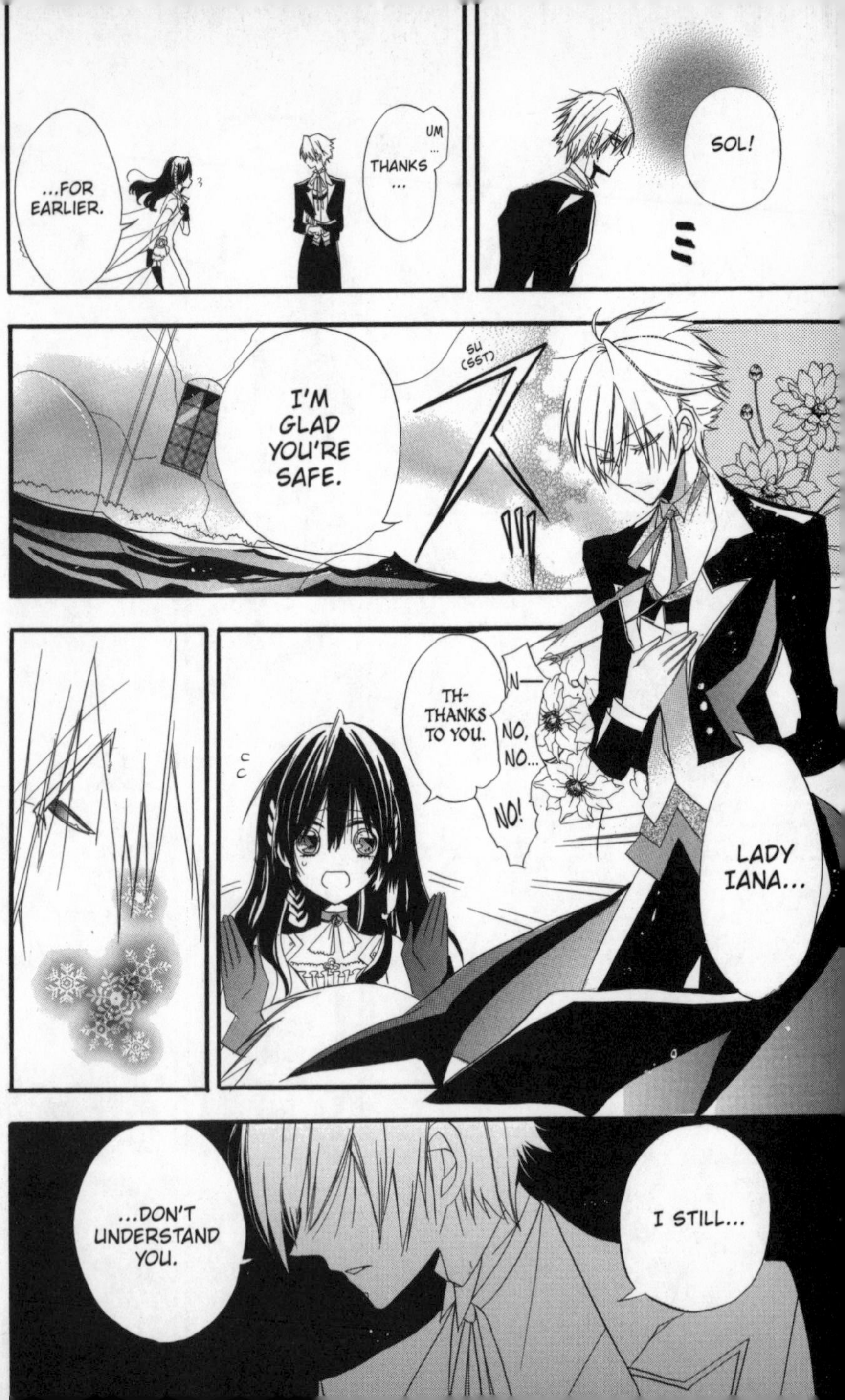
SOL!
UM ... THANKS ...
...FOR EARLIER.
SU (SST)
I'M GLAD YOU'RE SAFE.
TH-THANKS TO YOU.
N—
NO, NO...
NO!
LADY IANA...
I STILL...
...DON'T UNDERSTAND YOU.

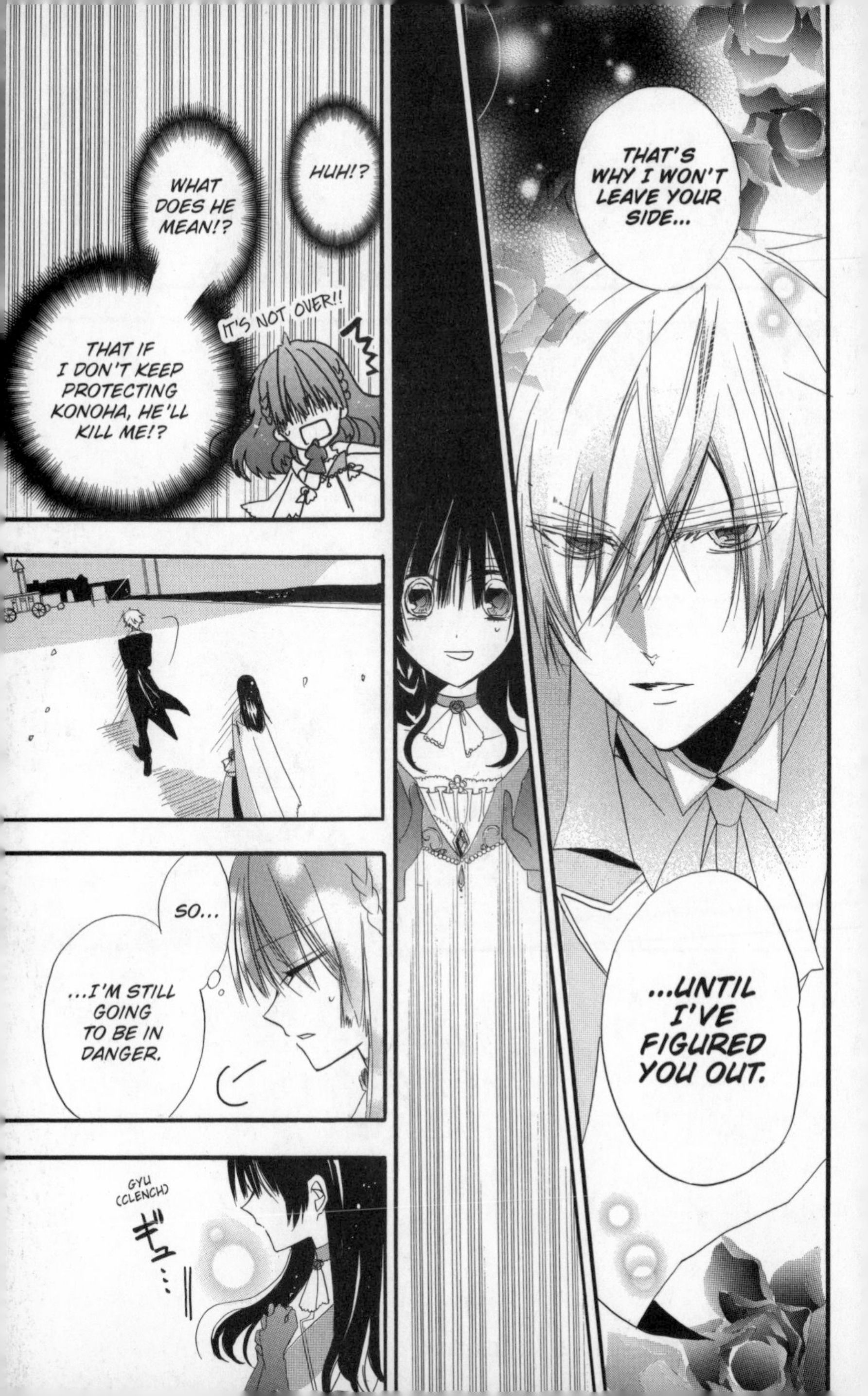
THAT'S WHY I WON'T LEAVE YOUR SIDE...
...UNTIL I'VE FIGURED YOU OUT.
HUH!?
WHAT DOES HE MEAN!?
IT'S NOT OVER!!
THAT IF I DON'T KEEP PROTECTING KONOHA, HE'LL KILL ME!?
SO...
...I'M STILL GOING TO BE IN DANGER.
GYU (CLENCH)
ギュ…

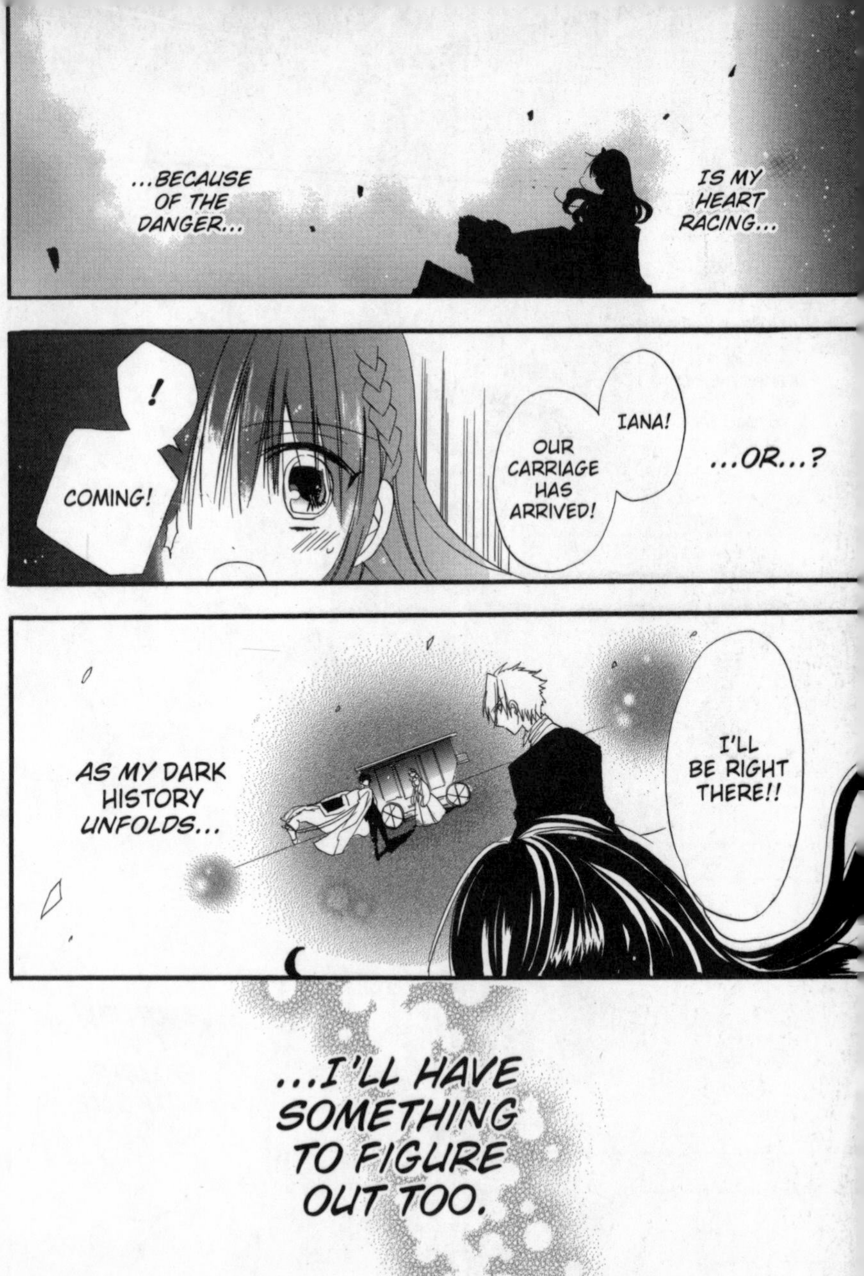
IS MY HEART RACING...
...BECAUSE OF THE DANGER...
...OR...?
IANA! OUR CARRIAGE HAS ARRIVED!
!
COMING!
I'LL BE RIGHT THERE!!
AS MY DARK HISTORY UNFOLDS...
...I'LL HAVE SOMETHING TO FIGURE OUT TOO.

THE DARK HISTORY OF THE REINCARNATED VILLAINESS ① END

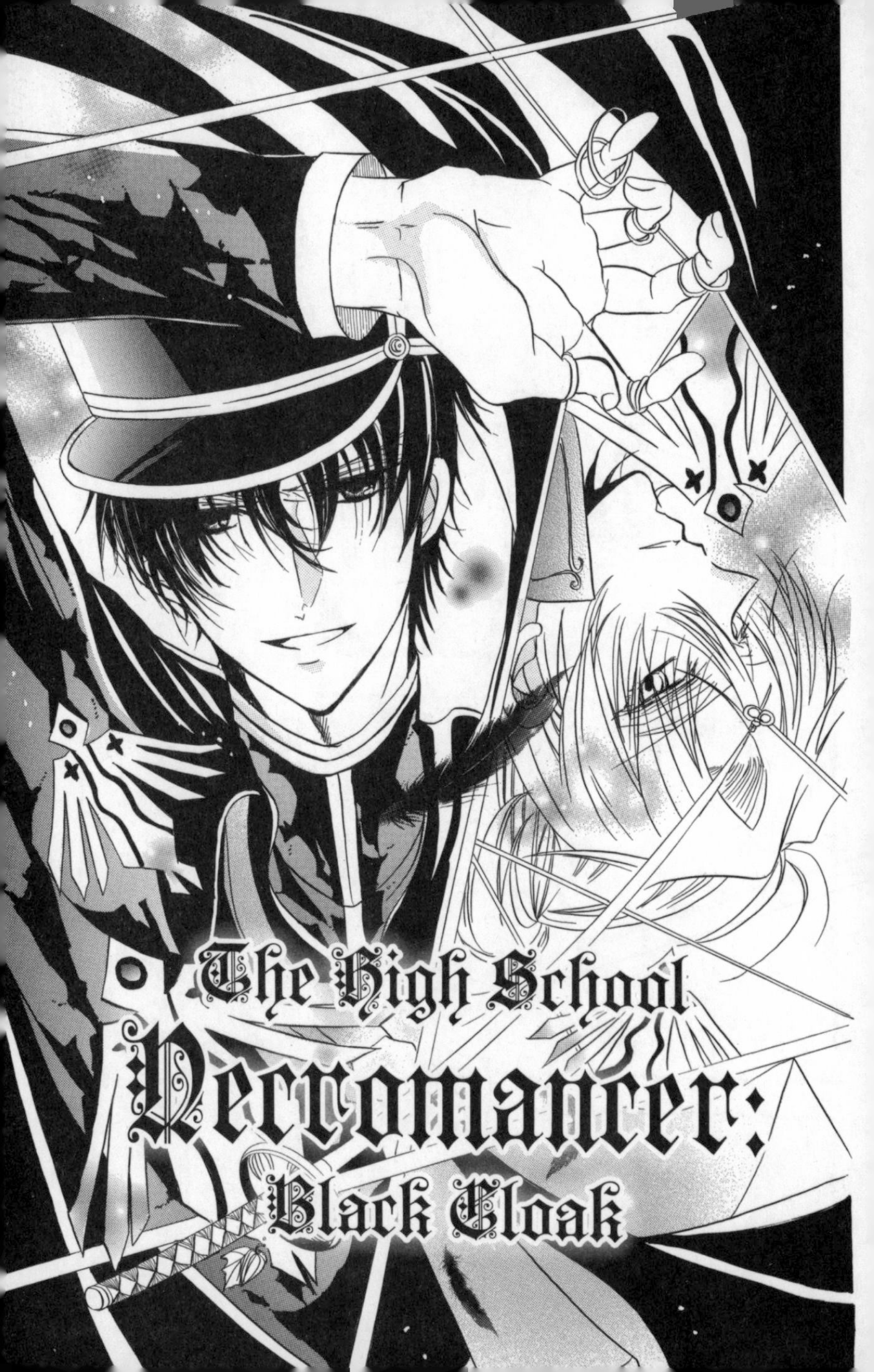
The High School
Necromancer:
Black Cloak

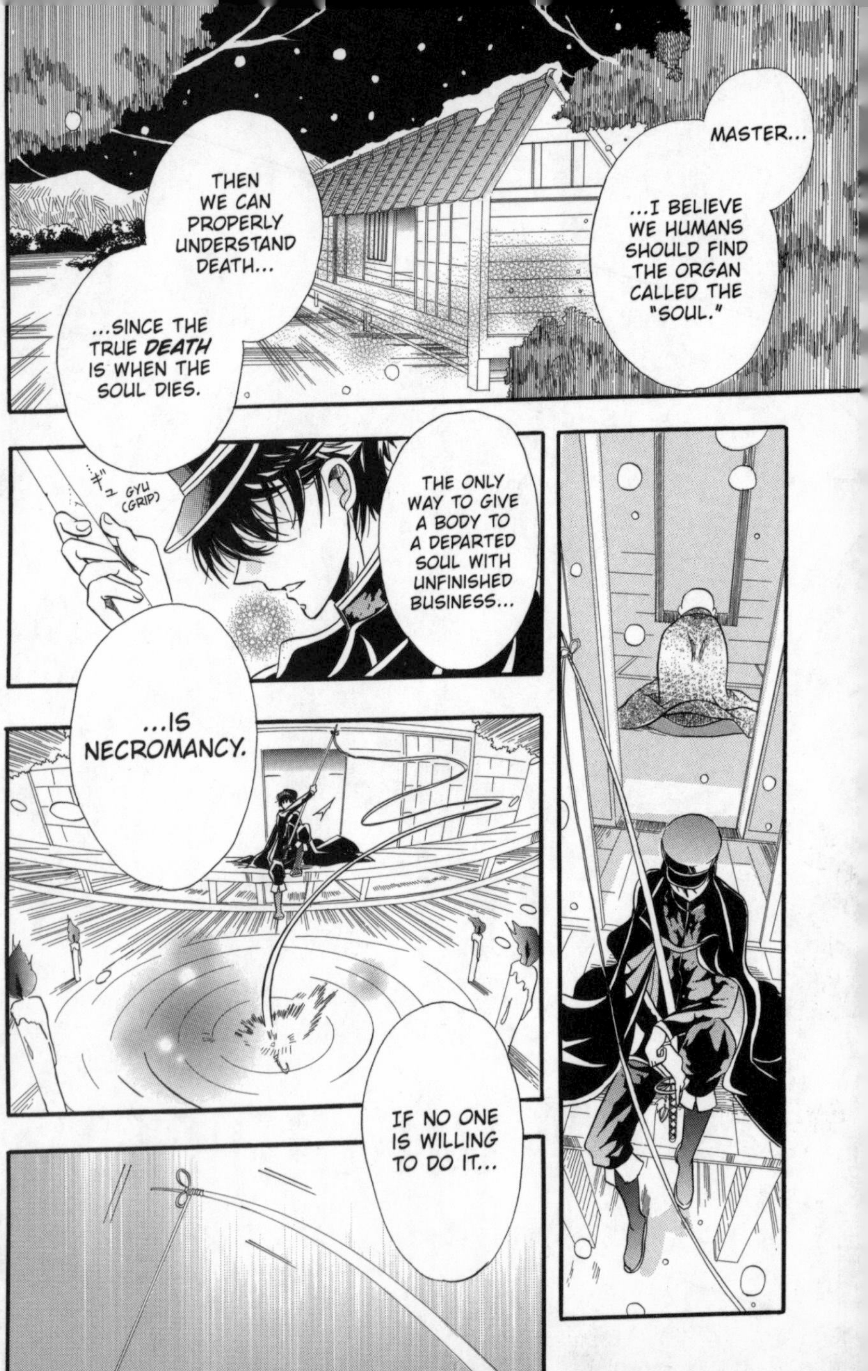
MASTER...
...I BELIEVE WE HUMANS SHOULD FIND THE ORGAN CALLED THE "SOUL."
THEN WE CAN PROPERLY UNDERSTAND DEATH...
...SINCE THE TRUE *DEATH* IS WHEN THE SOUL DIES.
THE ONLY WAY TO GIVE A BODY TO A DEPARTED SOUL WITH UNFINISHED BUSINESS...
ギュ
GYU (GRIP)
...IS NECROMANCY.
IF NO ONE IS WILLING TO DO IT...

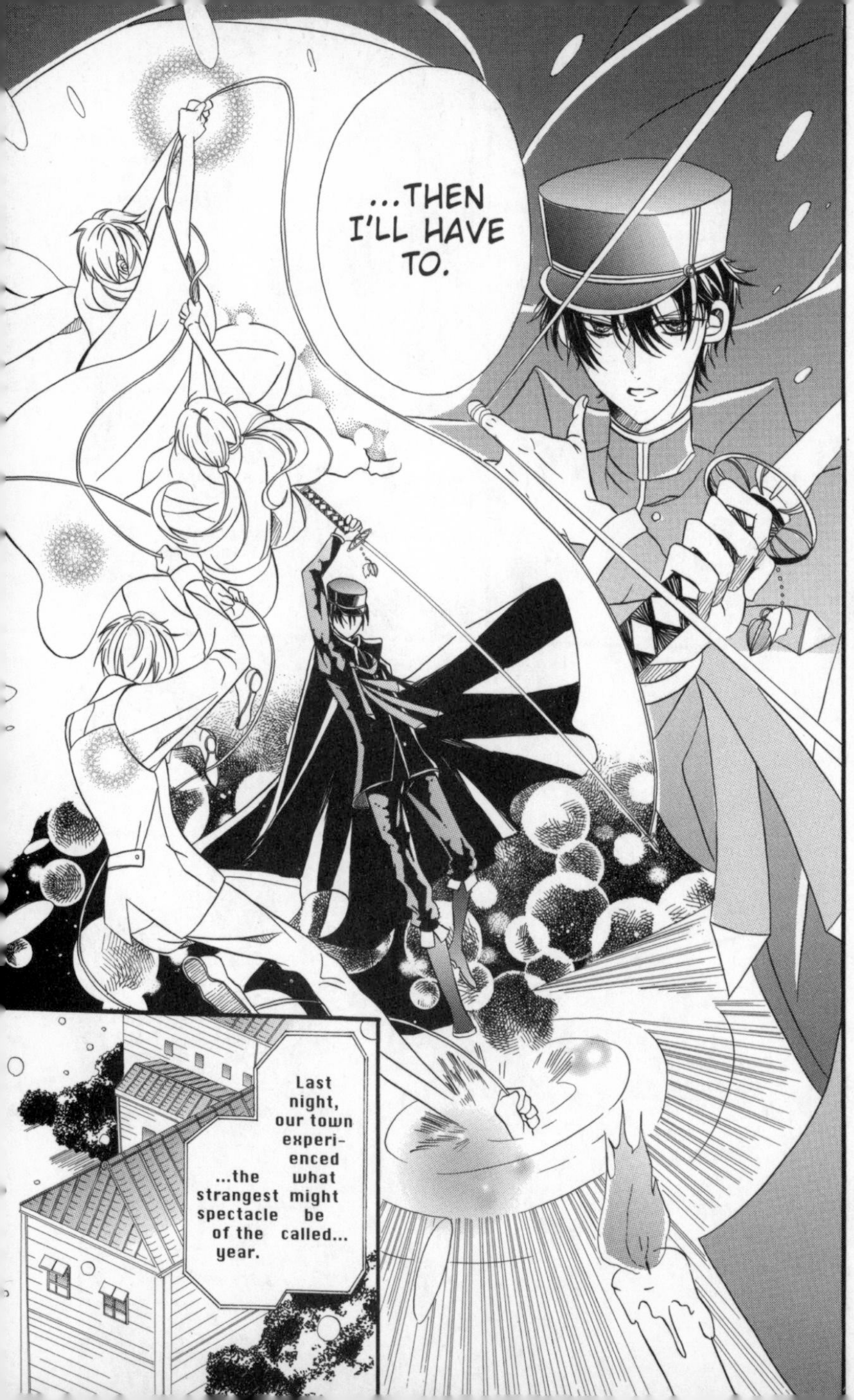
...THEN I'LL HAVE TO.
Last night, our town experienced what might be called...
...the strangest spectacle of the year.

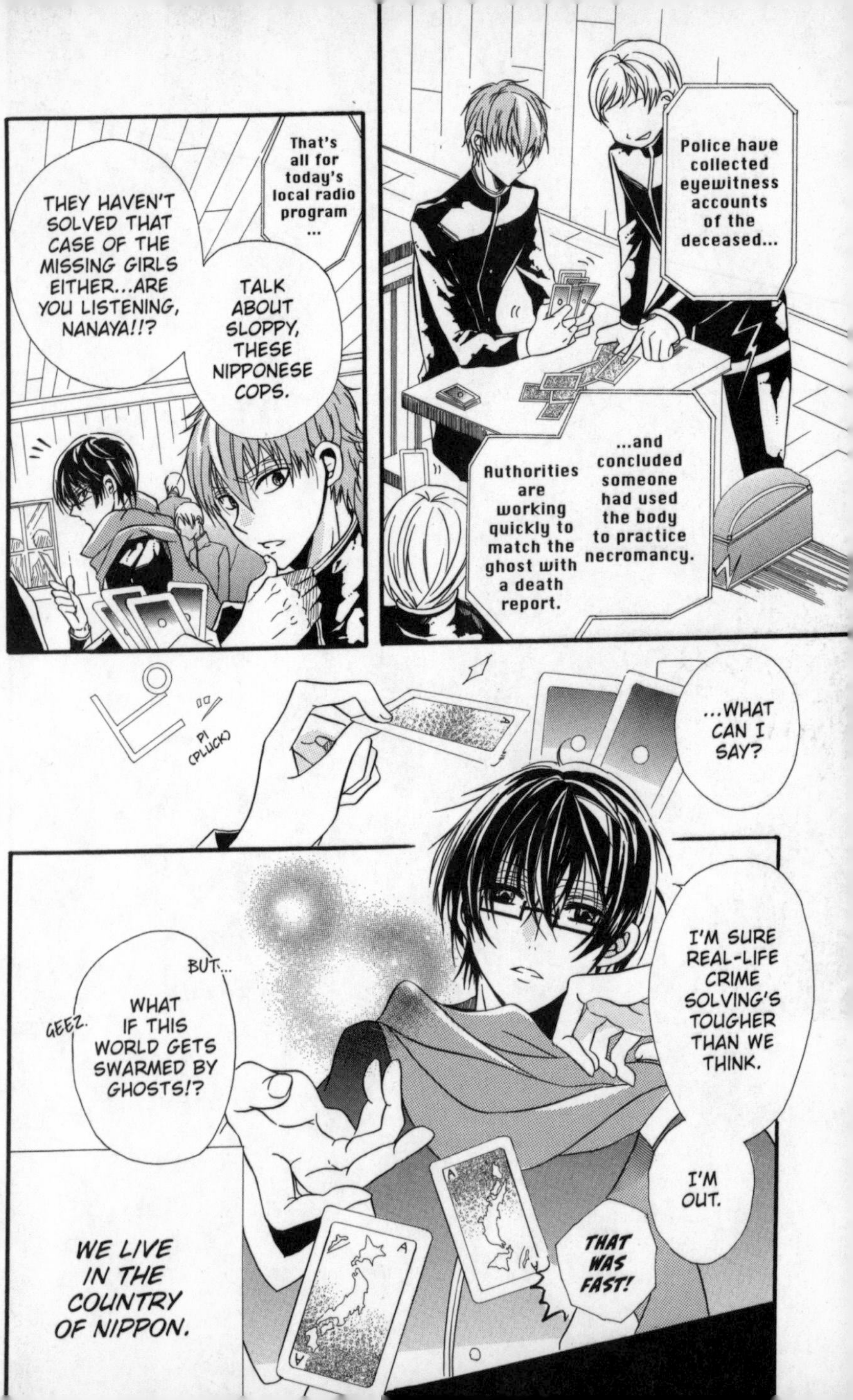
Police have collected eyewitness accounts of the deceased...
...and concluded someone had used the body to practice necromancy.
Authorities are working quickly to match the ghost with a death report.
That's all for today's local radio program ...
TALK ABOUT SLOPPY, THESE NIPPONESE COPS.
THEY HAVEN'T SOLVED THAT CASE OF THE MISSING GIRLS EITHER...ARE YOU LISTENING, NANAYA!!?
...WHAT CAN I SAY?
PI (PLUCK)
I'M SURE REAL-LIFE CRIME SOLVING'S TOUGHER THAN WE THINK.
I'M OUT.
THAT WAS FAST!
BUT...
WHAT IF THIS WORLD GETS SWARMED BY GHOSTS!?
GEEZ.
WE LIVE IN THE COUNTRY OF NIPPON.

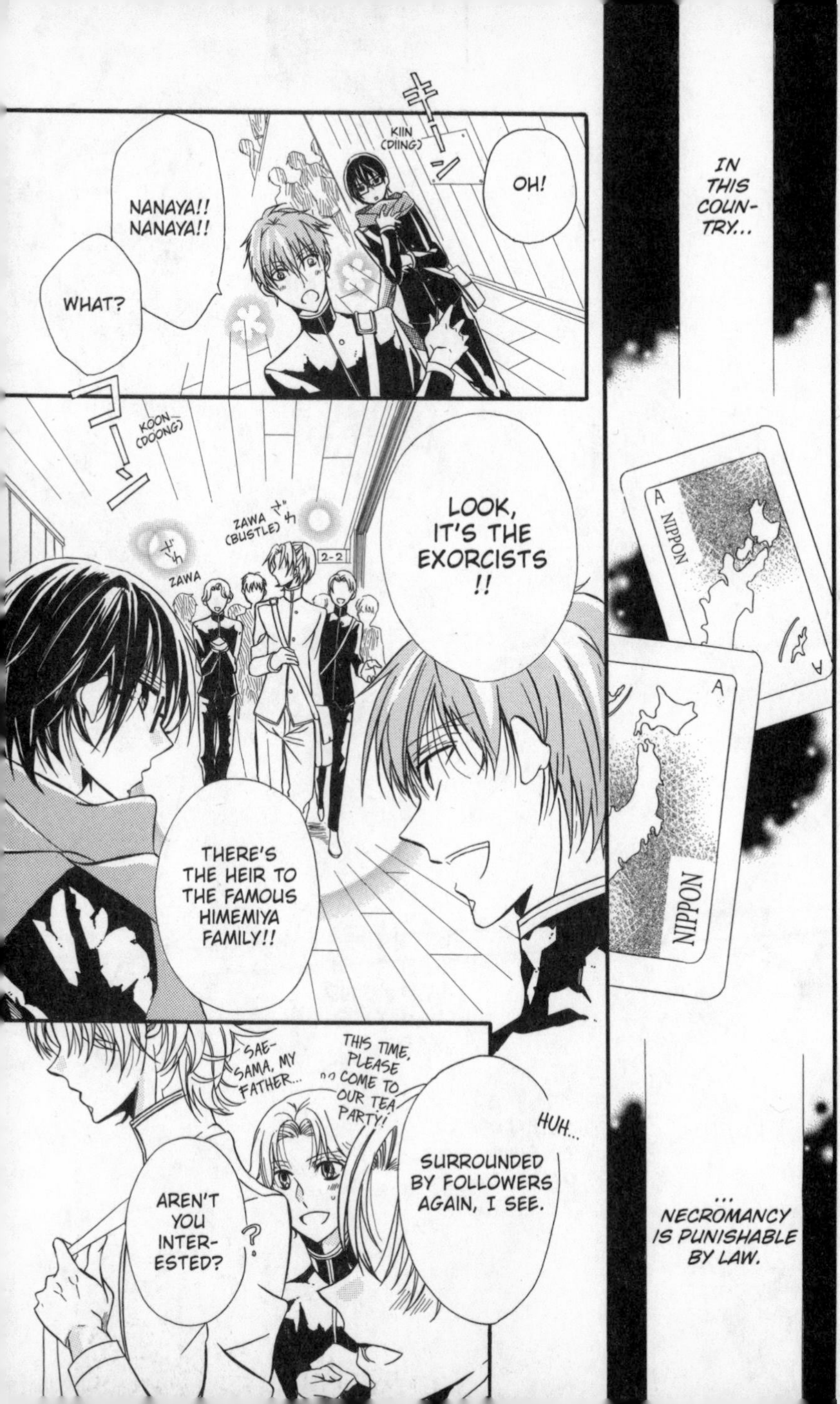
IN THIS COUN-TRY...
A
NIPPON
A
NIPPON
...NECROMANCY IS PUNISHABLE BY LAW.
OH!
KIIN (DIING)
NANAYA!! NANAYA!!
WHAT?
LOOK, IT'S THE EXORCISTS!!
KOON (DOONG)
ZAWA (BUSTLE)
ZAWA
2-2
THERE'S THE HEIR TO THE FAMOUS HIMEMIYA FAMILY!!
HUH...
SURROUNDED BY FOLLOWERS AGAIN, I SEE.
THIS TIME, PLEASE COME TO OUR TEA PARTY!
SAE-SAMA, MY FATHER...
AREN'T YOU INTERESTED?
?

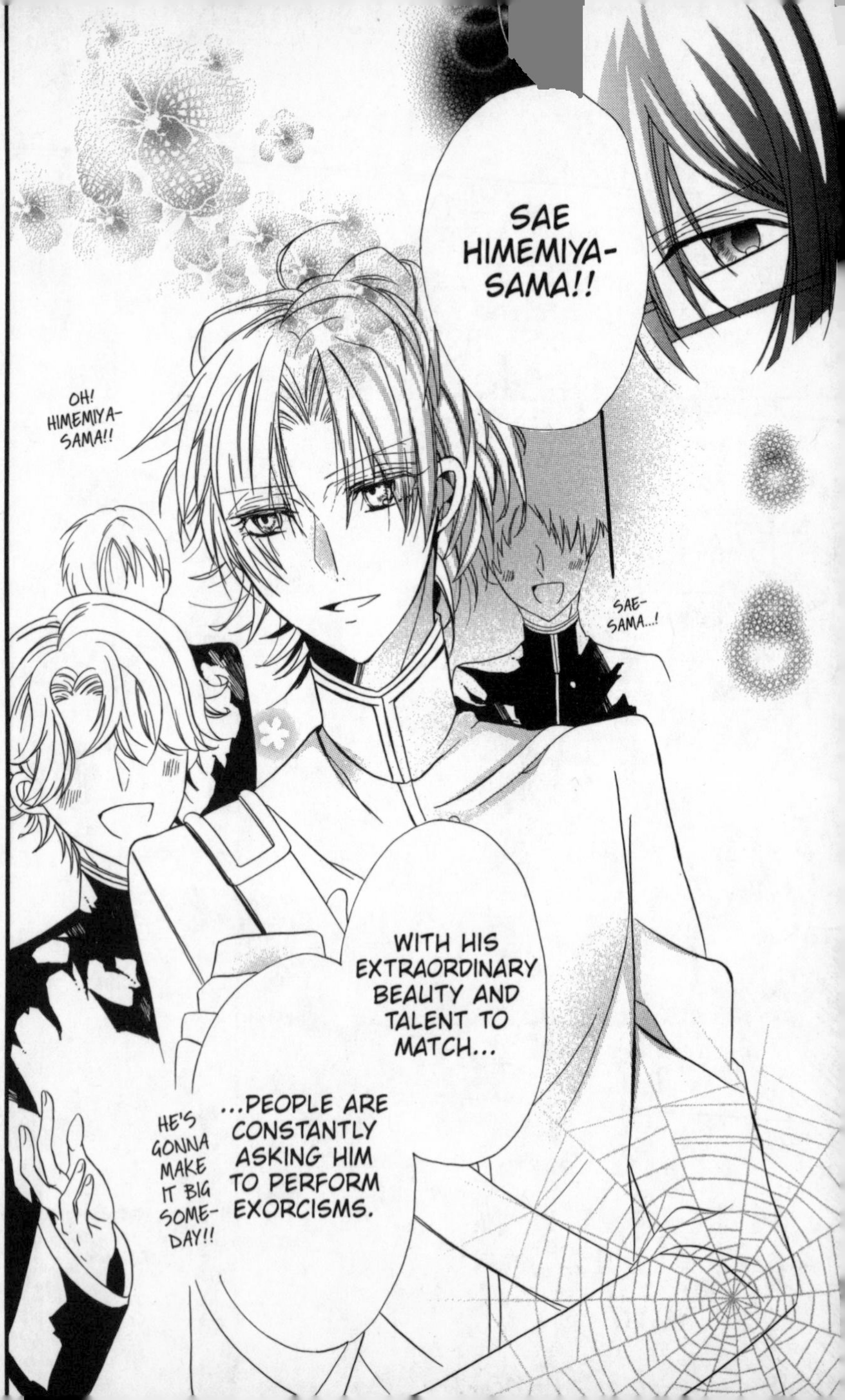
SAE HIMEMIYA-SAMA!!
SAE-SAMA...!
OH! HIMEMIYA-SAMA!!
WITH HIS EXTRAORDINARY BEAUTY AND TALENT TO MATCH...
...PEOPLE ARE CONSTANTLY ASKING HIM TO PERFORM EXORCISMS.
HE'S GONNA MAKE IT BIG SOME-DAY!!

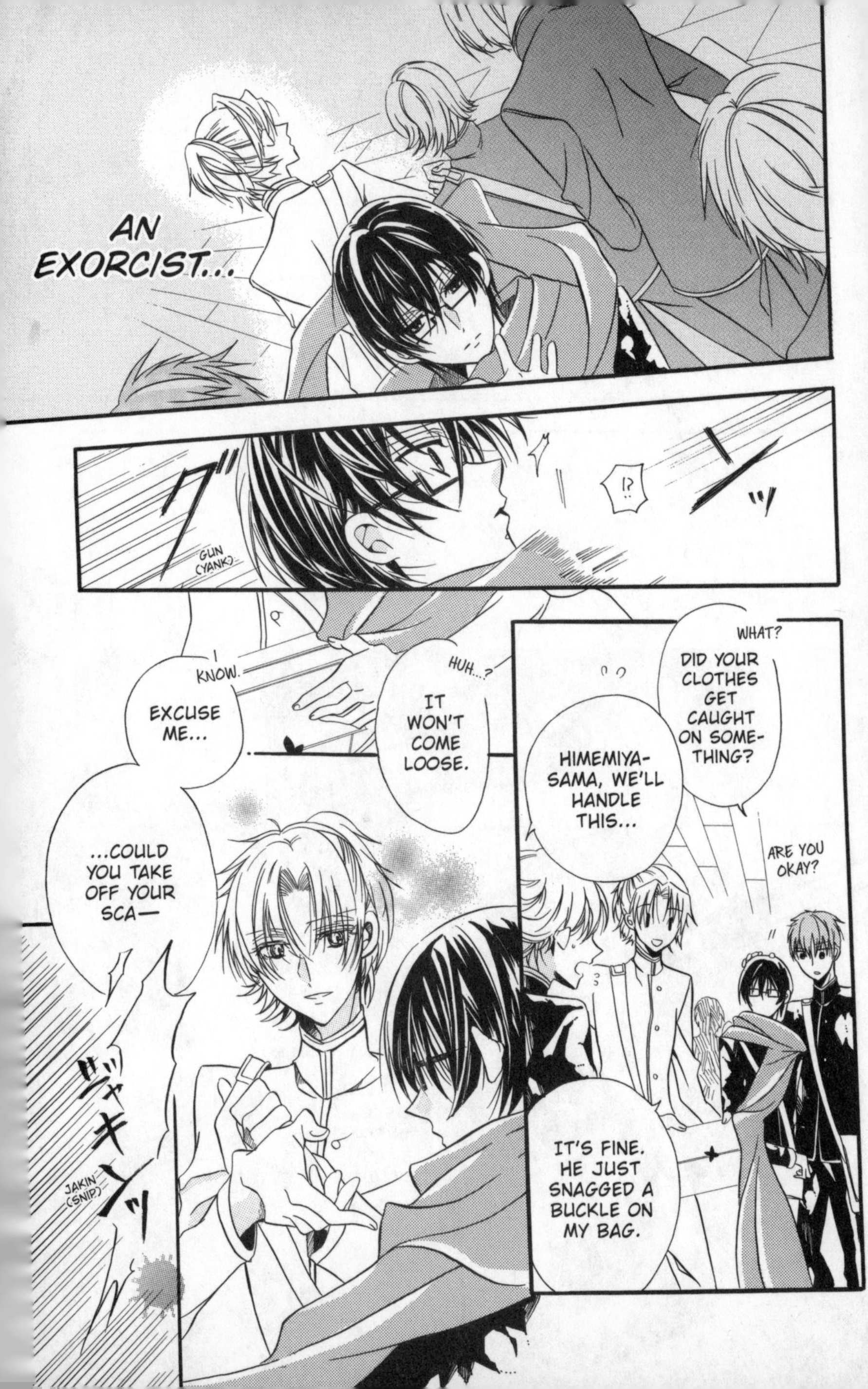
AN EXORCIST...
GUN (YANK)
!?
WHAT?
DID YOUR CLOTHES GET CAUGHT ON SOMETHING?
HIMEMIYA-SAMA, WE'LL HANDLE THIS...
ARE YOU OKAY?
IT'S FINE. HE JUST SNAGGED A BUCKLE ON MY BAG.
HUH...?
IT WON'T COME LOOSE.
I KNOW.
EXCUSE ME...
...COULD YOU TAKE OFF YOUR SCA—
JAKIN (SNIP)

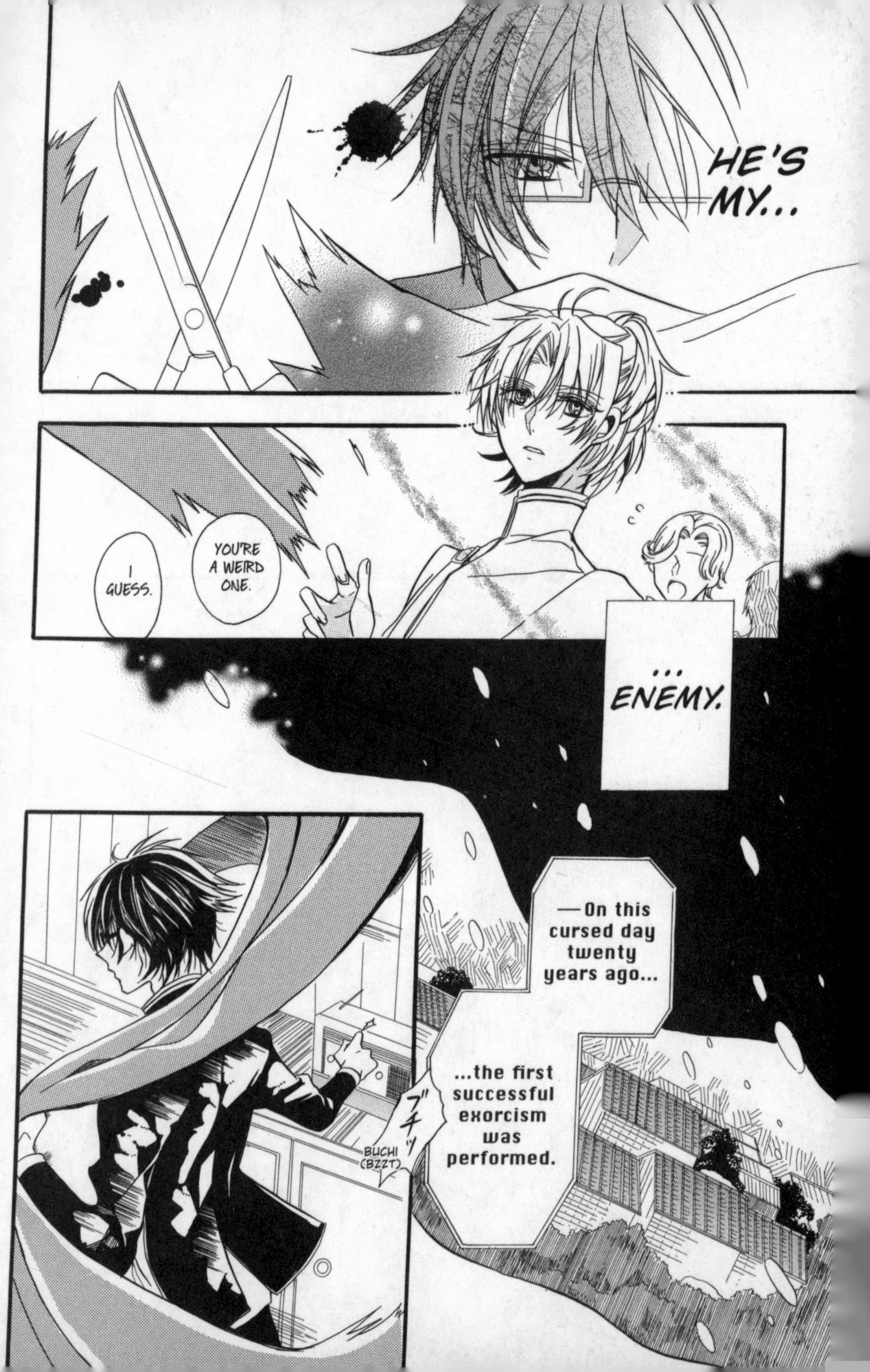
HE'S MY...
YOU'RE A WEIRD ONE.
I GUESS.
...ENEMY.
—On this cursed day twenty years ago...
...the first successful exorcism was performed.
ブチッ
BUCHI (BZZT)

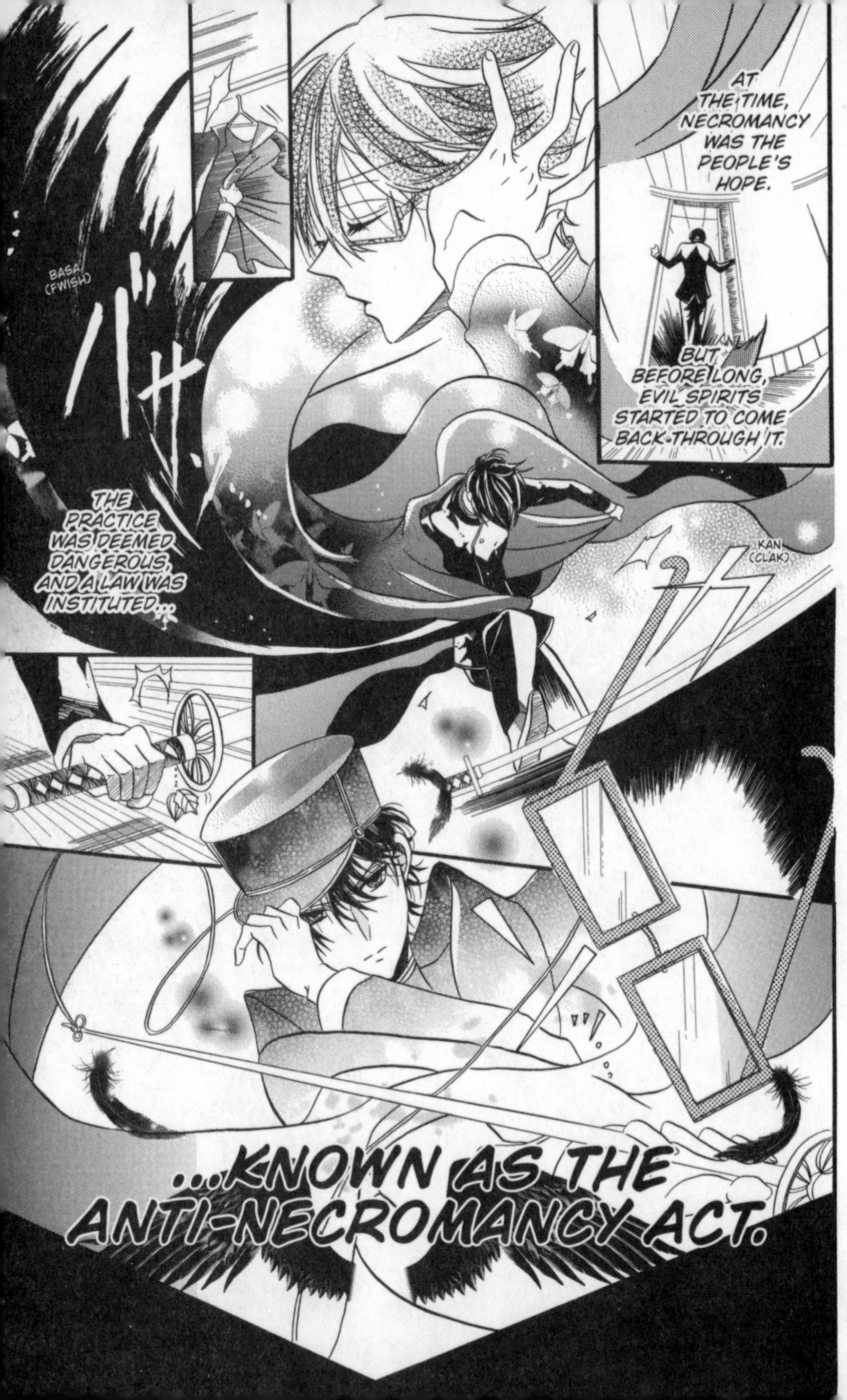
AT THE TIME, NECROMANCY WAS THE PEOPLE'S HOPE.
BUT BEFORE LONG, EVIL SPIRITS STARTED TO COME BACK THROUGH IT.
BASA (FWISH)
THE PRACTICE WAS DEEMED DANGEROUS, AND A LAW WAS INSTITUTED...
KAN (CLAK)
...KNOWN AS THE ANTI-NECROMANCY ACT.

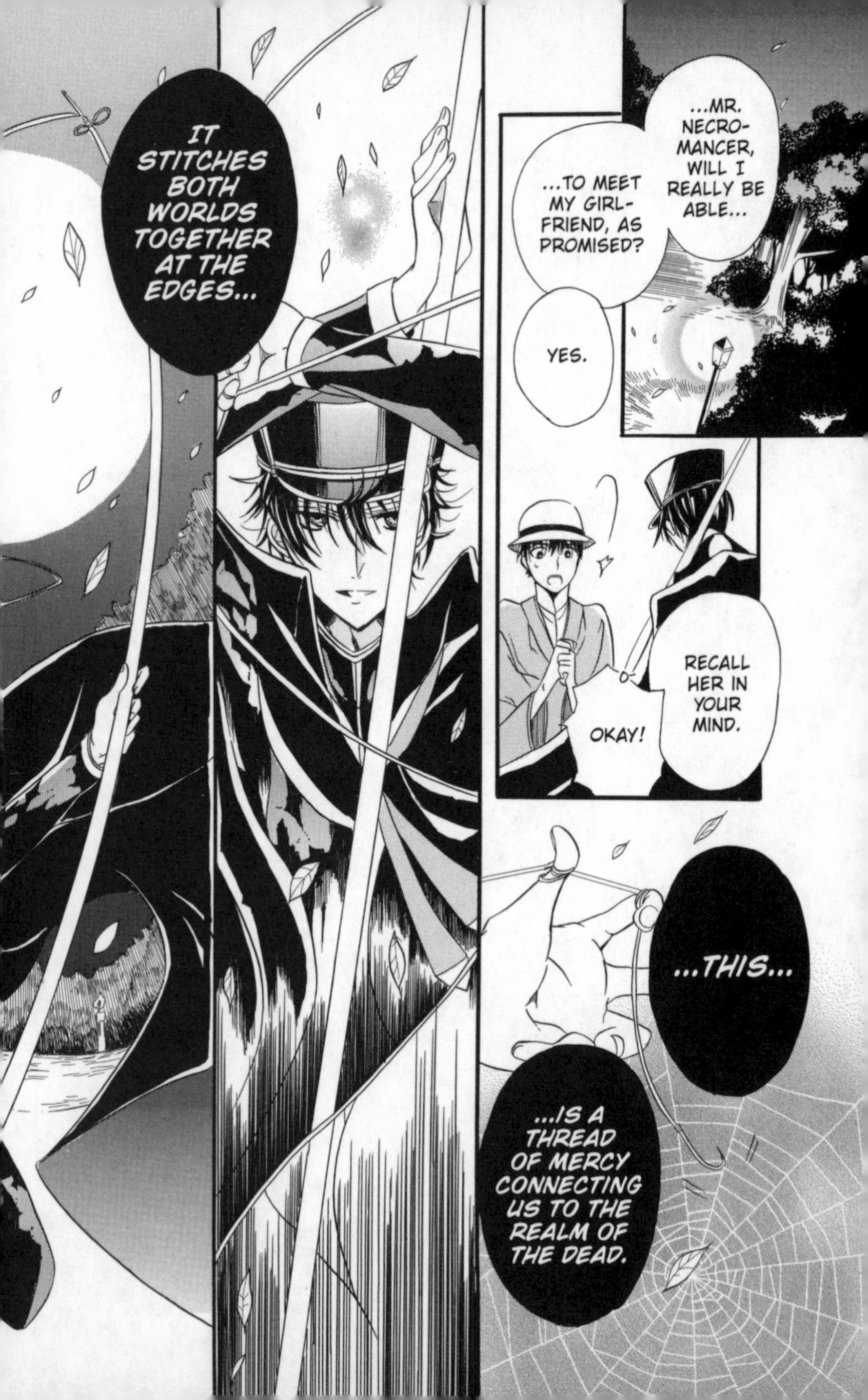
...MR. NECROMANCER, WILL I REALLY BE ABLE...
...TO MEET MY GIRLFRIEND, AS PROMISED?
YES.
RECALL HER IN YOUR MIND.
OKAY!
...THIS...
...IS A THREAD OF MERCY CONNECTING US TO THE REALM OF THE DEAD.
IT STITCHES BOTH WORLDS TOGETHER AT THE EDGES...

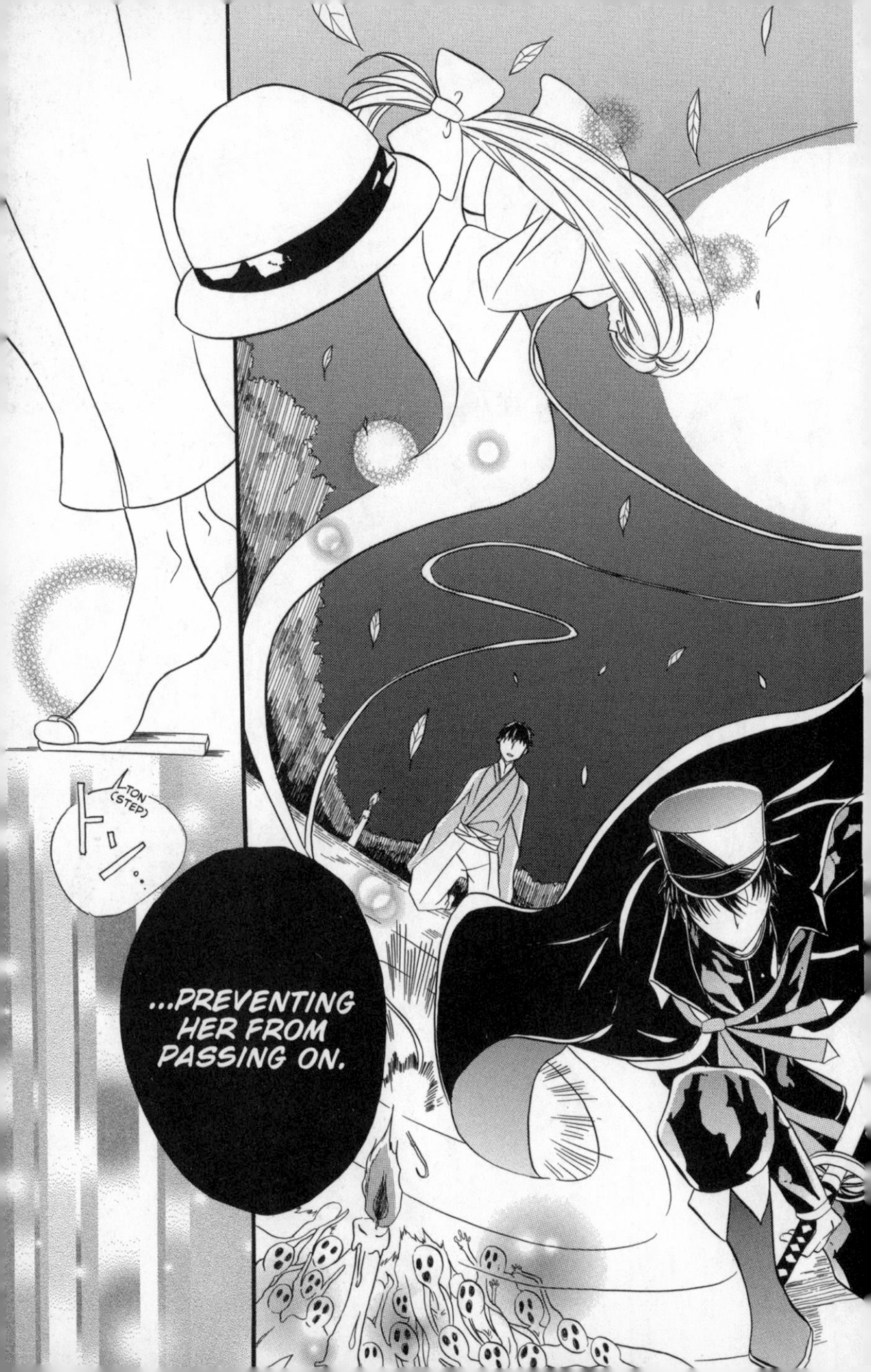
トン。。
TON (STEP)
...PREVENTING HER FROM PASSING ON.

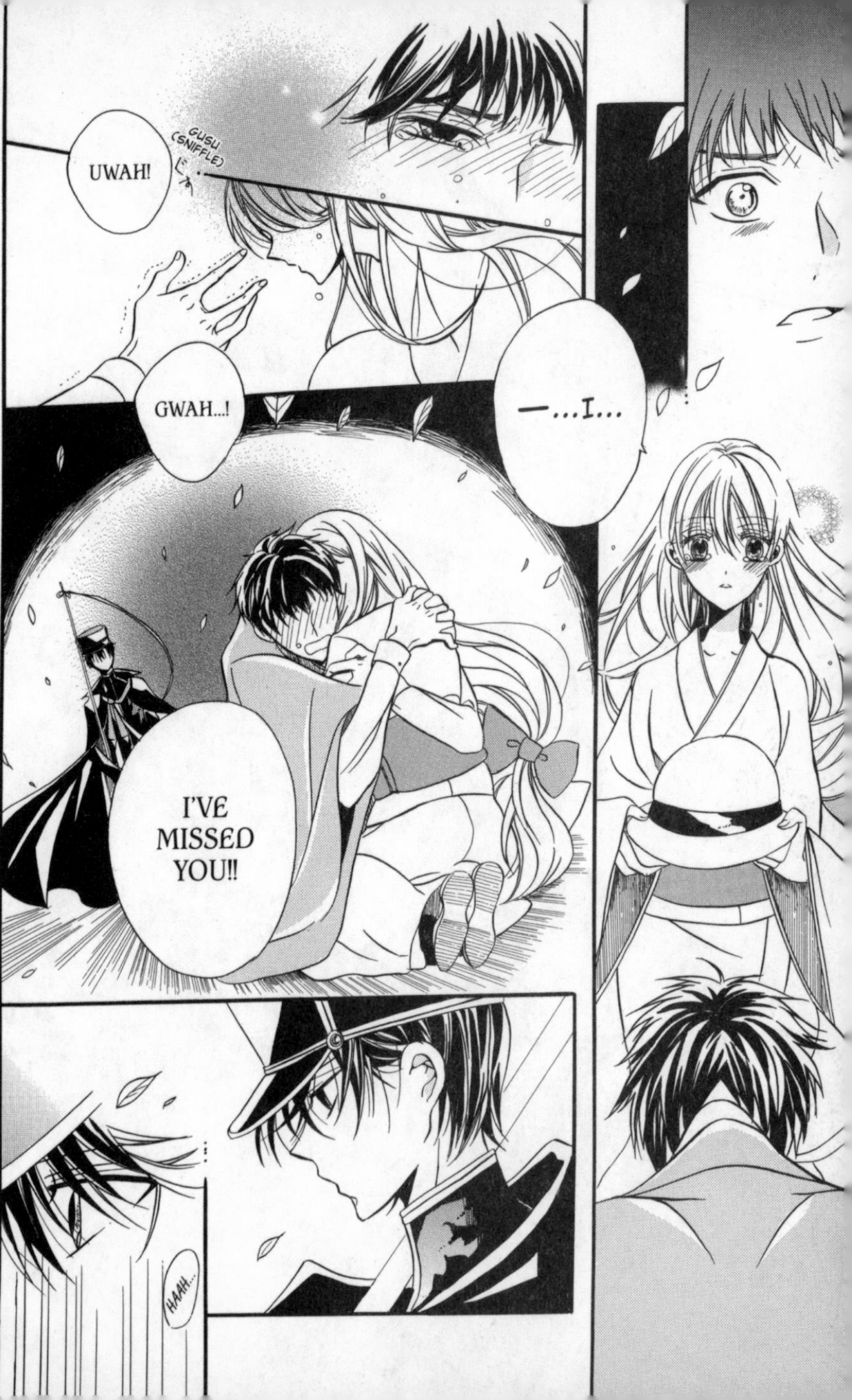
—...I...
UWAH!
GUSU (SNIFFLE)
GWAH...!
I'VE MISSED YOU!!
HAAH...

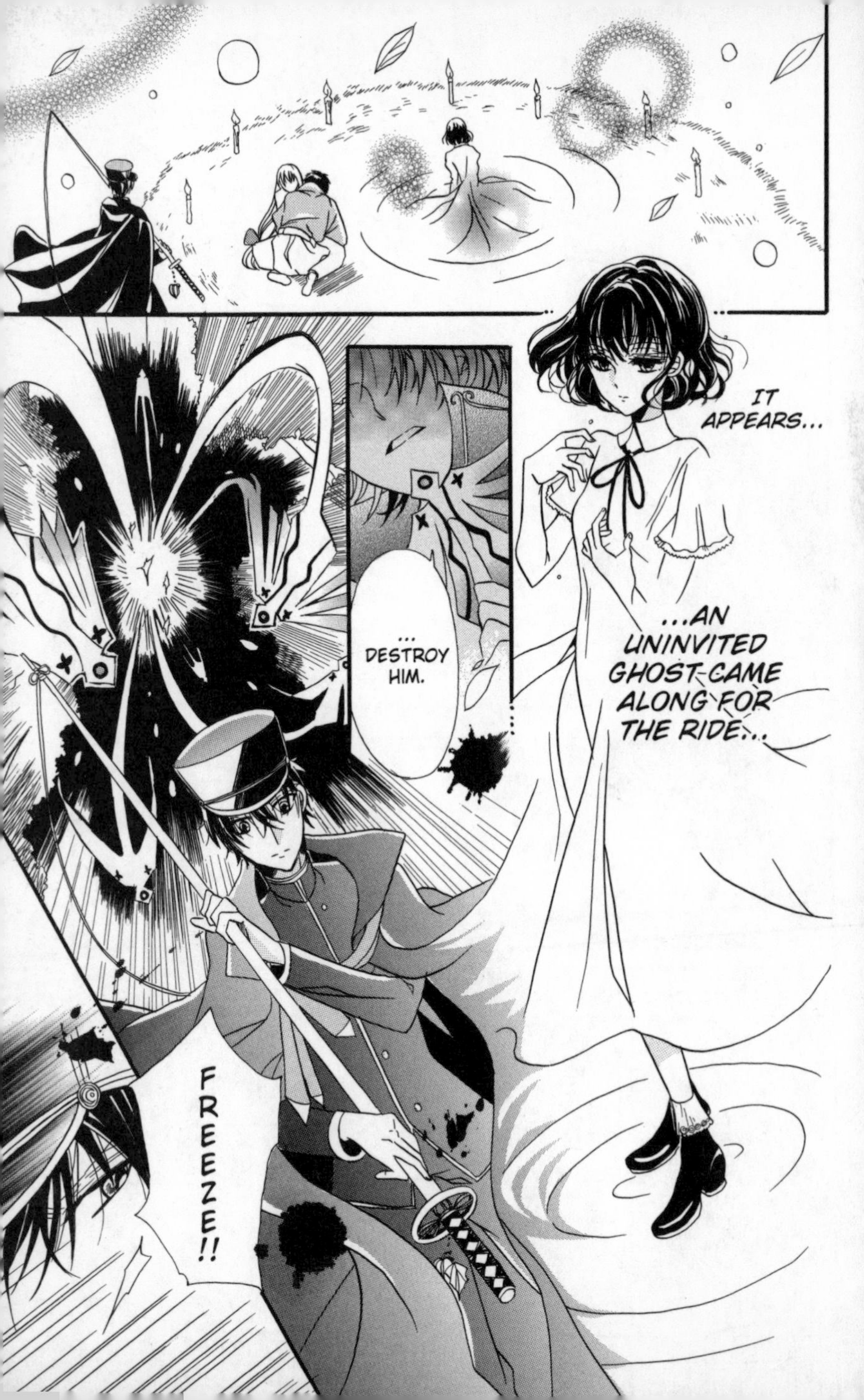
IT APPEARS...
...AN UNINVITED GHOST CAME ALONG FOR THE RIDE...
... DESTROY HIM.
FREEZE!!

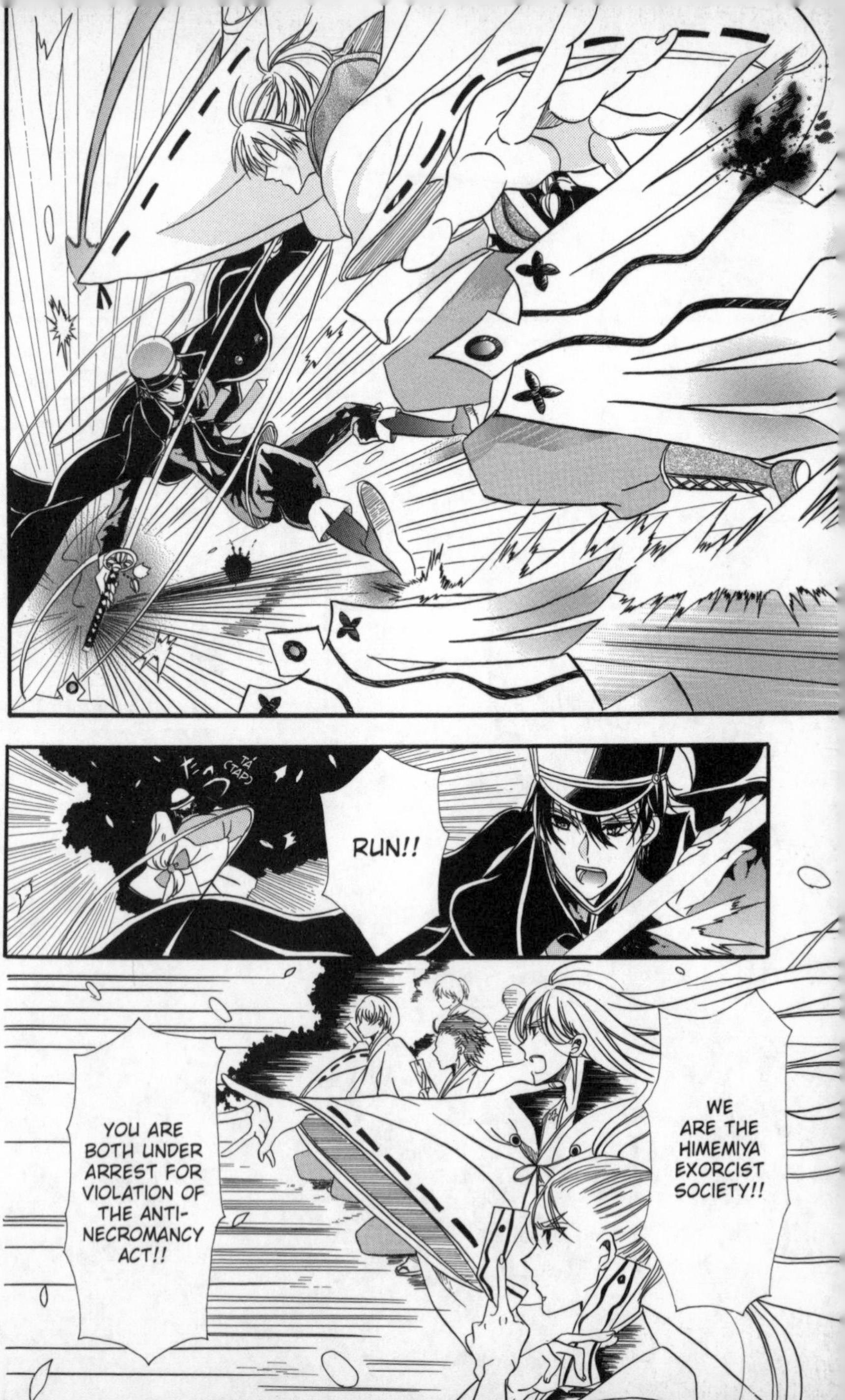
RUN!!
TA (TAP)
WE ARE THE HIMEMIYA EXORCIST SOCIETY!!
YOU ARE BOTH UNDER ARREST FOR VIOLATION OF THE ANTI-NECROMANCY ACT!!

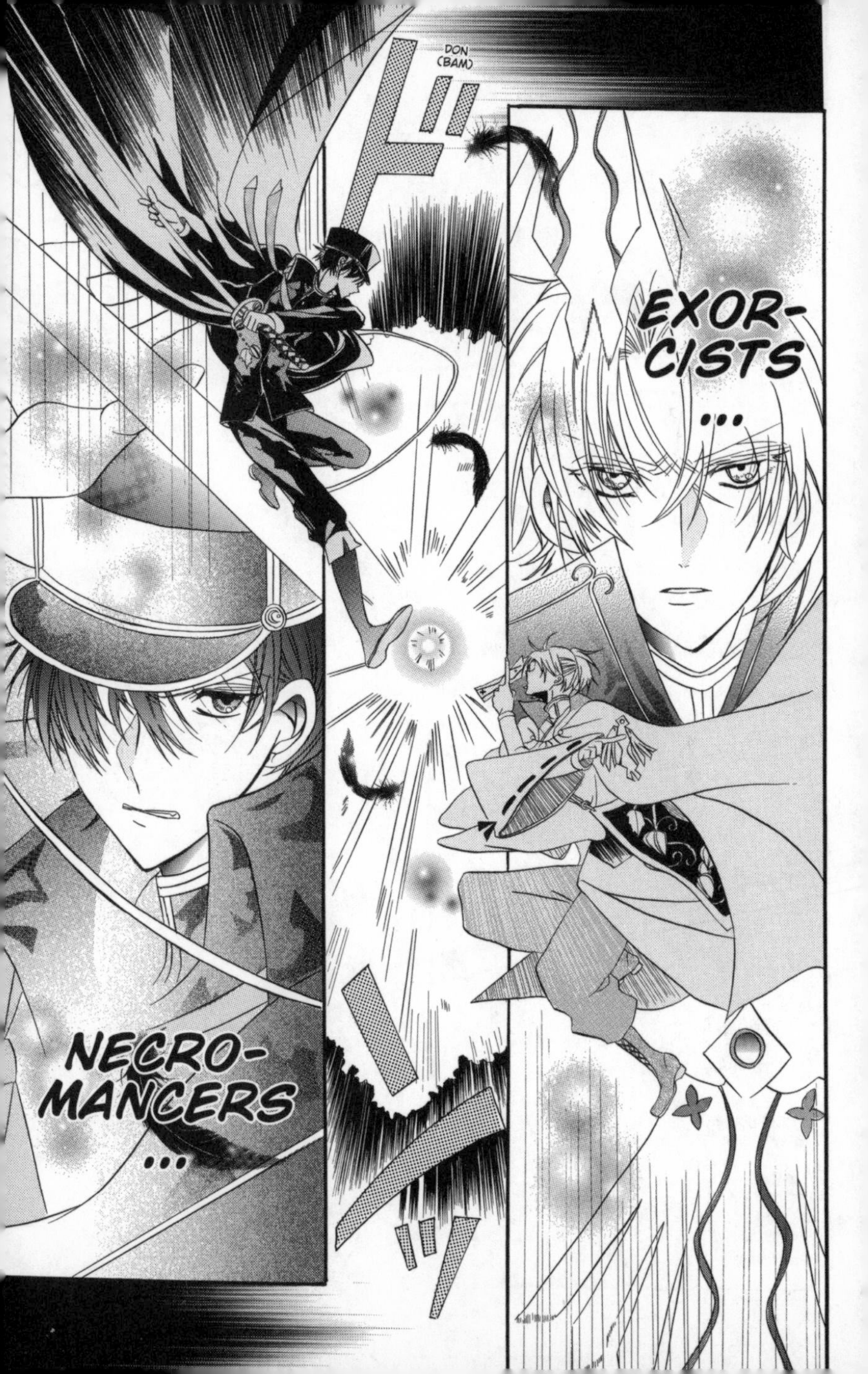
EXOR-
CISTS
...
DON
(BAM)
NECRO-
MANCERS
...

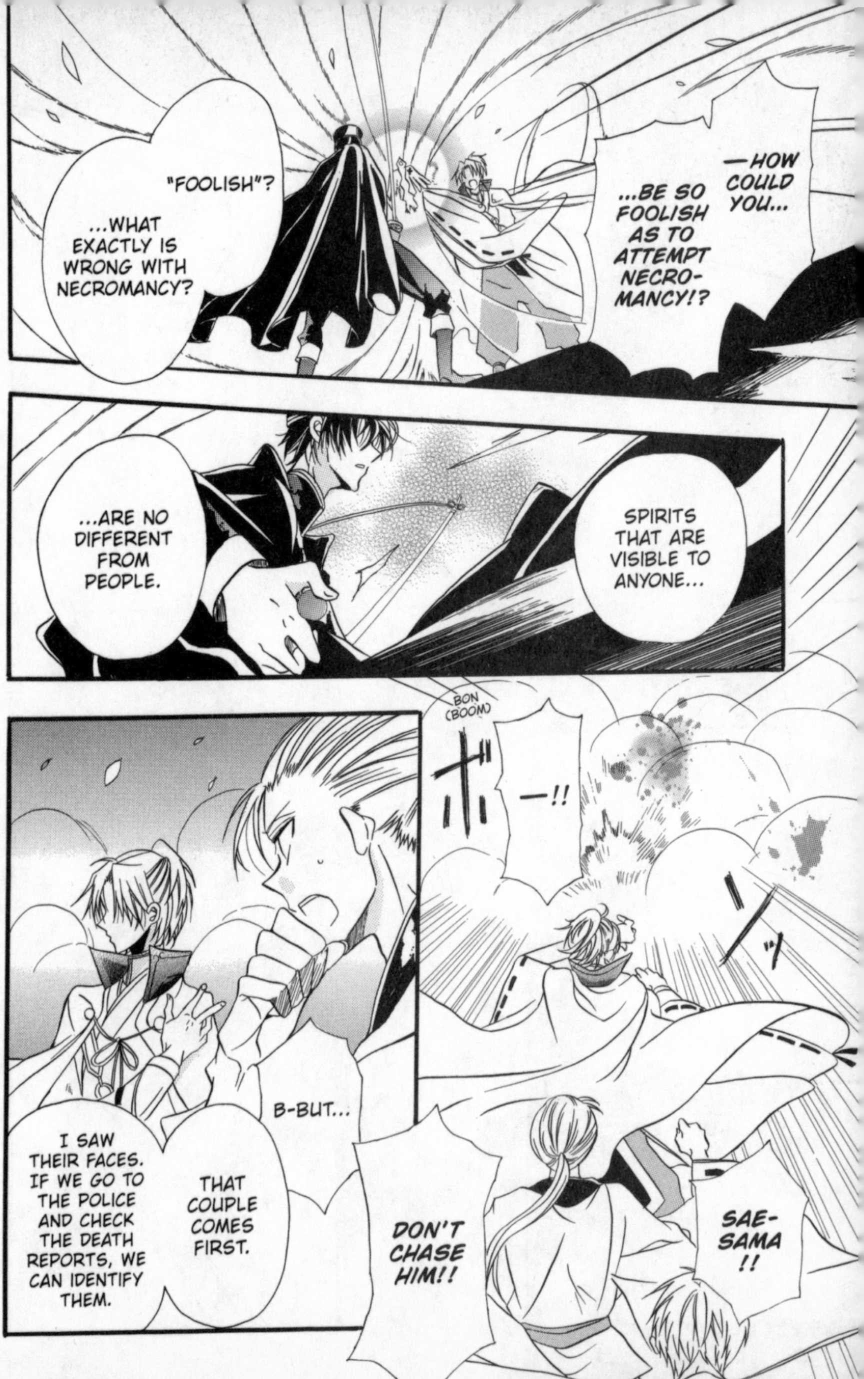
—HOW COULD YOU...
...BE SO FOOLISH AS TO ATTEMPT NECROMANCY!?
"FOOLISH"?
...WHAT EXACTLY IS WRONG WITH NECROMANCY?
SPIRITS THAT ARE VISIBLE TO ANYONE...
...ARE NO DIFFERENT FROM PEOPLE.
BON (BOOM)
—!!
SAE-SAMA!!
DON'T CHASE HIM!!
B-BUT...
THAT COUPLE COMES FIRST.
I SAW THEIR FACES. IF WE GO TO THE POLICE AND CHECK THE DEATH REPORTS, WE CAN IDENTIFY THEM.

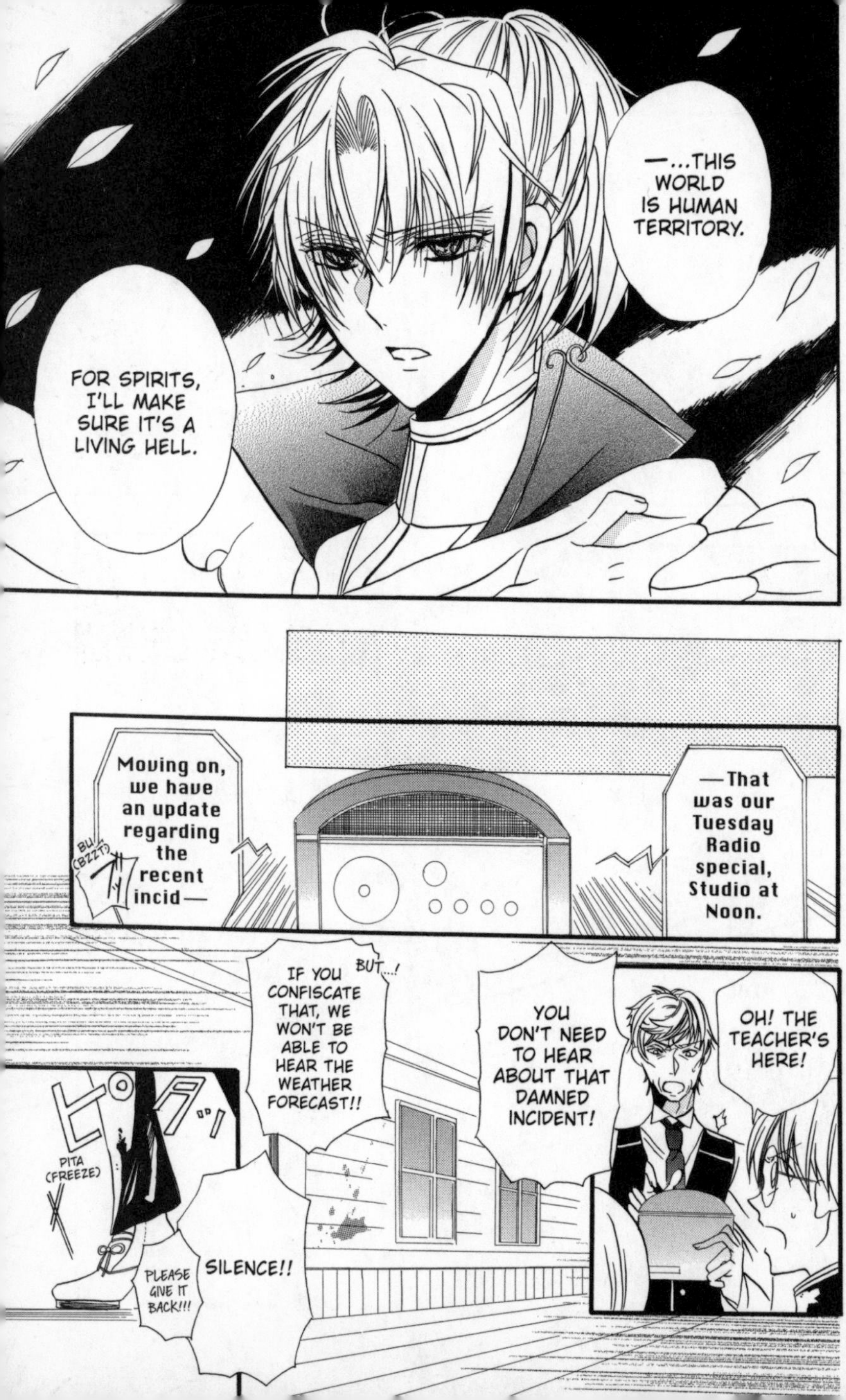
—...THIS WORLD IS HUMAN TERRITORY.
FOR SPIRITS, I'LL MAKE SURE IT'S A LIVING HELL.
—That was our Tuesday Radio special, Studio at Noon.
Moving on, we have an update regarding the recent incid—
BU... (BZZT)
OH! THE TEACHER'S HERE!
YOU DON'T NEED TO HEAR ABOUT THAT DAMNED INCIDENT!
BUT...!
IF YOU CONFISCATE THAT, WE WON'T BE ABLE TO HEAR THE WEATHER FORECAST!!
PITA (FREEZE)
SILENCE!!
PLEASE GIVE IT BACK!!!

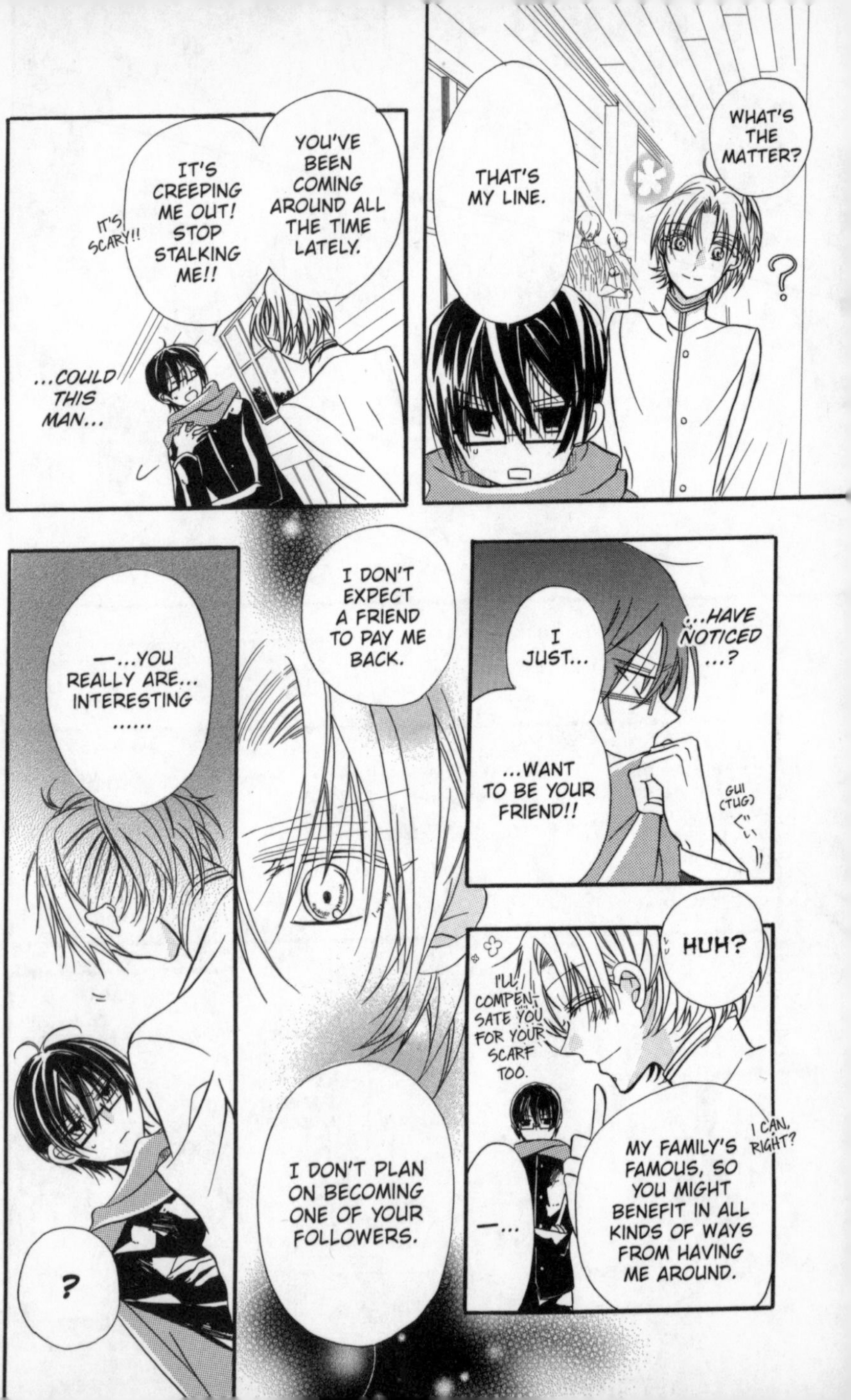
WHAT'S THE MATTER?
THAT'S MY LINE.
YOU'VE BEEN COMING AROUND ALL THE TIME LATELY.
IT'S CREEPING ME OUT! STOP STALKING ME!!
IT'S SCARY!!
...COULD THIS MAN...
...HAVE NOTICED ...?
I JUST...
...WANT TO BE YOUR FRIEND!!
GUI (TUG)
HUH?
I'LL COMPENSATE YOU FOR YOUR SCARF TOO.
I CAN, RIGHT?
MY FAMILY'S FAMOUS, SO YOU MIGHT BENEFIT IN ALL KINDS OF WAYS FROM HAVING ME AROUND.
—...
I DON'T EXPECT A FRIEND TO PAY ME BACK.
I DON'T PLAN ON BECOMING ONE OF YOUR FOLLOWERS.
—...YOU REALLY ARE... INTERESTING ......
?

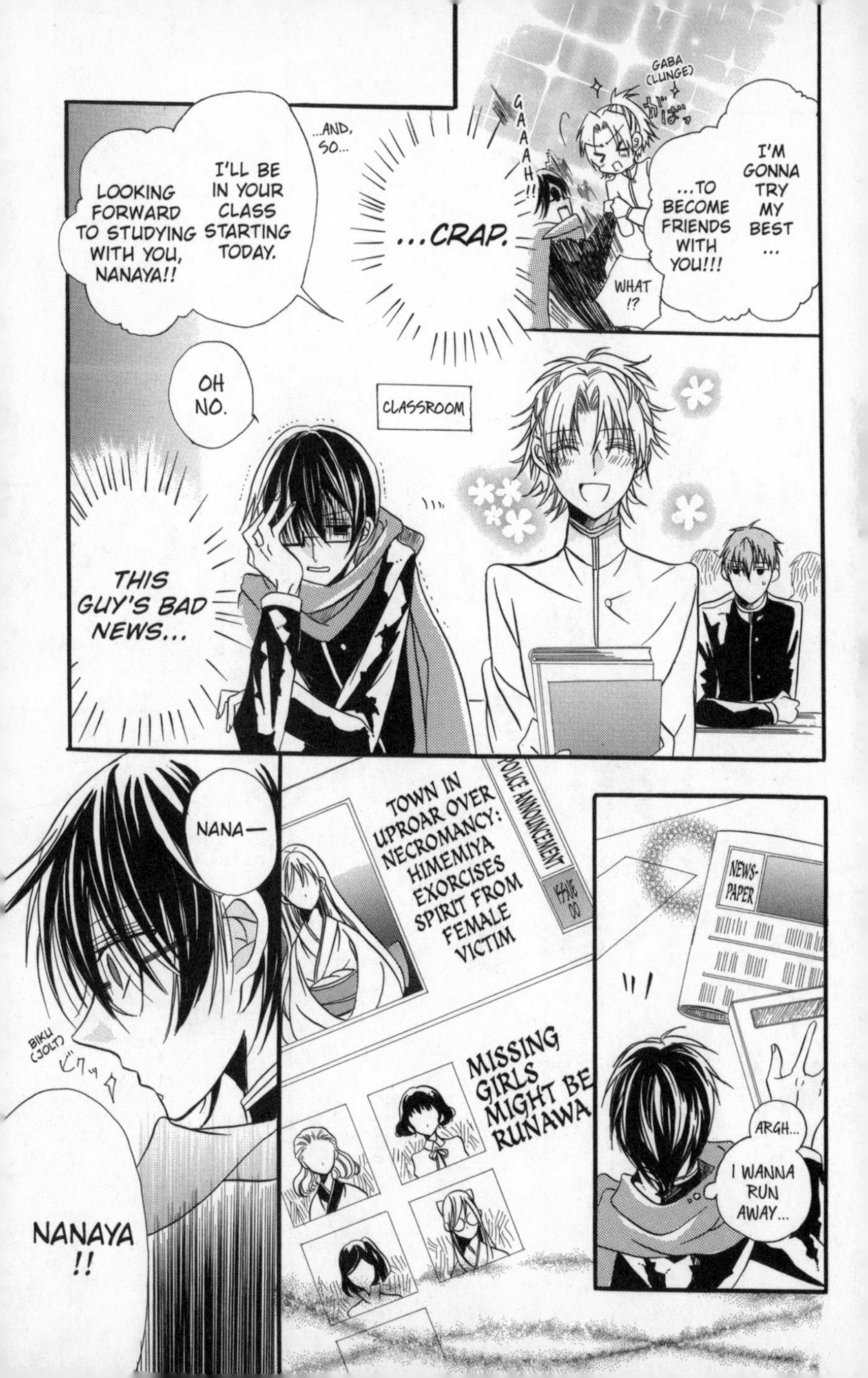
GABA (LUNGE)
I'M GONNA TRY MY BEST...
...TO BECOME FRIENDS WITH YOU!!!
WHAT!?
GAAAAH!!
...AND, SO...
I'LL BE IN YOUR CLASS STARTING TODAY.
LOOKING FORWARD TO STUDYING WITH YOU, NANAYA!!
...CRAP.
CLASSROOM
OH NO.
THIS GUY'S BAD NEWS...
NEWS-PAPER
ARGH...
I WANNA RUN AWAY...
POLICE ANNOUNCEMENT
TOWN IN UPROAR OVER NECROMANCY: HIMEMIYA EXORCISES SPIRIT FROM FEMALE VICTIM
MISSING GIRLS MIGHT BE RUNAWA
NANA—
BIKU (JOLT)
NANAYA!!

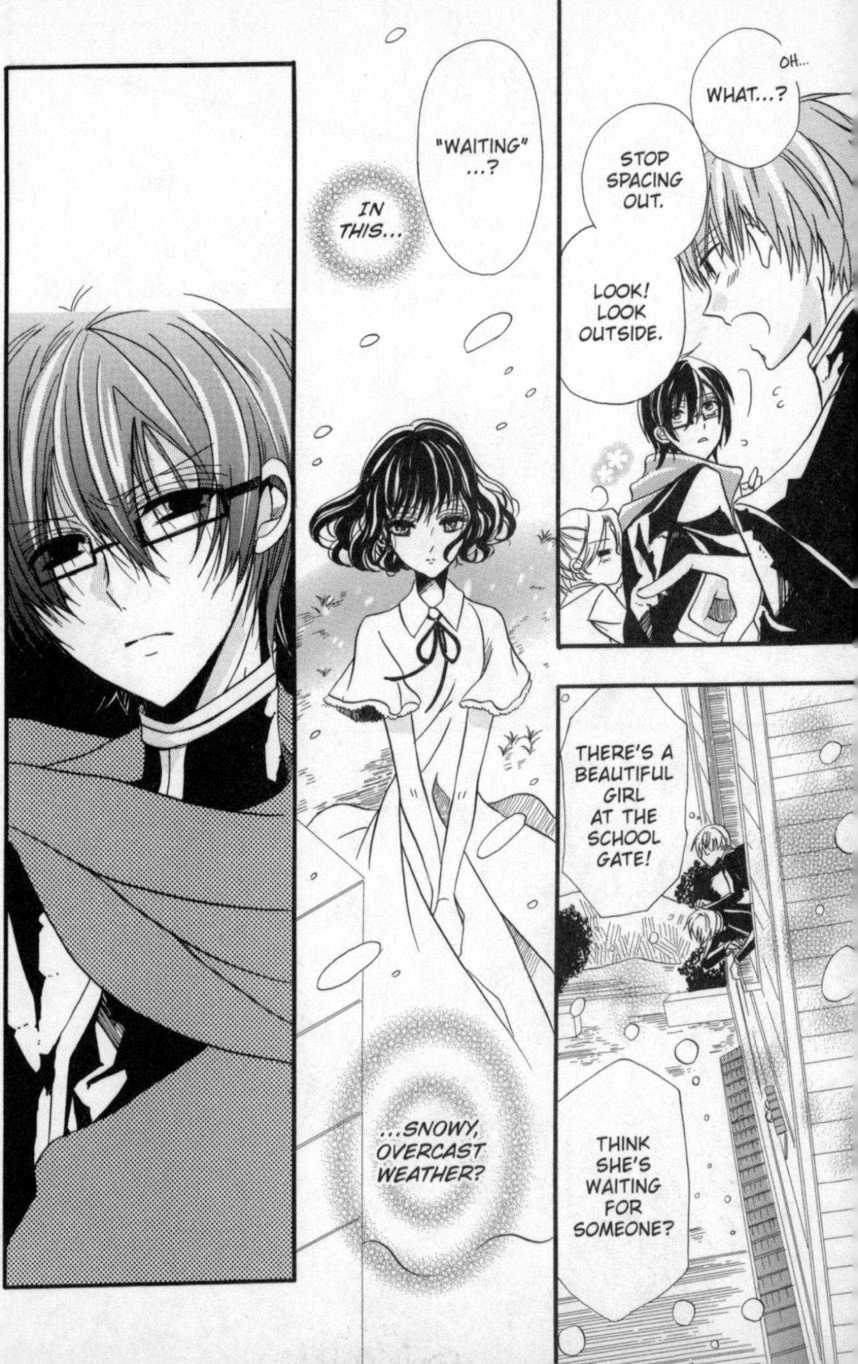
OH...
WHAT...?
STOP SPACING OUT.
LOOK! LOOK OUTSIDE.
THERE'S A BEAUTIFUL GIRL AT THE SCHOOL GATE!
THINK SHE'S WAITING FOR SOMEONE?
"WAITING" ...?
IN THIS...
...SNOWY, OVERCAST WEATHER?

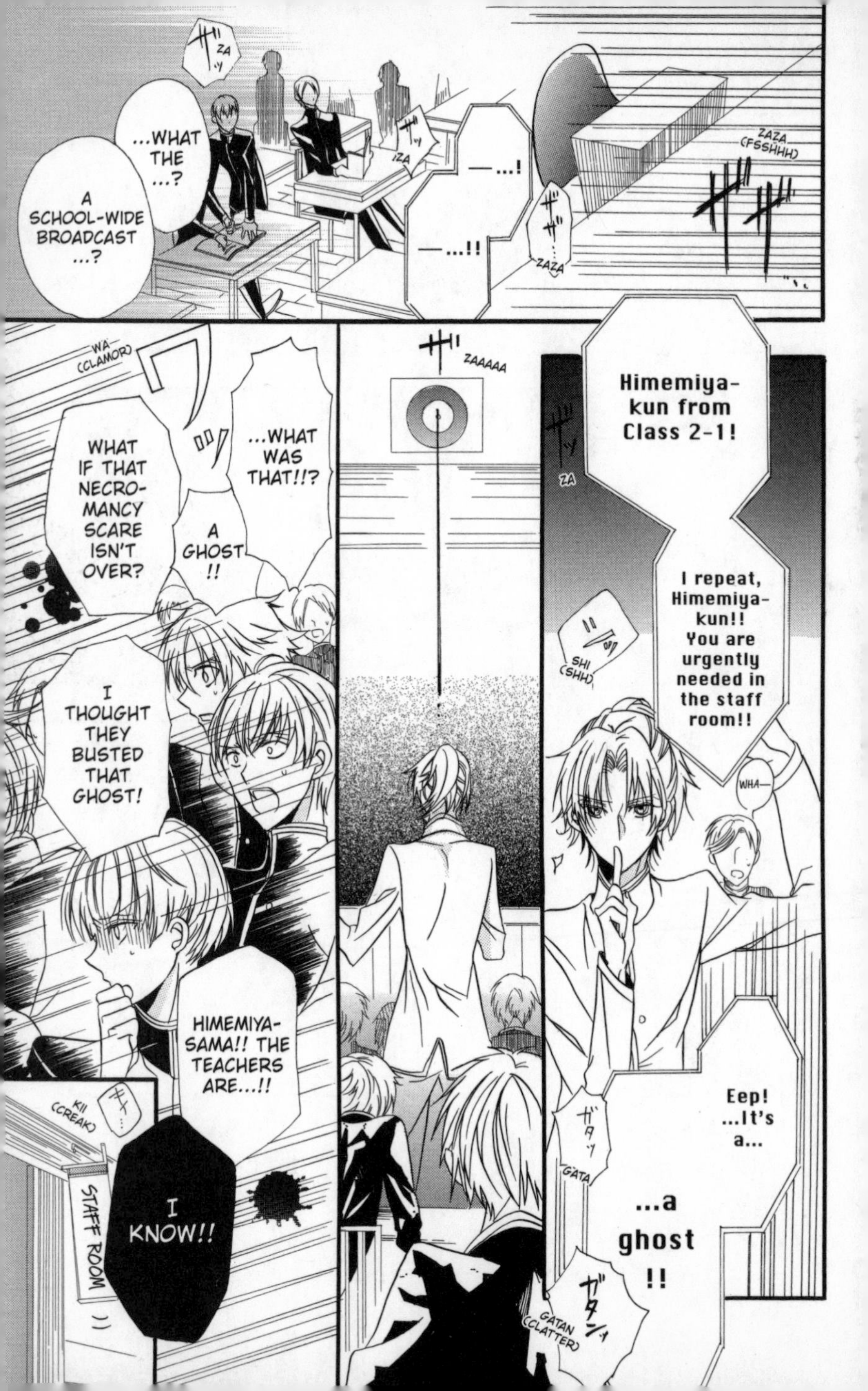
ZAZA (FSSHHH)
ZAZA
—...!
—...!!
ZA
...WHAT THE ...?
A SCHOOL-WIDE BROADCAST ...?
ZA
ZA
Himemiya-kun from Class 2-1!
I repeat, Himemiya-kun!! You are urgently needed in the staff room!!
SHI (SHH)
WHA—
Eep! ...It's a...
...a ghost !!
GATA
GATAN (CLATTER)
ZAAAAA
WA (CLAMOR)
...WHAT WAS THAT!!?
A GHOST !!
WHAT IF THAT NECRO-MANCY SCARE ISN'T OVER?
I THOUGHT THEY BUSTED THAT GHOST!
HIMEMIYA-SAMA!! THE TEACHERS ARE...!!
KII (CREAK)
I KNOW!!
STAFF ROOM

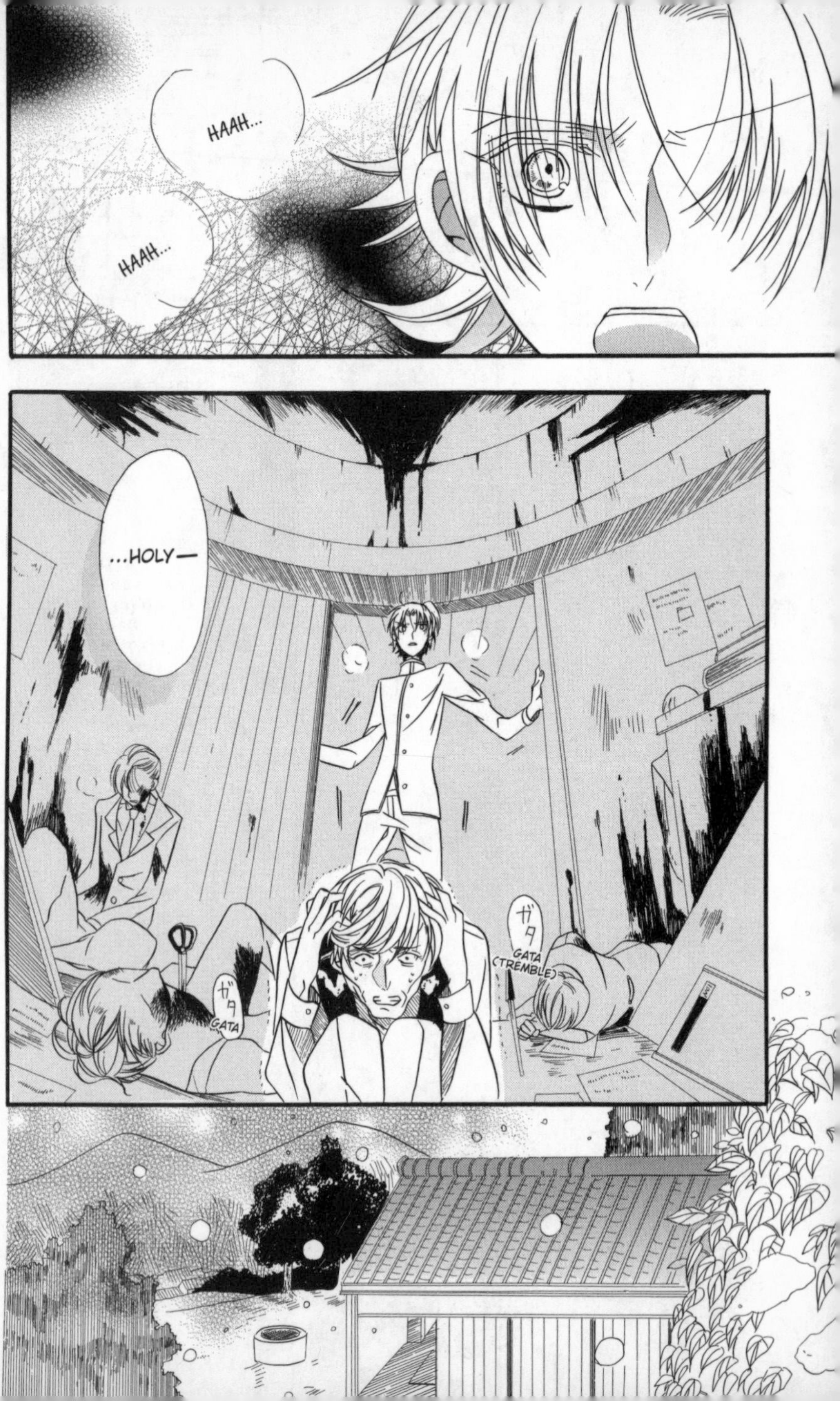
HAAH...
HAAH...
...HOLY—
ガタ
GATA (TREMBLE)
ガタ
GATA

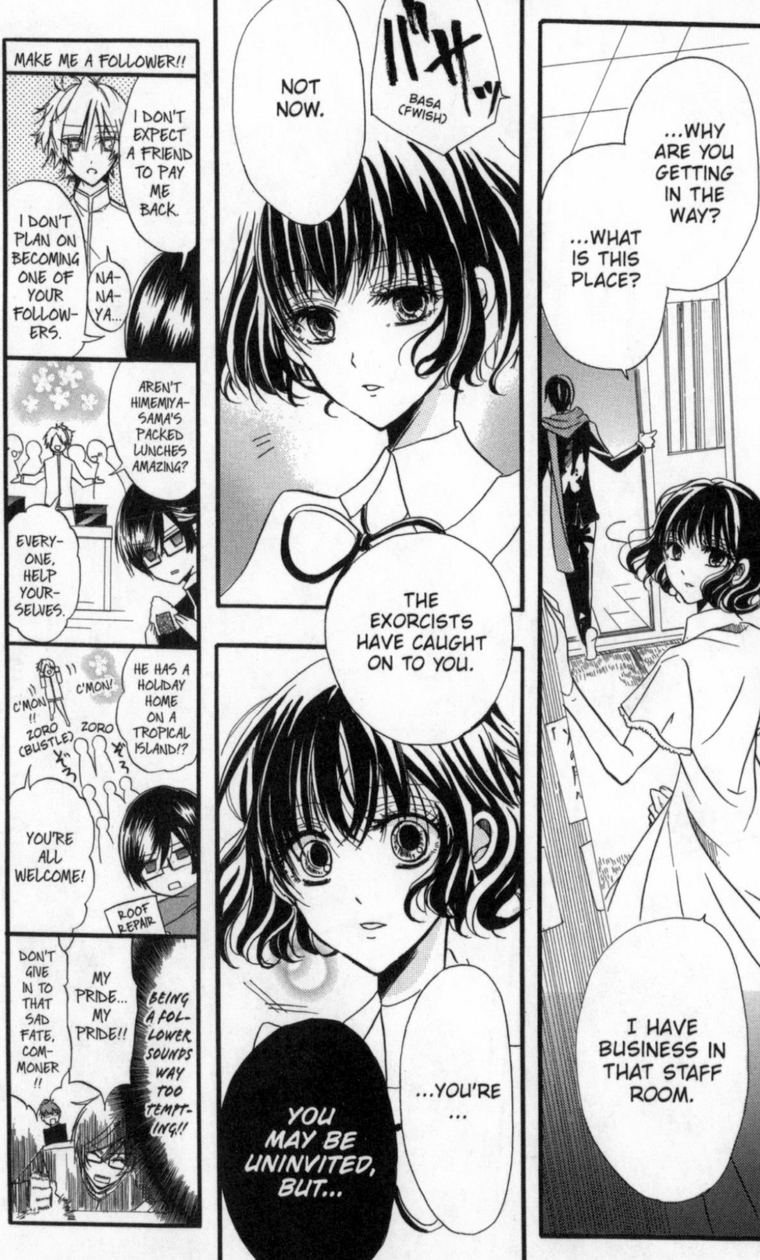
...WHY ARE YOU GETTING IN THE WAY?
...WHAT IS THIS PLACE?
I HAVE BUSINESS IN THAT STAFF ROOM.
BASA (FWISH)
NOT NOW.
THE EXORCISTS HAVE CAUGHT ON TO YOU.
...YOU'RE ...
YOU MAY BE UNINVITED, BUT...
MAKE ME A FOLLOWER!!
I DON'T EXPECT A FRIEND TO PAY ME BACK.
NA-NA-YA...
I DON'T PLAN ON BECOMING ONE OF YOUR FOLLOW-ERS.
AREN'T HIMEMIYA-SAMA'S PACKED LUNCHES AMAZING?
EVERY-ONE, HELP YOUR-SELVES.
HE HAS A HOLIDAY HOME ON A TROPICAL ISLAND!?
C'MON!
C'MON!!
ZORO
ZORO (BUSTLE)
YOU'RE ALL WELCOME!
ROOF REPAIR
BEING A FOL-LOWER SOUNDS WAY TOO TEMPT-ING!!
MY PRIDE... MY PRIDE!!
DON'T GIVE IN TO THAT SAD FATE, COM-MONER!!

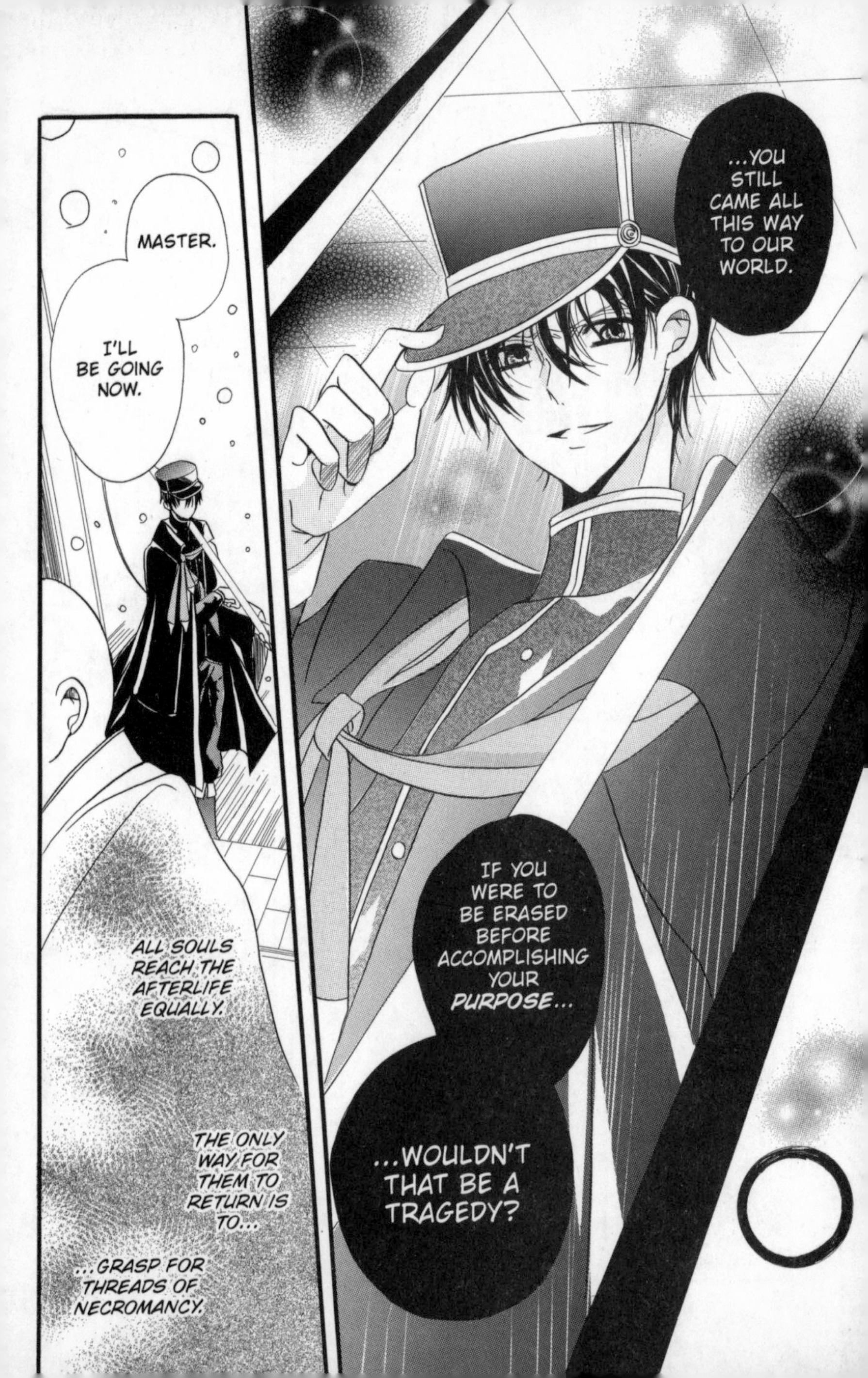
...YOU STILL CAME ALL THIS WAY TO OUR WORLD.
IF YOU WERE TO BE ERASED BEFORE ACCOMPLISHING YOUR PURPOSE...
...WOULDN'T THAT BE A TRAGEDY?
MASTER.
I'LL BE GOING NOW.
ALL SOULS REACH THE AFTERLIFE EQUALLY.
THE ONLY WAY FOR THEM TO RETURN IS TO...
...GRASP FOR THREADS OF NECROMANCY.

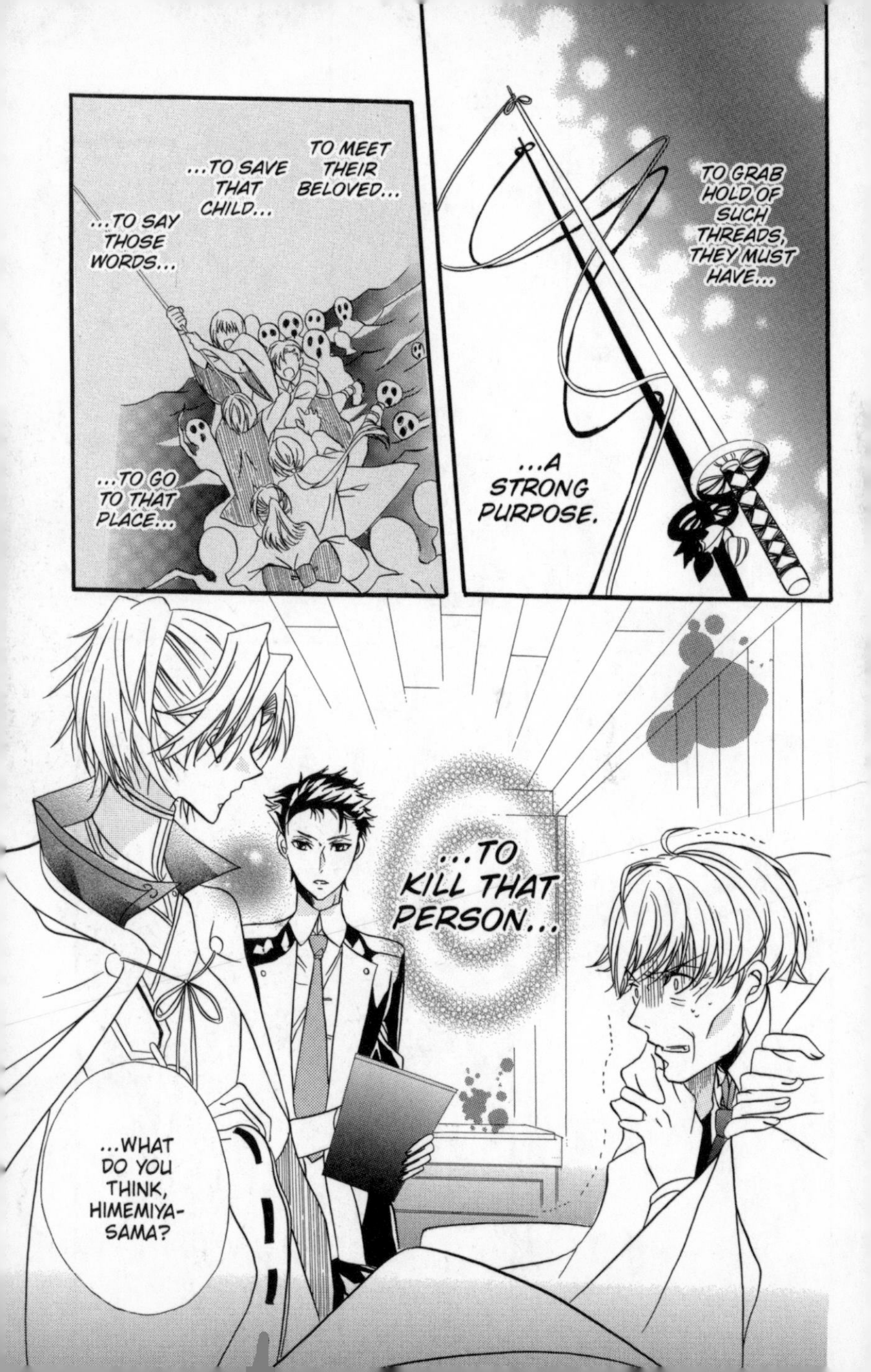
TO GRAB HOLD OF SUCH THREADS, THEY MUST HAVE...
...A STRONG PURPOSE.
TO MEET THEIR BELOVED...
...TO SAVE THAT CHILD...
...TO SAY THOSE WORDS...
...TO GO TO THAT PLACE...
...TO KILL THAT PERSON...
...WHAT DO YOU THINK, HIMEMIYA-SAMA?

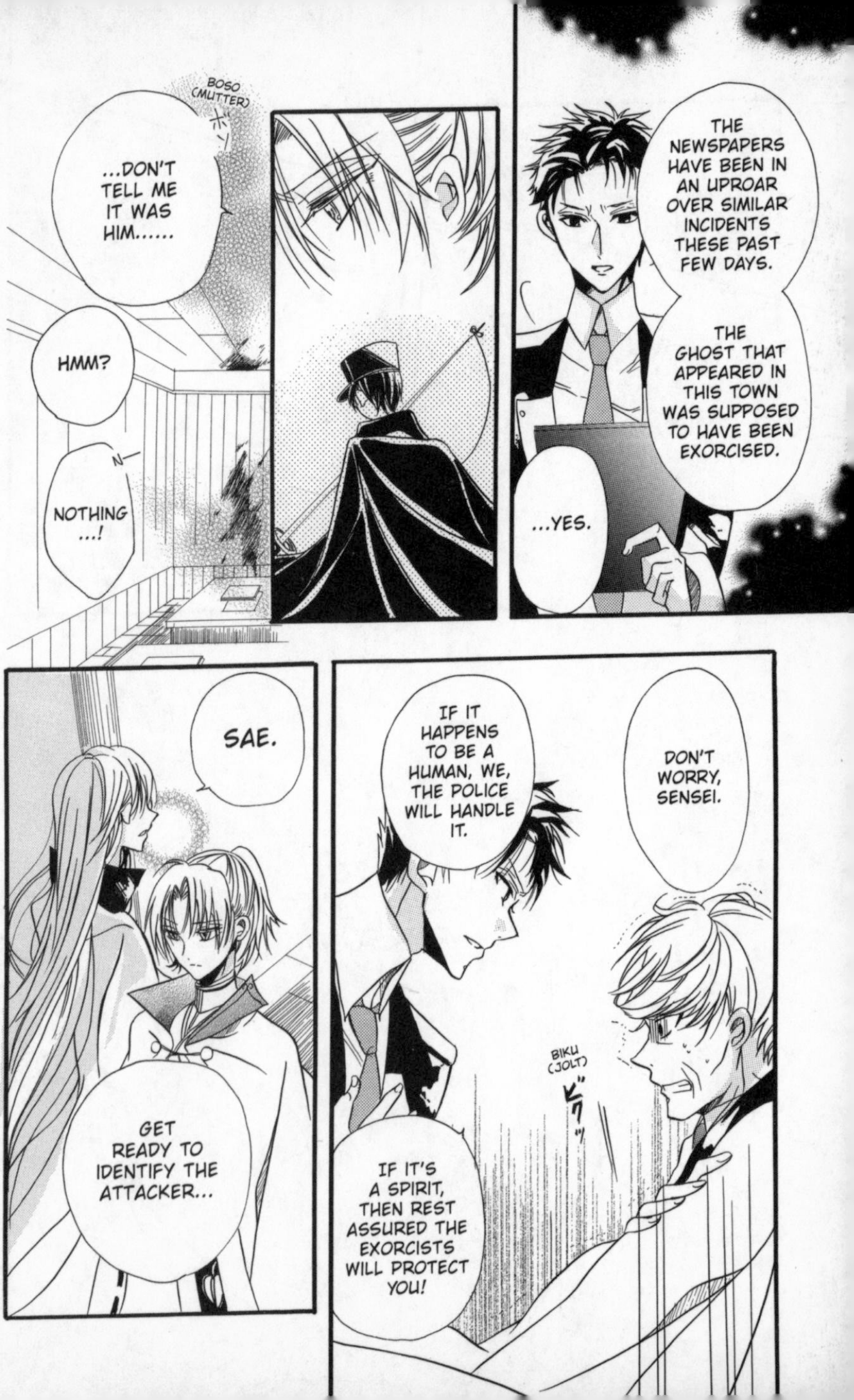
THE NEWSPAPERS HAVE BEEN IN AN UPROAR OVER SIMILAR INCIDENTS THESE PAST FEW DAYS.
THE GHOST THAT APPEARED IN THIS TOWN WAS SUPPOSED TO HAVE BEEN EXORCISED.
...YES.
BOSO (MUTTER)
...DON'T TELL ME IT WAS HIM......
HMM?
N—
NOTHING ...!
DON'T WORRY, SENSEI.
IF IT HAPPENS TO BE A HUMAN, WE, THE POLICE WILL HANDLE IT.
BIKU (JOLT)
IF IT'S A SPIRIT, THEN REST ASSURED THE EXORCISTS WILL PROTECT YOU!
SAE.
GET READY TO IDENTIFY THE ATTACKER...

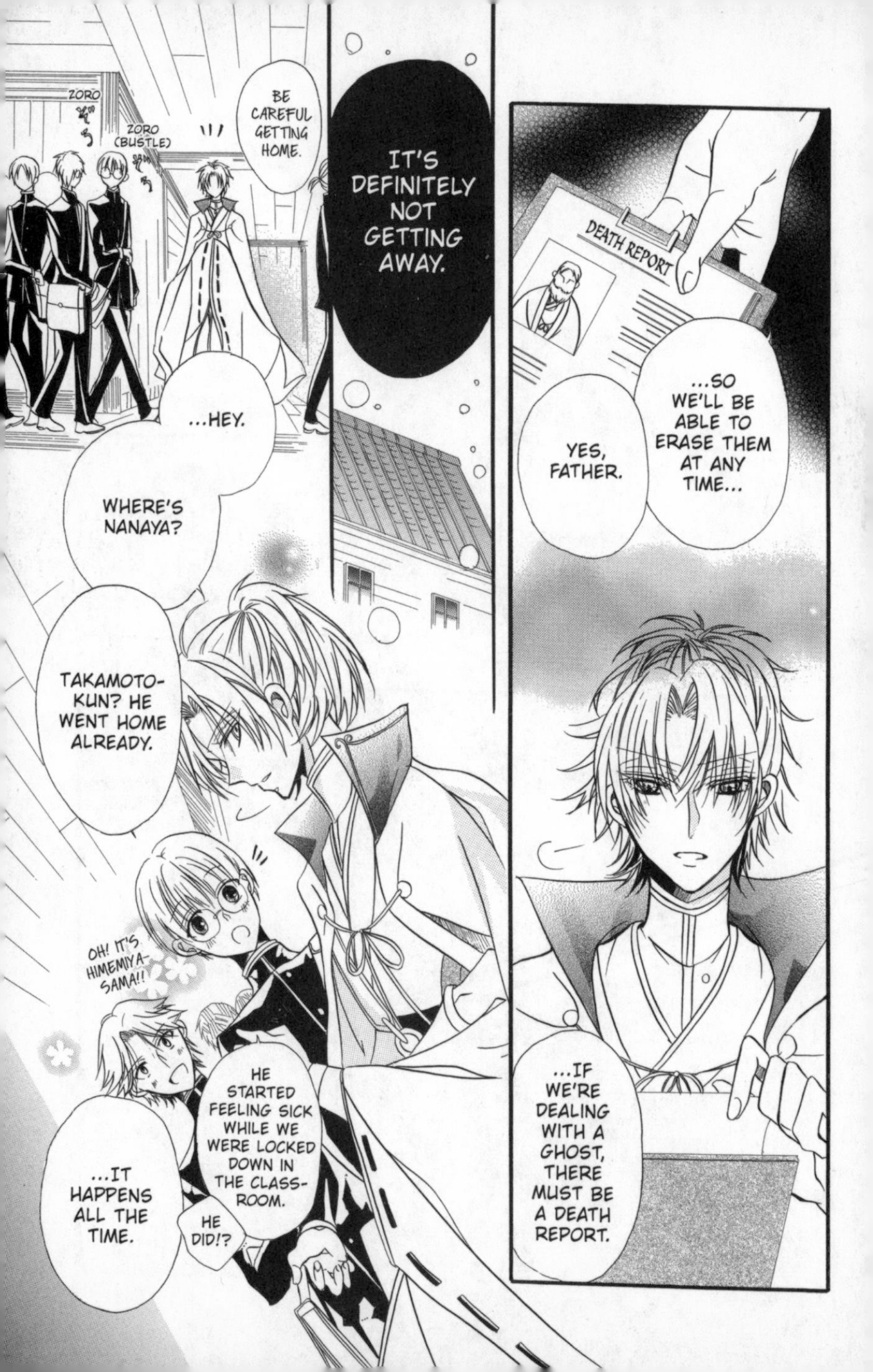
DEATH REPORT
...SO WE'LL BE ABLE TO ERASE THEM AT ANY TIME...
YES, FATHER.
...IF WE'RE DEALING WITH A GHOST, THERE MUST BE A DEATH REPORT.
IT'S DEFINITELY NOT GETTING AWAY.
BE CAREFUL GETTING HOME.
ZORO
ZORO (BUSTLE)
...HEY.
WHERE'S NANAYA?
TAKAMOTO-KUN? HE WENT HOME ALREADY.
OH! IT'S HIMEMIYA-SAMA!!
HE STARTED FEELING SICK WHILE WE WERE LOCKED DOWN IN THE CLASS-ROOM.
HE DID!?
...IT HAPPENS ALL THE TIME.

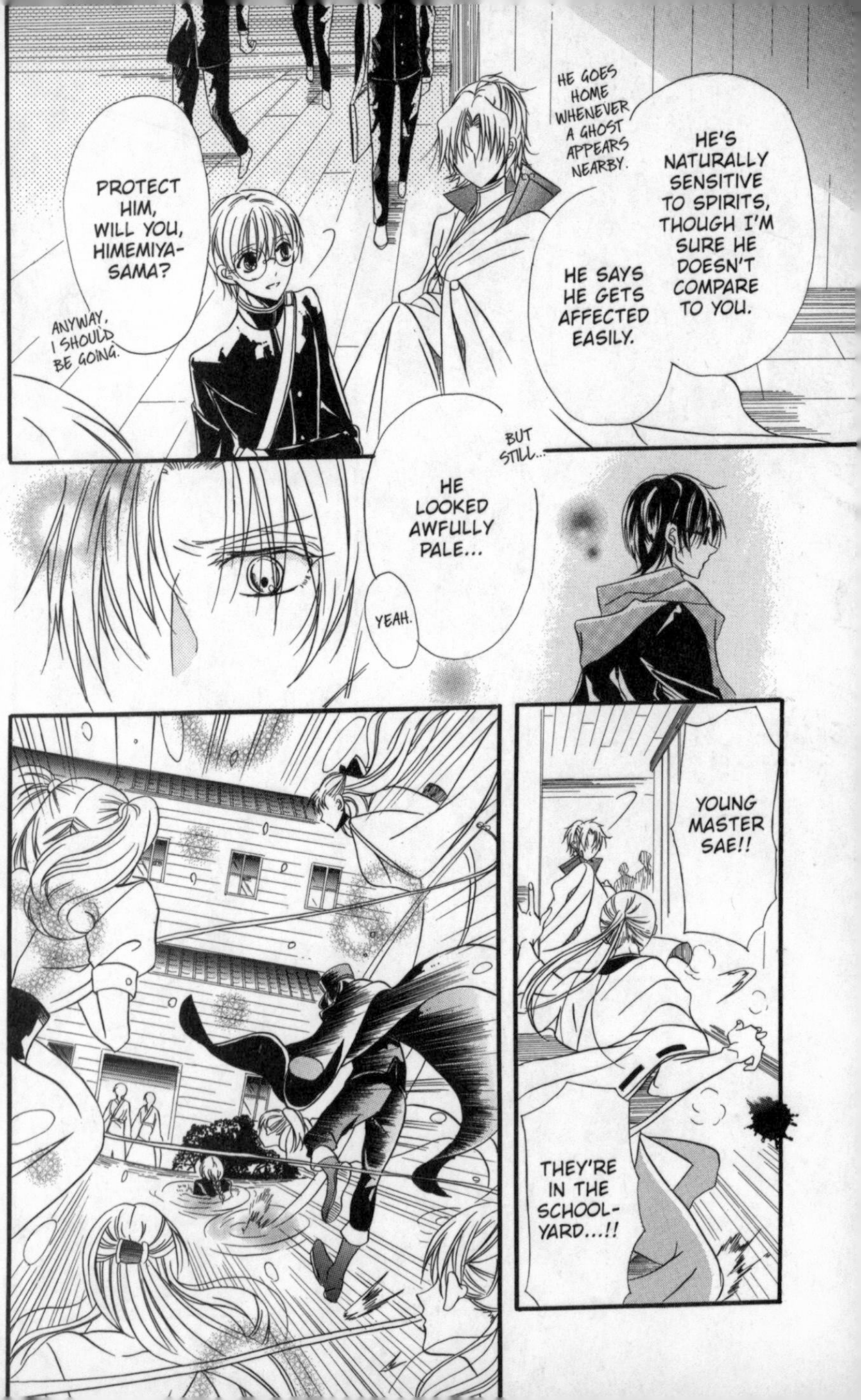
HE GOES HOME WHENEVER A GHOST APPEARS NEARBY.
HE'S NATURALLY SENSITIVE TO SPIRITS, THOUGH I'M SURE HE DOESN'T COMPARE TO YOU.
HE SAYS HE GETS AFFECTED EASILY.
PROTECT HIM, WILL YOU, HIMEMIYA-SAMA?
ANYWAY, I SHOULD BE GOING.
BUT STILL...
HE LOOKED AWFULLY PALE...
YEAH.
YOUNG MASTER SAE!!
THEY'RE IN THE SCHOOL-YARD...!!

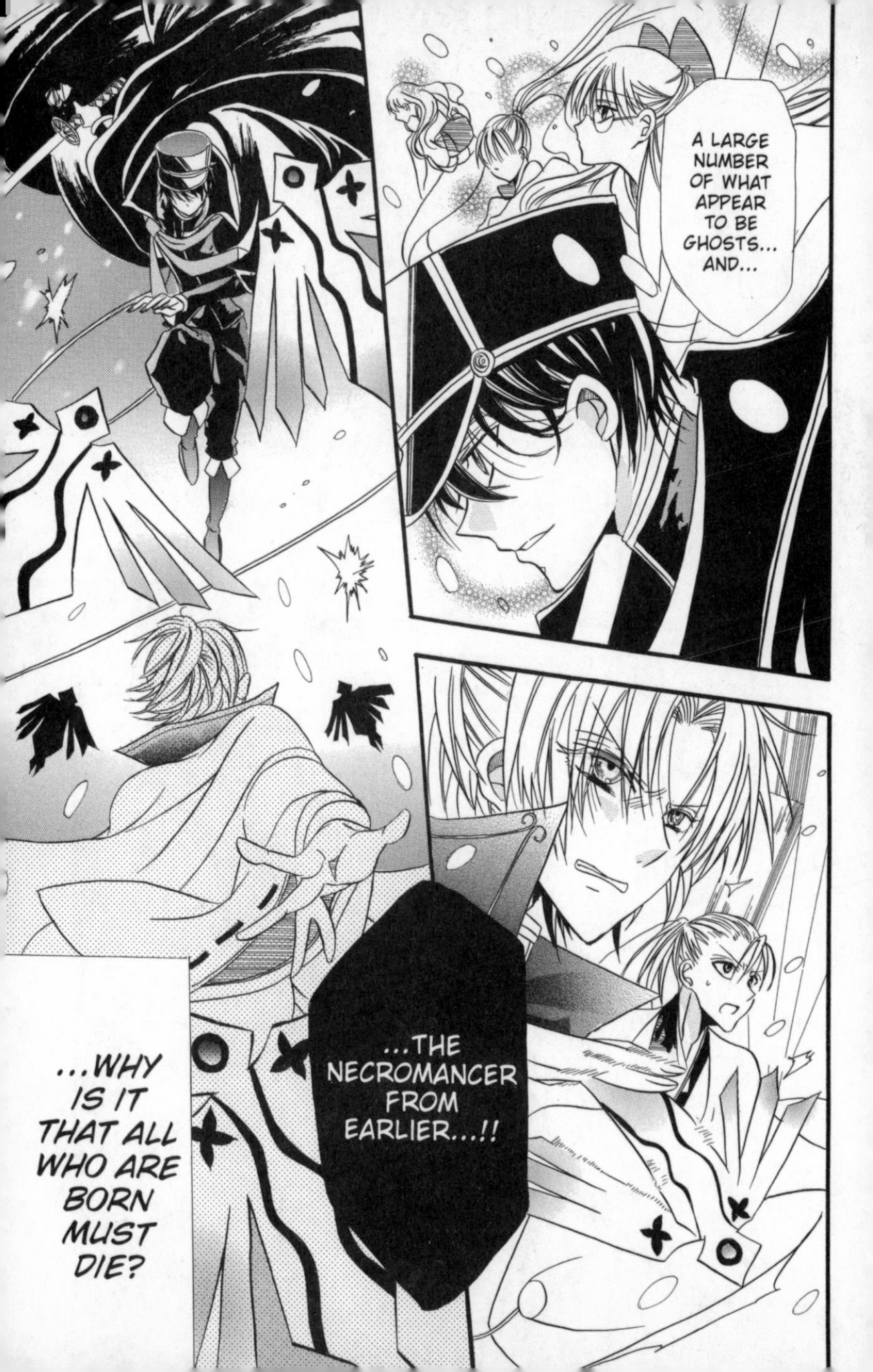
A LARGE NUMBER OF WHAT APPEAR TO BE GHOSTS... AND...
...THE NECROMANCER FROM EARLIER...!!
...WHY IS IT THAT ALL WHO ARE BORN MUST DIE?

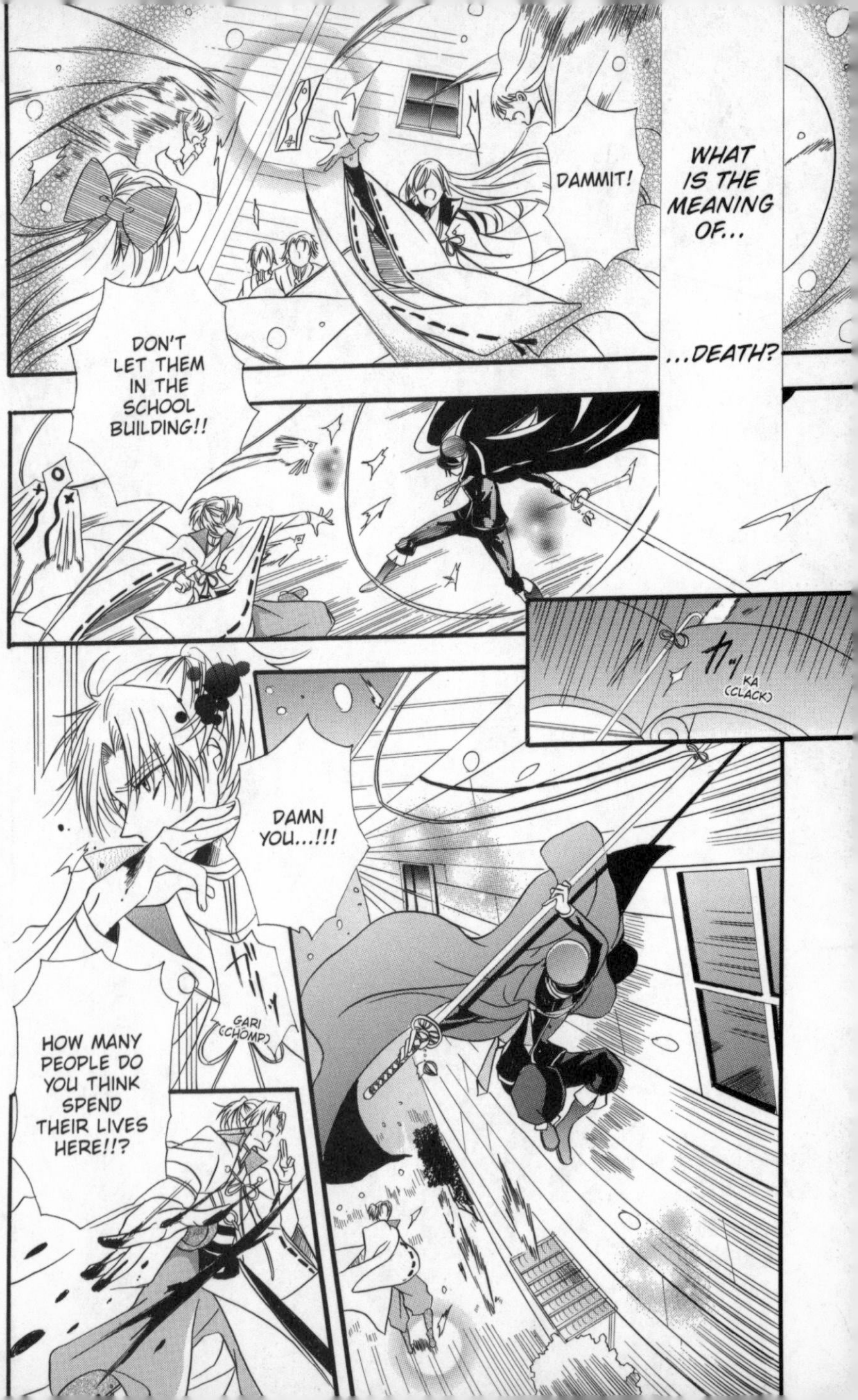

WHAT IS THE MEANING OF...
DAMMIT!
...DEATH?
DON'T LET THEM IN THE SCHOOL BUILDING!!
カッ
KA (CLACK)
DAMN YOU...!!!
GARI (CHOMP)
HOW MANY PEOPLE DO YOU THINK SPEND THEIR LIVES HERE!!?

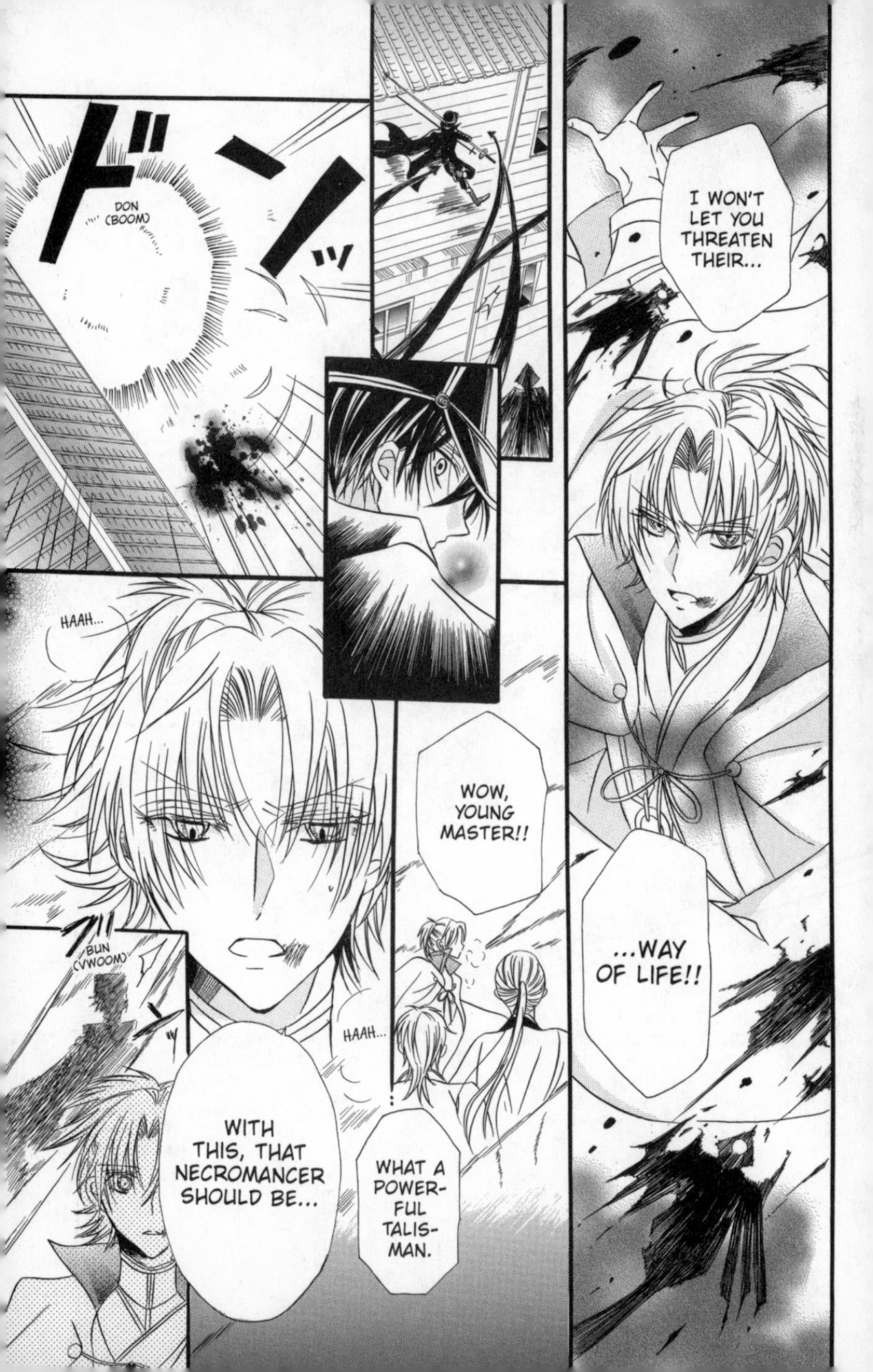
I WON'T LET YOU THREATEN THEIR...
...WAY OF LIFE!!
ドーン
DON (BOOM)
WOW, YOUNG MASTER!!
HAAH...
WHAT A POWERFUL TALISMAN.
HAAH...
WITH THIS, THAT NECROMANCER SHOULD BE...
BUN (VWOOM)

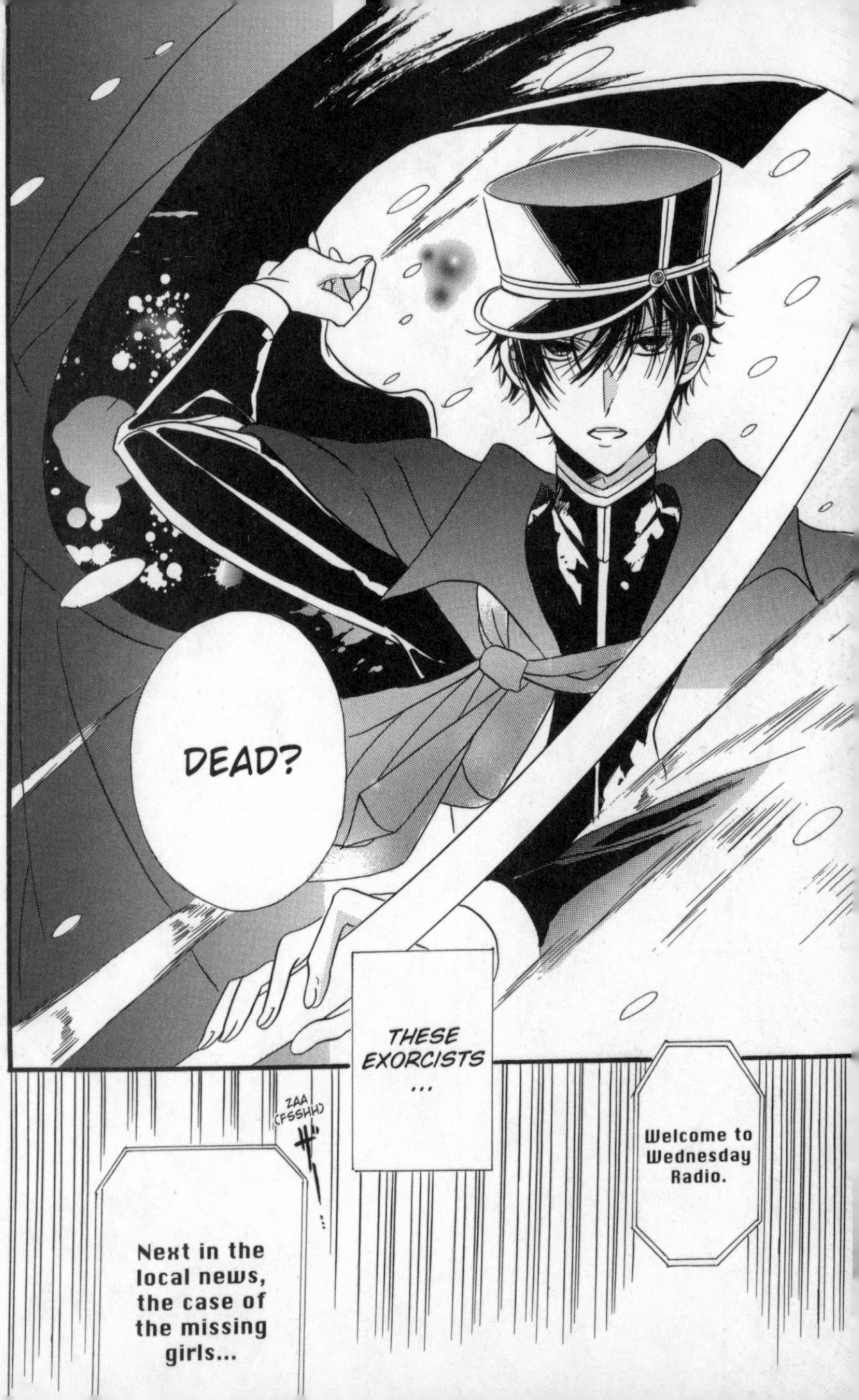
DEAD?
THESE EXORCISTS ...
Welcome to Wednesday Radio.
ZAA (FSSHH)
Next in the local news, the case of the missing girls...

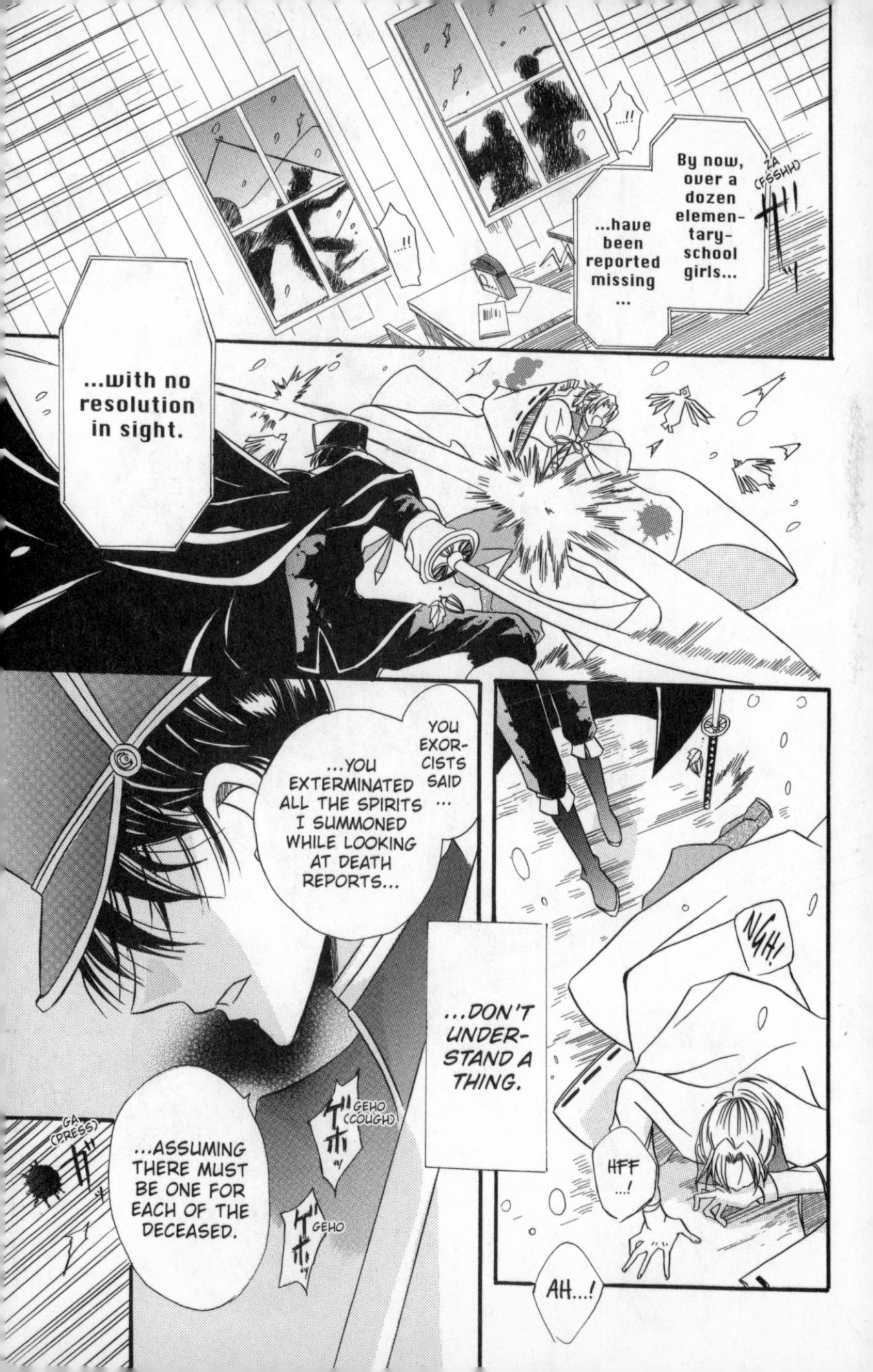
...!!
By now, over a dozen elementary-school girls...
ZA (FSSHH)
...!!
...have been reported missing ...
...with no resolution in sight.
NGH!
...DON'T UNDERSTAND A THING.
HFF ...!
AH...!
YOU EXORCISTS SAID ...
...YOU EXTERMINATED ALL THE SPIRITS I SUMMONED WHILE LOOKING AT DEATH REPORTS...
GEHO (COUGH)
GA (PRESS)
...ASSUMING THERE MUST BE ONE FOR EACH OF THE DECEASED.
GEHO

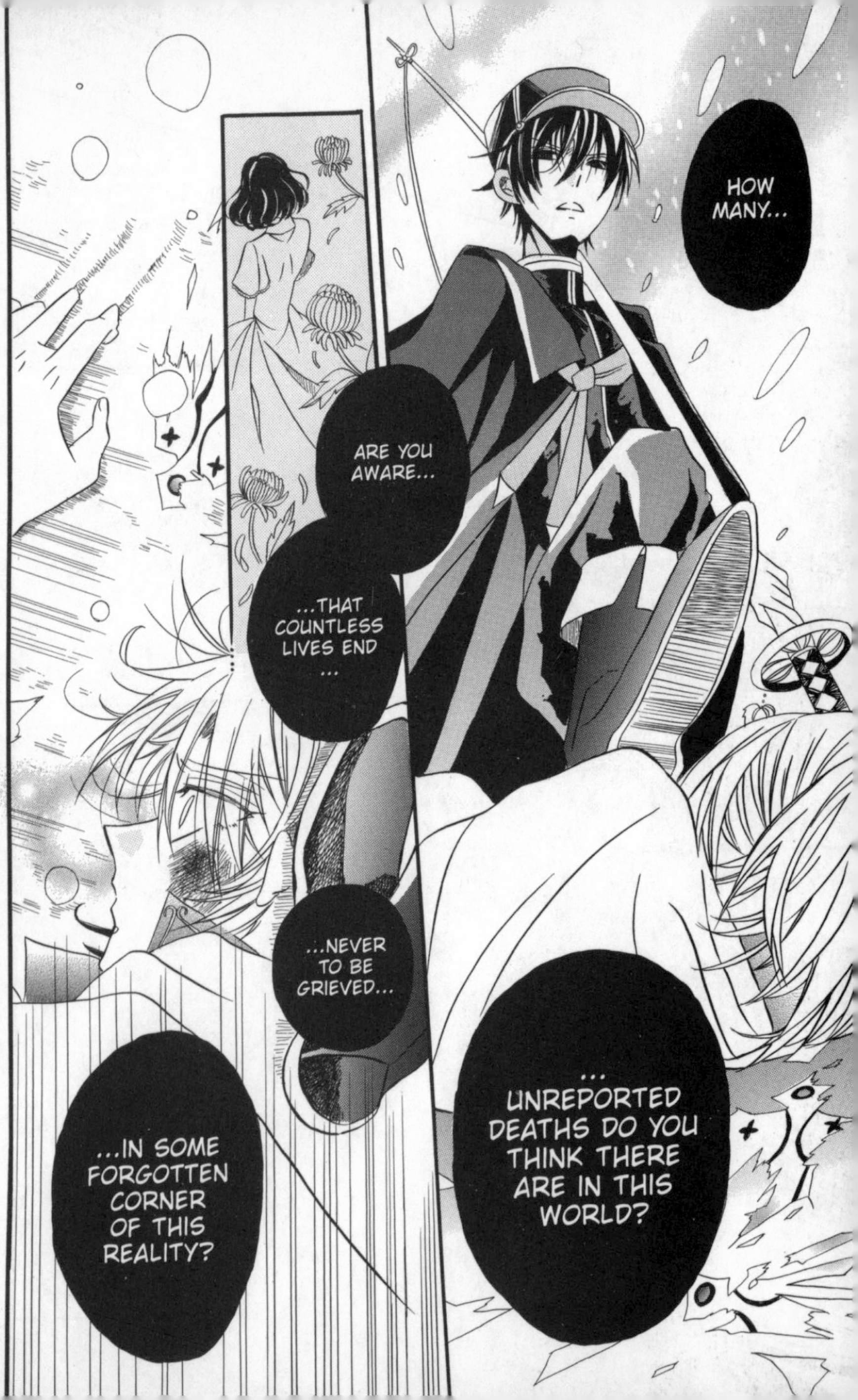
HOW MANY...
...UNREPORTED DEATHS DO YOU THINK THERE ARE IN THIS WORLD?
ARE YOU AWARE...
...THAT COUNTLESS LIVES END...
...NEVER TO BE GRIEVED...
...IN SOME FORGOTTEN CORNER OF THIS REALITY?

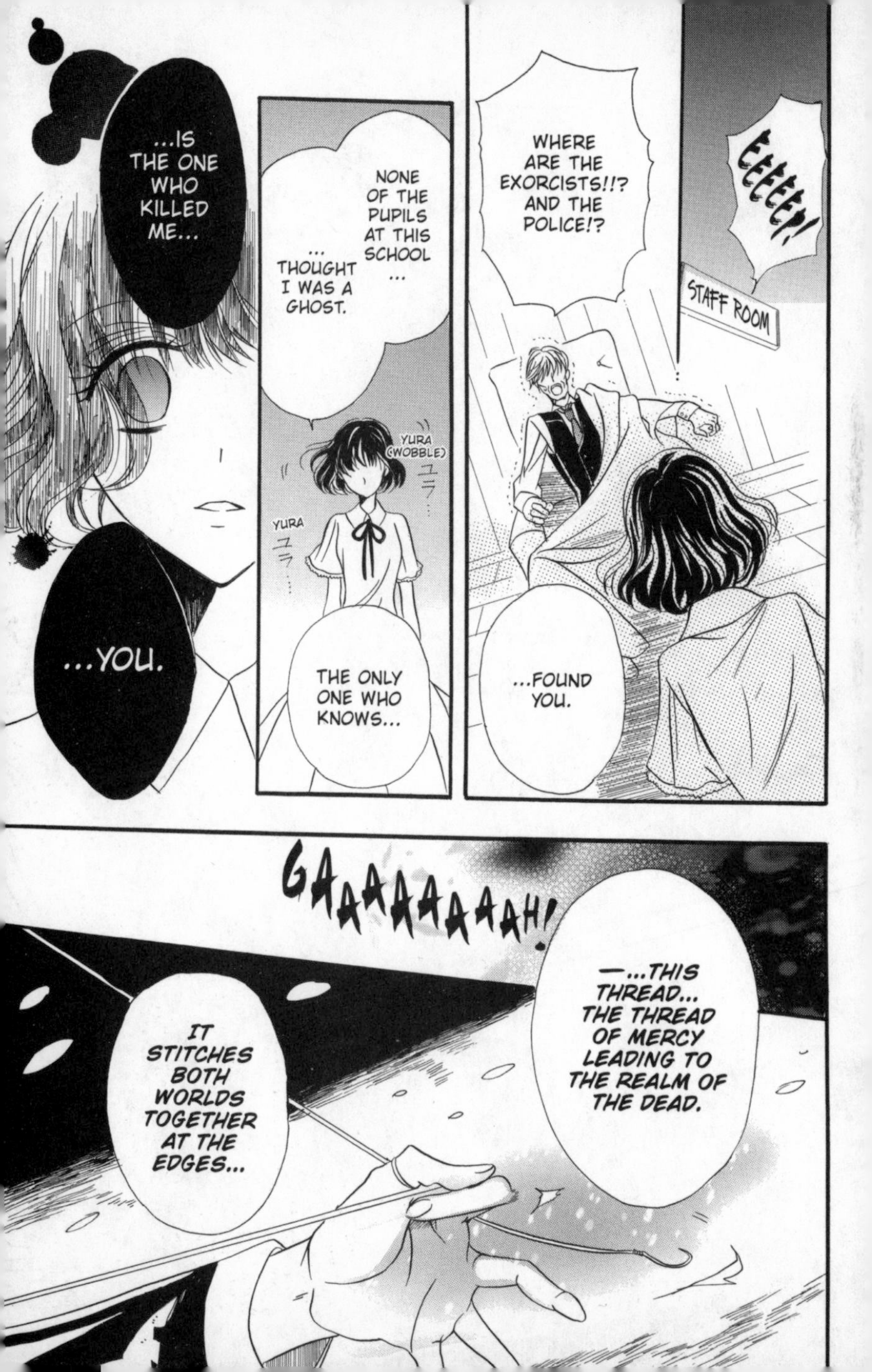
EEEEP!
STAFF ROOM
WHERE ARE THE EXORCISTS!!? AND THE POLICE!?
...FOUND YOU.
NONE OF THE PUPILS AT THIS SCHOOL ...
... THOUGHT I WAS A GHOST.
YURA (WOBBLE) ユラ
YURA ユラ
THE ONLY ONE WHO KNOWS...
...IS THE ONE WHO KILLED ME...
...YOU.
GAAAAAAAAAH!
—...THIS THREAD... THE THREAD OF MERCY LEADING TO THE REALM OF THE DEAD.
IT STITCHES BOTH WORLDS TOGETHER AT THE EDGES...

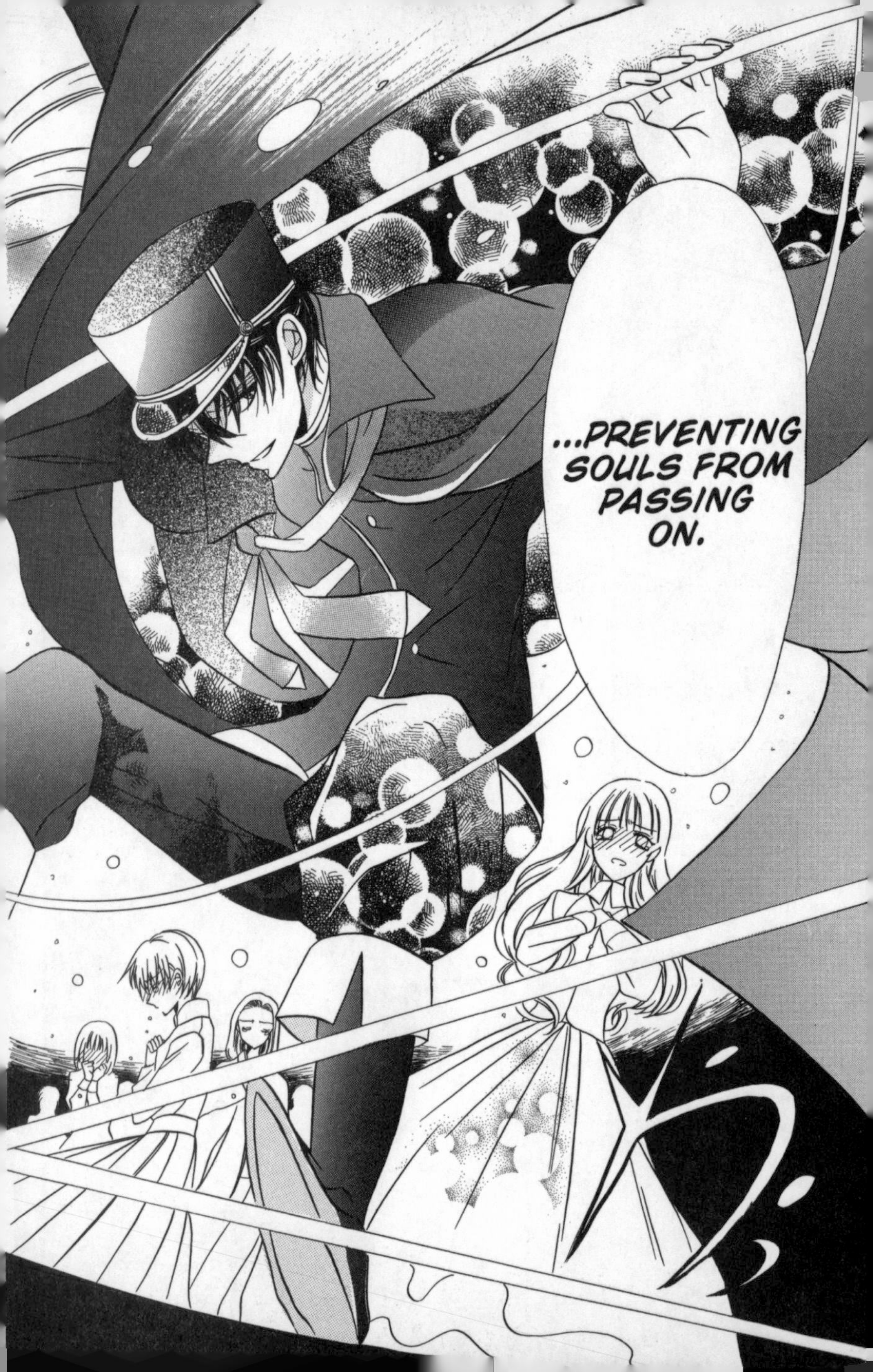
...PREVENTING SOULS FROM PASSING ON.

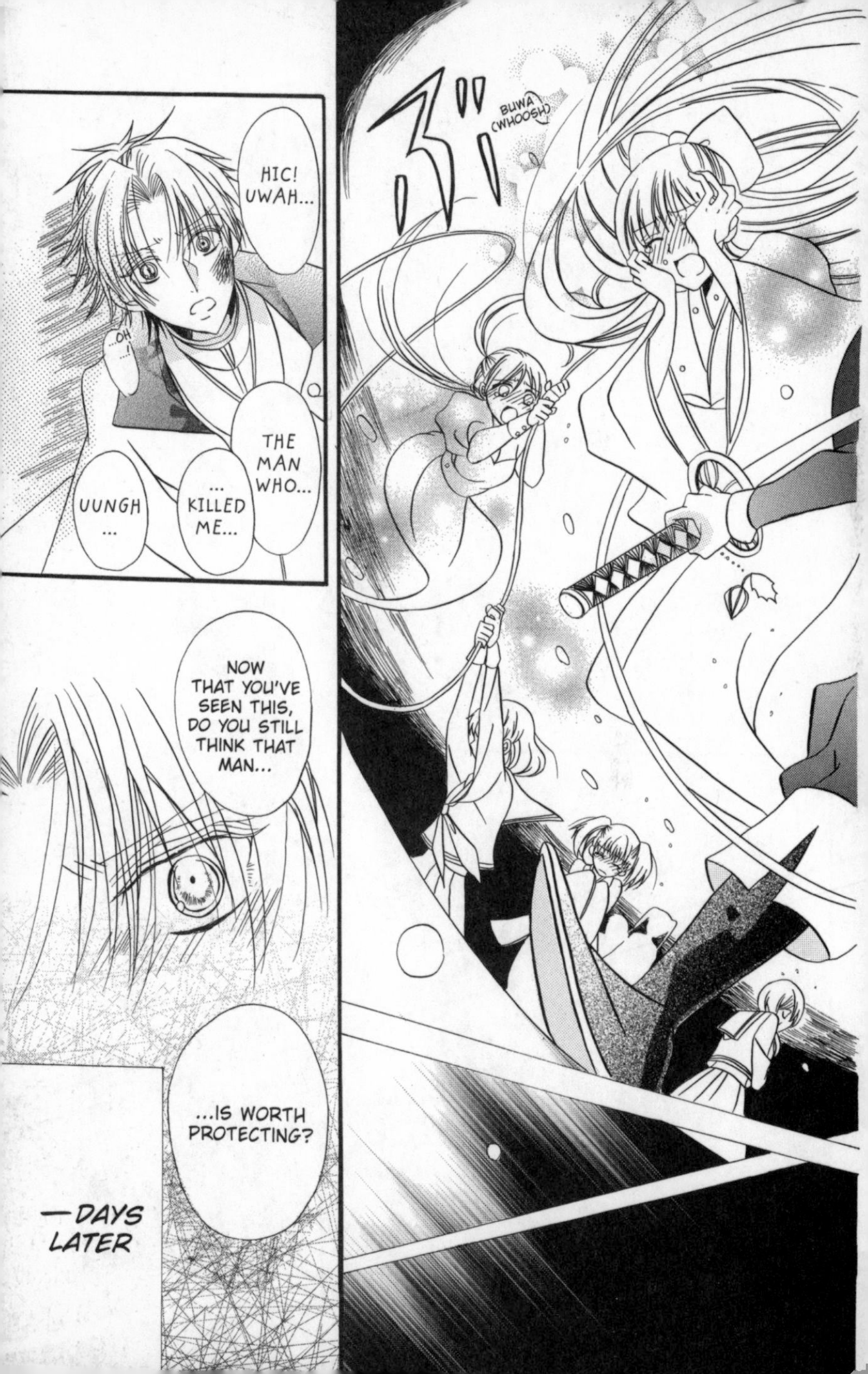
BUWA (WHOOSH)
HIC! UWAH...
THE MAN WHO...
... KILLED ME...
UUNGH ...
NOW THAT YOU'VE SEEN THIS, DO YOU STILL THINK THAT MAN...
...IS WORTH PROTECTING?
—DAYS LATER

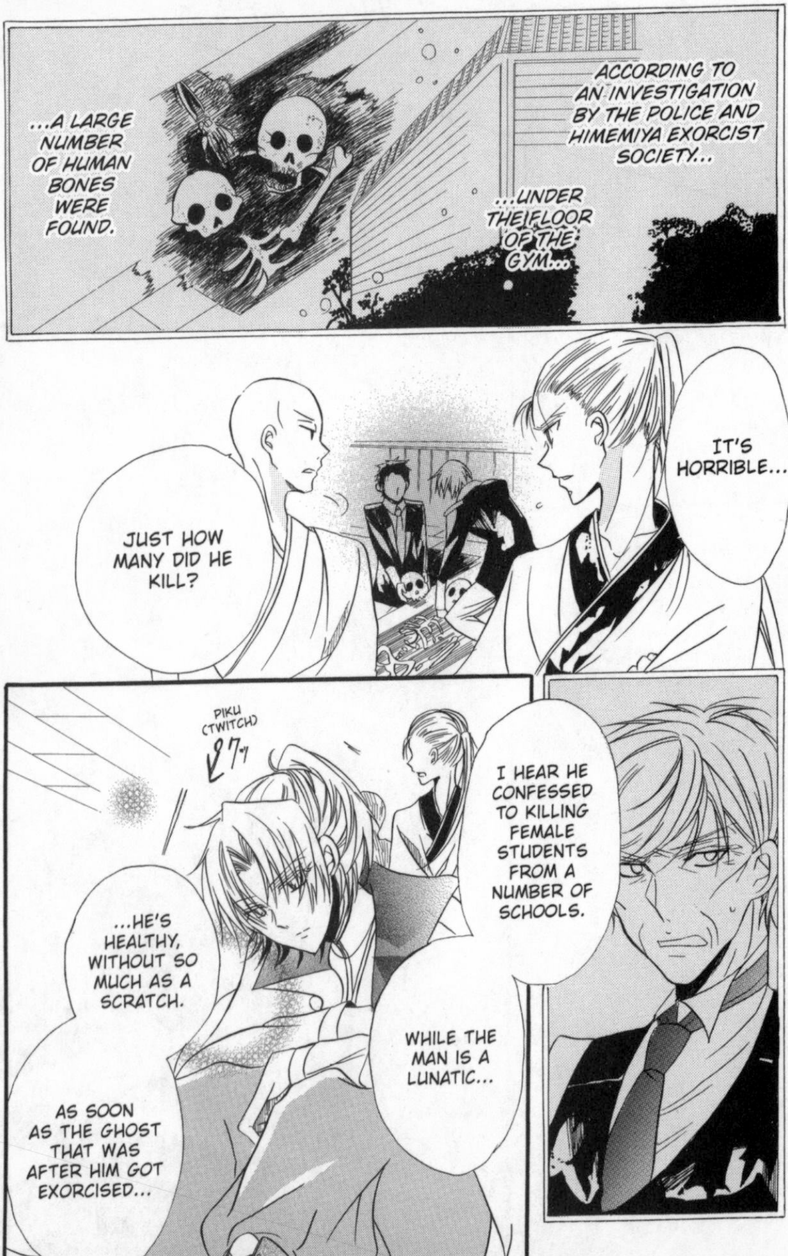
ACCORDING TO AN INVESTIGATION BY THE POLICE AND HIMEMIYA EXORCIST SOCIETY...
...UNDER THE FLOOR OF THE GYM...
...A LARGE NUMBER OF HUMAN BONES WERE FOUND.
IT'S HORRIBLE...
JUST HOW MANY DID HE KILL?
I HEAR HE CONFESSED TO KILLING FEMALE STUDENTS FROM A NUMBER OF SCHOOLS.
WHILE THE MAN IS A LUNATIC...
PIKU (TWITCH)
...HE'S HEALTHY, WITHOUT SO MUCH AS A SCRATCH.
AS SOON AS THE GHOST THAT WAS AFTER HIM GOT EXORCISED...

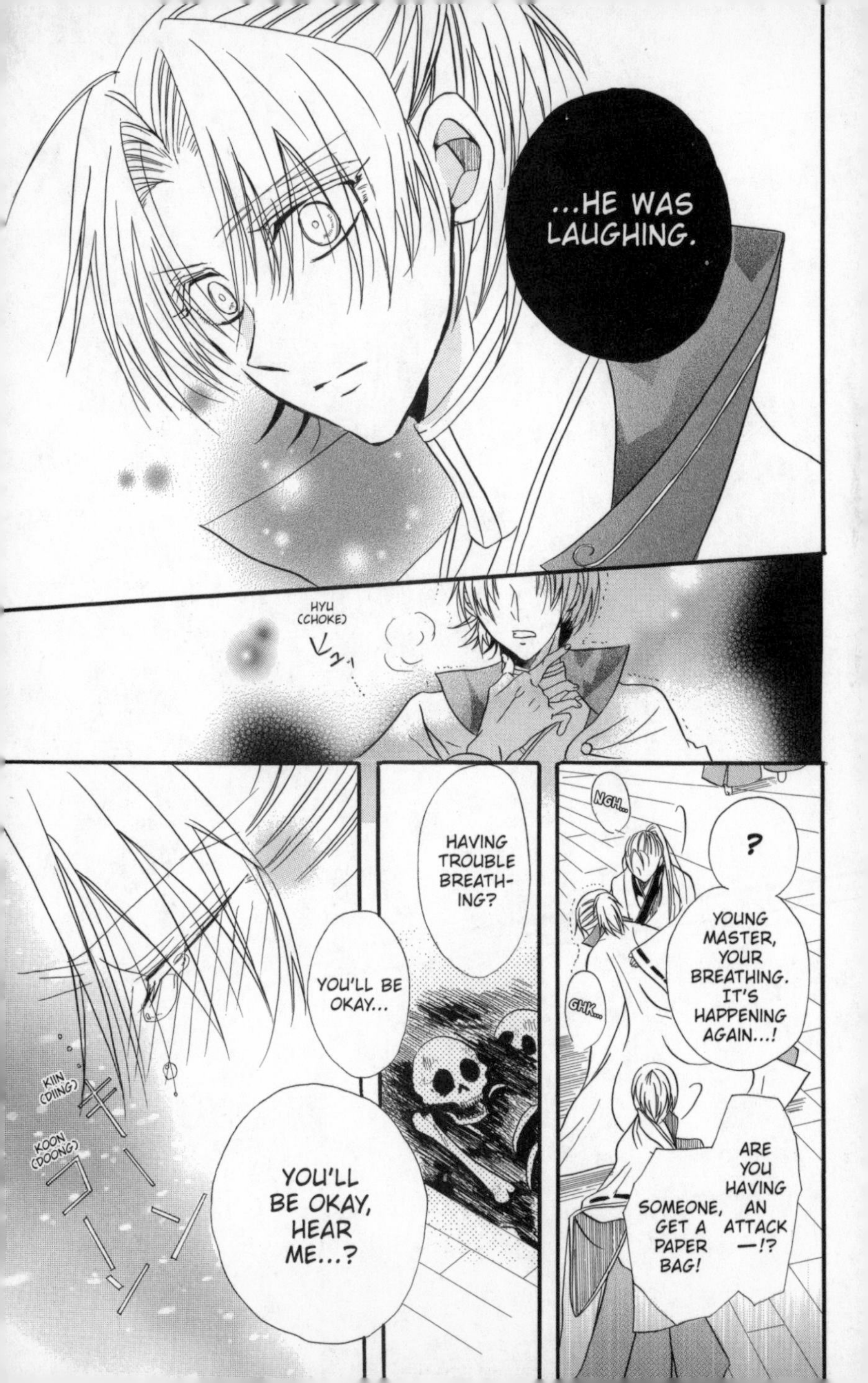
...HE WAS LAUGHING.
HYU (CHOKE)
NGH...
?
YOUNG MASTER, YOUR BREATHING. IT'S HAPPENING AGAIN...!
GHK...
ARE YOU HAVING AN ATTACK—!?
SOMEONE, GET A PAPER BAG!
HAVING TROUBLE BREATH-ING?
YOU'LL BE OKAY...
YOU'LL BE OKAY, HEAR ME...?
KIIN (DIING)
KOON (DOONG)

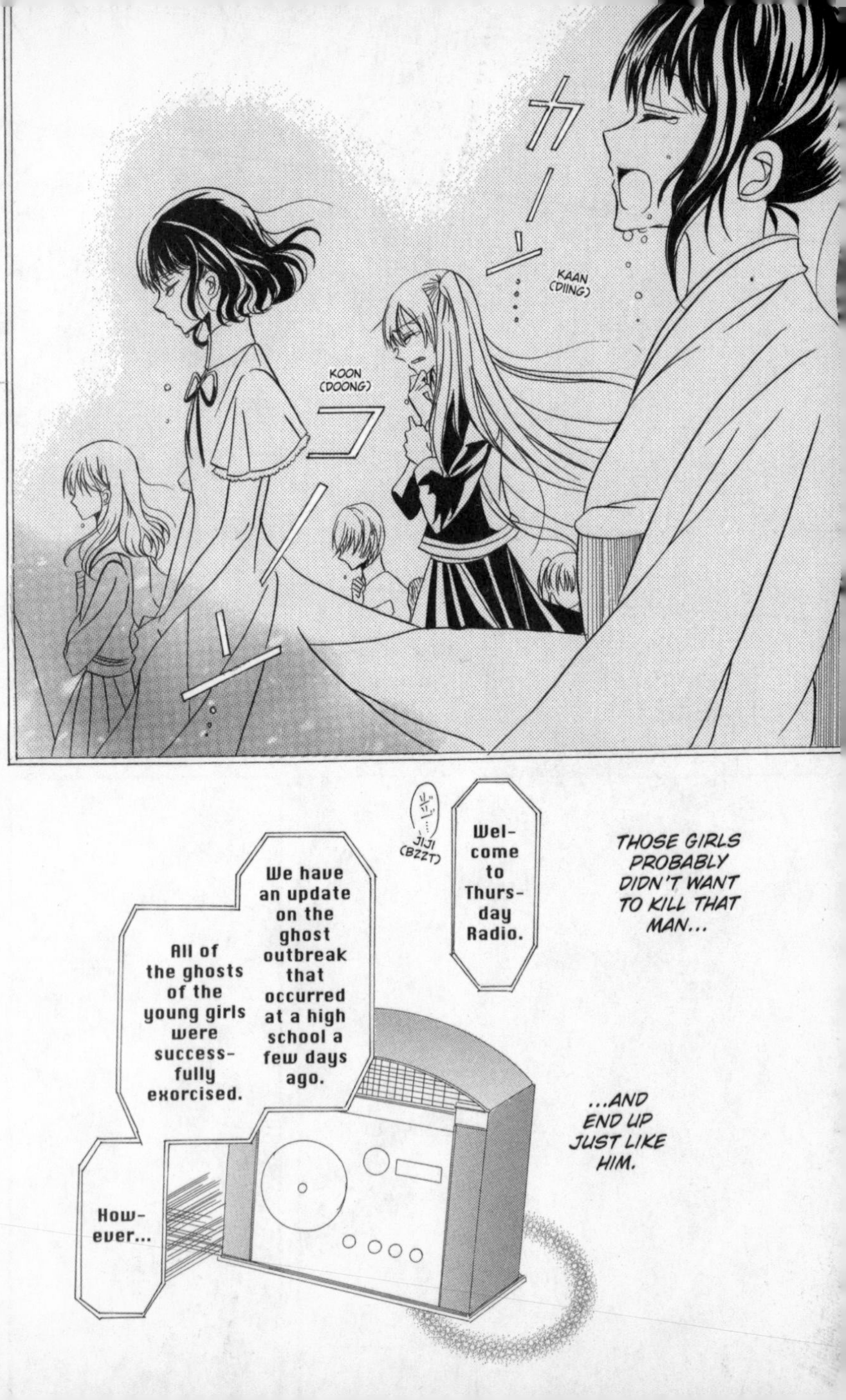
KAAN (DIING)
KOON (DOONG)
THOSE GIRLS PROBABLY DIDN'T WANT TO KILL THAT MAN...
...AND END UP JUST LIKE HIM.
JIJI (BZZT)
Welcome to Thursday Radio.
We have an update on the ghost outbreak that occurred at a high school a few days ago.
All of the ghosts of the young girls were successfully exorcised.
However...

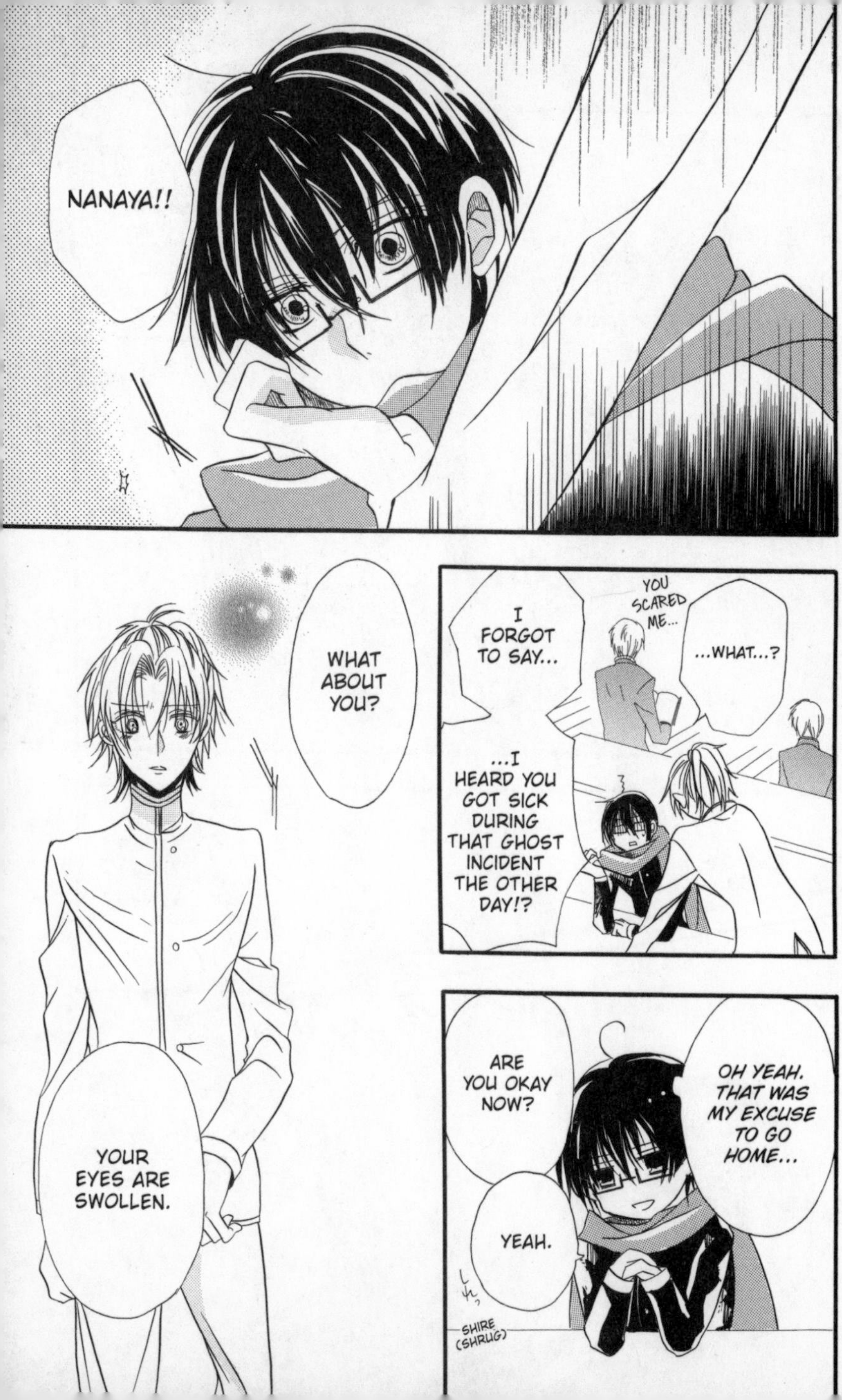
NANAYA!!
...WHAT...?
YOU SCARED ME...
I FORGOT TO SAY...
...I HEARD YOU GOT SICK DURING THAT GHOST INCIDENT THE OTHER DAY!?
OH YEAH. THAT WAS MY EXCUSE TO GO HOME...
ARE YOU OKAY NOW?
YEAH.
SHIRE (SHRUG)
WHAT ABOUT YOU?
YOUR EYES ARE SWOLLEN.

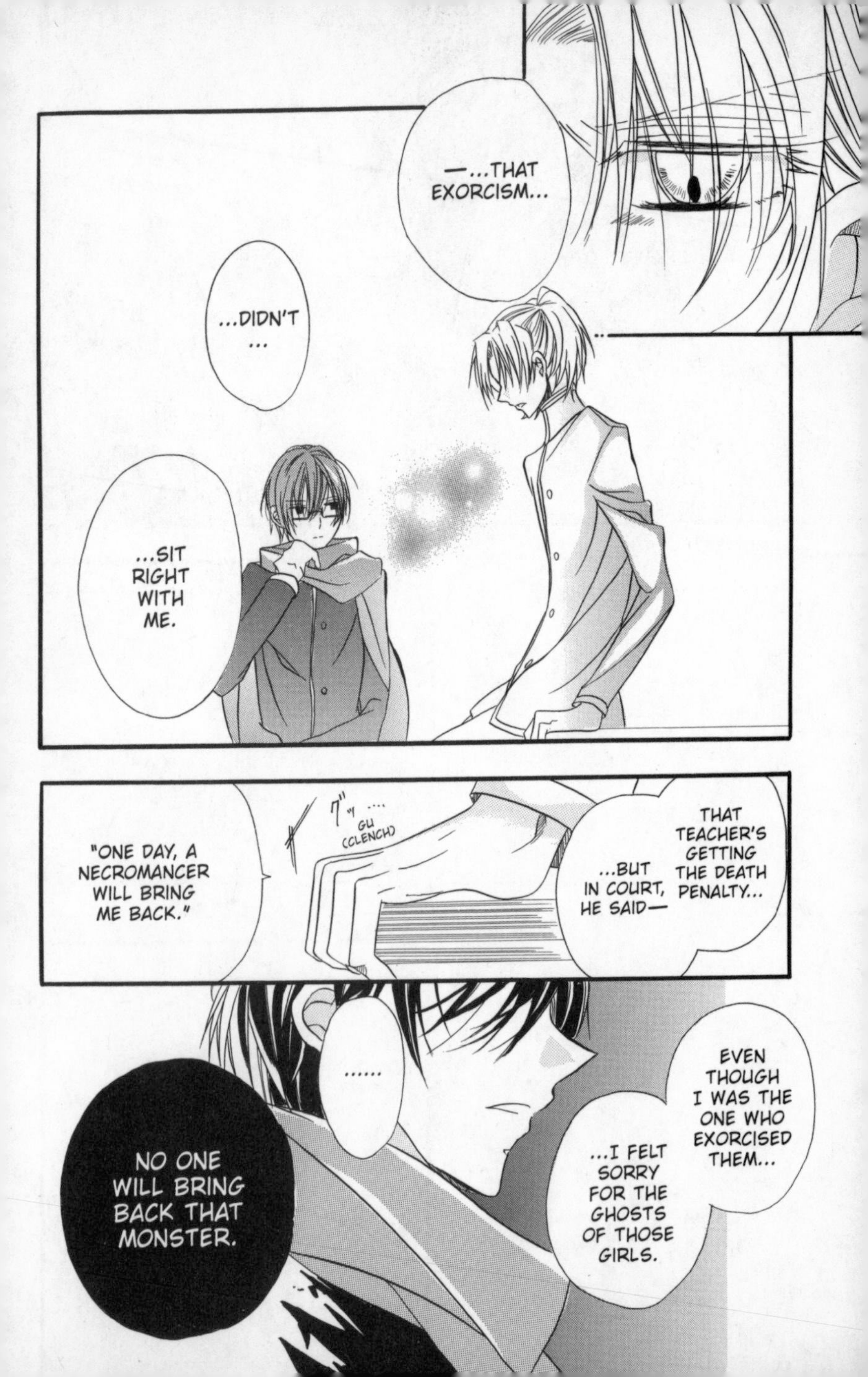
—...THAT EXORCISM...
...DIDN'T ...
...SIT RIGHT WITH ME.
THAT TEACHER'S GETTING THE DEATH PENALTY...
...BUT IN COURT, HE SAID—
グッ GU (CLENCH)
"ONE DAY, A NECROMANCER WILL BRING ME BACK."
EVEN THOUGH I WAS THE ONE WHO EXORCISED THEM...
...I FELT SORRY FOR THE GHOSTS OF THOSE GIRLS.
......
NO ONE WILL BRING BACK THAT MONSTER.

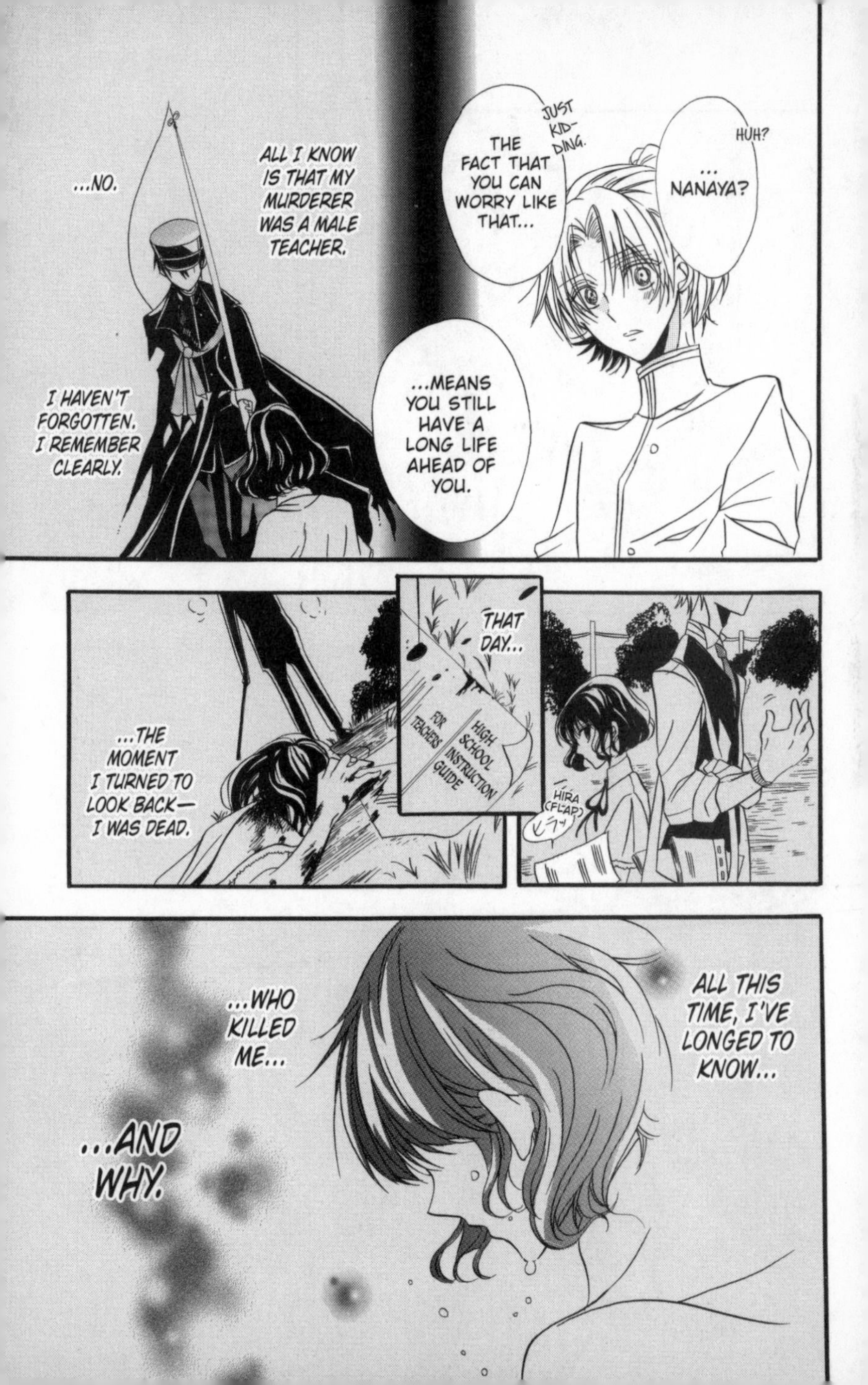
HUH?
...NANAYA?
THE FACT THAT YOU CAN WORRY LIKE THAT...
JUST KIDDING.
...MEANS YOU STILL HAVE A LONG LIFE AHEAD OF YOU.
ALL I KNOW IS THAT MY MURDERER WAS A MALE TEACHER.
...NO.
I HAVEN'T FORGOTTEN. I REMEMBER CLEARLY.
HIRA (FLAP)
ヒラッ
THAT DAY...
HIGH SCHOOL INSTRUCTION GUIDE
FOR TEACHERS
...THE MOMENT I TURNED TO LOOK BACK—
I WAS DEAD.
ALL THIS TIME, I'VE LONGED TO KNOW...
...WHO KILLED ME...
...AND WHY.

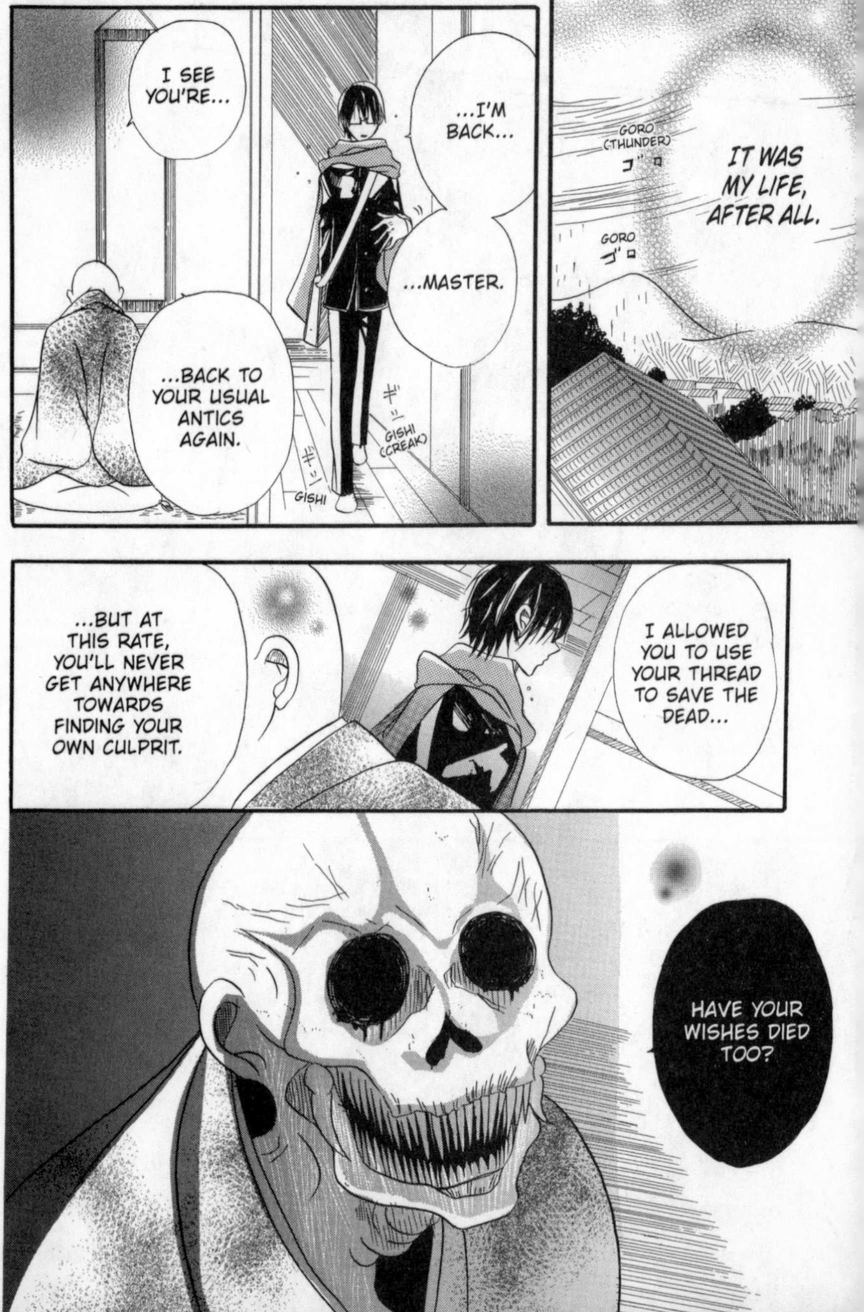
IT WAS MY LIFE, AFTER ALL.
GORO (THUNDER) ゴロ
GORO ゴロ
...I'M BACK...
...MASTER.
I SEE YOU'RE...
...BACK TO YOUR USUAL ANTICS AGAIN.
GISHI (CREAK) ギシ
GISHI ギシ
I ALLOWED YOU TO USE YOUR THREAD TO SAVE THE DEAD...
...BUT AT THIS RATE, YOU'LL NEVER GET ANYWHERE TOWARDS FINDING YOUR OWN CULPRIT.
HAVE YOUR WISHES DIED TOO?

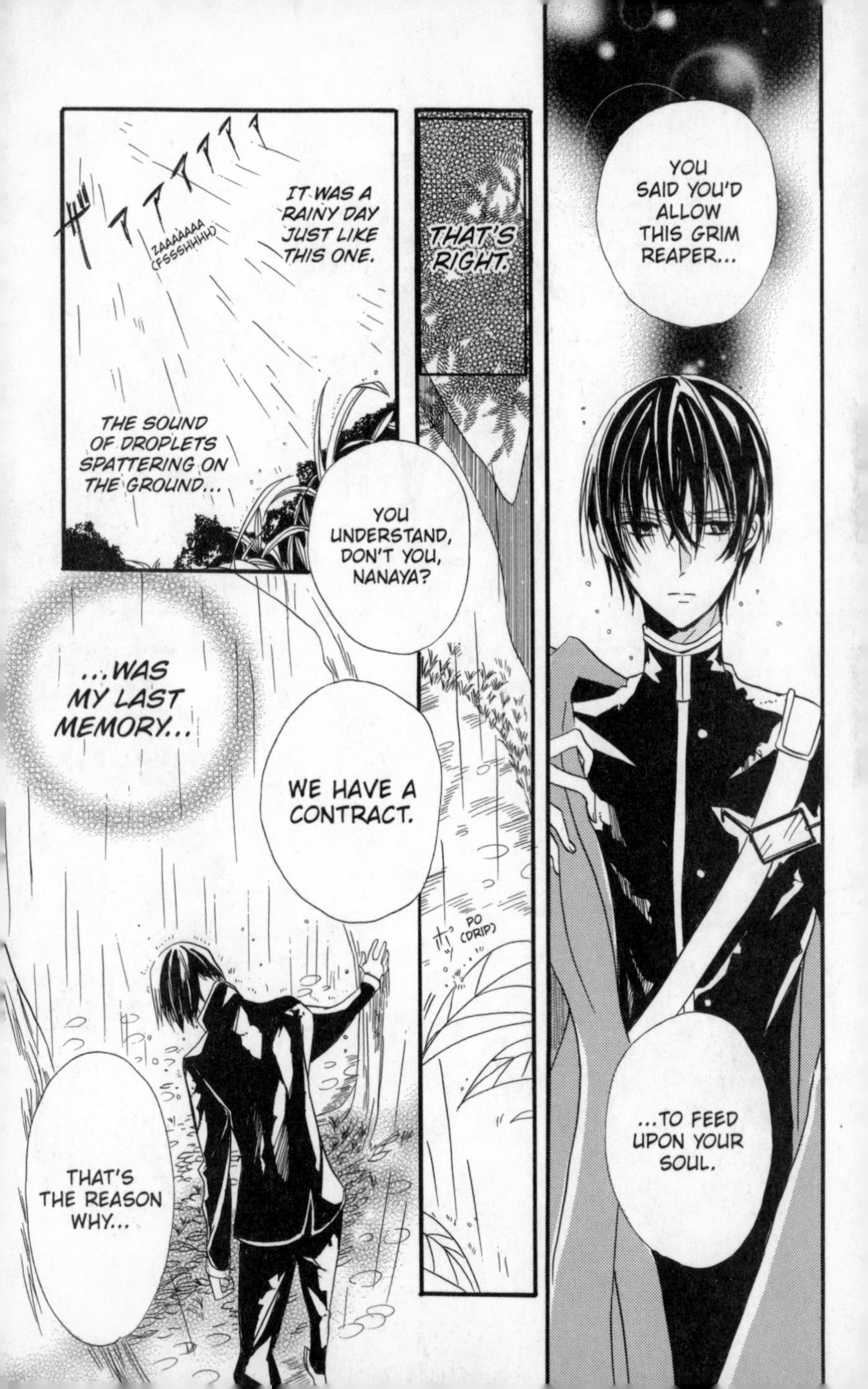
YOU SAID YOU'D ALLOW THIS GRIM REAPER...
...TO FEED UPON YOUR SOUL.
THAT'S RIGHT.
IT WAS A RAINY DAY JUST LIKE THIS ONE.
ZAAAAAAA (FSSSHHHH)
THE SOUND OF DROPLETS SPATTERING ON THE GROUND...
YOU UNDERSTAND, DON'T YOU, NANAYA?
WE HAVE A CONTRACT.
PO (DRIP)
...WAS MY LAST MEMORY...
THAT'S THE REASON WHY...

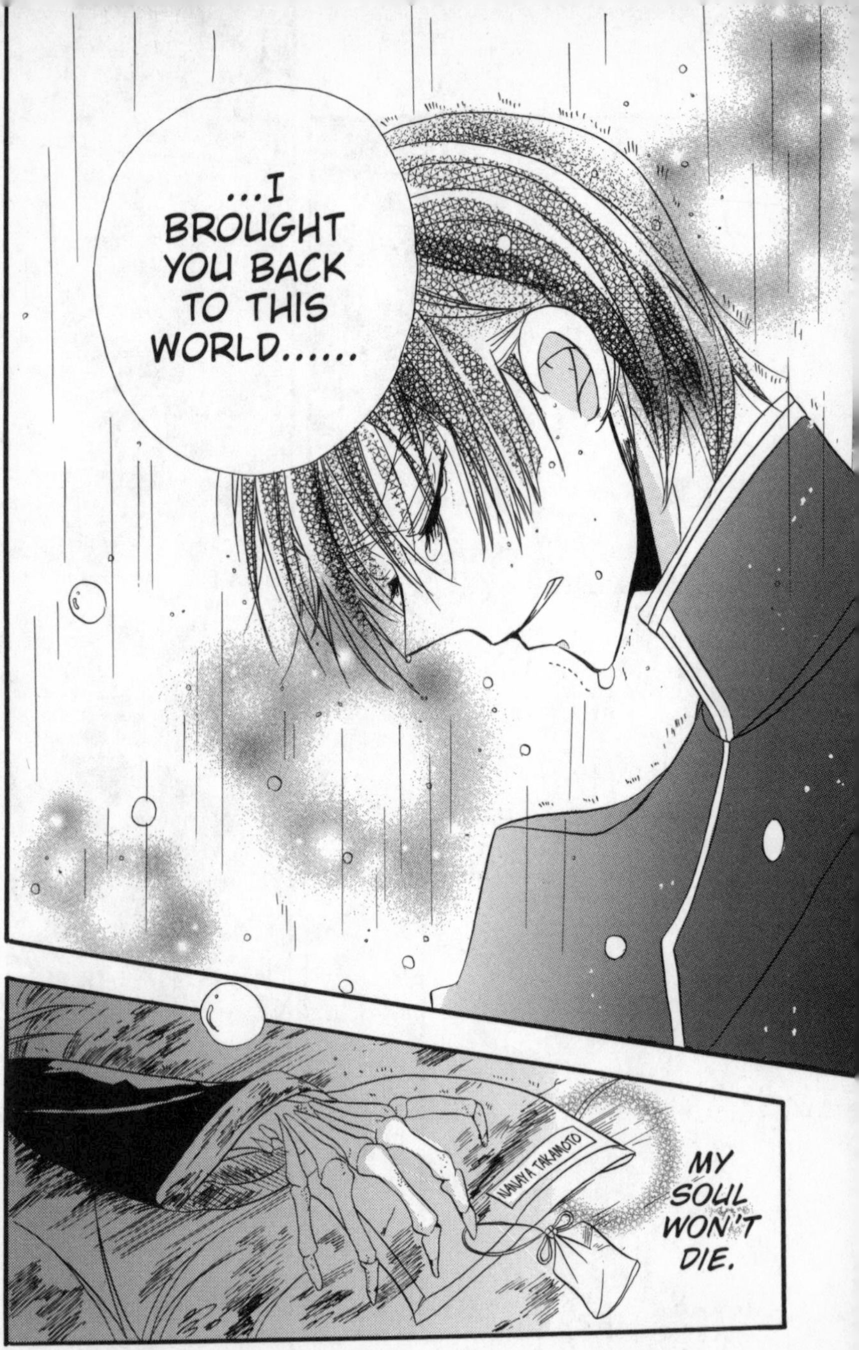
...I BROUGHT YOU BACK TO THIS WORLD......
NANAYA TAKAMOTO
MY SOUL WON'T DIE.

IT'S KEPT ALIVE BY REGRET.

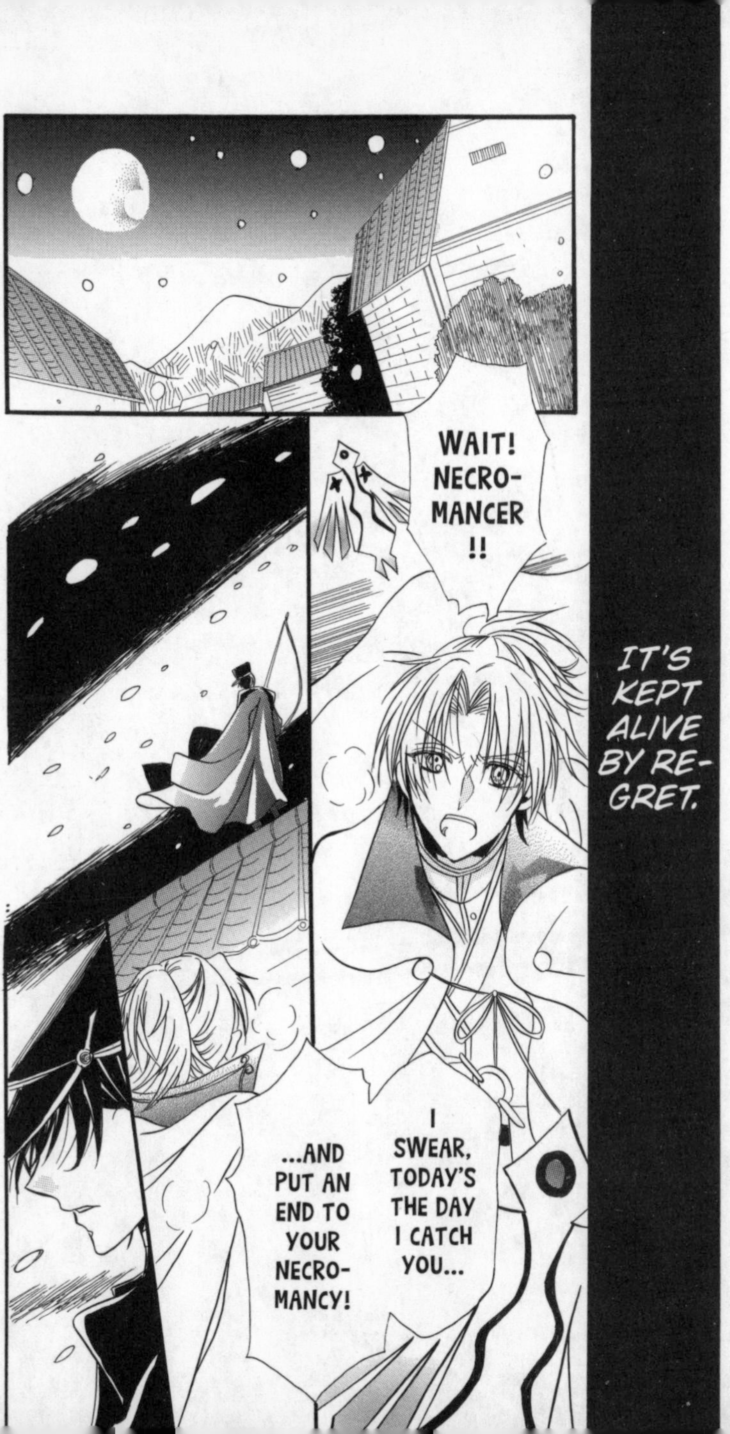
WAIT! NECROMANCER!!
I SWEAR, TODAY'S THE DAY I CATCH YOU...
...AND PUT AN END TO YOUR NECROMANCY!

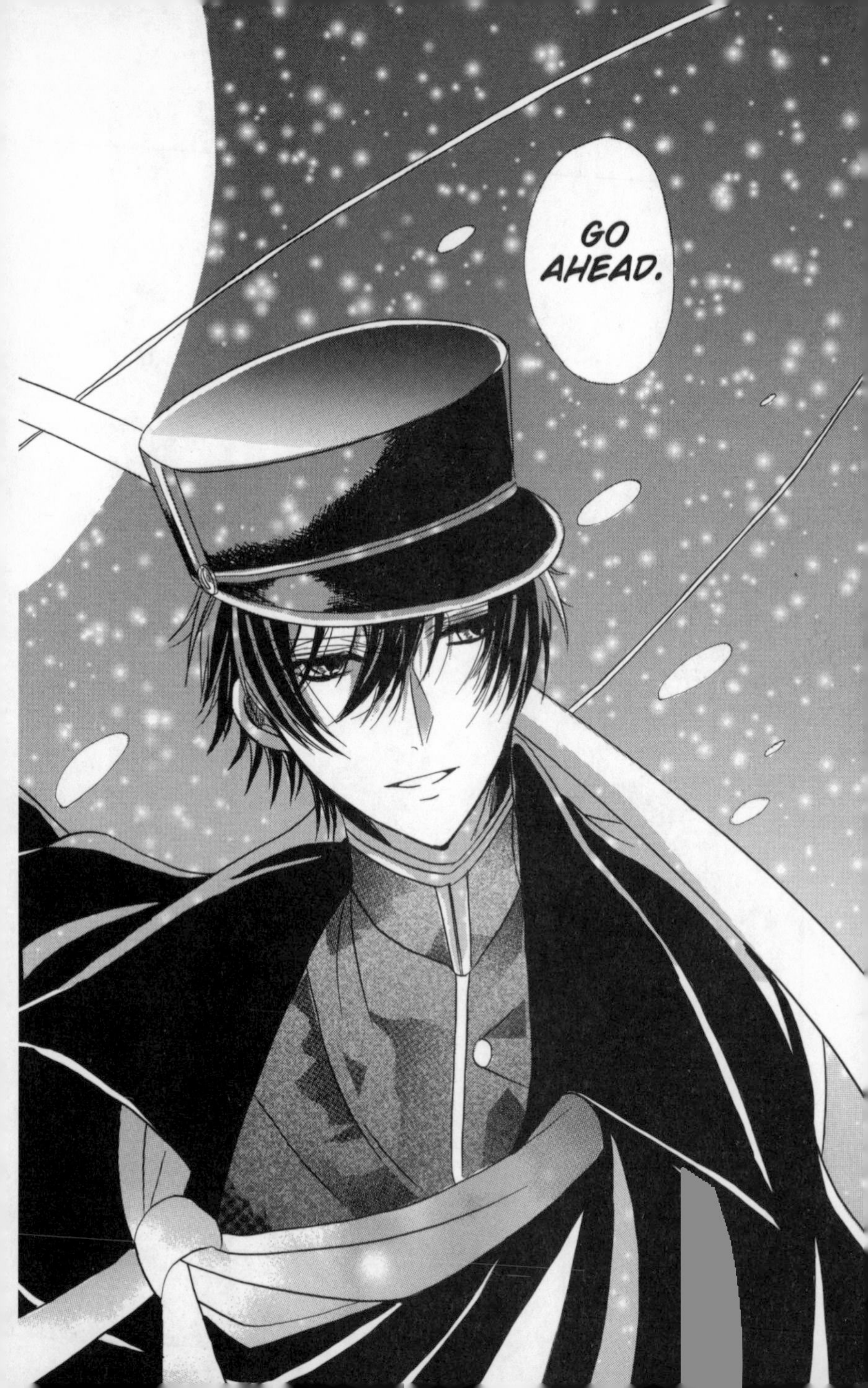
GO AHEAD.

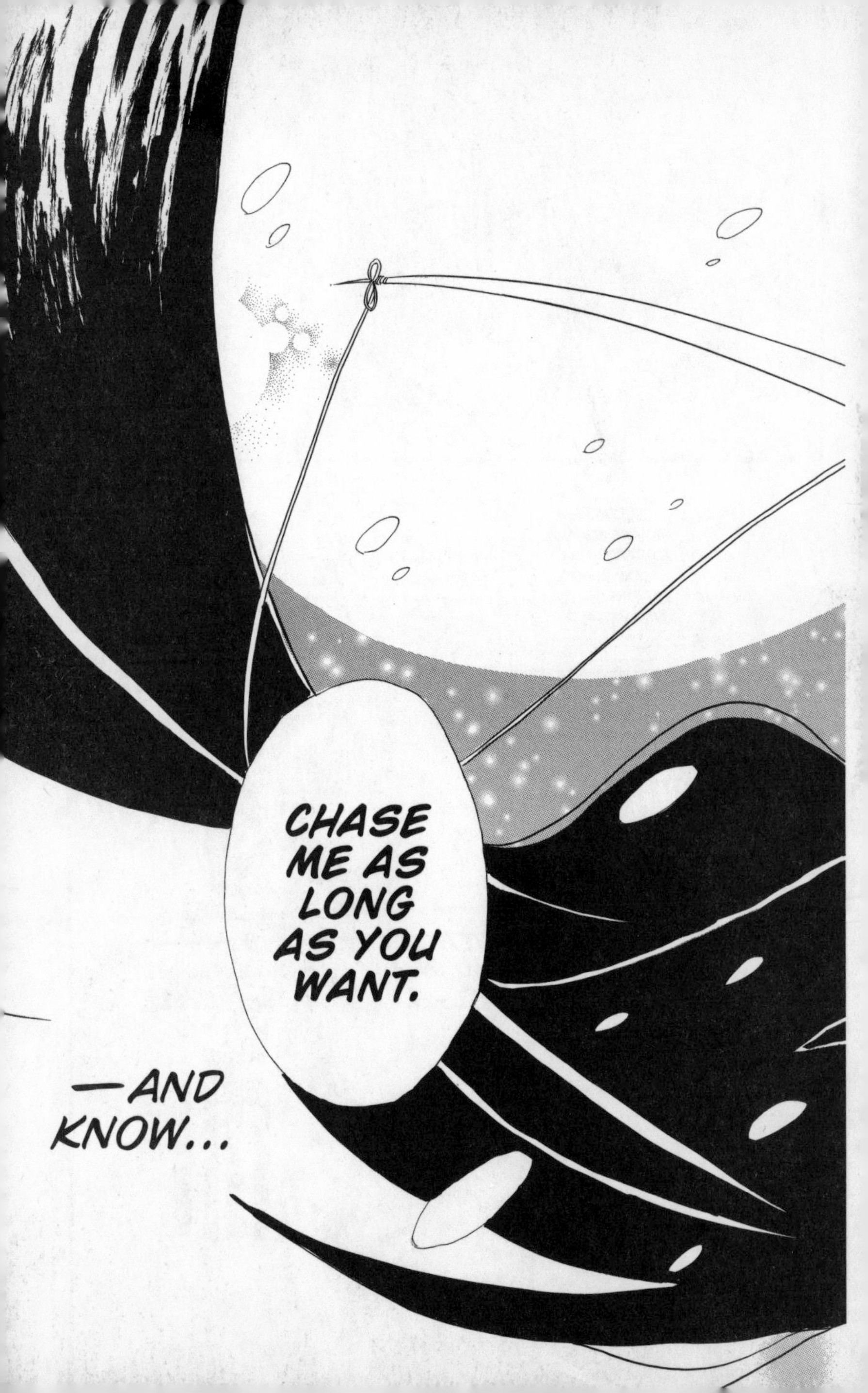
CHASE ME AS LONG AS YOU WANT.
—AND KNOW...

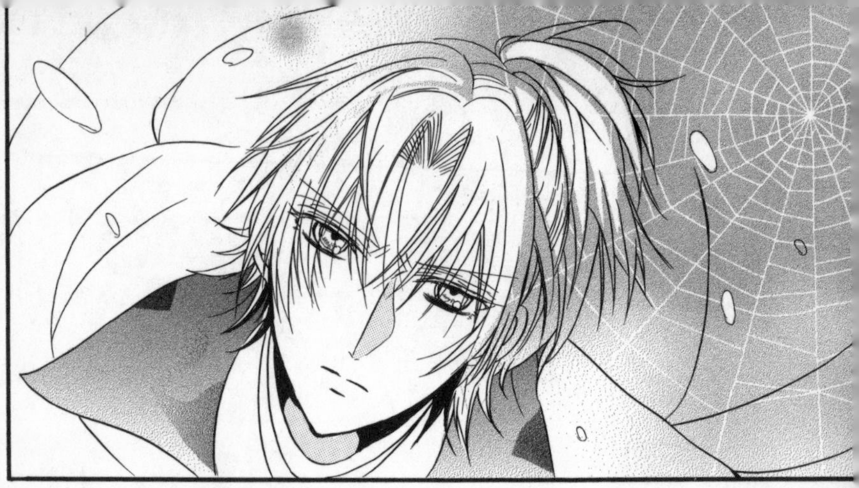

...THAT WITH MY THREADS OF NECROMANCY, I'LL REEL IN THOSE DARK BONDS...

...BETWEEN HUMANS AND SPIRITS WHO LONG TO DESCEND TO THIS WORLD...

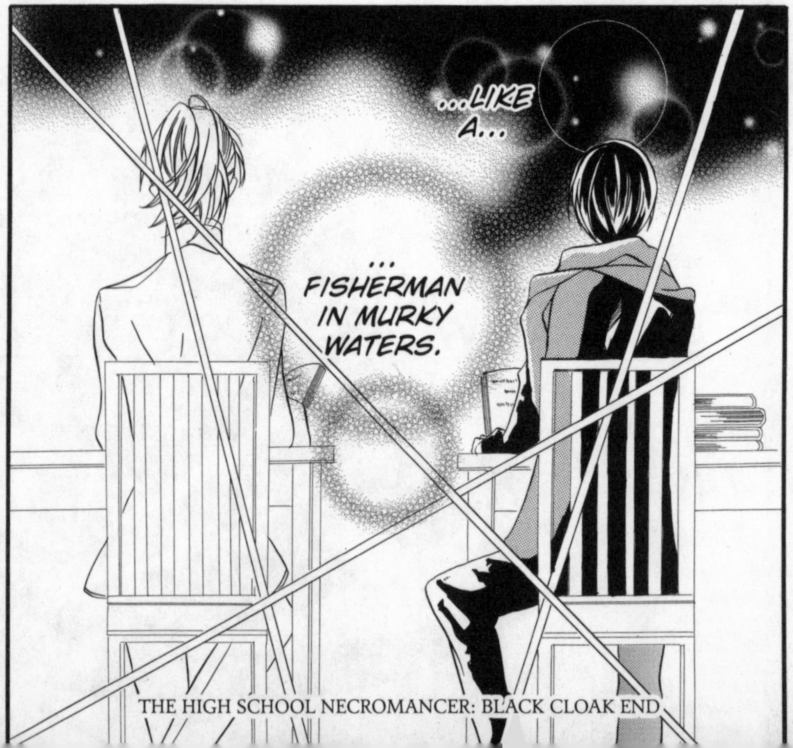
...LIKE A...
... FISHERMAN IN MURKY WATERS.

THE HIGH SCHOOL NECROMANCER: BLACK CLOAK END

AFTERWORD: BLACK CLOAK

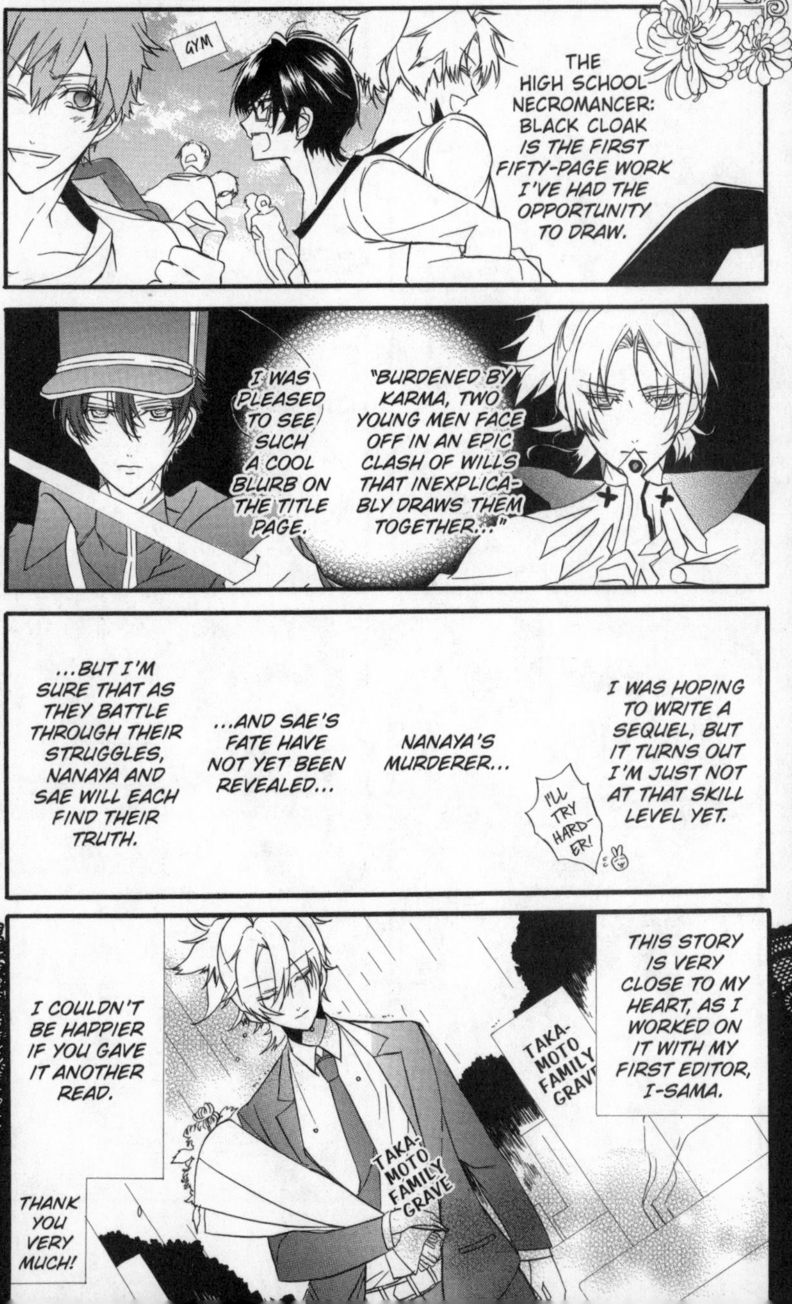
GYM
THE HIGH SCHOOL NECROMANCER: BLACK CLOAK IS THE FIRST FIFTY-PAGE WORK I'VE HAD THE OPPORTUNITY TO DRAW.
"BURDENED BY KARMA, TWO YOUNG MEN FACE OFF IN AN EPIC CLASH OF WILLS THAT INEXPLICA-BLY DRAWS THEM TOGETHER..."
I WAS PLEASED TO SEE SUCH A COOL BLURB ON THE TITLE PAGE.
I WAS HOPING TO WRITE A SEQUEL, BUT IT TURNS OUT I'M JUST NOT AT THAT SKILL LEVEL YET.
I'LL TRY HARD-ER!
NANAYA'S MURDERER...
...AND SAE'S FATE HAVE NOT YET BEEN REVEALED...
...BUT I'M SURE THAT AS THEY BATTLE THROUGH THEIR STRUGGLES, NANAYA AND SAE WILL EACH FIND THEIR TRUTH.
THIS STORY IS VERY CLOSE TO MY HEART, AS I WORKED ON IT WITH MY FIRST EDITOR, I-SAMA.
TAKA-MOTO FAMILY GRAVE
TAKA-MOTO FAMILY GRAVE
I COULDN'T BE HAPPIER IF YOU GAVE IT ANOTHER READ.
THANK YOU VERY MUCH!

SEE THE NEXT PAGE FOR FOUR-PANEL COMICS OF THE DARK HISTORY OF THE REINCARNATED VILLAINESS!

A FULL-FACE SMILE FOR HIS BELOVED

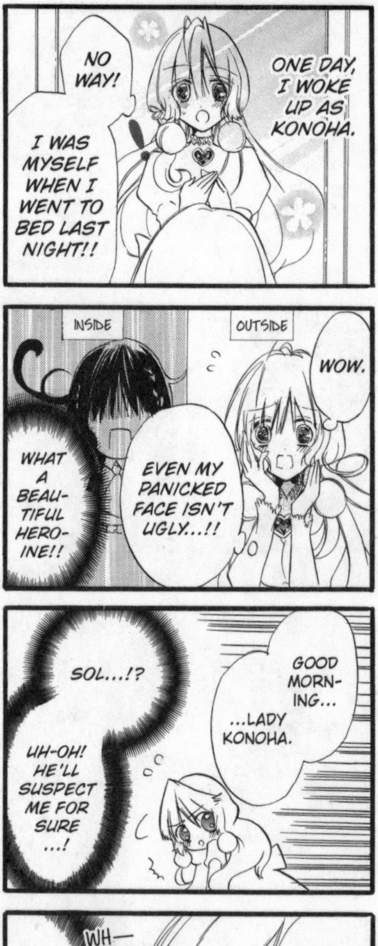
ONE DAY, I WOKE UP AS KONOHA.
NO WAY!
I WAS MYSELF WHEN I WENT TO BED LAST NIGHT!!
OUTSIDE
WOW.
INSIDE
EVEN MY PANICKED FACE ISN'T UGLY...!!
WHAT A BEAUTIFUL HEROINE!!
GOOD MORNING...
...LADY KONOHA.
SOL...!?
UH-OH! HE'LL SUSPECT ME FOR SURE...!
IS SOMETHING WRONG?
WH—
WHO IS THAAAT!!?

EVERY GREETING WITH A KISS ON THE FOREHEAD OR THE HAND OR A REGULAR KISS

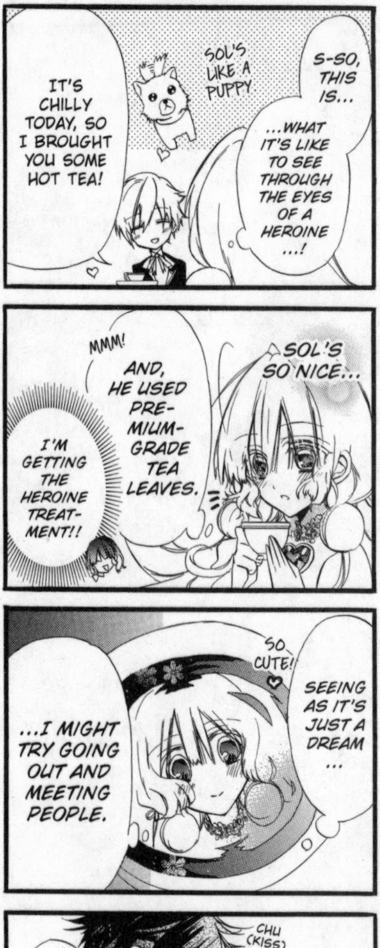
S-SO, THIS IS...
...WHAT IT'S LIKE TO SEE THROUGH THE EYES OF A HEROINE...!
SOL'S LIKE A PUPPY
IT'S CHILLY TODAY, SO I BROUGHT YOU SOME HOT TEA!
SOL'S SO NICE...
AND, HE USED PREMIUM-GRADE TEA LEAVES.
MMM!
I'M GETTING THE HEROINE TREATMENT!!
SO CUTE!
SEEING AS IT'S JUST A DREAM...
...I MIGHT TRY GOING OUT AND MEETING PEOPLE.
LIKE, GINO—
CHU (KISS)
GOOD MORNING, KONOHA.
I'VE MISSED YOU.

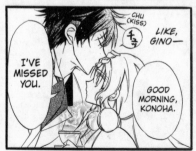

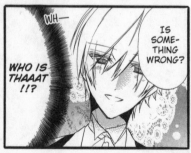

KONOHA SATOU'S DREAM IN MIDDLE SCHOOL

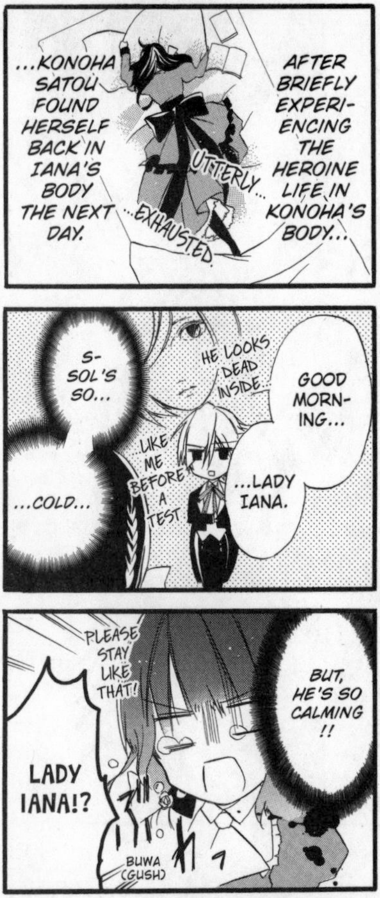

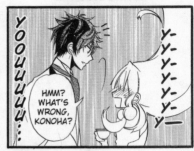

Y-Y-Y-Y-Y-Y-Y—
HMM? WHAT'S WRONG, KONOHA?
YOOUUUUUU...
DO YOU HAVE A FEVER?
ぴと PITO (PRESS)
EEP!
I...
I'M ALL RIGHT...
WHAT THE HELL!!?
THE HERO AND HEROINE ARE JUST TOO SWEET TOGETHER!
KAAAA (BLUSH)
WHO WROTE THIS DRIVEL—!?
KONOHA SATOU.
ME.

NO TALENT FOR BEING A HEROINE

AFTER BRIEFLY EXPERIENCING THE HEROINE LIFE IN KONOHA'S BODY...
UTTERLY... ...EXHAUSTED.
...KONOHA SATOU FOUND HERSELF BACK IN IANA'S BODY THE NEXT DAY.
GOOD MORNING...
...LADY IANA.
HE LOOKS DEAD INSIDE...
LIKE ME BEFORE A TEST
S-SOL'S SO...
...COLD...
BUT, HE'S SO CALMING!!
PLEASE STAY LIKE THAT!
LADY IANA!?
BUWA (GUSH)
...DID YOU HAVE A SCARY DREAM, PERHAPS?
YEAH. YOU COULD SAY THAT.
ONCE AGAIN, SHE EXPERIENCED THE JOY OF BEING THE VILLAINESS...
...IANA.

BONUS/END

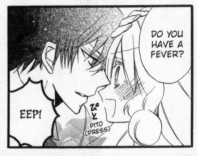

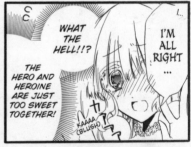

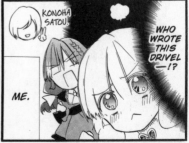

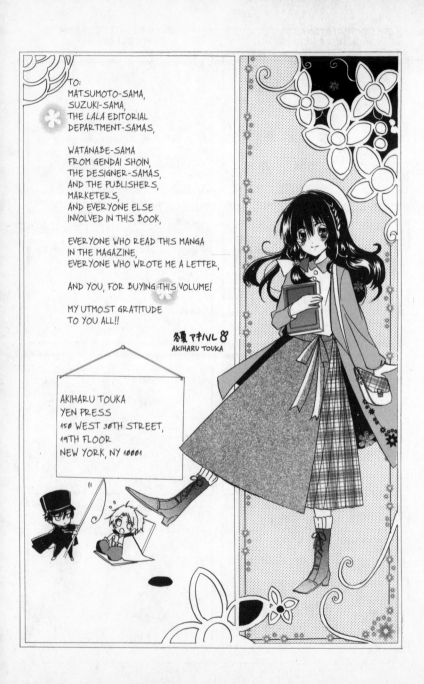

TO:
MATSUMOTO-SAMA,
SUZUKI-SAMA,
THE LALA EDITORIAL
DEPARTMENT-SAMAS,

WATANABE-SAMA
FROM GENDAI SHOIN,
THE DESIGNER-SAMAS,
AND THE PUBLISHERS,
MARKETERS,
AND EVERYONE ELSE
INVOLVED IN THIS BOOK,

EVERYONE WHO READ THIS MANGA
IN THE MAGAZINE,
EVERYONE WHO WROTE ME A LETTER,

AND YOU, FOR BUYING THIS VOLUME!

MY UTMOST GRATITUDE
TO YOU ALL!!

冬夏アキハル
AKIHARU TOUKA

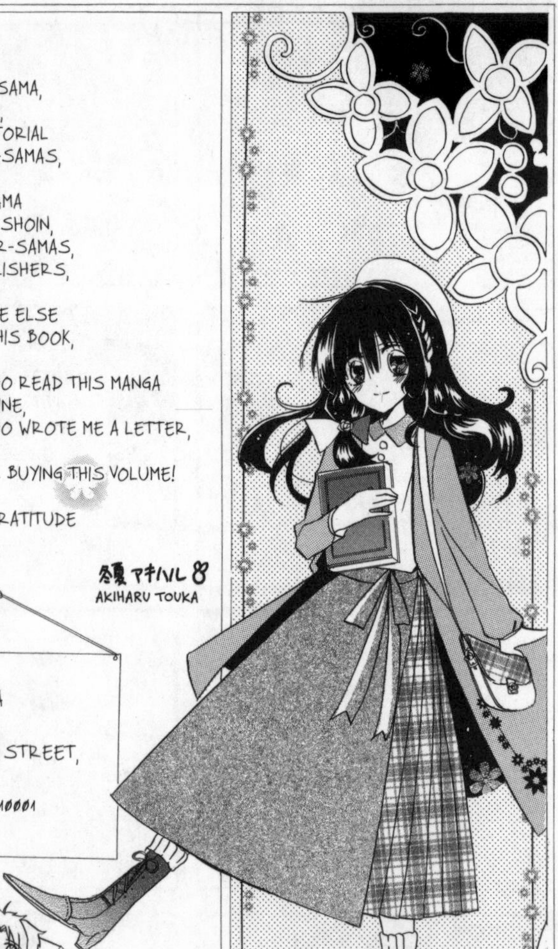

AKIHARU TOUKA
YEN PRESS
150 WEST 30TH STREET,
19TH FLOOR
NEW YORK, NY 10001

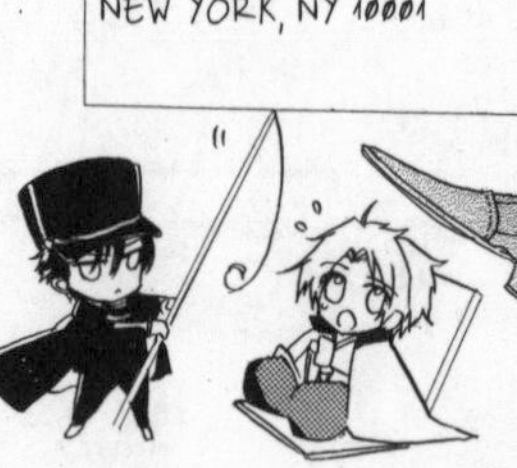